Illinois

Scott Foresman

Science

The Diamond Edition

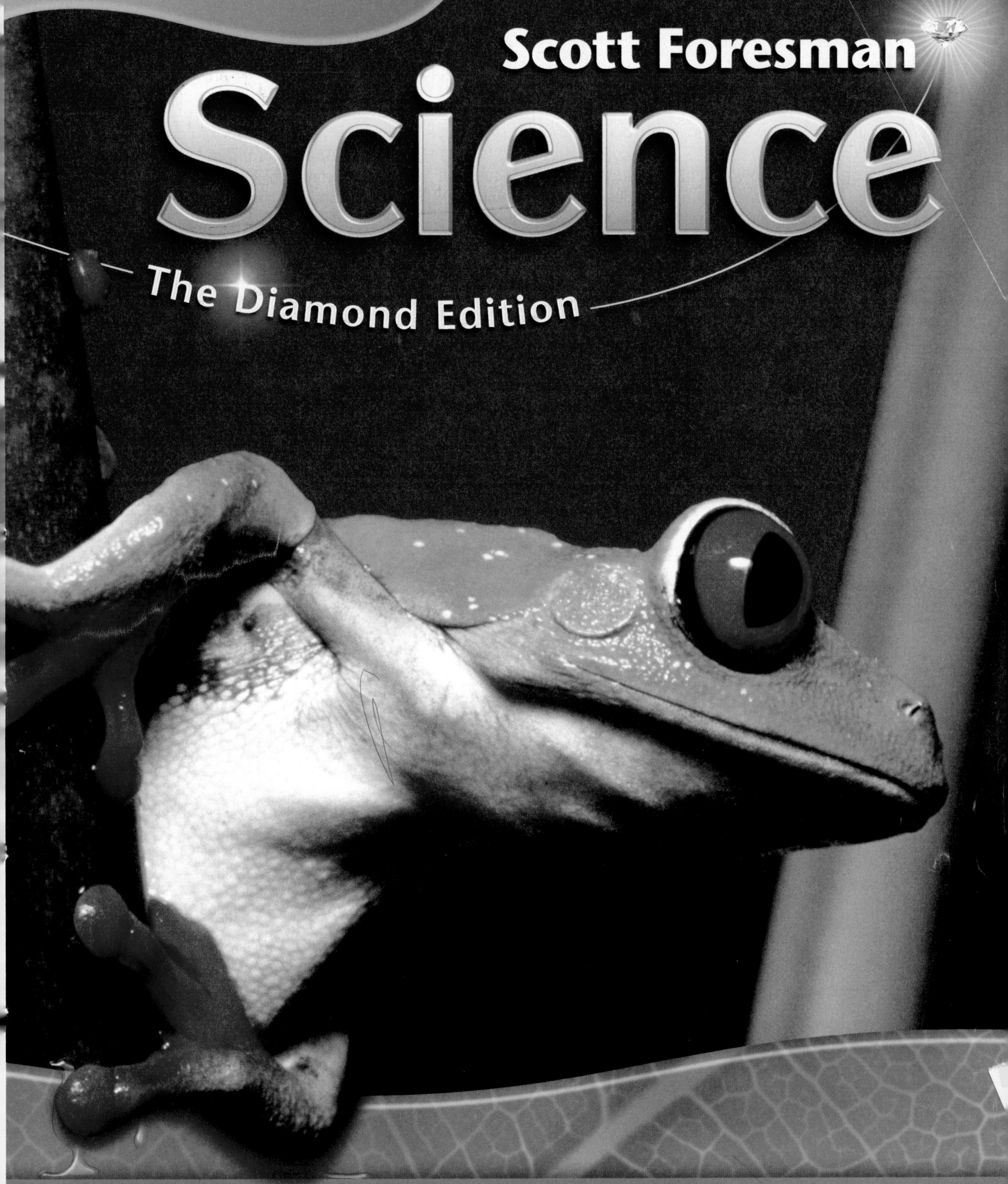

PEARSON
Scott Foresman

Editorial Offices: Glenview, Illinois • Parsippany, New Jersey • New York, New York
Sales Offices: Boston, Massachusetts • Duluth, Georgia • Glenview, Illinois
Coppell, Texas • Sacramento, California • Mesa, Arizona
www.pearsonsuccessnet.com

Series Authors

Dr. Timothy Cooney
Professor of Earth Science and Science Education
University of Northern Iowa (UNI)
Cedar Falls, Iowa

Dr. Jim Cummins
Professor
Department of Curriculum, Teaching, and Learning
University of Toronto
Toronto, Canada

Dr. James Flood
Distinguished Professor of Literacy and Language
School of Teacher Education
San Diego State University
San Diego, California

Barbara Kay Foots, M.Ed.
Science Education Consultant
Houston, Texas

Dr. M. Jenice Goldston
Associate Professor of Science Education
Department of Elementary Education Programs
University of Alabama
Tuscaloosa, Alabama

Dr. Shirley Gholston Key
Associate Professor of Science Education
Instruction and Curriculum Leadership Department
College of Education
University of Memphis
Memphis, Tennessee

Dr. Diane Lapp
Distinguished Professor of Reading and Language Arts in Teacher Education
San Diego State University
San Diego, California

Sheryl A. Mercier
Classroom Teacher
Dunlap Elementary School
Dunlap, California

Karen L. Ostlund, Ph.D.
UTeach Specialist
College of Natural Sciences
The University of Texas at Austin
Austin, Texas

Dr. Nancy Romance
Professor of Science Education & Principal Investigator
NSF/IERI Science IDEAS Project
Charles E. Schmidt College of Science
Florida Atlantic University
Boca Raton, Florida

Dr. William Tate
Chair and Professor of Education and Applied Statistics
Department of Education
Washington University
St. Louis, Missouri

Dr. Kathryn C. Thornton
Former NASA Astronaut
Professor
School of Engineering and Applied Science
University of Virginia
Charlottesville, Virginia

Dr. Leon Ukens
Professor Emeritus
Department of Physics, Astronomy, and Geosciences
Towson University
Towson, Maryland

Steve Weinberg
Consultant
Connecticut Center for Advanced Technology
East Hartford, Connecticut

ISBN–13: 978-0-328-30703-6
ISBN–10: 0-328-30703-3

3 4 5 6 7 8 9 10 V063 15 14 13 12 11 10 09

Maps
MapQuest, Inc.
Photographs
Every effort has been made to secure permission and provide appropriate credit for photographic material. The publisher deeply regrets any omission and pledges to correct errors called to its attention in subsequent editions. Unless otherwise acknowledged, all photographs are the property of Scott Foresman, a division of Pearson Education. Photo locators denoted as follows: Top (T), Center (C), Bottom (B), Left (L), Right (R), Background (Bkgd)
Earth Science: 1 Mark Gibson/Index Stock Imagery; 2 Carolina Biological Supply Company/Phototake; 3 (CL) Phil Degginger/Alamy Images, (B, T) E.R. Degginger/Bruce Coleman Inc.; 4 David Bell/Corbis
Life Science: 1 John G. Shedd Aquarium; 2 (T) Adam Jones/ Photo Researchers, Inc., (B) Kevin Schafer/Corbis; 3 Illinois Department of Natural Resources; 4 John G. Shedd Aquarium
Physical Science: 2 (T) ©Mark E. Gibson Stock Photography, (BL) ©Robert Frerck/Odyssey/Chicago ; 3 Getty Images
Space and Technology: 2 (TL) Harold Theissen/Alamy Images, (TR) Peter Cade/Getty Images, (BL) Barry Runk/Grant Heilman Photography, (BR) Dan Lim/Masterfile Corporation; 3 NASA; 4 Richard Cummins/Corbis

Consulting Author

Dr. Michael P. Klentschy
Superintendent
El Centro Elementary School District
El Centro, California

Science Content Consultants

Dr. Frederick W. Taylor
Senior Research Scientist
Institute for Geophysics
Jackson School of Geosciences
The University of Texas at Austin
Austin, Texas

Dr. Ruth E. Buskirk
Senior Lecturer
School of Biological Sciences
The University of Texas at Austin
Austin, Texas

Dr. Cliff Frohlich
Senior Research Scientist
Institute for Geophysics
Jackson School of Geosciences
The University of Texas at Austin
Austin, Texas

Brad Armosky
McDonald Observatory
The University of Texas at Austin
Austin, Texas

NASA Content Consultants

Adena Williams Loston, Ph.D.
Chief Education Officer
Office of the Chief Education Officer

Clifford W. Houston, Ph.D.
Deputy Chief Education Officer for Education Programs
Office of the Chief Education Officer

Frank C. Owens
Senior Policy Advisor
Office of the Chief Education Officer

Deborah Brown Biggs
Manager, Education Flight Projects Office
Space Operations Mission Directorate, Education Lead

Erika G. Vick
NASA Liaison to Pearson Scott Foresman
Education Flight Projects Office

William E. Anderson
Partnership Manager for Education
Aeronautics Research Mission Directorate

Anita Krishnamurthi
Program Planning Specialist
Space Science Education and Outreach Program

Bonnie J. McClain
Chief of Education
Exploration Systems Mission Directorate

Diane Schweizer
Program Scientist
Earth Science Education

Deborah Rivera
Strategic Alliances Manager
Office of Public Affairs
NASA Headquarters

Douglas D. Peterson
Public Affairs Officer, Astronaut Office
Office of Public Affairs
NASA Johnson Space Center

Nicole Cloutier
Public Affairs Officer, Astronaut Office
Office of Public Affairs
NASA Johnson Space Center

Dr. Jennifer J. Wiseman
Hubble Space Scientist
Program Scientist
NASA Headquarters

Reviewers

Dr. Maria Aida Alanis
Administrator
Austin ISD
Austin Texas

Melissa Barba
Teacher
Wesley Mathews Elementary
Miami, Florida

Dr. Marcelline Barron
Supervisor/K-12 Math and Science
Fairfield Public Schools
Fairfield, Connecticut

Jane Bates
Teacher
Hickory Flat Elementary
Canton, Georgia

Denise Bizjack
Teacher Dr. N. H. Jones Elementary
Ocala, Florida

Latanya D. Bragg
Teacher
Davis Magnet School
Jackson, Mississippi

Richard Burton
Teacher
George Buck Elementary School 94
Indianapolis, Indiana

Dawn Cabrera
Teacher E.W.F. Stirrup School
Miami, Florida

Barbara Calabro
Teacher
Compass Rose Foundation
Ft. Myers, Florida

Lucille Calvin
Teacher
Weddington Math & Science School
Greenville, Mississippi

Patricia Carmichael
Teacher
Teasley Middle School
Canton, Georgia

Martha Cohn
Teacher
An Wang Middle School
Lowell, Massachusetts

Stu Danzinger
Supervisor
Community Consolidated School District 59
Arlington Heights, Illinois

Esther Draper
Supervisor/Science Specialist
Belair Math Science Magnet School
Pine Bluff, Arkansas

Sue Esser
Teacher
Loretto Elementary
Jacksonville, Florida

Dr. Richard Fairman
Teacher
Antioch University
Yellow Springs, Ohio

Joan Goldfarb
Teacher
Indialantic Elementary
Indialantic, Florida

Deborah Gomes
Teacher
A J Gomes Elementary
New Bedford, Massachusetts

Sandy Hobart
Teacher
Mims Elementary
Mims, Florida

Tom Hocker
Teacher/Science Coach
Boston Latin Academy
Dorchester, Massachusetts

Shelley Jaques
Science Supervisor
Moore Public Schools
Moore, Oklahoma

Marguerite W. Jones
Teacher
Spearman Elementary
Piedmont, South Carolina

Kelly Kenney
Teacher
Kansas City Missouri School District
Kansas City, Missouri

Carol Kilbane
Teacher
Riverside Elementary School
Wichita, Kansas

Robert Kolenda
Teacher
Neshaminy School District
Langhorne, Pennsylvania

Karen Lynn Kruse
Teacher
St. Paul the Apostle
Yonkers, New York

Elizabeth Loures
Teacher
Point Fermin Elementary School
San Pedro, California

Susan MacDougall
Teacher
Brick Community Primary Learning Center
Brick, New Jersey

Jack Marine
Teacher
Raising Horizons Quest Charter School
Philadelphia, Pennsylvania

Nicola Micozzi Jr.
Science Coordinator
Plymouth Public Schools
Plymouth, Massachusetts

Paula Monteiro
Teacher
A J Gomes Elementary
New Bedford, Massachusetts

Tracy Newallis
Teacher
Taper Avenue Elementary
San Pedro, California

Dr. Eugene Nicolo
Supervisor, Science K-12
Moorestown School District
Moorestown, New Jersey

Jeffry Pastrak
School District of Philadelphia
Philadelphia, Penslyvania

Helen Pedigo
Teacher
Mt. Carmel Elementary
Huntsville Alabama

Becky Peltonen
Teacher
Patterson Elementary School
Panama City, Florida

Sherri Pensler
Teacher/ESOL
Claude Pepper Elementary
Miami, Florida

Virginia Rogliano
Teacher
Bridgeview Elementary
South Charleston, West Virginia

Debbie Sanders
Teacher
Thunderbolt Elementary
Orange Park, Florida

Grethel Santamarina
Teacher
E.W.F. Stirrup School
Miami, Florida

Migdalia Schneider
Teacher/Bilingual
Lindell School
Long Beach, New York

Susan Shelly
Teacher
Bonita Springs Elementary
Bonita Springs, Florida

Peggy Terry
Teacher
Madison Elementary
South Holland, Illinois

Jane M. Thompson
Teacher
Emma Ward Elementary
Lawrenceburg, Kentucky

Martha Todd
Teacher
W. H. Rhodes Elementary
Milton, Florida

Renee Williams
Teacher
Bloomfield Schools
Central Primary
Bloomfield, New Mexico

Myra Wood
Teacher
Madison Street Academy
Ocala, Florida

Marion Zampa
Teacher
Shawnee Mission School District
Overland Park, Kansas

Science

See learning in a whole new light

How do plants live in their habitats?

Life Science in Illinois

Chapter 1 • All About Plants

Chapter 2 • All About Animals

How are animals different from each other?

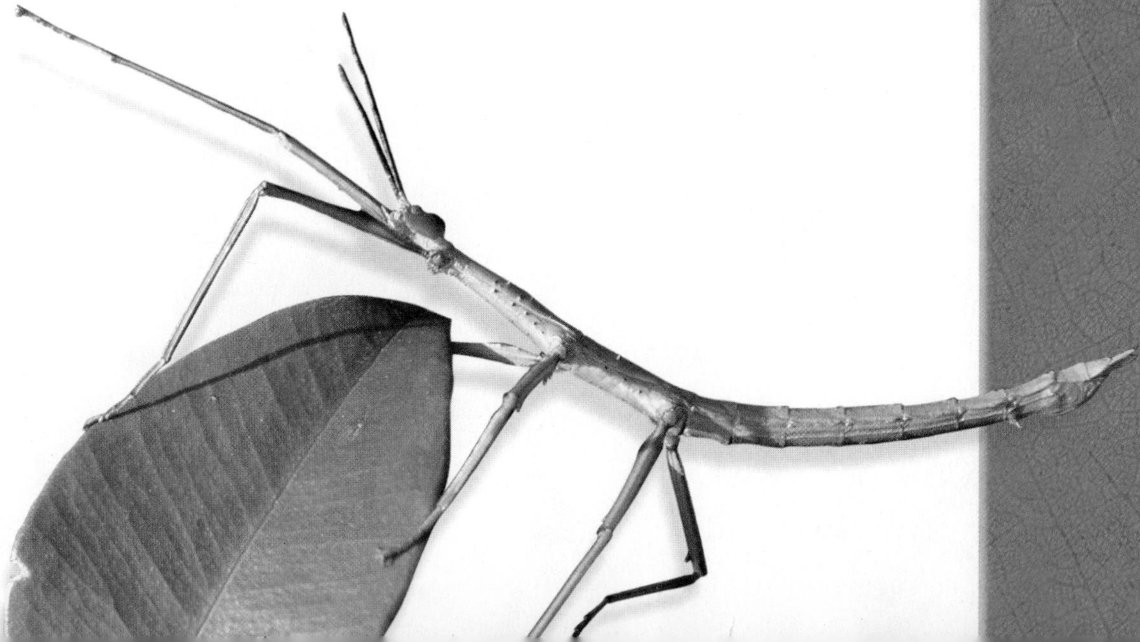

Chapter 3 • How Plants and Animals Live Together

How do living things help each other?

Chapter 4 • How Living Things Grow and Change

How do living things grow in different ways?

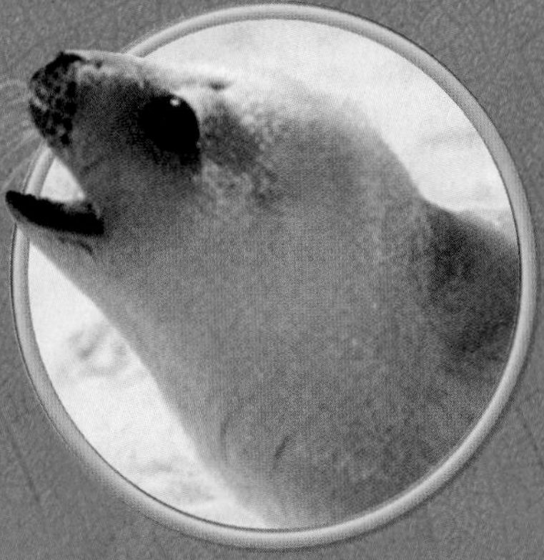

What are Earth's natural resources?

Earth Science in Illinois

Chapter 5 • Earth's Land, Air, and Water

Chapter 6 • Earth's Weather and Seasons

How does weather change?

Unit B Earth Science

How can people learn about the Earth long ago?

Chapter 7 • Fossils and Dinosaurs

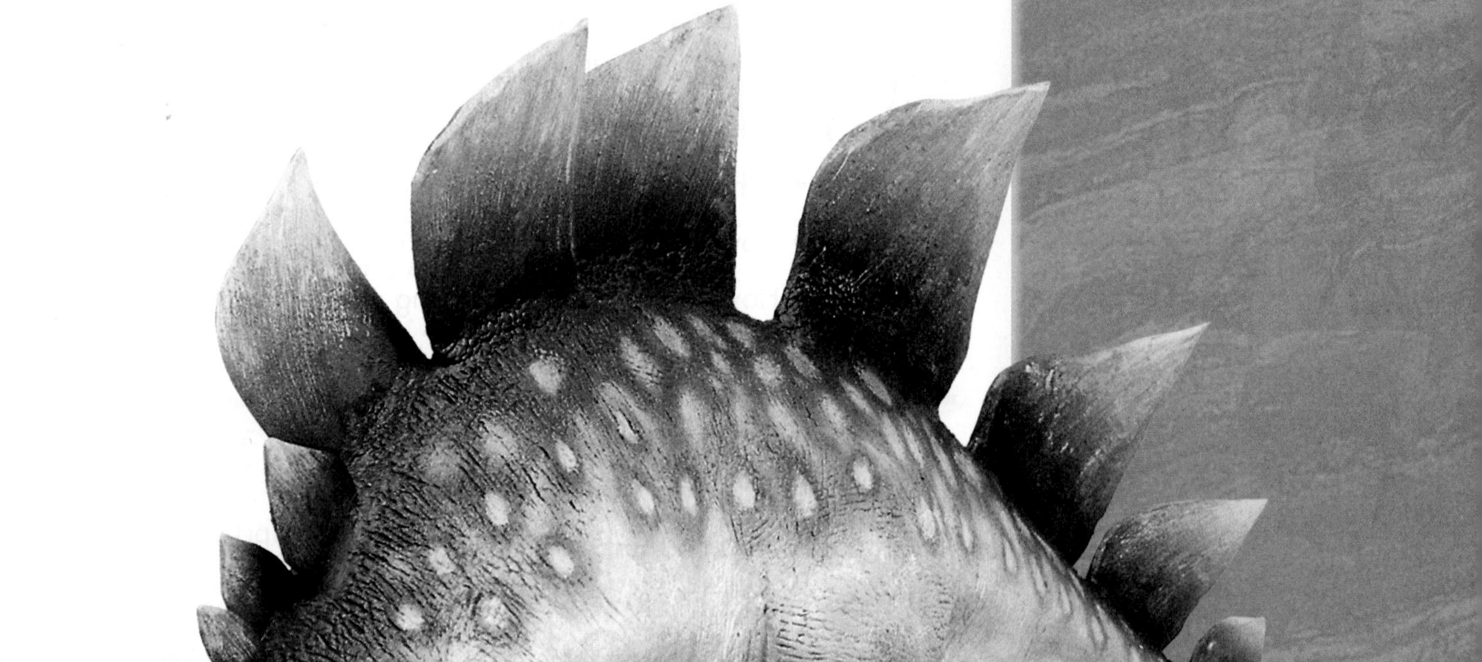

Science Process Skills

Scientists use process skills to find out about things. You will use these skills when you do the activities in this book. Suppose scientists want to learn more about space. Which process skills might they use?

Space

Observe
A scientist who wants to find out more about space observes many things. You use your senses to find out about things too.

Classify
Scientists classify objects in space. You classify when you sort or group things by their properties.

Estimate and Measure
Scientists build machines to explore space. First scientists make a careful guess about the size or amount of the parts of the machine. Then they measure each part.

Infer
Scientists are always learning about space. Scientists draw a conclusion or make a guess from what they already know.

What are some properties of matter?

Physical Science in Illinois

Chapter 8 • Properties of Matter

Chapter 9 • Energy

What are some kinds of energy?

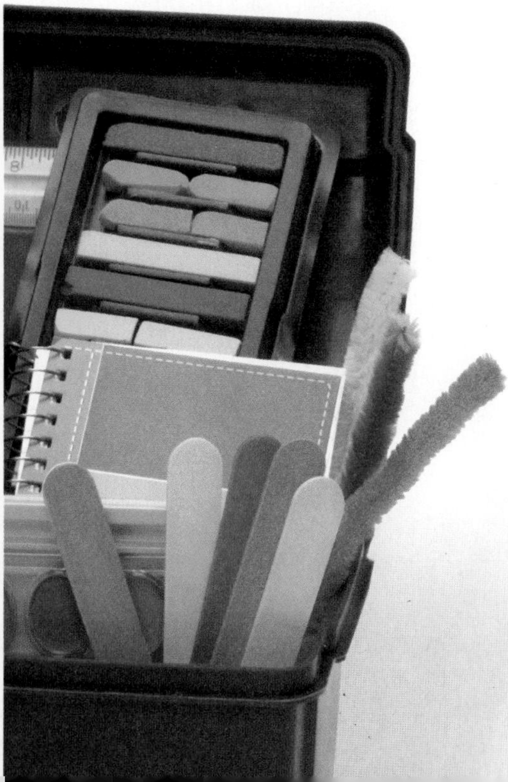

Unit C Physical Science

Chapter 10 • Forces and Motion

How do forces cause objects to move?

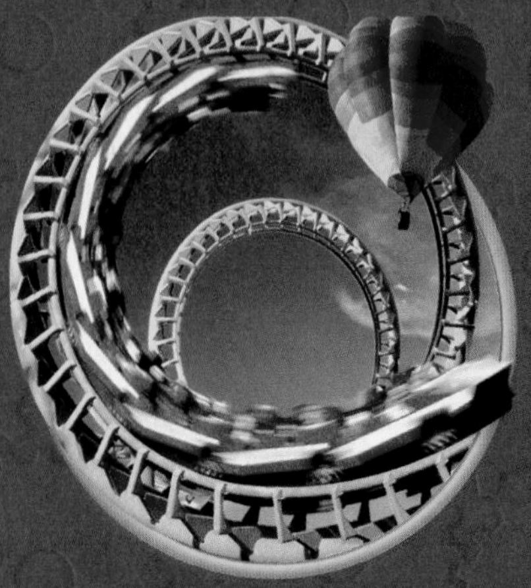

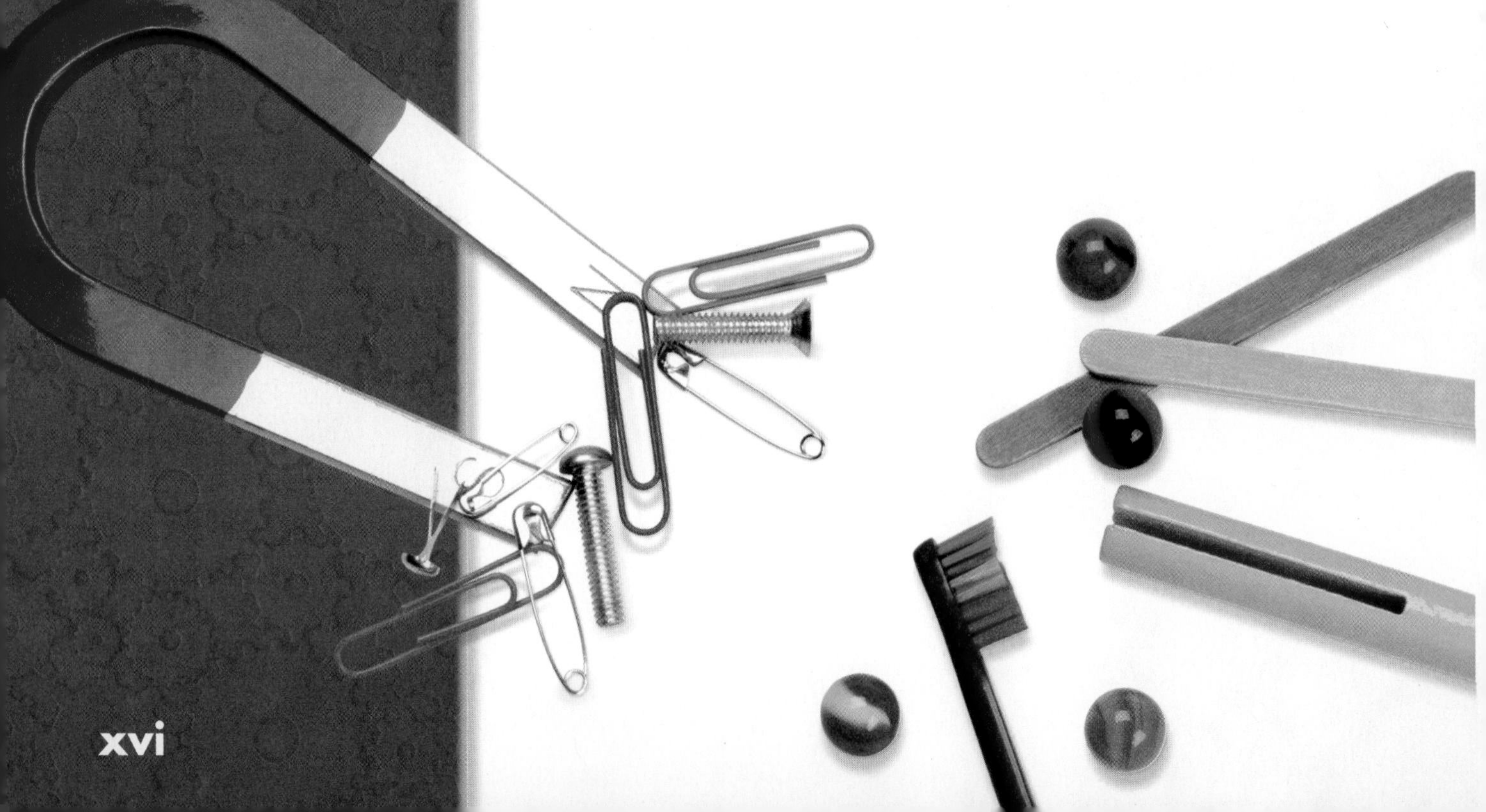

Chapter 11 • Sound

How is sound made?

Unit D Space and Technology

What are some ways the Earth moves?

Space and Technology in Illinois

Chapter 12 • Earth and Space

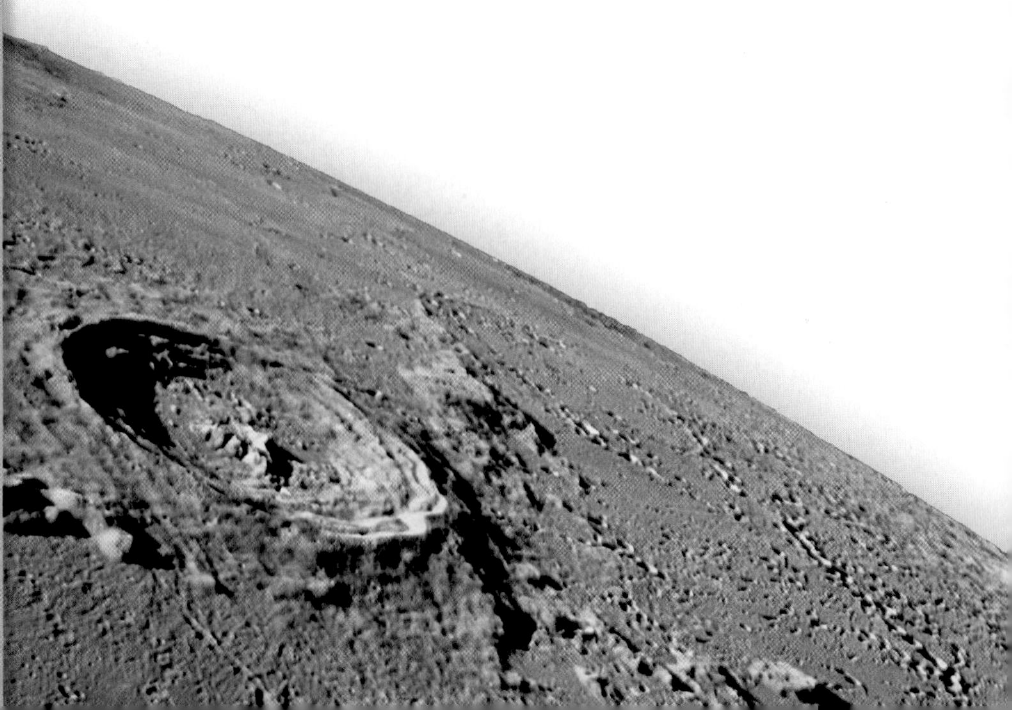

Chapter 13 • Technology in Our World

What are some ways technology helps us?

How to Read Science

Each chapter in your book has a page like this one. This page shows you how to use a reading skill.

Before reading
First, read the Build Background page. Next, read the How To Read Science page. Then, think about what you already know. Last, make a list of what you already know.

Target Reading Skill
Each page has a target reading skill. The target reading skill will help you understand what you read.

Real-World Connection
Each page has an example of something you will learn.

Graphic Organizer
A graphic organizer can help you think about what you learn.

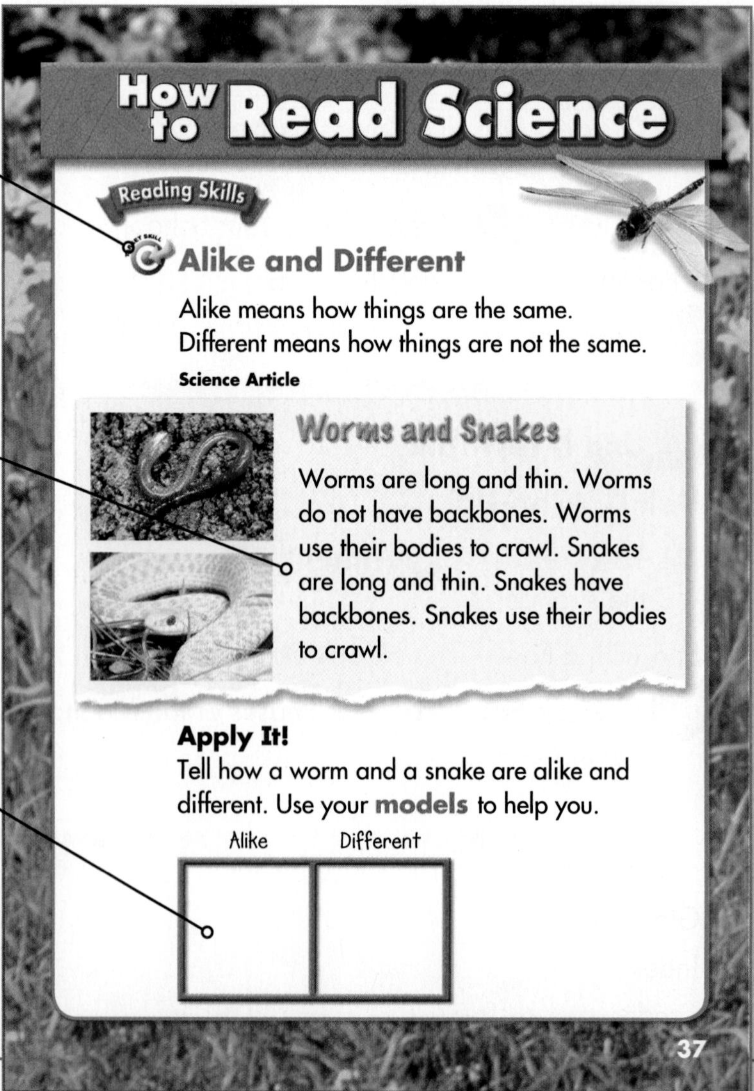
How to Read Science

Reading Skills

Alike and Different

Alike means how things are the same.
Different means how things are not the same.

Science Article

Worms and Snakes

Worms are long and thin. Worms do not have backbones. Worms use their bodies to crawl. Snakes are long and thin. Snakes have backbones. Snakes use their bodies to crawl.

Apply It!
Tell how a worm and a snake are alike and different. Use your **models** to help you.

Alike	Different

37

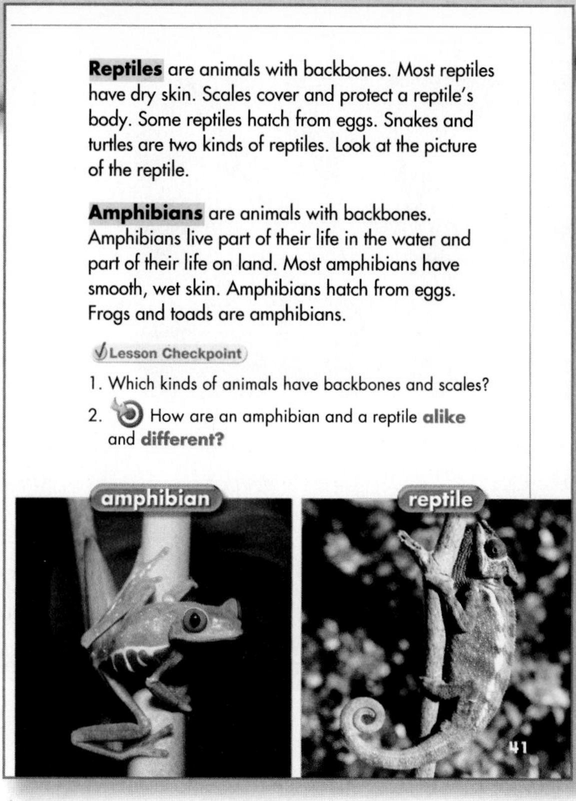
Reptiles are animals with backbones. Most reptiles have dry skin. Scales cover and protect a reptile's body. Some reptiles hatch from eggs. Snakes and turtles are two kinds of reptiles. Look at the picture of the reptile.

Amphibians are animals with backbones. Amphibians live part of their life in the water and part of their life on land. Most amphibians have smooth, wet skin. Amphibians hatch from eggs. Frogs and toads are amphibians.

Lesson Checkpoint

1. Which kinds of animals have backbones and scales?
2. How are an amphibian and a reptile **alike** and **different?**

amphibian

reptile

41

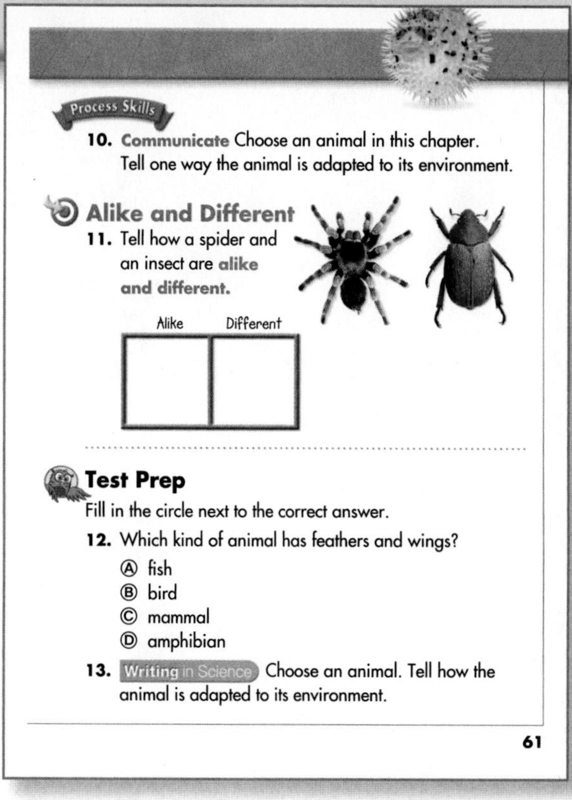
Process Skills

10. **Communicate** Choose an animal in this chapter. Tell one way the animal is adapted to its environment.

Alike and Different

11. Tell how a spider and an insect are **alike and different.**

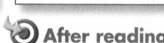

Alike	Different

Test Prep

Fill in the circle next to the correct answer.

12. Which kind of animal has feathers and wings?

Ⓐ fish
Ⓑ bird
Ⓒ mammal
Ⓓ amphibian

13. Writing in Science Choose an animal. Tell how the animal is adapted to its environment.

61

During reading

Use the checkpoint as you read the lesson. This will help you check how much you understand.

After reading

Think about what you have learned. Compare what you learned with the list you made before you read the chapter. Answer the questions in the Chapter Review.

Target Reading Skills

These are some target reading skills that appear in this book.

- Cause and Effect
- Alike and Different
- Put Things in Order
- Predict
- Draw Conclusions
- Picture Clues
- Important Details

Science Process Skills

Scientists use process skills to find out about things. You will use these skills when you do the activities in this book. Suppose scientists want to learn more about space. Which process skills might they use?

Observe
A scientist who wants to find out more about space observes many things. You use your senses to find out about things too.

Classify
Scientists classify objects in space. You classify when you sort or group things by their properties.

Estimate and Measure
Scientists build machines to explore space. First scientists make a careful guess about the size or amount of the parts of the machine. Then they measure each part.

Infer
Scientists are always learning about space. Scientists draw a conclusion or make a guess from what they already know.

Space

Predict

First scientists tell what they think will happen. Then they do an experiment.

Make and Use Models

Scientists might make and use models of a machine to use in space. Models show what scientists already know.

Make Definitions

Scientists use what they know to tell what something means.

Science Process Skills

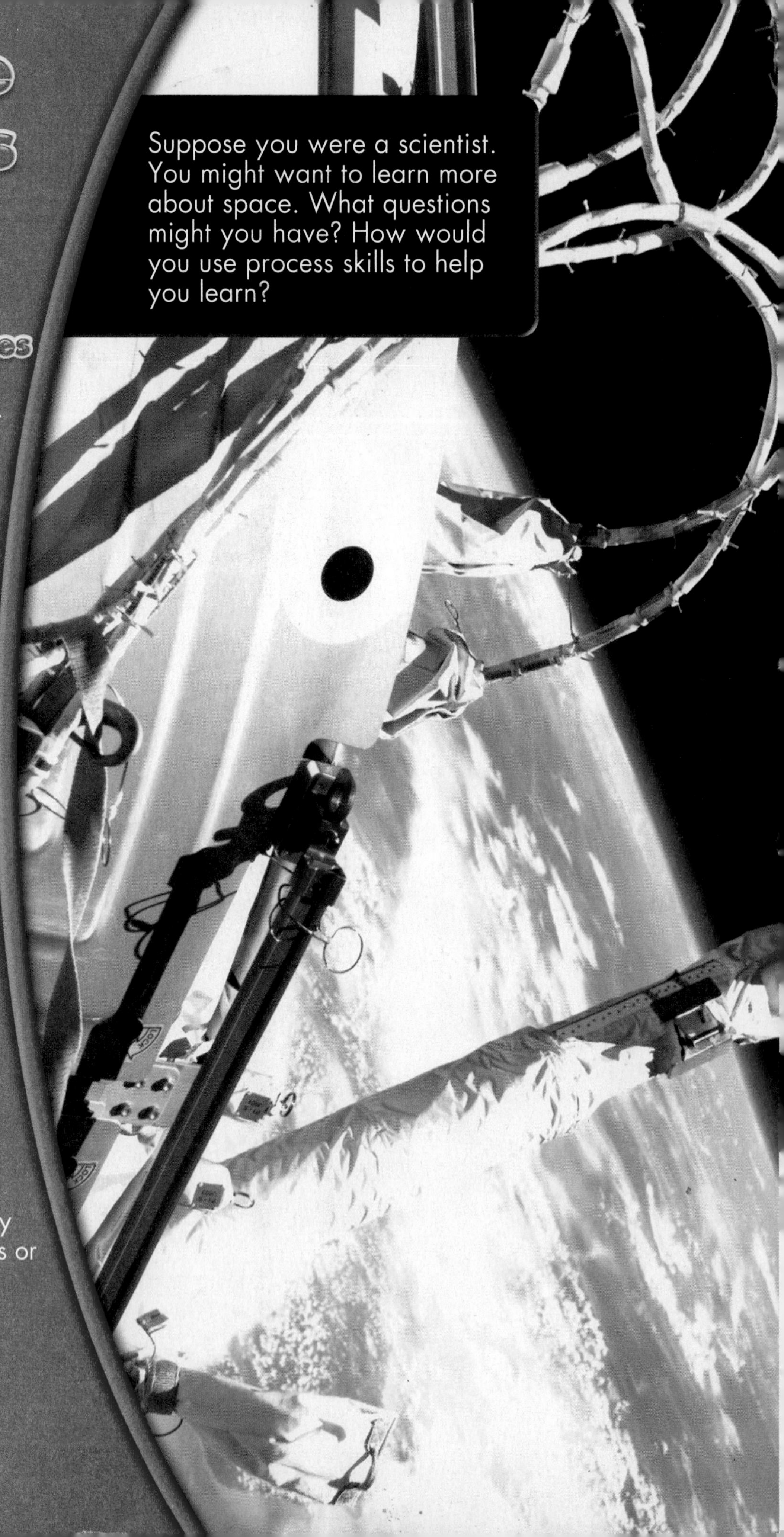

Suppose you were a scientist. You might want to learn more about space. What questions might you have? How would you use process skills to help you learn?

Make Hypotheses

Think of a question you have about space. Make a statement that you can test to answer your question.

Collect Data

Scientists record what they observe and measure. Scientists put this data into charts or graphs.

Interpret Data

Scientists use what they learn to solve problems or answer questions.

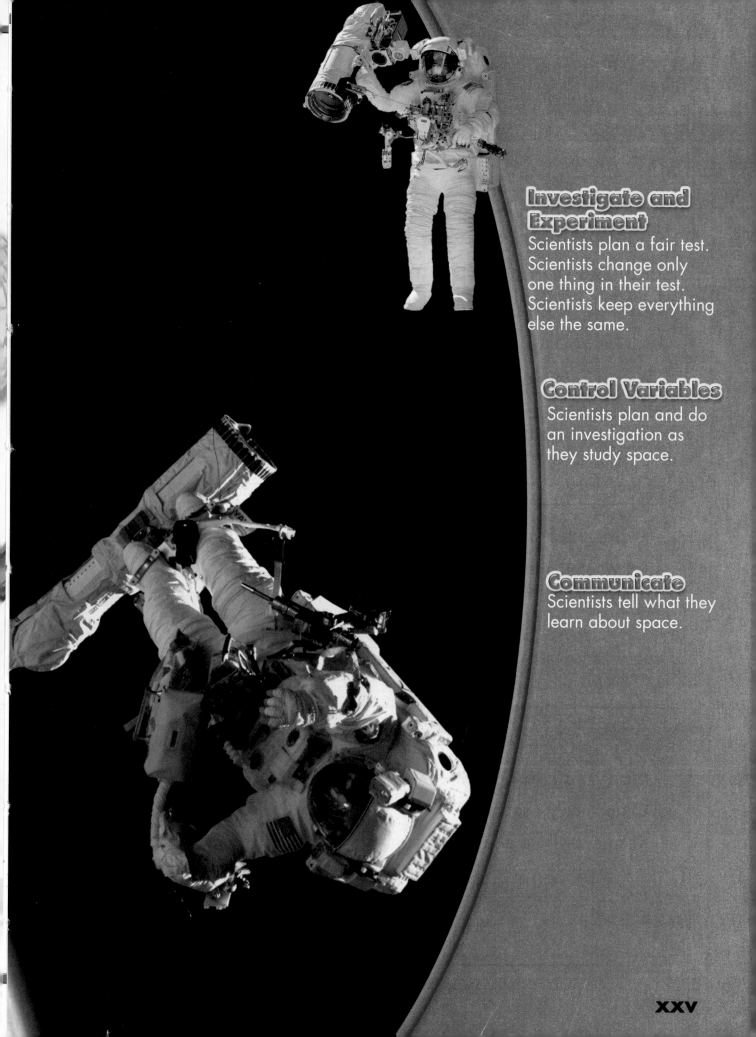

Investigate and Experiment

Scientists plan a fair test. Scientists change only one thing in their test. Scientists keep everything else the same.

Control Variables

Scientists plan and do an investigation as they study space.

Communicate

Scientists tell what they learn about space.

Science Tools

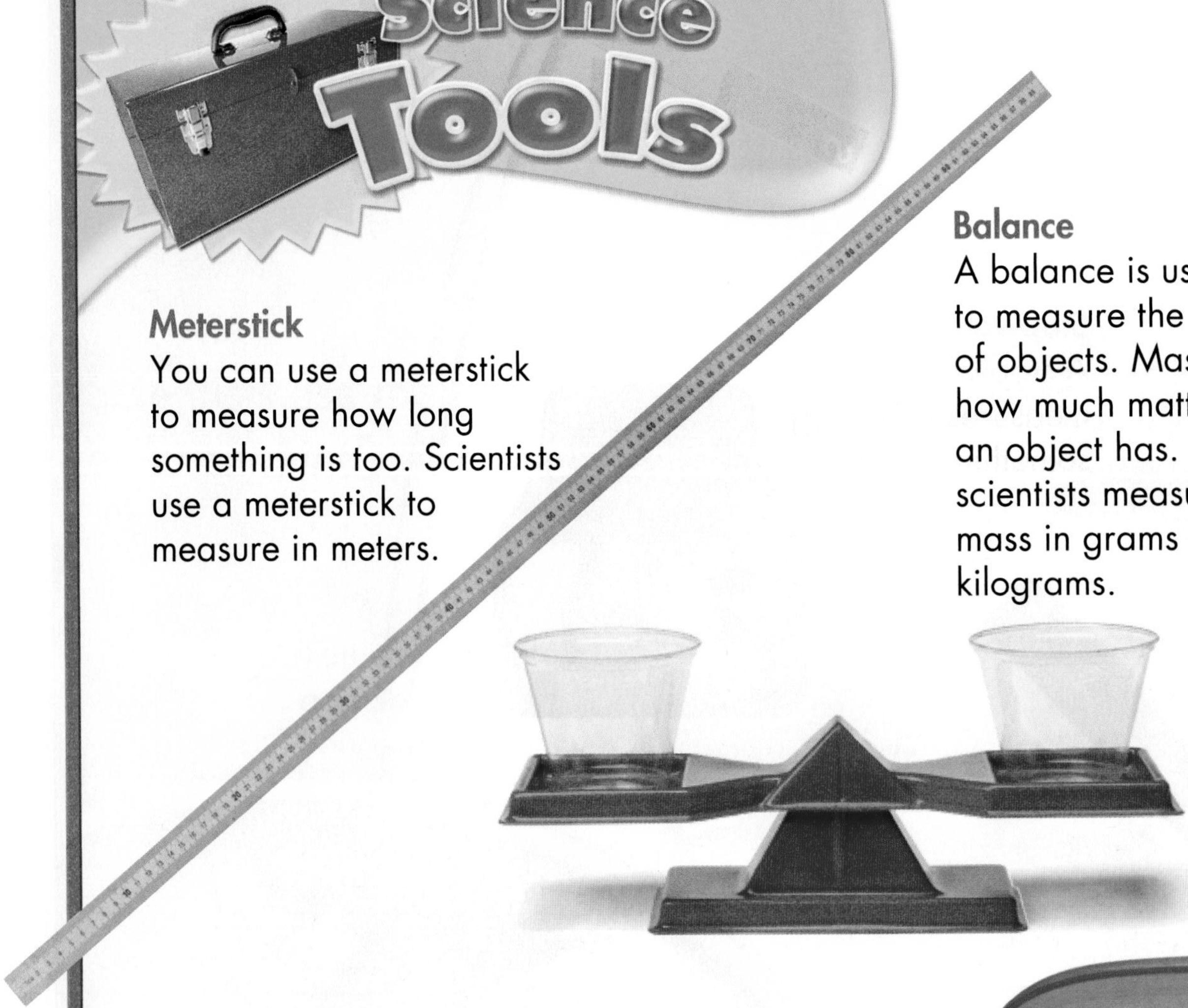

Meterstick

You can use a meterstick to measure how long something is too. Scientists use a meterstick to measure in meters.

Balance

A balance is used to measure the mass of objects. Mass is how much matter an object has. Most scientists measure mass in grams or kilograms.

Measuring cup

You can use a measuring cup to measure volume. Volume is how much space something takes up.

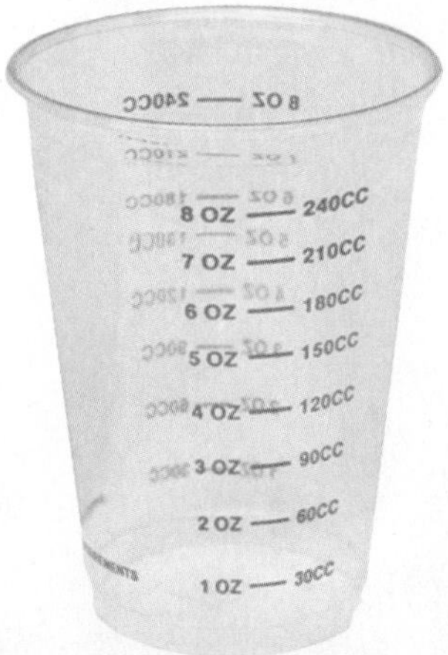

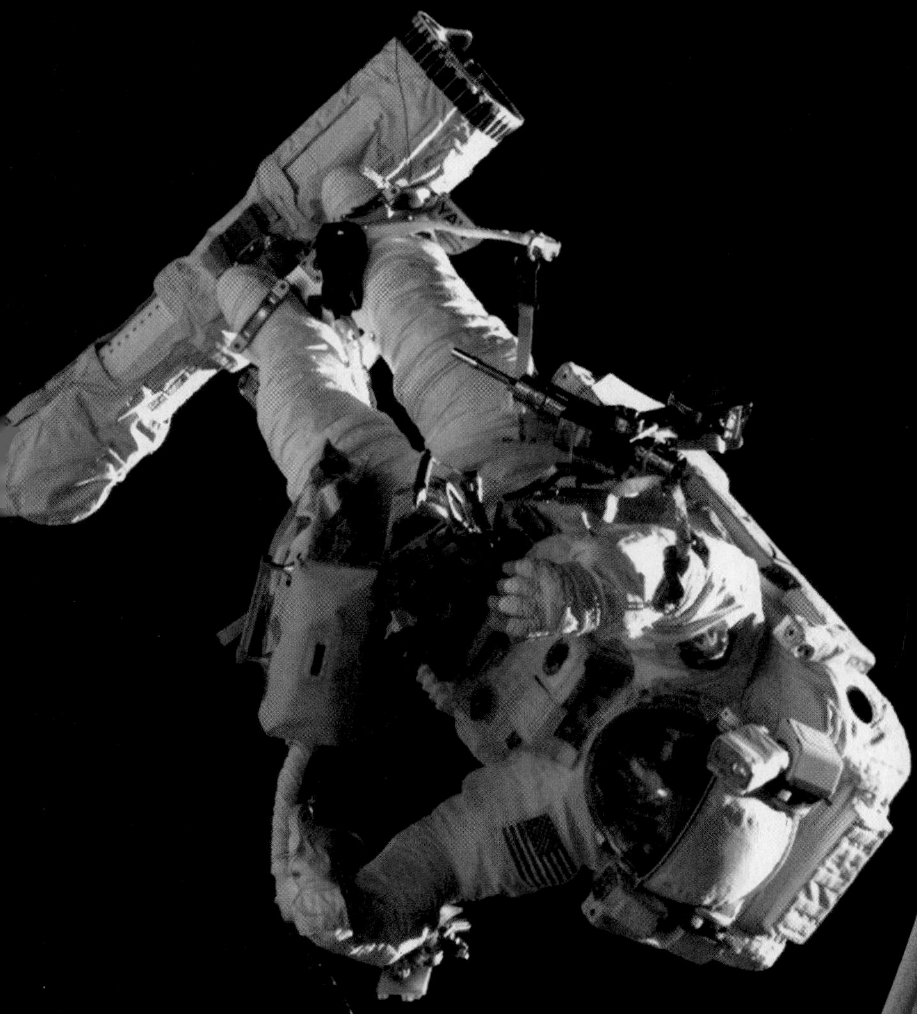

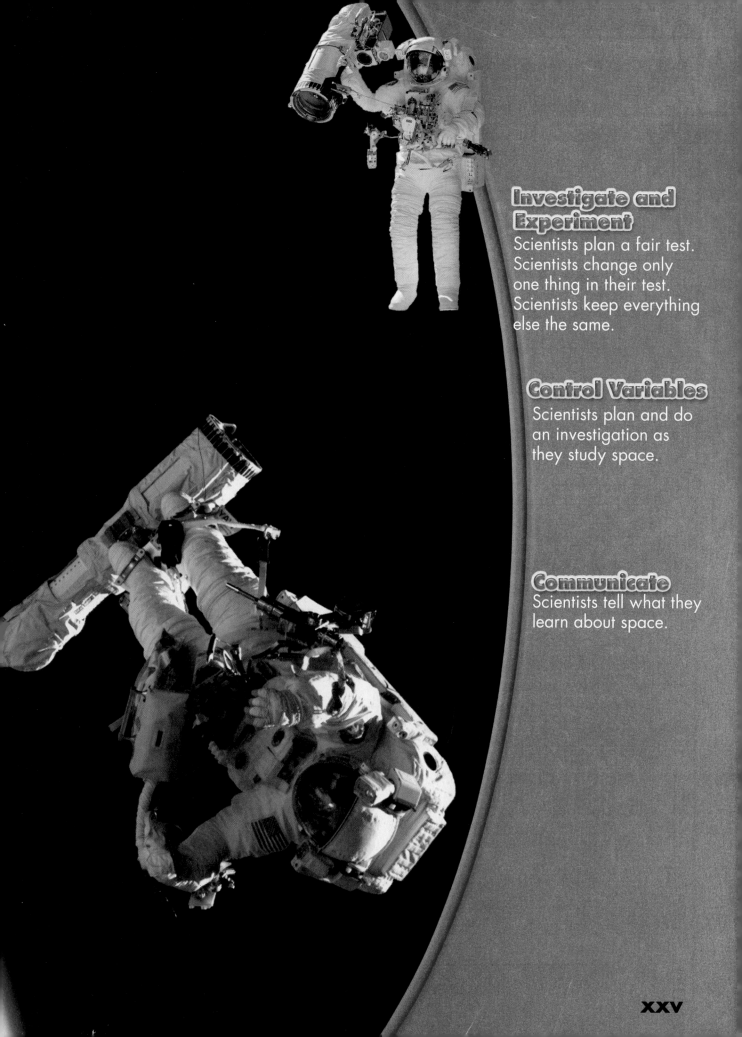

Investigate and Experiment

Scientists plan a fair test. Scientists change only one thing in their test. Scientists keep everything else the same.

Control Variables

Scientists plan and do an investigation as they study space.

Communicate

Scientists tell what they learn about space.

Lab zone

Using Scientific Methods

Scientific methods are ways of finding answers. Scientific methods have these steps. Sometimes scientists do the steps in a different order. Scientists do not always do all of the steps.

Ask a question.

Ask a question that you want answered.

Do seeds need water to grow?

Make your hypothesis.

Tell what you think the answer is to your question.

If seeds are watered, then they will grow.

Plan a fair test.

Change only one thing.

Keep everything else the same.

Water one pot with seeds.

water

no water

Do your test.

Test your hypothesis. Do your test more than once. See if your results are the same.

Collect and record your data.

Keep records of what you find out. Use words or drawings to help.

Tell your conclusion.

Observe the results of your test. Decide if your hypothesis is right or wrong. Tell what you decide.

Seeds need water to grow.

no water

water

Go further.

Use what you learn. Think of new questions or better ways to do a test.

Science Tools

Scientists use many different kinds of tools.

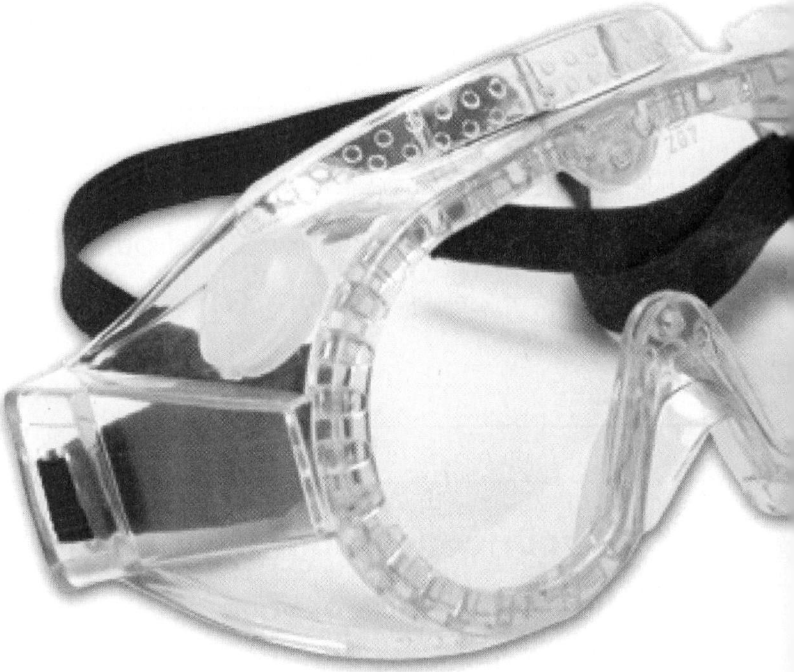

Safety goggles
You can use safety goggles to protect your eyes.

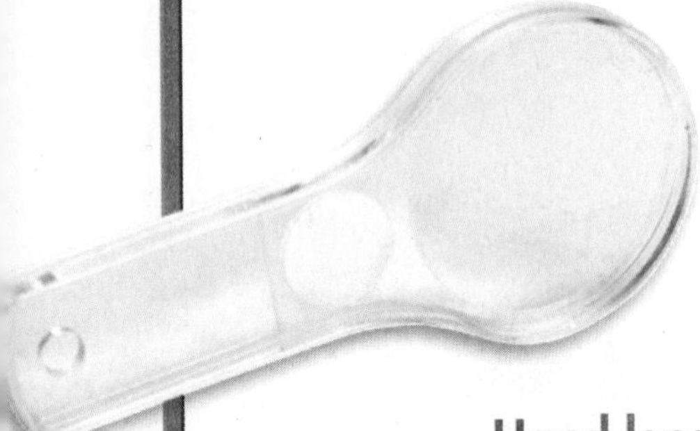

Hand lens
A hand lens makes objects look larger.

Clock
A clock measures time.

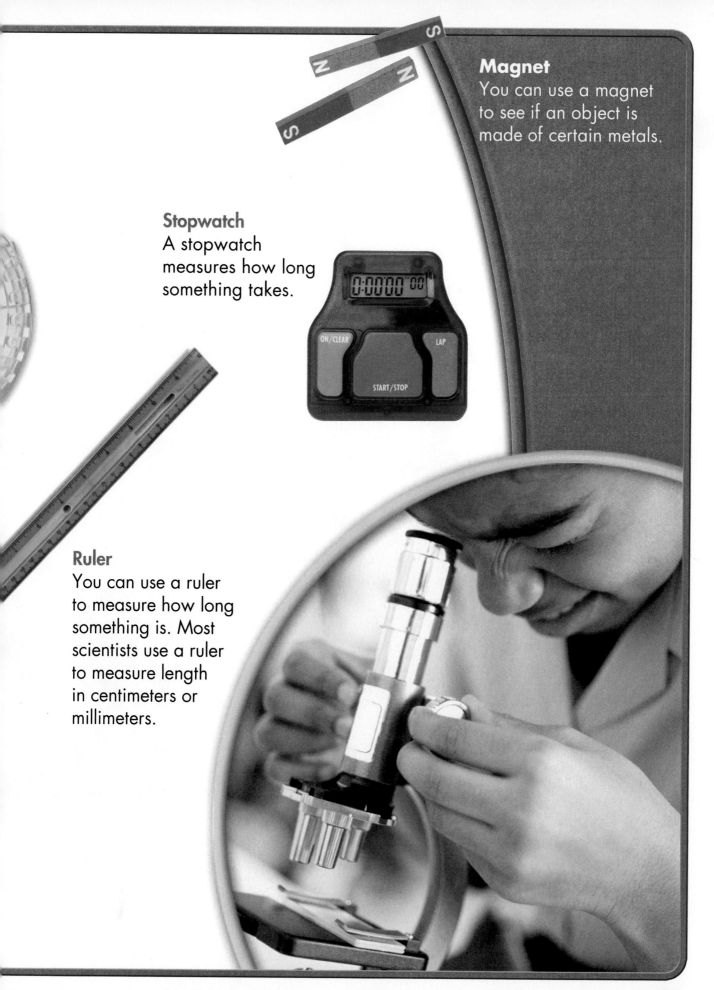

Magnet
You can use a magnet to see if an object is made of certain metals.

Stopwatch
A stopwatch measures how long something takes.

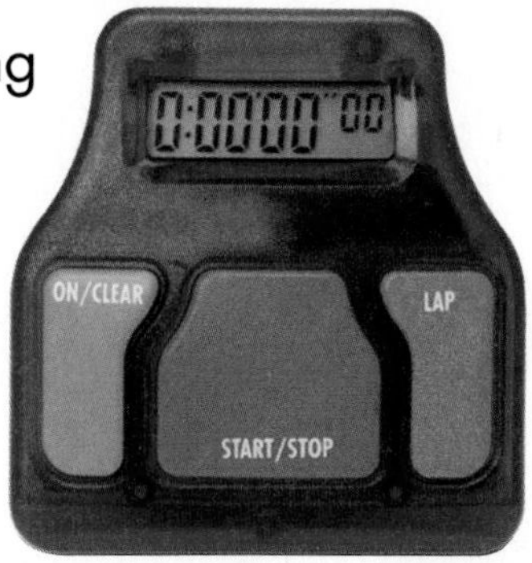

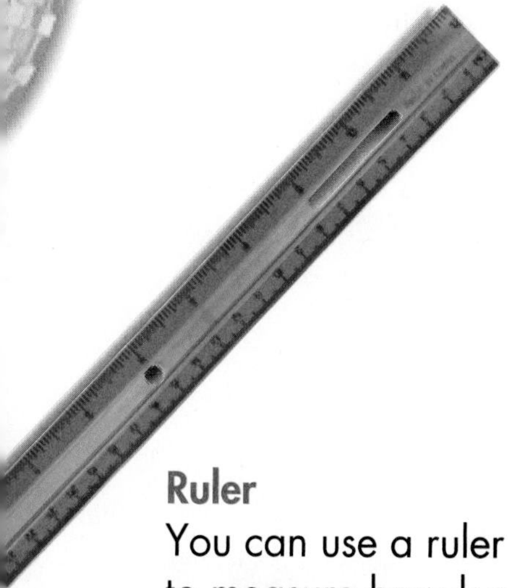

Ruler
You can use a ruler to measure how long something is. Most scientists use a ruler to measure length in centimeters or millimeters.

Science Tools

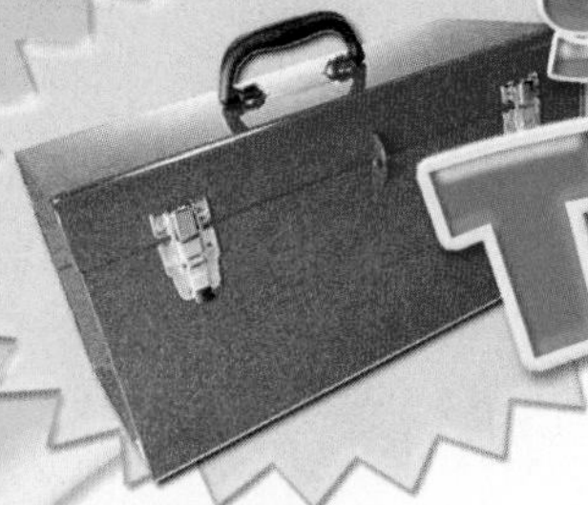

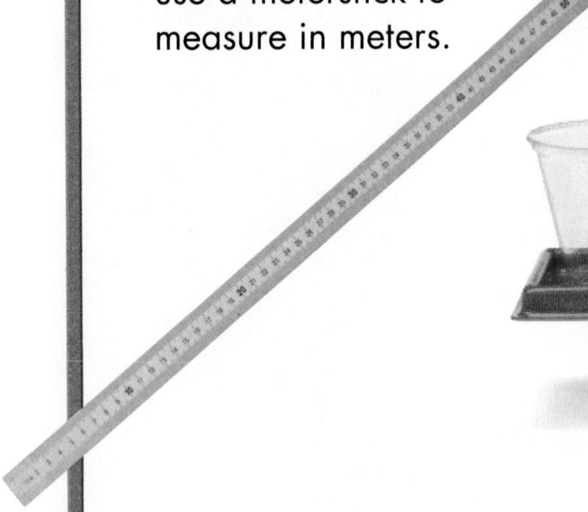

Meterstick
You can use a meterstick to measure how long something is too. Scientists use a meterstick to measure in meters.

Balance
A balance is used to measure the mass of objects. Mass is how much matter an object has. Most scientists measure mass in grams or kilograms.

Measuring cup
You can use a measuring cup to measure volume. Volume is how much space something takes up.

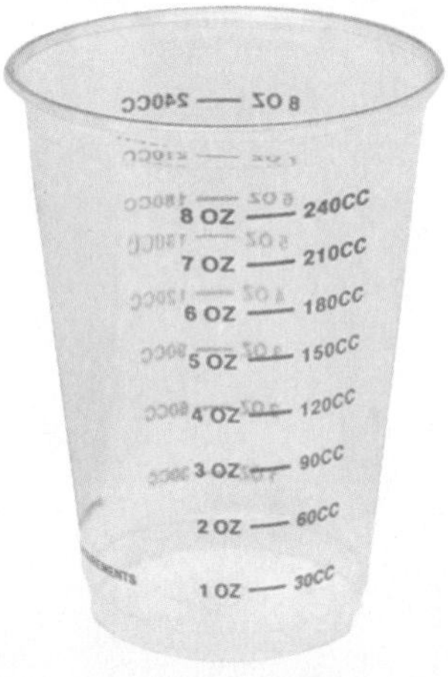

Calculator

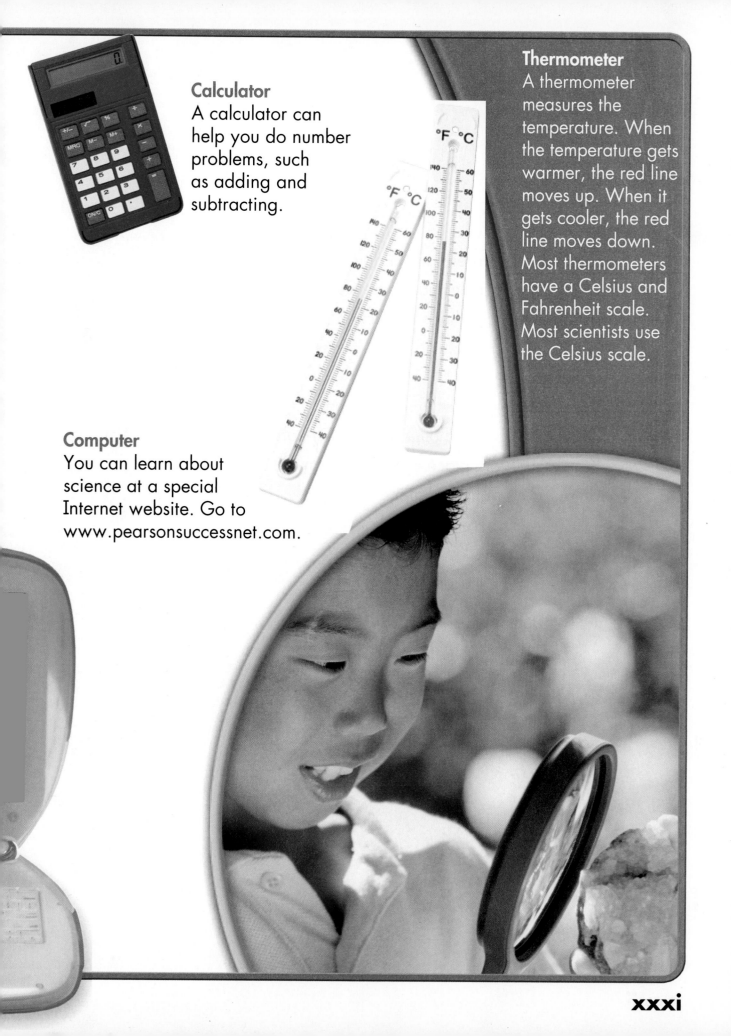

A calculator can help you do number problems, such as adding and subtracting.

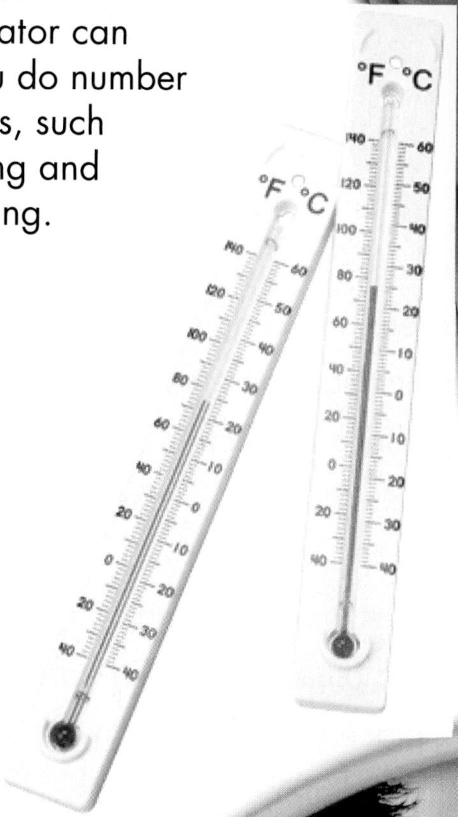

Thermometer

A thermometer measures the temperature. When the temperature gets warmer, the red line moves up. When it gets cooler, the red line moves down. Most thermometers have a Celsius and Fahrenheit scale. Most scientists use the Celsius scale.

Computer

You can learn about science at a special Internet website. Go to www.pearsonsuccessnet.com.

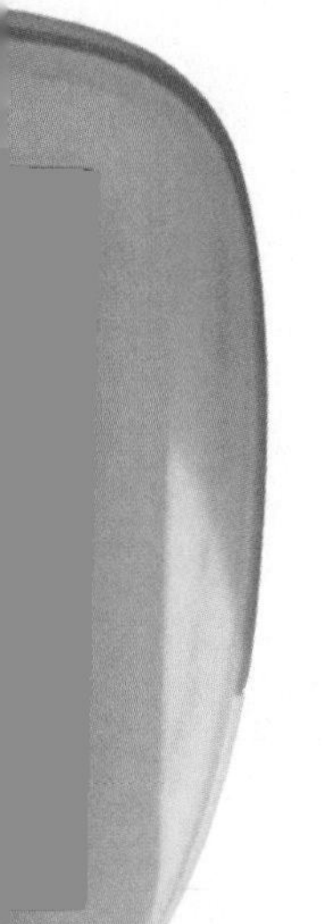

Safety in Science

You need to be careful when doing science activities. This page includes safety tips to remember:

- Listen to your teacher's instructions.
- Never taste or smell materials unless your teacher tells you to.
- Wear safety goggles when needed.
- Handle scissors and other equipment carefully.
- Keep your work place neat and clean.
- Clean up spills immediately.
- Tell your teacher immediately about accidents or if you see something that looks unsafe.
- Wash your hands well after every activity.

Unit A

Life Science in Illinois

Did you know that you can learn about sea animals in Chicago? The Oceanarium at the Shedd Aquarium is the largest indoor aquarium in the world.

ILLINOIS

Field Trip

Shedd Aquarium

You can learn how plants and animals live together at the Shedd Aquarium in Chicago. Many of the fish and other animals are from places that are far from Illinois. You can learn about coral reefs and places with rocks. You can also learn about fish and other animals living in lakes and rivers in Illinois.

Find out more:

Research to find out more about the different fish at the Shedd Aquarium.

- Draw a picture of a fish.
- Write the name of the fish.
- Write about what the fish eats and where it lives.

IL CRU 10 9 8 7 6 5 4 3 2 1

Unit A

Life Science in Illinois

Did you know that you can learn about sea animals in Chicago? The Oceanarium at the Shedd Aquarium is the largest indoor aquarium in the world.

Life Science in Illinois

How are wildflowers, bobcats, and fish alike? They can all be found in Illinois. You will learn more about the science behind them in Unit A.

Woodland Wildflowers

You can see wildflowers during the spring in Illinois. Many wildflowers grow after winter. Wildflowers can be different colors and sizes. You will learn more about plants in Chapter 1.

Badgers, Beavers, and Bobcats

Badgers live in grasslands. Beavers live near water. Bobcats live in forests. They are all mammals in Illinois. They live in different environments that meet their needs. You will learn more about animals and their needs in Chapter 2.

Argyle Lake State Park

Argyle Lake State Park is near Colchester. Bass, trout, and catfish live in Argyle Lake. Some people catch the fish to eat. Some fish are food for birds and other animals. You will learn more about how plants and animals live together in Chapter 3.

ISAT Prep

Answer the questions below. Write your answers on a separate sheet of paper.

Multiple-Choice Questions

1 Which animal lives in Illinois forests?

A. badger
B. beaver
C. bat
D. bobcat

2 In which season do many Illinois wildflowers grow?

A. winter
B. spring
C. fall
D. summer

3 Fish from Illinois lakes are NOT food for

A. people
B. birds
C. other animals
D. wildflowers

Short-Response Questions

4 Name three kinds of fish that live in Argyle Lake.

5 What are three mammals that live in Illinois?

ILLINOIS

Field Trip

Shedd Aquarium

You can learn how plants and animals live together at the Shedd Aquarium in Chicago. Many of the fish and other animals are from places that are far from Illinois. You can learn about coral reefs and places with rocks. You can also learn about fish and other animals living in lakes and rivers in Illinois.

Find out more:

Research to find out more about the different fish at the Shedd Aquarium.

- Draw a picture of a fish.
- Write the name of the fish.
- Write about what the fish eats and where it lives.

IL CRU 10 9 8 7 6 5 4 3 2 1

You Will Discover

- how each part of a plant helps the plant live.
- where different kinds of plants live.

Chapter 1
All About Plants

online Student Edition
pearsonsuccessnet.com

Build Background

How do plants live in their habitats?

nutrients

Nutrients are materials that living things need to live and grow.

Chapter 1 Vocabulary

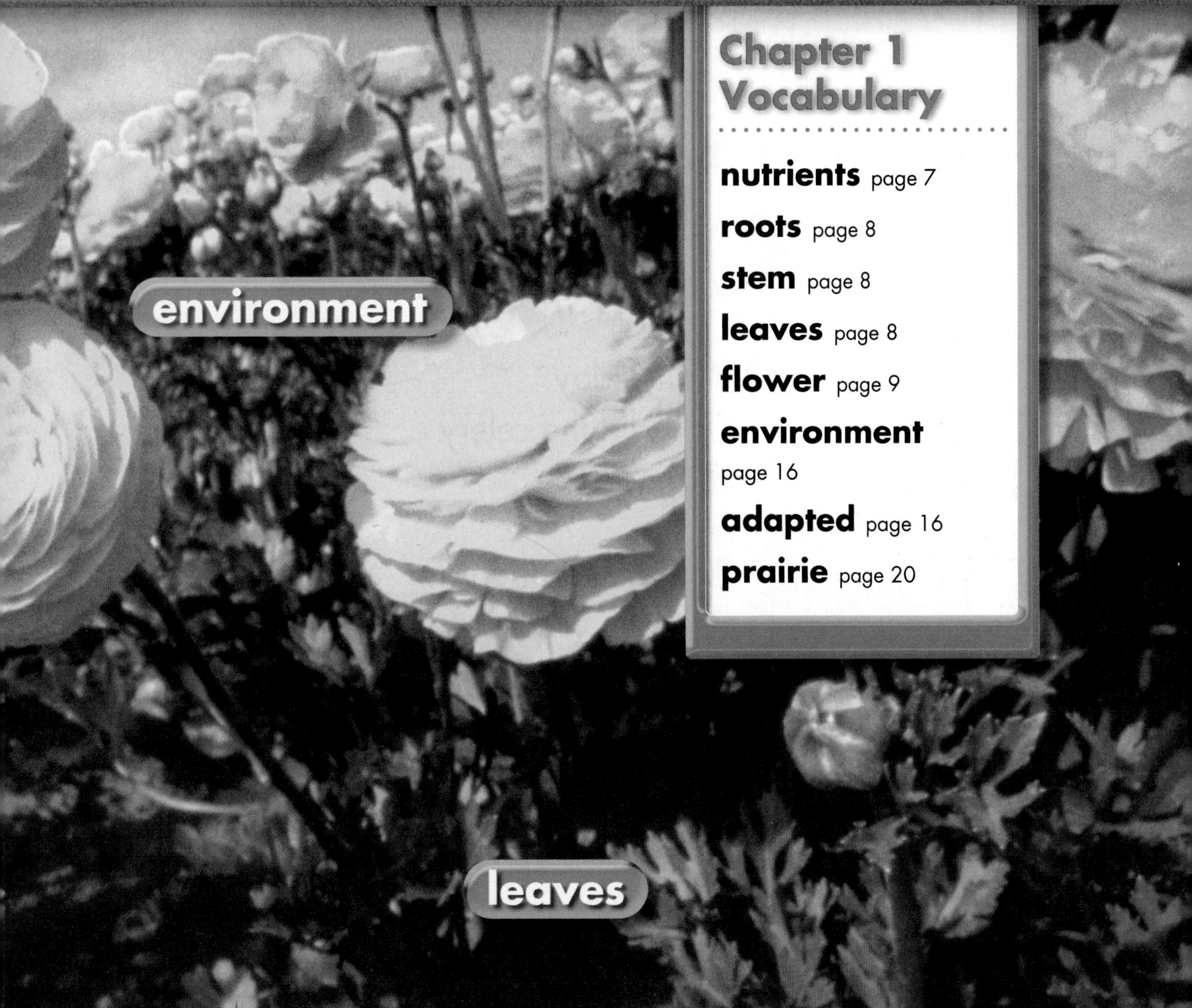

Lab zone Directed Inquiry

Explore Do plants need water?

Materials

celery

jar

water

What to Do

1. Put celery in the jar. Look at the celery.

2. Wait 1 day. How did the celery change?

3. Put water in the jar. **Predict** what will happen to the celery.

4. Wait 1 day. How did the celery change? Why did it change?

Process Skills

You **predict** when you tell what you think might happen.

Explain Your Results

Predict What will happen if you take the celery out of the water?

How to Read Science

Reading Skills

Target Skill: Predict

Predict means to tell what you think might happen next.

Science Story

Workers plant celery seeds in little pots. When the seeds begin to grow, farmers move the young plants to fields. The farmers cut the celery when it is grown.

Apply It!

Predict what will happen to the celery next. Make a graphic organizer to help you.

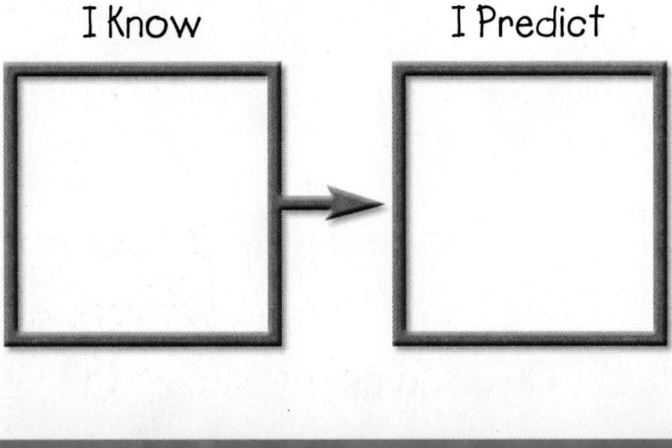

You Are There

Plants

Sung to the tune of "Where, Oh, Where Has My Little Dog Gone?"
Lyrics by Gerri Brioso & Richard Freitas/The Dovetail Group, Inc.

Plants have roots that grow in soil,
And hold the plant in place.
The roots take in water and nutrients,
And carry them up to the stem.

CAMdeN

Lesson 1

What are the parts of a plant?

Plants need water, air, and sunlight. Plants need space to grow. Plants need nutrients. **Nutrients** are materials that living things need to live and grow. Many plants get nutrients from soil and water.

The parts of a plant help it get food, water, air, and sunlight.

Plant Parts

Plants have different parts. The four main parts are the roots, stem, leaves, and flowers.

Roots grow down into the soil. Roots hold the plant in place. Roots take water and nutrients from the soil to the stem.

The **stem** carries water and nutrients to the leaves. The stem holds up the plant.

Green **leaves** take in sunlight and air. They use sunlight, air, water, and nutrients to make food for the plant.

Many plants have flowers. A **flower** makes seeds. These seeds might grow into new plants.

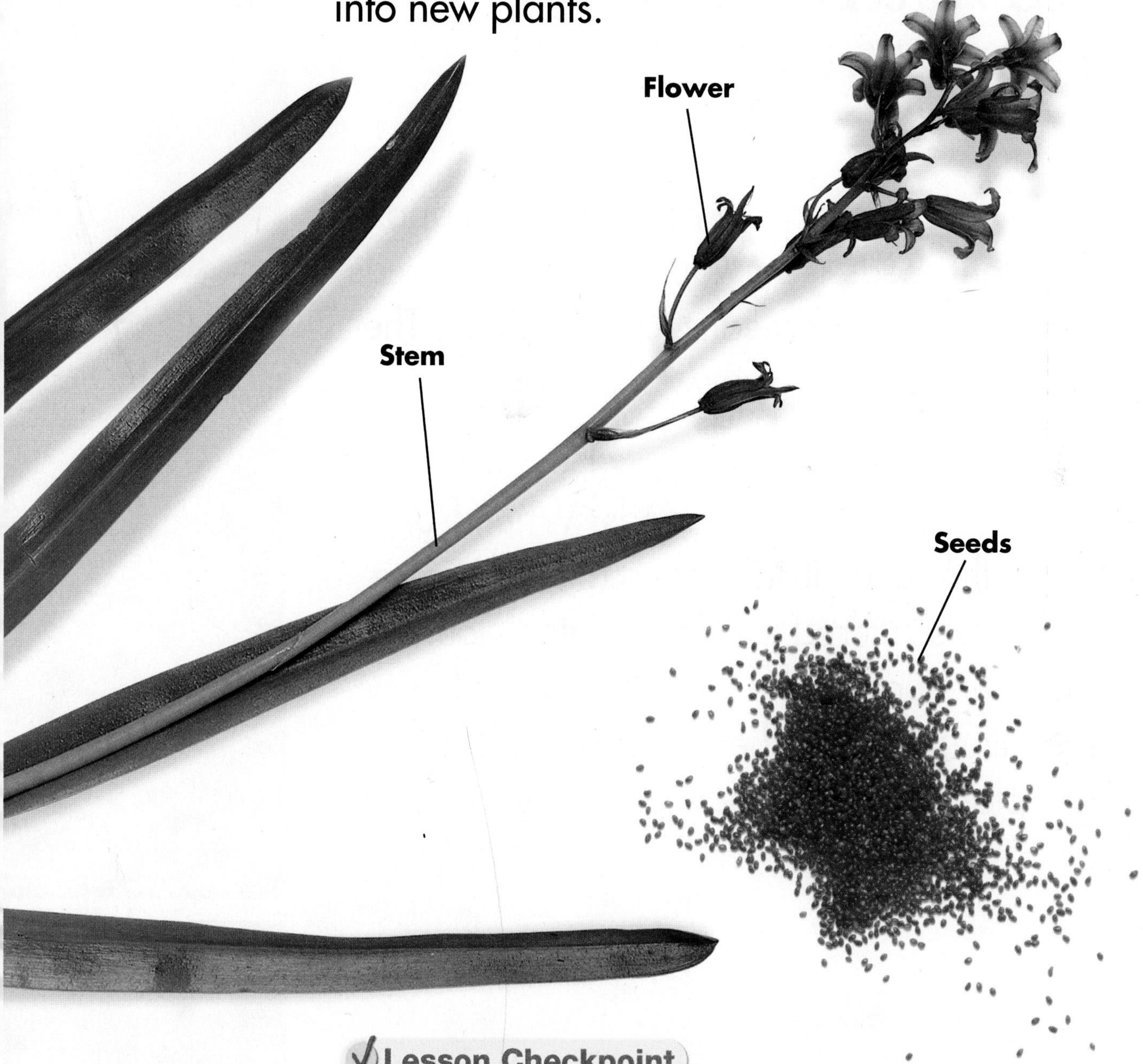

✓ Lesson Checkpoint

1. What are the four main parts of a plant?
2. **Writing in Science**
   Write a sentence in your journal. Tell why the stem of a plant is important.

Lesson 2

How are seeds scattered?

Many new plants grow from seeds. Suppose you plant seeds. You would scatter the seeds in the soil. Scatter means to spread out. The seeds have space to grow.

Fruits cover and protect seeds. When fruits travel, the seeds inside are scattered. Some fruits are scattered by air or water. Some fruits get stuck on the fur or feathers of animals. Scattering helps carry seeds to new places where they might grow.

Lesson Checkpoint

1. Name 3 ways that seeds travel.
2. **Predict** A maple tree fruit spins to the ground. It lands in an open field. What do you think might happen next?

The fruits of a maple tree are shaped like wings. This shape helps them travel through the air.

The fruits of the water lily float on lakes and streams.

Burrs are fruits.
Burrs travel by sticking on clothing or fur. This dog has burrs stuck to its fur.

Lesson 3

How are plants grouped?

Plants can be grouped into two kinds. One kind of plant has flowers. The other kind of plant does not have flowers.

Plants with flowers grow in different places. Trees are plants. Some trees have flowers. The flowers form fruits that cover and protect the seeds inside.

Peach trees grow flowers. Peaches are a fruit. You can eat peaches.

Cactus plants grow in the desert. Their flowers form seeds. Some seeds fall into the sand. New cactus plants might grow.

Saguaro cactus flowers open during cool nights.

1. Checkpoint How are plants grouped?
2. Health in Science Name some fruits that you can eat.

Plants Without Flowers

Not all plants have flowers. Some plants have cones. Seeds grow inside the cones. When a cone opens, the seeds fall out. Some seeds grow into new trees.

Mosses are tiny plants that do not have flowers. Mosses do not make seeds or fruits. Mosses do not have leaves, roots, or stems.

Ferns do not have flowers. Ferns do not make seeds. Ferns have leaves, roots, and stems.

✓ Lesson Checkpoint

1. What grows inside cones?
2. **Art in Science** Draw a forest. Label trees, mosses, and ferns.

Pine trees have cones.

Mosses often grow on wet rocks.

Some ferns live in warm, shady, wet places.

Lesson 4

How are some woodland plants adapted?

Plants live almost everywhere. A plant's **environment** is all the living and nonliving things around it.

Living things have **adapted,** or changed, to live in their environment.

Many kinds of plants grow in a woodland environment. Pine trees are adapted to live in cold weather. Pine trees have small leaves that are shaped like needles.

Pine tree leaves are adapted to keep from drying out in cold weather.

Maple tree leaves turn color in the fall.

Maple trees are adapted to live where summers are warm and winters are cold. Maple trees have large flat leaves. The maple tree loses its leaves in winter. This helps the tree keep the water it needs to live in winter.

1. **✓Checkpoint** How are pine trees adapted to their environment?
2. **Math in Science** Find a leaf outside. Use paper clips and counters to measure it.

Plants That Live Near Water

Some plants in a woodland environment live near rivers and streams.

Plants that grow near rivers and streams are adapted to live where it is very wet.

This red plant is called a cardinal plant. The roots of a cardinal plant are adapted to get nutrients from the moist soil in a woodland.

Cardinal plant

✓Lesson Checkpoint

1. How is a fanwort adapted to its wet habitat?
2. **Social Studies** in Science
   Look at a map. Find a river or stream in your state.

The stinging nettle has tiny, sharp hairs on its stem. The hairs protect the plant from animals that want to eat it.

The fanwort is adapted to live in water. Water can move through the thin leaves of the plant.

Lesson 5

How are some prairie plants adapted?

A **prairie** is flat land with lots of grass and few trees. Many prairies have hot summers with little rain. Some prairie plants are adapted to keep water when there is not enough rain.

Goldenrod plants have stiff stems and leaves. The stems and leaves help the plants keep the water they need to live.

Goldenrod

✓ Lesson Checkpoint

1. How are goldenrod plants adapted?
2. **Writing in Science** Write a sentence in your **science journal.** Tell how prairie plants are different from woodland plants.

Prairie smoke has fuzz on its stems and leaves. The fuzz helps the plant keep the water it needs.

Prairie grasses have thin leaves. The leaves help the plants keep the water they need.

Lesson 6

How are some desert plants adapted?

Many deserts are sunny and hot during the day. Deserts can be cool at night. Very little rain falls in a desert environment.

Some desert plants are adapted to hold water for a long time. The desert almond has leaves that grow in different directions. Some leaves get less sunlight than others. Leaves that get less sunlight can keep the water they need to live.

Desert almond

✓ Lesson Checkpoint

1. Tell about the leaves of a desert almond.
2. **Social Studies** in Science
   Find Arizona on a map. Name a desert in Arizona.

The saguaro cactus has a long, thick stem that holds water.

The octopus tree has long spines. The spines protect the plant from animals that want to eat the leaves.

Lesson 7

How are some marsh plants adapted?

A marsh is an environment that is very wet. The soil in a marsh may not have the nutrients plants need. The plants in a marsh are adapted to get nutrients in other ways.

Cattails are plants. Cattails are adapted to grow in very wet soil. Cattails get the nutrients they need from the water.

Cattails

Lesson Checkpoint

1. How does a sundew plant trap insects?
2. **Predict** An insect lands on the leaf of a Venus's-flytrap. Predict what will happen next.

A sundew plant gets some nutrients from insects. The plant has sticky hairs on each leaf. Insects land on a leaf and stick to the hairs.

A Venus's-flytrap also gets some nutrients from insects. An insect lands on the plant's leaves. Then the leaves snap shut.

Lab zone

Guided Inquiry

Investigate Do plants need light?

Plants need water, air, sunlight, and nutrients to live and grow. What might happen if plants do not get light?

Materials

2 cups with grass

water

What to Do

1. Water both plants.

You can paint your cups!

2. Put one plant in sunlight.

3. Put the other plant in a dark place.

Process Skills

You **observe** when you look closely at the plants.

4. How do you think the plants will look after 1 week? **Observe** the plants every day for 1 week.

	Sunlight	Dark

Day 1		
Day 2		

5. Fill in the chart. Draw pictures to show the plants each day.

Go Further

What will happen if you move the plant from the dark place to a sunny place? Try it and find out.

Explain Your Results

1. Which plant grew better?
2. **Infer** What will happen if a plant does not get sunlight?

Math in Science

Leaf Patterns

Ash tree leaves

Beech tree leaves

Leaves grow on branches in different patterns. Ash tree leaves grow in pairs. Two leaves grow across from each other. One leaf is on one side of a stalk. One leaf is on the other side.

Beech tree leaves grow in a different pattern. One leaf grows on one side of a stalk. Farther down, another leaf grows on the other side of the branch. This pattern repeats.

Copy the leaf pictures below. Use what you know about leaf patterns. Predict where the next two leaves will grow. Draw two more leaves on each stalk.

Lab zone Take-Home Activity

Take your drawings home. Discuss what you have learned about the way leaves grow with your family.

Chapter 1 Review and Test Prep

Vocabulary

Which picture goes with each word?

1. stem
2. leaf
3. flowers
4. prairie
5. roots

A

B

C

D

E

What did you learn?

6. What are nutrients?
7. What is a plant's environment?
8. How is prairie smoke adapted to live on a prairie?

Process Skills

9. **Infer** What might happen if a plant does not get enough space to live and grow?

Predict

10. The leaves on a maple tree change color from green to red. **Predict** what will happen next.

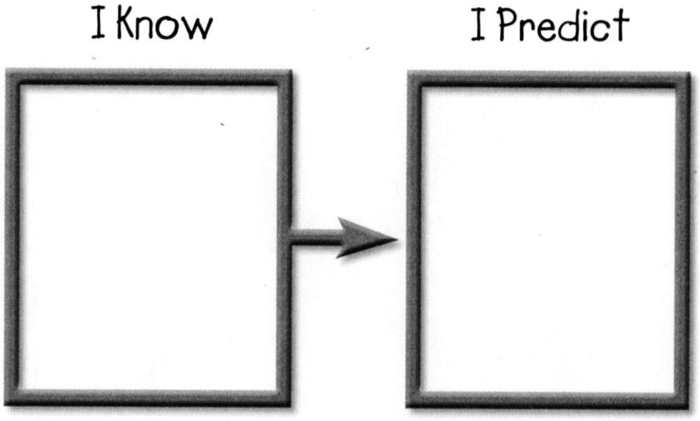

Test Prep

Fill in the circle next to the correct answer.

11. Which part of a plant brings water up to the leaves?

Ⓐ stem
Ⓑ cone
Ⓒ roots
Ⓓ flower

12. **Writing in Science** Name the 4 main parts of a plant. Tell how each part helps the plant.

Biography

Mary Agnes Chase

Read Together

Mary Agnes Chase was born in 1869. She liked to collect plants when she was young. She drew pictures of the plants.

When she was older, Mary Agnes Chase became a plant scientist. She went all over the world studying plants. She kept drawing pictures of all the different plants.

Mary Agnes Chase wrote books to help other people learn about plants. Her drawings were in her books.

Mary Agnes Chase enjoyed learning about and drawing grasses.

Lab zone Take-Home Activity

Find a grass plant or other plant growing outside. Draw a picture of it. Talk to your family about your drawing.

EC CRU 10 9 8 7 6 5 4 3 2 1

You Will Discover

- that there are many different kinds of animals.
- how animals are adapted to different kinds of environments.

Chapter 2
All About Animals

Web Games
Take It to the Net
pearsonsuccessnet.com

online
Student Edition
pearsonsuccessnet.com

How are animals different from each other?

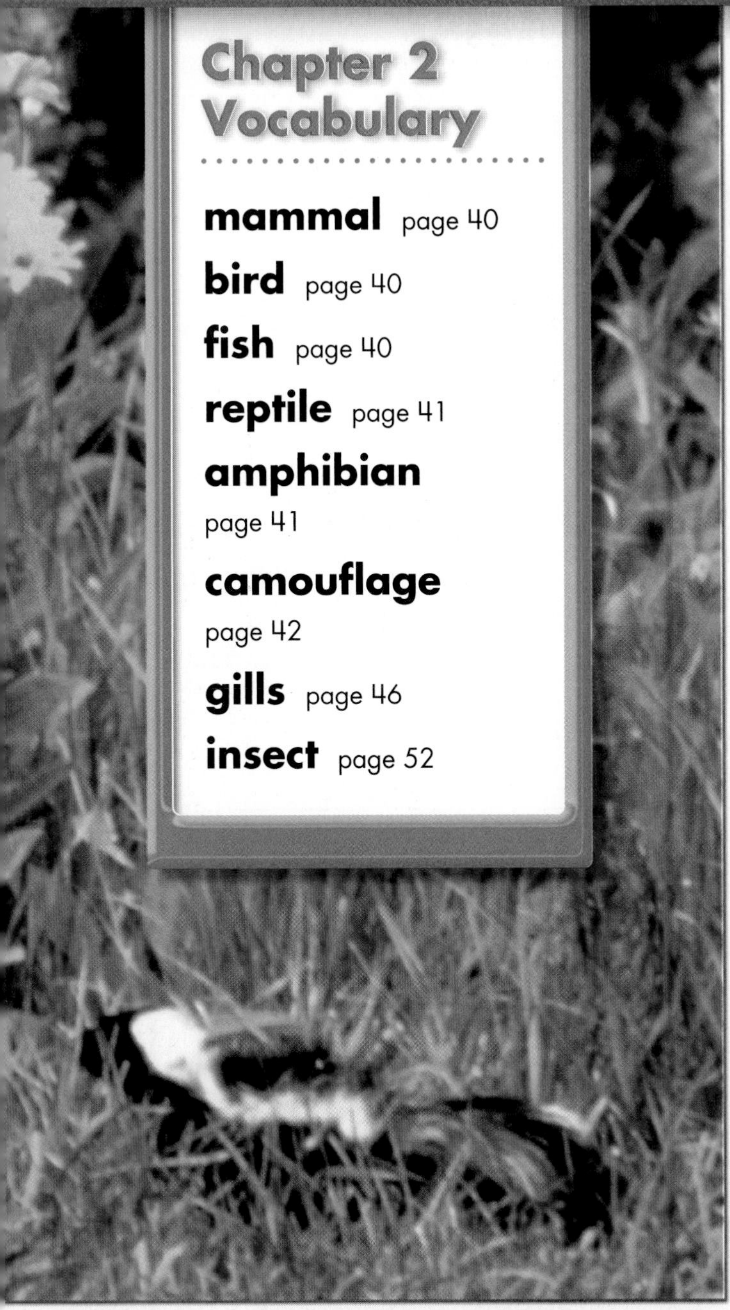

Chapter 2 Vocabulary

mammal page 40

bird page 40

fish page 40

reptile page 41

amphibian page 41

camouflage page 42

gills page 46

insect page 52

Lab zone Directed Inquiry

Explore How are worms and snakes alike and different?

Materials

short tape

long tape

7 cotton squares

pipe cleaner

14 pieces of pasta

What to Do

Make models of a worm and a snake.

Worm

1. Roll up.
Pinch the ends.

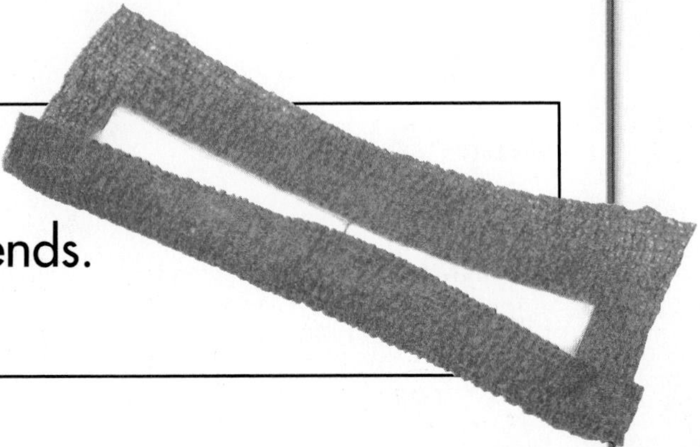

Snake

2. String the pasta.
3. Roll up.
Pinch the ends.

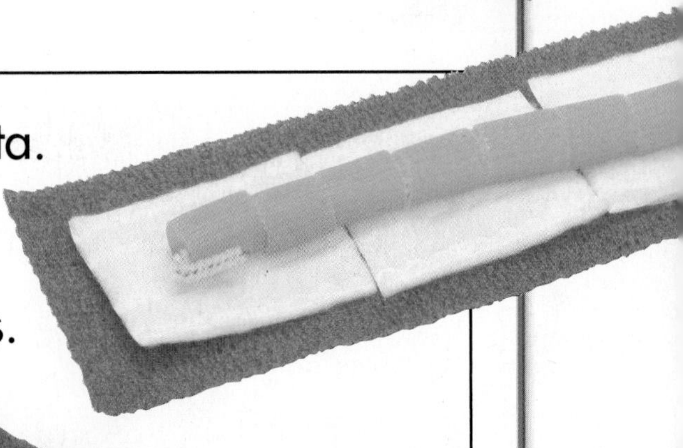

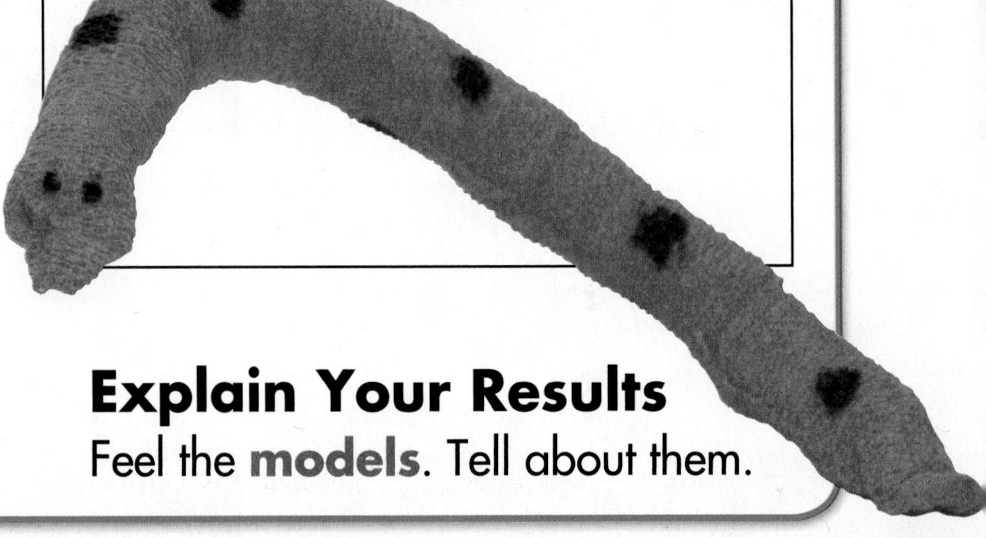

Process Skills

Models show how animals are alike and different.

Explain Your Results

Feel the **models**. Tell about them.

How to Read Science

Reading Skills

Target Skill

Alike and Different

Alike means how things are the same.
Different means how things are not the same.

Science Article

Worms and Snakes

Worms are long and thin. Worms do not have backbones. Worms use their bodies to crawl. Snakes are long and thin. Snakes have backbones. Snakes use their bodies to crawl.

Apply It!

Tell how a worm and a snake are alike and different. Use your **models** to help you.

Alike	Different

You Are There

What Has Backbones?

Sung to the tune of "There's a Hole In The Bucket"
Lyrics by Gerri Brioso & Richard Freitas/The Dovetail Group, Inc.

There are animals with backbones,
Like mammals.
Yes, mammals.
Dogs and cats,
Skunks and chipmunks,
All have backbones.

Lesson 1

What are some animals with backbones?

There are many different kinds of animals. One main group of animals has backbones.

Bones help give an animal shape. Bones can help an animal move. Bones can help protect some body parts of animals.

A skunk has a backbone.

Animals with Backbones

Mammals are animals with backbones.
A mammal usually has hair or fur on its body.
Young mammals get milk from their mother.
Dogs and cats are two kinds of mammals.
The chipmunk in the picture is a mammal.

Birds are animals with backbones. Birds have feathers and wings. Birds hatch from eggs.

Fish are animals with backbones. Fish live in water. Most fish are covered with scales. Fish have fins. Most fish hatch from eggs.

Reptiles are animals with backbones. Most reptiles have dry skin. Scales cover and protect a reptile's body. Some reptiles hatch from eggs. Snakes and turtles are two kinds of reptiles.

Amphibians are animals with backbones. Amphibians live part of their life in the water and part of their life on land. Most amphibians have smooth, wet skin. Amphibians hatch from eggs. Frogs and toads are amphibians.

✓ Lesson Checkpoint

1. Which kinds of animals have backbones and scales?
2. How are an amphibian and a reptile **alike** and **different?**

Lesson 2

What are some ways mammals are adapted?

Mammals live almost everywhere in the world. Like plants, mammals have adapted to live in their environment. An animal's environment is all the living and nonliving things around it.

Like many animals, mule deer are adapted to their environment by camouflage. **Camouflage** is a color or shape that makes a plant or animal hard to see.

The mule deer's fur is brown in summer.

In winter, the mule deer's fur turns color. The deer is harder to see in the snow.

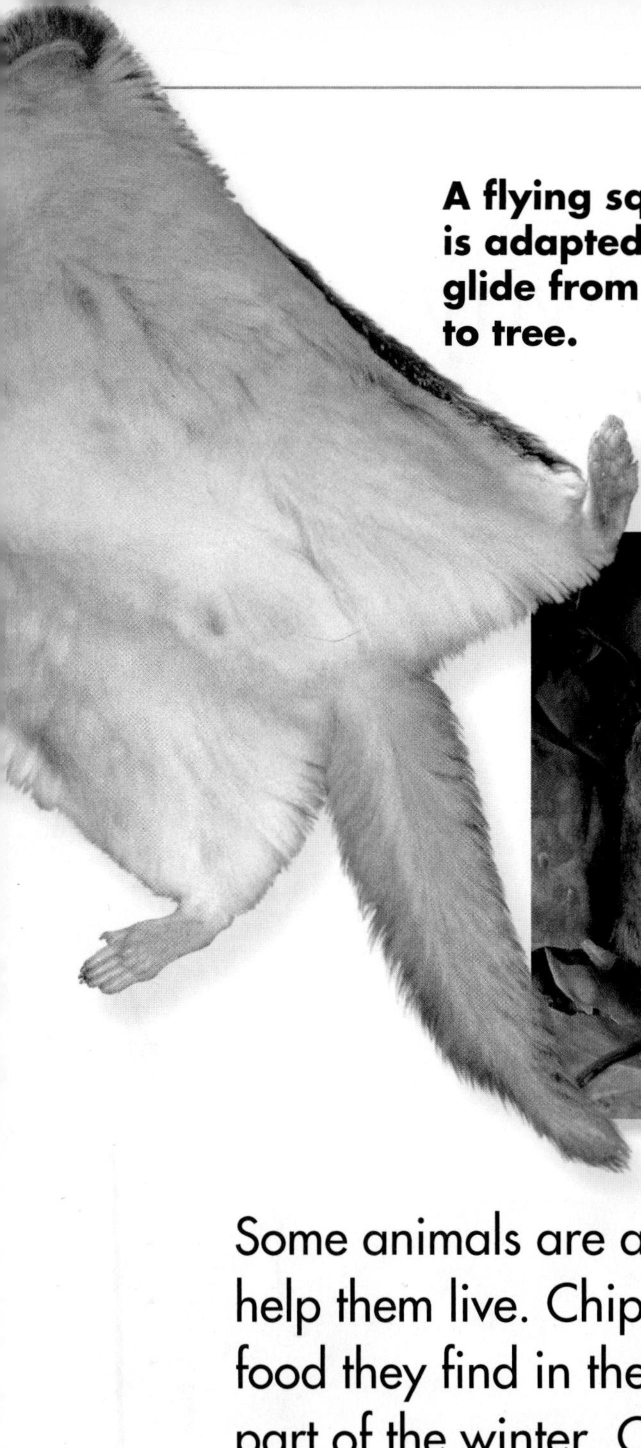

A flying squirrel is adapted to glide from tree to tree.

A chipmunk sleeps for part of the winter.

Some animals are adapted to act in ways that help them live. Chipmunks store some of the food they find in the summer. They sleep for part of the winter. Chipmunks eat some of the food they store every time they wake up.

Lesson Checkpoint

1. How does a mule deer's fur change in winter?
2. **Art in Science** Draw a picture of a mammal that you have seen.

Lesson 3

What are some ways birds are adapted?

Many birds are adapted to fly. Wings and feathers help birds fly.

This bird is called a nightjar.

The nightjar lives in fields. Its feathers look like the ground. This camouflage helps the bird hide from animals that might eat it.

Hmmm!
A hummingbird's beak is adapted. A hummingbird uses its beak to drink liquid from flowers.

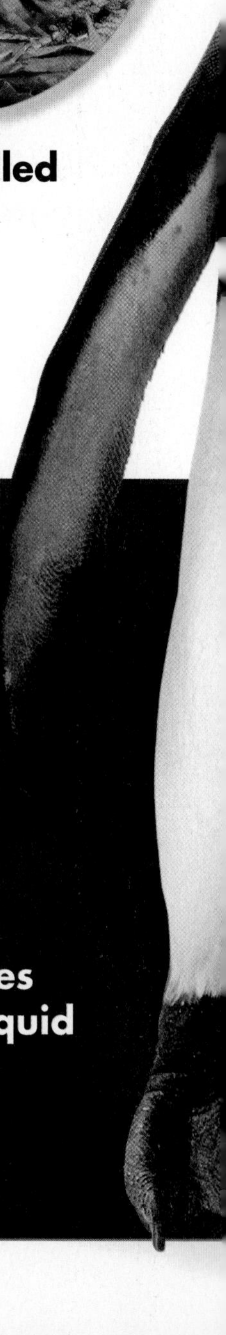

Most penguins live where it is very cold.

A penguin's top feathers are waterproof. These feathers help keep the penguin dry. Tiny feathers below the top feathers trap air. The trapped air helps keep the penguin warm.

Penguins do not fly. Their wings are adapted for swimming.

Lesson Checkpoint

1. How does camouflage protect the nightjar?
2. How are hummingbirds and penguins **alike?** How are they **different?**

Lesson 4

What are some ways fish are adapted?

Fish are adapted to life in the water. Fish have gills. **Gills** are body parts that help fish get oxygen from the water. Fish have fins to help them swim.

This porcupine fish is adapted to protect itself. The porcupine fish can make itself big. Sharp spikes stick out from its body when it is big.

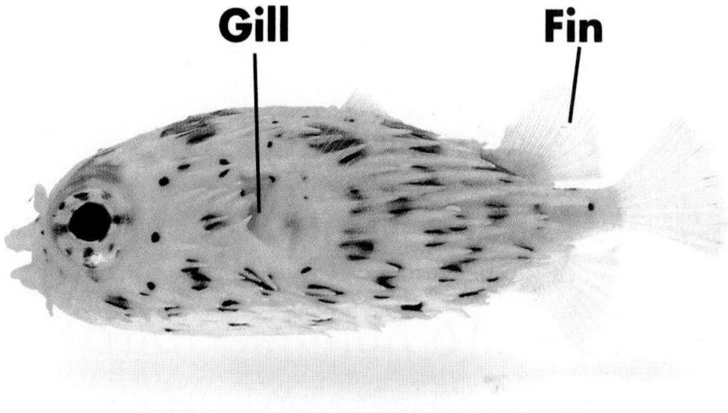

This tiny porcupine fish can become very big.

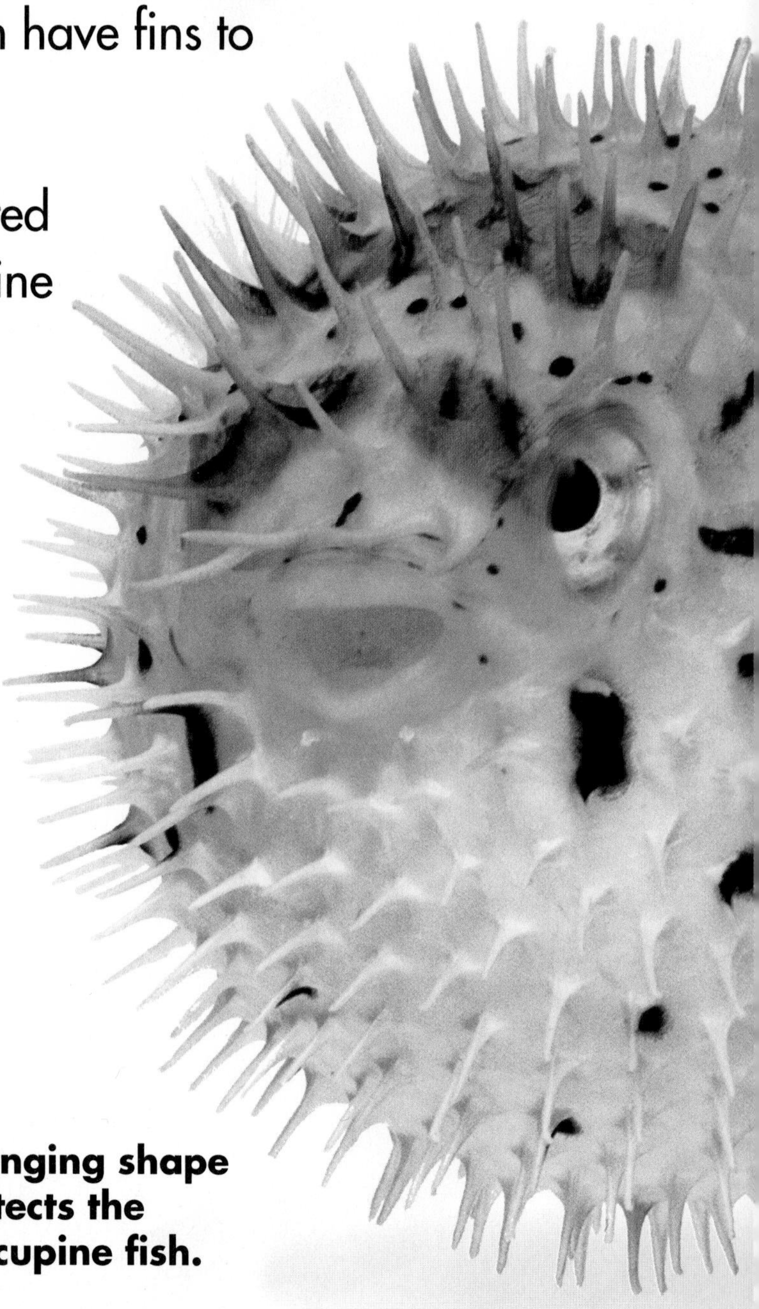

Changing shape protects the porcupine fish.

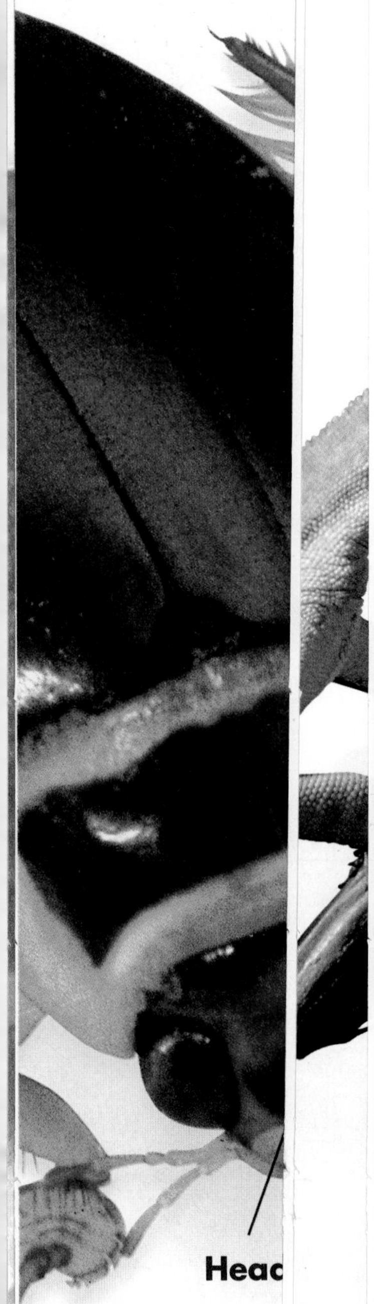

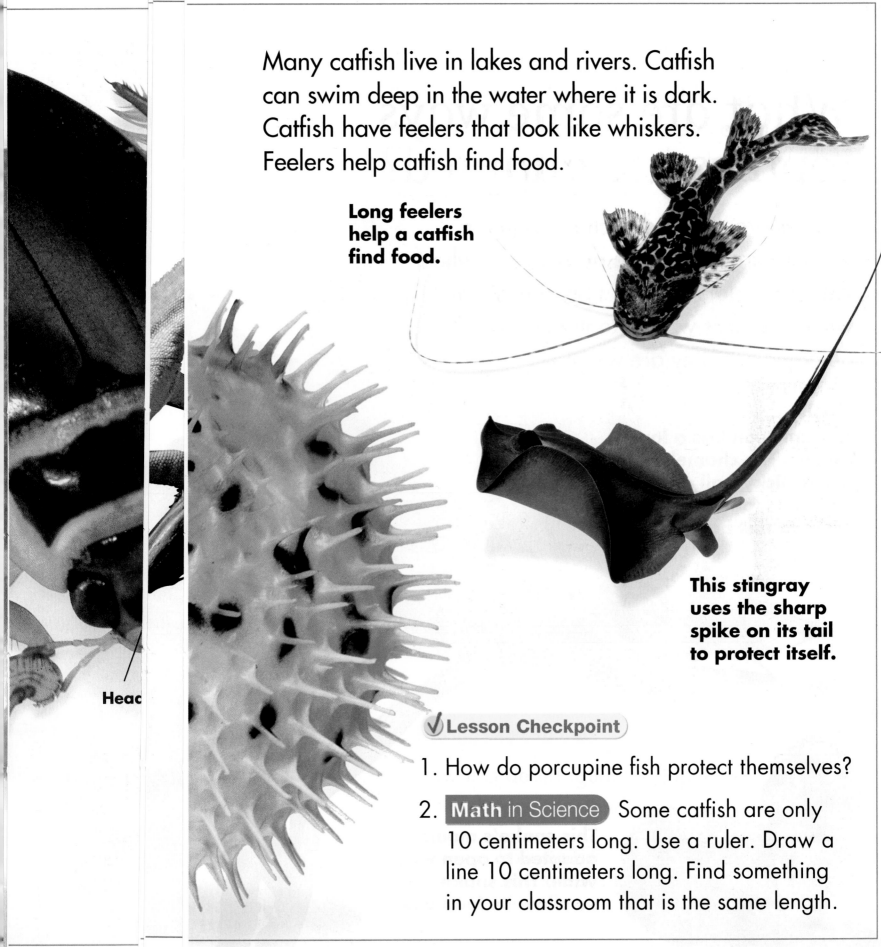

Many catfish live in lakes and rivers. Catfish can swim deep in the water where it is dark. Catfish have feelers that look like whiskers. Feelers help catfish find food.

Long feelers help a catfish find food.

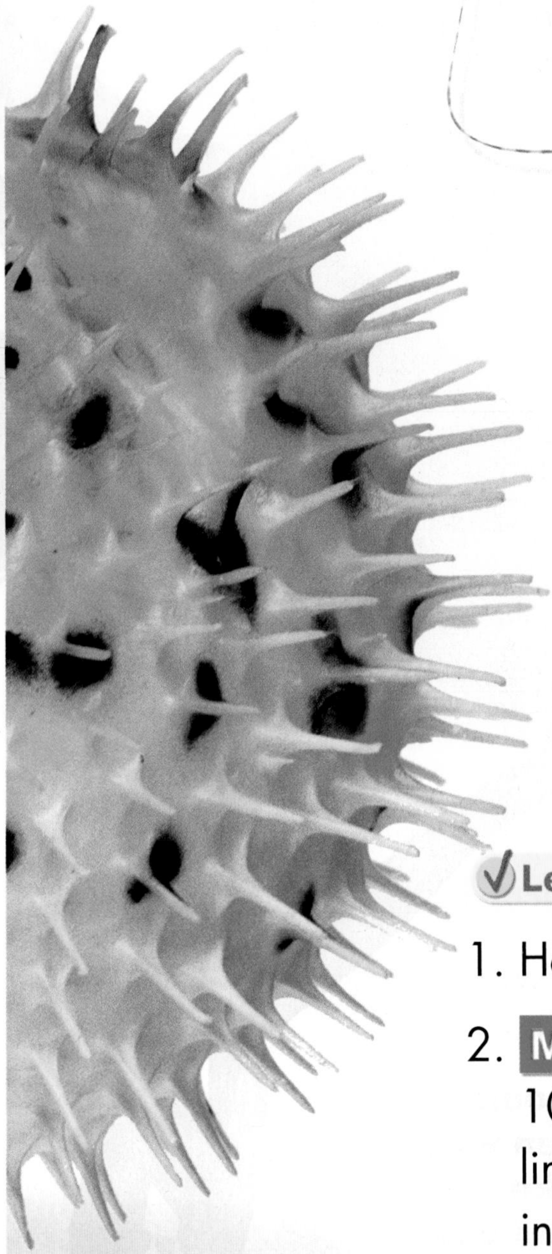

This stingray uses the sharp spike on its tail to protect itself.

✓ Lesson Checkpoint

1. How do porcupine fish protect themselves?
2. **Math** in Science Some catfish are only 10 centimeters long. Use a ruler. Draw a line 10 centimeters long. Find something in your classroom that is the same length.

Lessc

Wh
an
ba

One r
backb
anima
Most l
have l

Insec
not ho
three
parts
and th
legs.
smell,

Math in Science

Sorting Animals

Sort these animals into 2 groups. One group has animals with backbones. Count the number of animals with backbones. The other group has animals without backbones. Count the number of animals without backbones.

Some kinds of honeypot ants are adapted to store water and food in their abdomens.

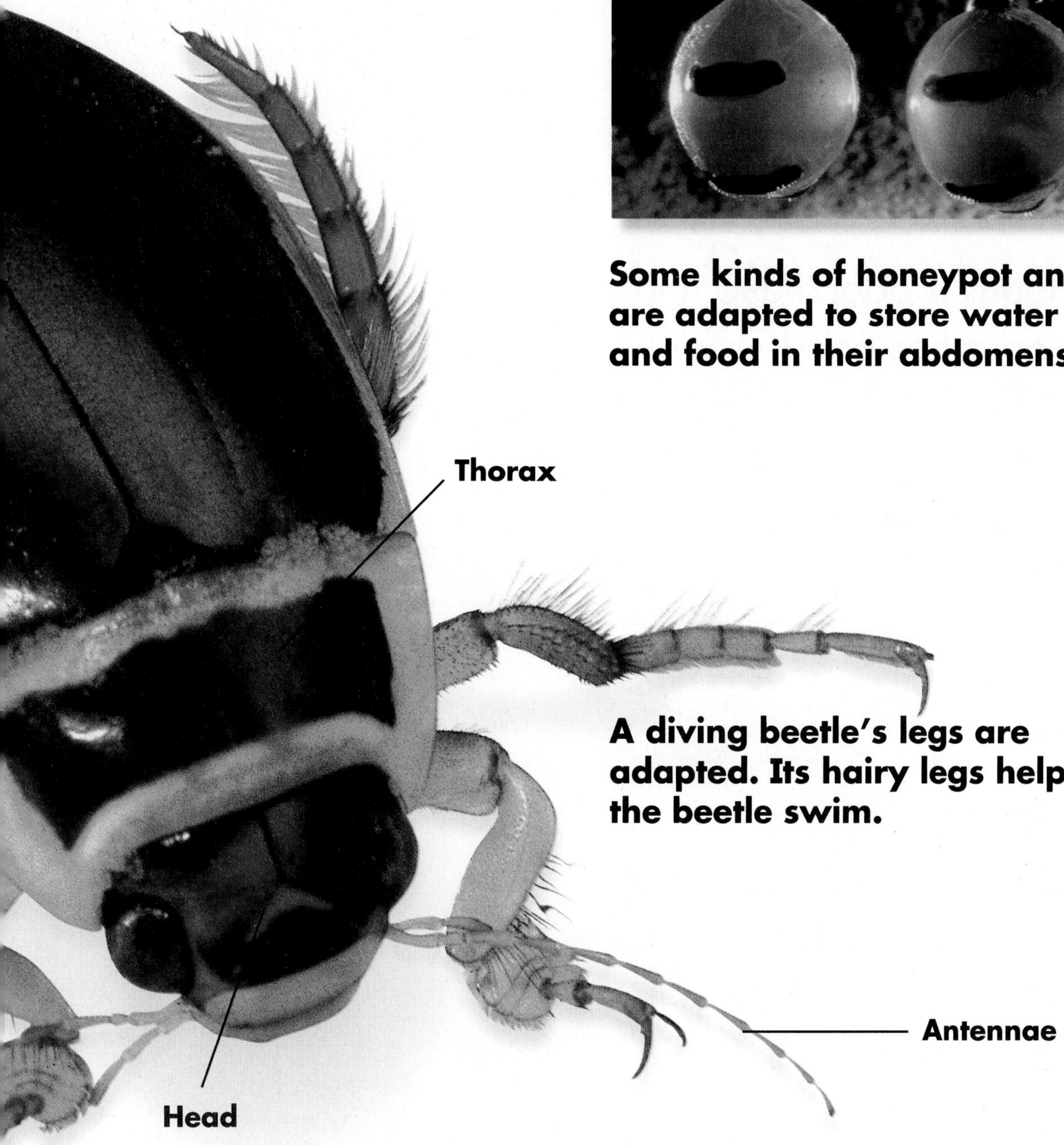

A diving beetle's legs are adapted. Its hairy legs help the beetle swim.

1. ✓Checkpoint How is the diving beetle adapted to life in water?
2. Technology in Science Tell about inventions that help people move in water.

Other Animals Without Backbones

An octopus lives in the ocean. An octopus is an animal without a backbone.

An octopus is adapted to find and catch food. An octopus has good eyesight. Its eyesight helps it find food. The suction cups on its arms help the octopus hold its food.

An octopus has 8 arms.

Spiders are animals without backbones. Spiders have eight legs. Spiders are adapted to spin webs. The webs trap insects that spiders eat.

This spider builds a web to trap insects.

✓ Lesson Checkpoint

1. Tell how the octopus is adapted to find food.
2. **Math** in Science A spider has 8 legs. How many legs will 2 spiders have in all? Write a number sentence to show your answer.

Lab zone

Guided Inquiry

Investigate How can an octopus use its arms?

An octopus has suction cups on its 8 arms. It can use its arms to pick things up. Billye the octopus uses its arms to solve a problem. Billye can open a jar to get a fish inside.

Materials

scissors

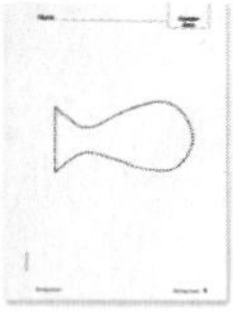

fish

jar

8 suction cups

What to Do

1. Cut out the fish.

2. Put the fish in the jar. **Predict** how many suction cups you will need to open a jar.

Process Skills

When you share your ideas, you **communicate** with classmates.

 More Lab zone Activities Take It to the Net pearsonsuccessnet.com

3. Work with your group. Take turns. Try to open the jar with suction cups. Where should you put them?

4. How many suction cups did you predict? How many did you use?

How many suction cups will open a jar?								
Predict								
Test								
	1	2	3	4	5	6	7	8

Number of Suction Cups

Explain Your Results

Communicate Tell how you used the suction cups.

Go Further

What other problems can you solve using suction cups? Try to solve the problems!

Math in Science

Sorting Animals

Sort these animals into 2 groups. One group has animals with backbones. Count the number of animals with backbones. The other group has animals without backbones. Count the number of animals without backbones.

Make a graph like this one. Color in your graph to show the number of animals in each group.

Animal Groups

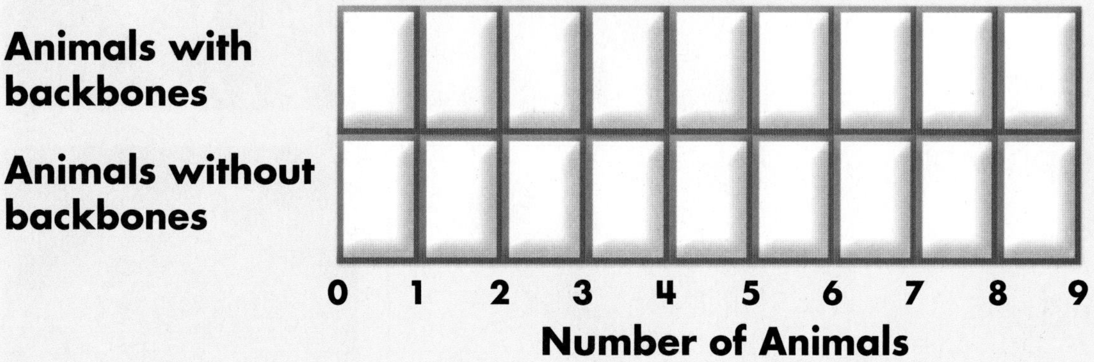

1. Which group has the most animals?
2. Which group has the fewest animals?

snake

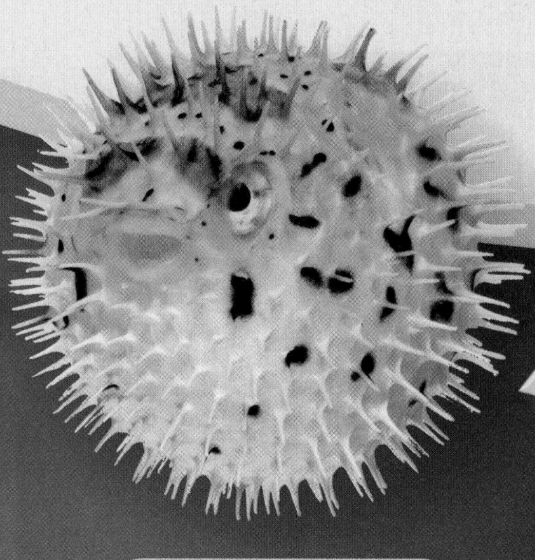

porcupine fish

Lab zone Take-Home Activity

Take a nature walk. List all of the animals you see. Sort the animals into groups.

Chapter 2 Review and Test Prep

Vocabulary

Which picture goes with each word?

1. insect
2. mammal
3. amphibian
4. fish
5. bird
6. reptile

A

B

C
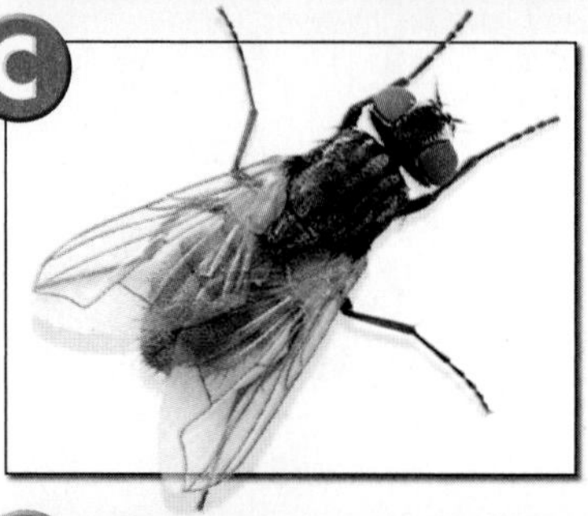

D
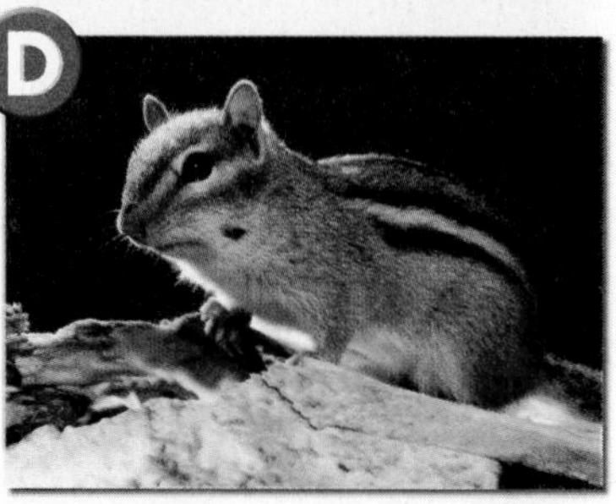

E

F

What did you learn?

7. How do fish use gills?
8. How does camouflage help protect animals?
9. Name 2 kinds of animals with backbones. Name 2 kinds of animals without backbones.

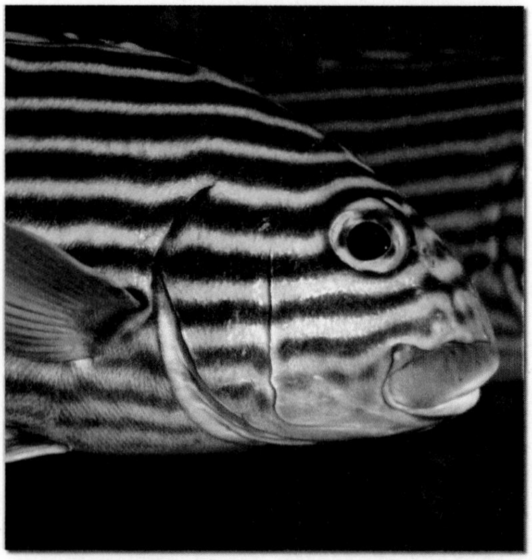

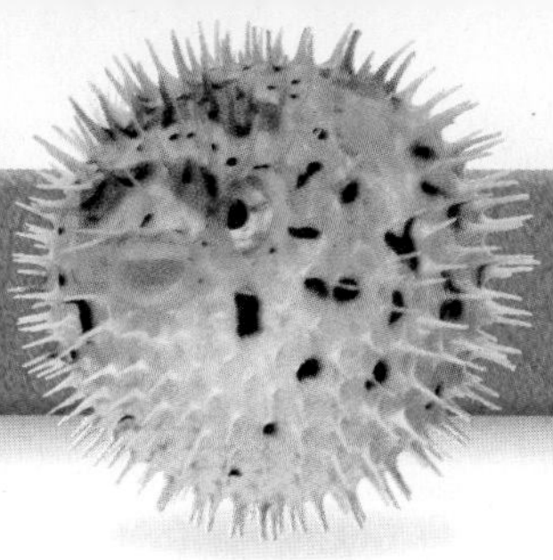

Process Skills

10. **Communicate** Choose an animal in this chapter. Tell one way the animal is adapted to its environment.

Alike and Different

11. Tell how a spider and an insect are **alike and different.**

Alike	Different

Test Prep

Fill in the circle next to the correct answer.

12. Which kind of animal has feathers and wings?

Ⓐ fish
Ⓑ bird
Ⓒ mammal
Ⓓ amphibian

13. **Writing** in Science Choose an animal. Tell how the animal is adapted to its environment.

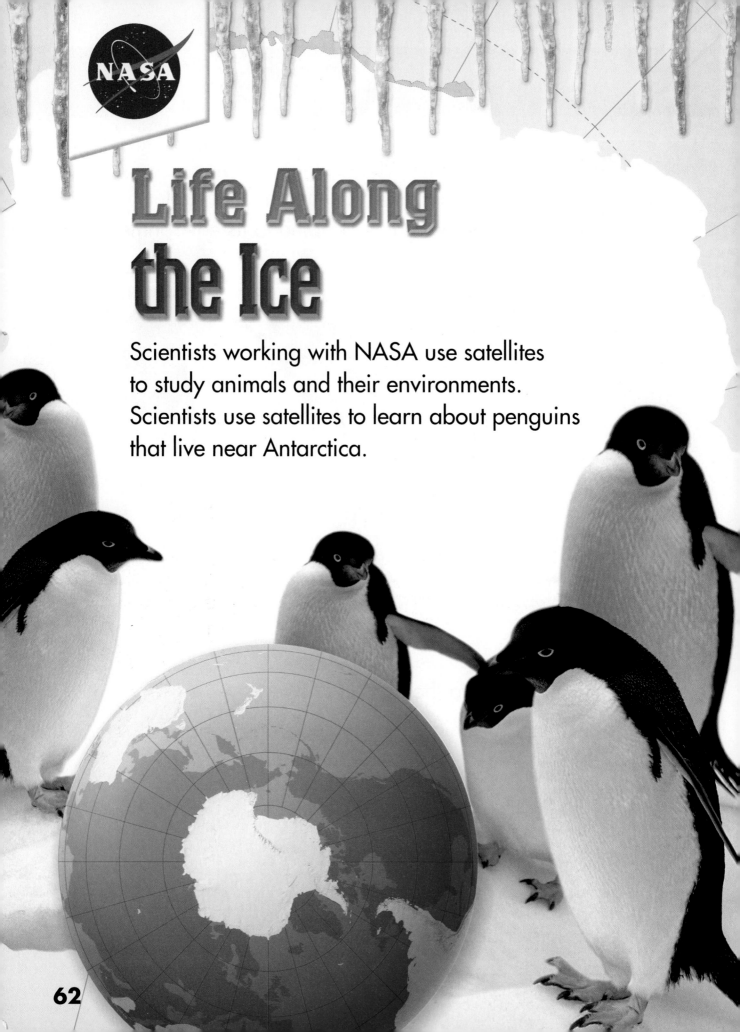

Life Along the Ice

Scientists working with NASA use satellites to study animals and their environments. Scientists use satellites to learn about penguins that live near Antarctica.

Antarctica is very cold. Most of the ocean water near Antarctica is full of ice. The wind blows holes in the ice. Plants called algae can grow in the holes in the ice. Tiny animals called krill eat the algae. Penguins eat krill.

Scientists have learned that when there are more algae, there are more krill. When there are more krill, there are more penguins. When there are fewer krill, there are fewer penguins.

Satellites send information about the ocean back to Earth.

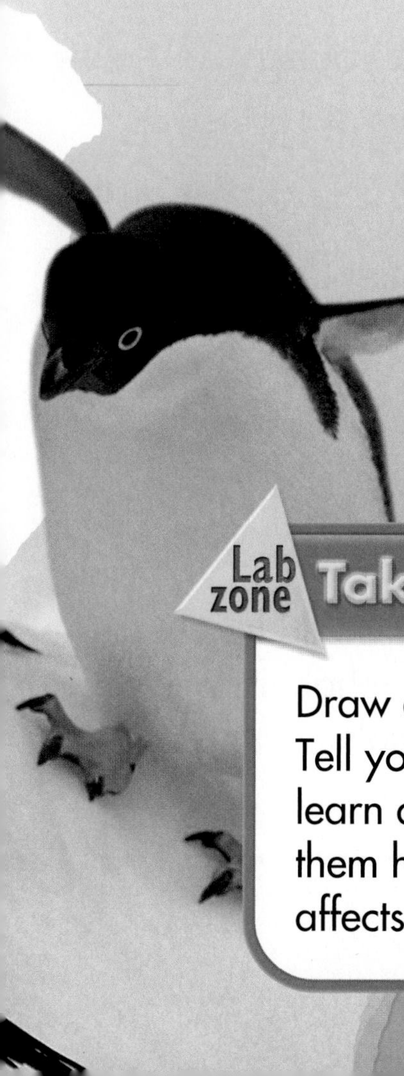

Lab zone Take-Home Activity

Draw a picture of a penguin. Tell your family how scientists learn about the ocean. Tell them how the amount of krill affects the number of penguins.

Career

Wildlife Rehabilitator

Read Together

What happens when animals that live in forests or oceans are hurt? Are there ways people can help?

Wildlife rehabilitators are people that help hurt or sick animals. They know what animals need to live in their environment. A wildlife rehabilitator can even teach young animals how to hunt for food.

Wildlife rehabilitators know that it is important that animals get the care they need to survive.

A wildlife rehabilitator saved this sea turtle.

Lab zone Take-Home Activity

Write about what it would be like to be a wildlife rehabilitator. What kinds of animals would you like to help?

EC CRU 10987654321

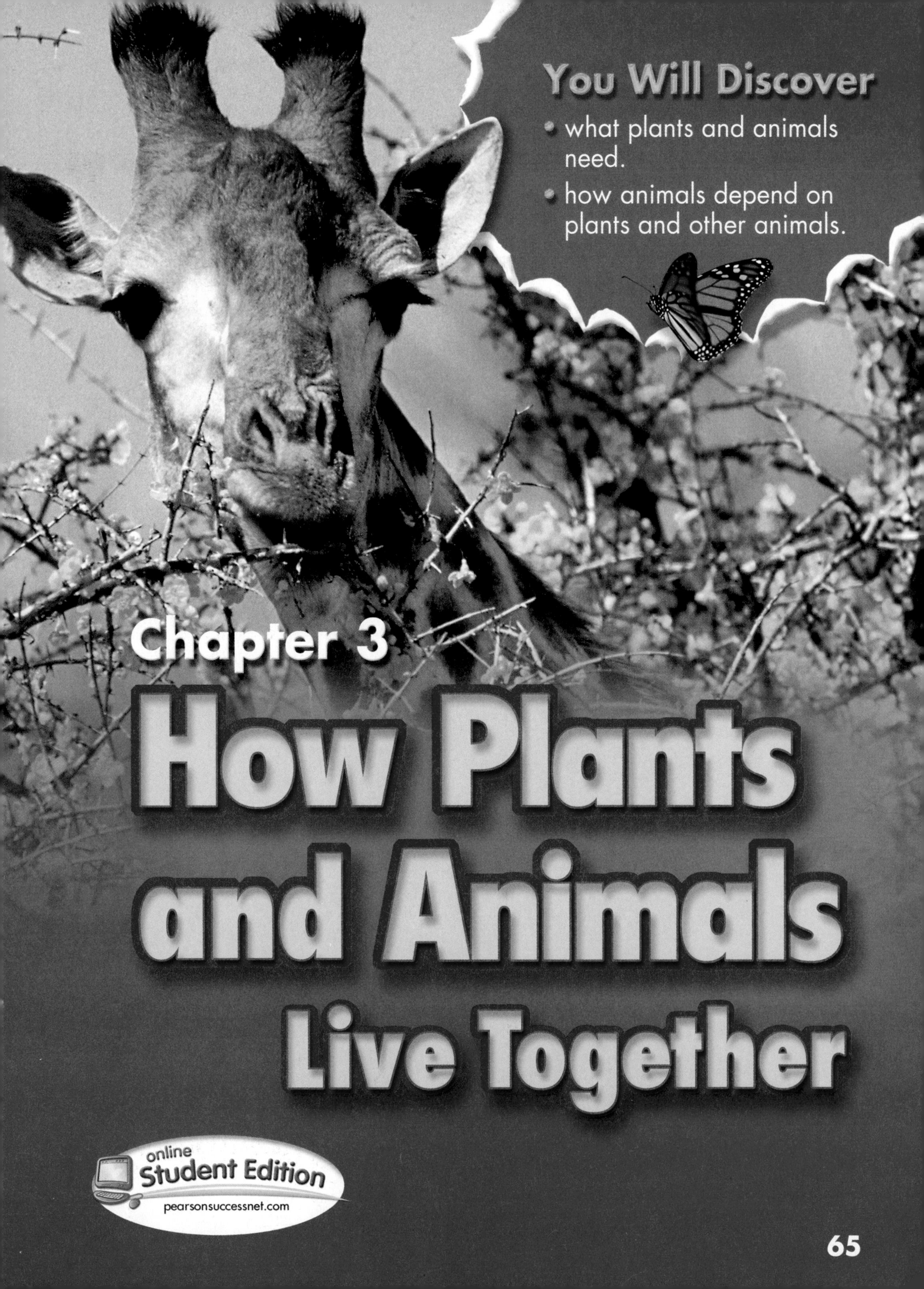

You Will Discover

- what plants and animals need.
- how animals depend on plants and other animals.

Chapter 3
How Plants and Animals Live Together

online
Student Edition
pearsonsuccessnet.com

Build Background

How do living things help each other?

producer

consumer

predator

prey

Chapter 3 Vocabulary

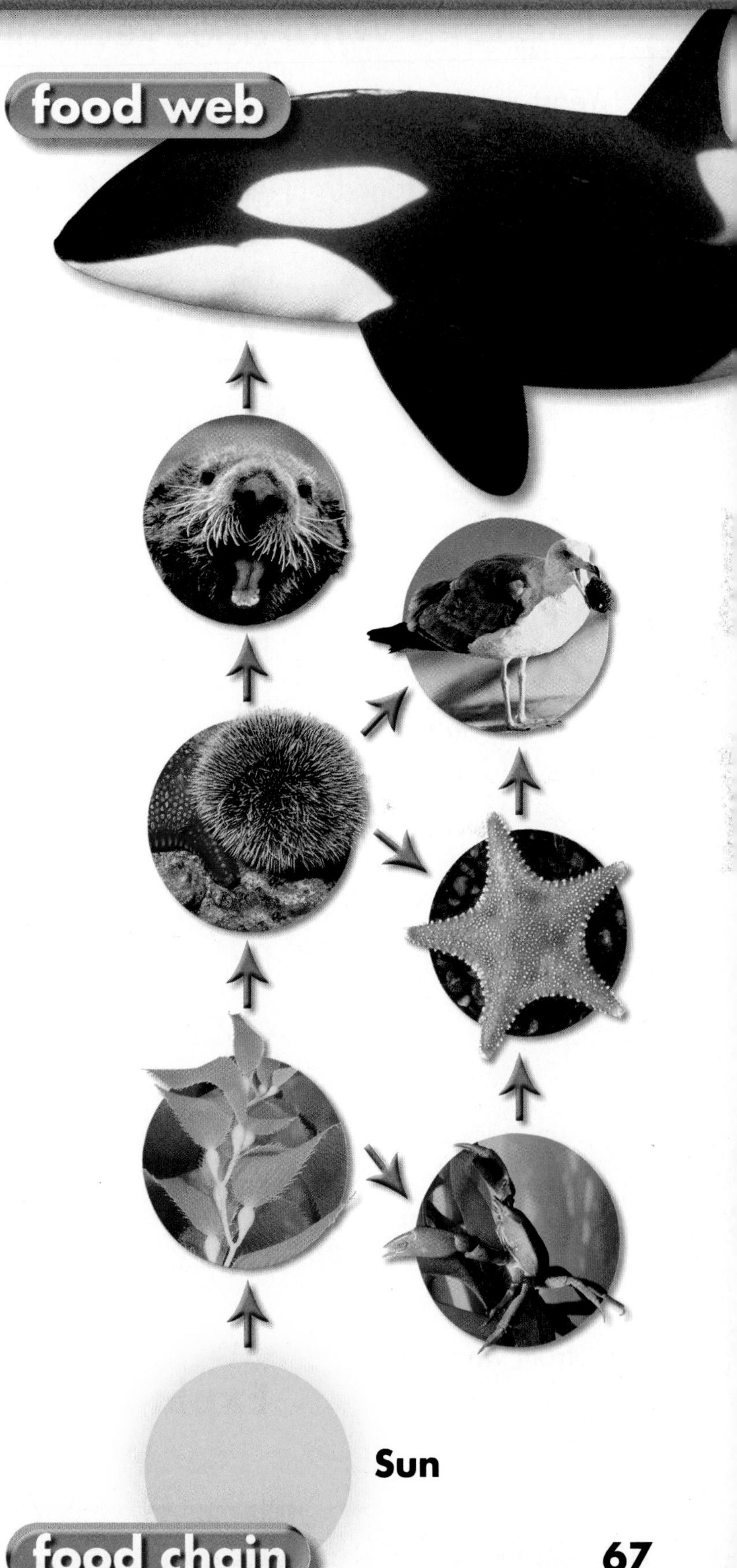

Lab zone Directed Inquiry

Explore What does yeast need to grow?

Yeast are tiny living things.
They cannot make their own food.
They must get food from where they live.

Be careful! Don't slip! Clean up spills.

Materials

cup with yeast

cup with warm water

cup with sugar

spoon

What to Do

1. Put water in the cup with yeast.

2. Add sugar and stir.
   Watch the yeast.

Look at the tiny bubbles!

3. **Estimate**
   How long did it take to see tiny bubbles?

Process Skills

You can **infer** from what you observe with your senses.

Explain Your Results

Infer What made the yeast change?

How to Read Science

Reading Skills

Cause and Effect

A cause is why something happens.
An effect is what happens.

Science Activity

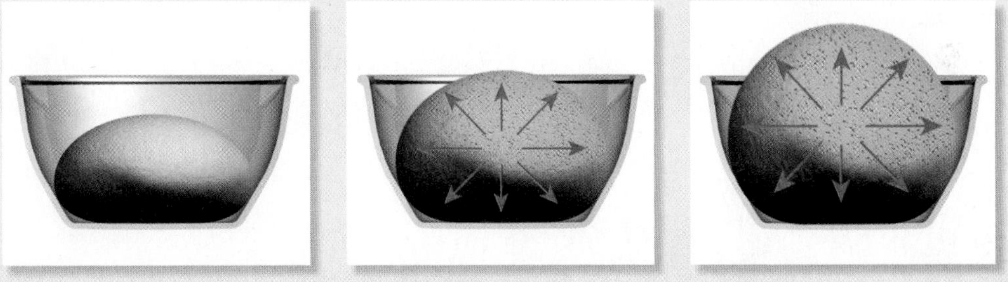

Yeast is added to bread dough. The yeast causes air bubbles to form in the bread dough. The air bubbles make the bread dough rise.

Apply It!

Infer What would happen to the bread dough without the yeast?

You Are There

Good Partners

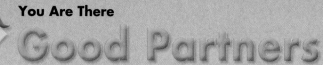

Sung to the tune of "Frere Jacques"
Lyrics by Gerri Brioso & Richard Freitas/The Dovetail Group, Inc.

Plants and animals
Are good partners.
Yes they are.
Yes they are.

Lesson 1

What do plants and animals need?

You learned that plants need air, water, sunlight, nutrients, and space to grow. Most green plants are producers. A **producer** is a living thing that can make its own food.

Animals need air, water, shelter, and space to live. Animals need food. Animals are consumers. A **consumer** cannot make its own food. Consumers get food from their habitat.

These giraffes are consumers.

Different Needs

Many plants and animals live together in a habitat. Plants and animals depend on each other and their habitat to meet their needs.

Large animals often need a lot of food, water, and space. Large animals need a large shelter. Small animals often do not need as much to eat and drink as large animals. Small animals can live in small spaces.

These plants and animals live in the same habitat.

These animals both need water. Which animal do you think needs more water?

Sometimes a habitat does not have enough food for all of the animals that live there. When this happens, some of the animals might die.

✓ Lesson Checkpoint

1. What do all animals need?
2. **Cause and Effect** What might happen if there is not enough food for all of the animals in a habitat?

Lesson 2

How do plants and animals get food in a grassland?

All living things need food. Most plants make food. Some animals eat plants. Other animals eat those animals. This is called a **food chain.**

Food chains start with the Sun. Plants use energy from the Sun to make food. Animals get energy from the food they eat. Look at the pictures of the food chain. Energy passes from sunlight to the mountain lion.

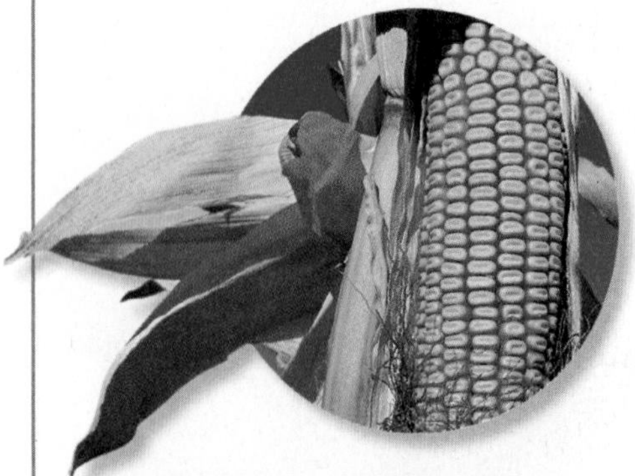

The corn plant uses water, air, and energy from sunlight to make food.

Crunch! The vole eats the corn for energy.

All food chains have predators and prey. A **predator** is an animal that catches and eats another animal. **Prey** is an animal that is caught and eaten. Look at the animals in the food chain. The coyote and mountain lion are predators. Which animals are their prey?

1. ✓ Checkpoint Give an example of a predator and its prey.
2. **Art** in Science Draw a picture of this grassland food chain. Label your picture.

Gulp! The coyote eats the vole. The vole is the coyote's prey.

Pounce! The mountain lion catches and eats the coyote.

A Food Web in a Grassland

Habitats usually have more than one food chain. The food chains in a habitat make up a **food web.** The plants and animals in a food web need each other for energy.

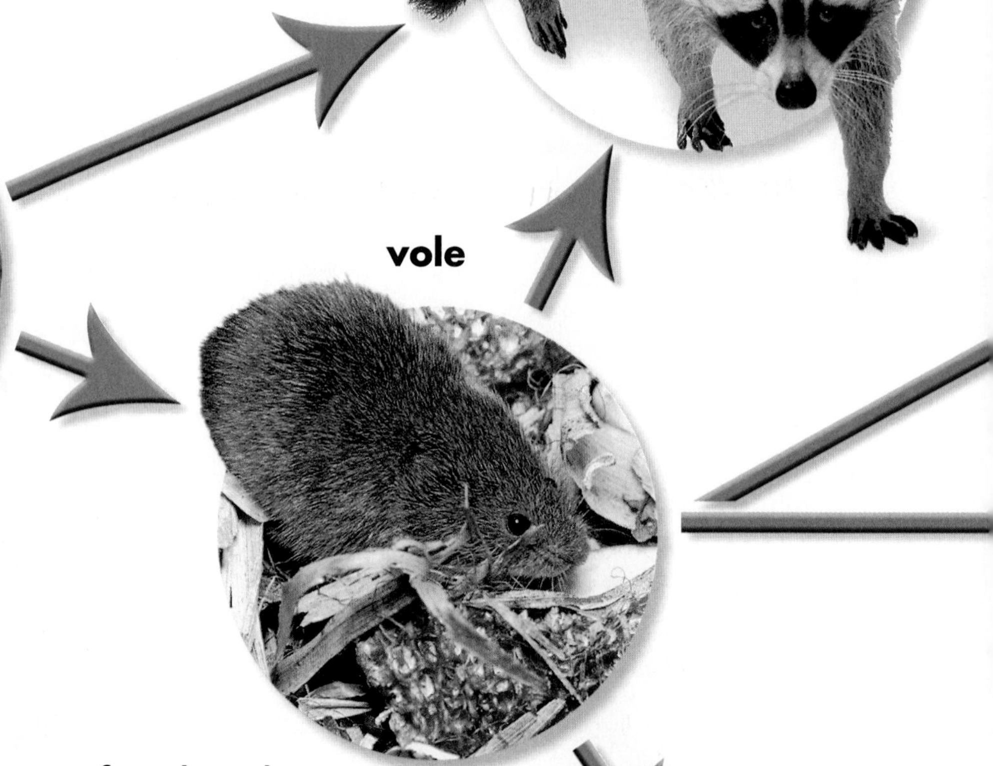

These pages show a food web in a grassland. Energy passes from sunlight to the corn. Use your finger to trace how energy moves from the corn to the vole to the fox. This is one food chain. What other food chains can you find on these two pages?

Lesson Checkpoint

1. Describe a food web.
2. **Math in Science** How many animals in this food web eat the corn? How many animals eat the vole? How many more animals eat the vole than the corn? Write a number sentence.

Lesson 3

How do plants and animals get food in an ocean?

An ocean has food chains and food webs too. Many different plants and animals live in an ocean. The pictures on these pages show an ocean food chain.

Kelp grows in an ocean. Kelp uses energy from sunlight to make food.

Sea urchins eat kelp.

Crunch! A sea star eats the sea urchin.

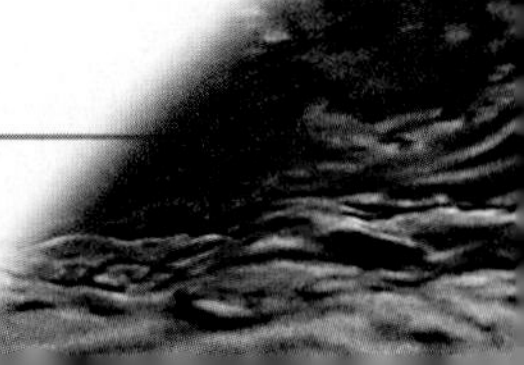

Remember that energy is passed through each step in a food chain. Trace how energy in this food chain passes from the Sun to the sea otter.

1. **Checkpoint** Where does a sea otter get energy?

2. **Writing in Science** Write 2 or 3 sentences. Tell how energy moves through this food chain.

Chomp! The sea otter eats the sea star. The sea otter gets the energy it needs from the sea star.

A Food Web in an Ocean

Look at this simple ocean food web. Energy passes from sunlight to the kelp. Use your finger to trace the food chains. How many food chains can you count?

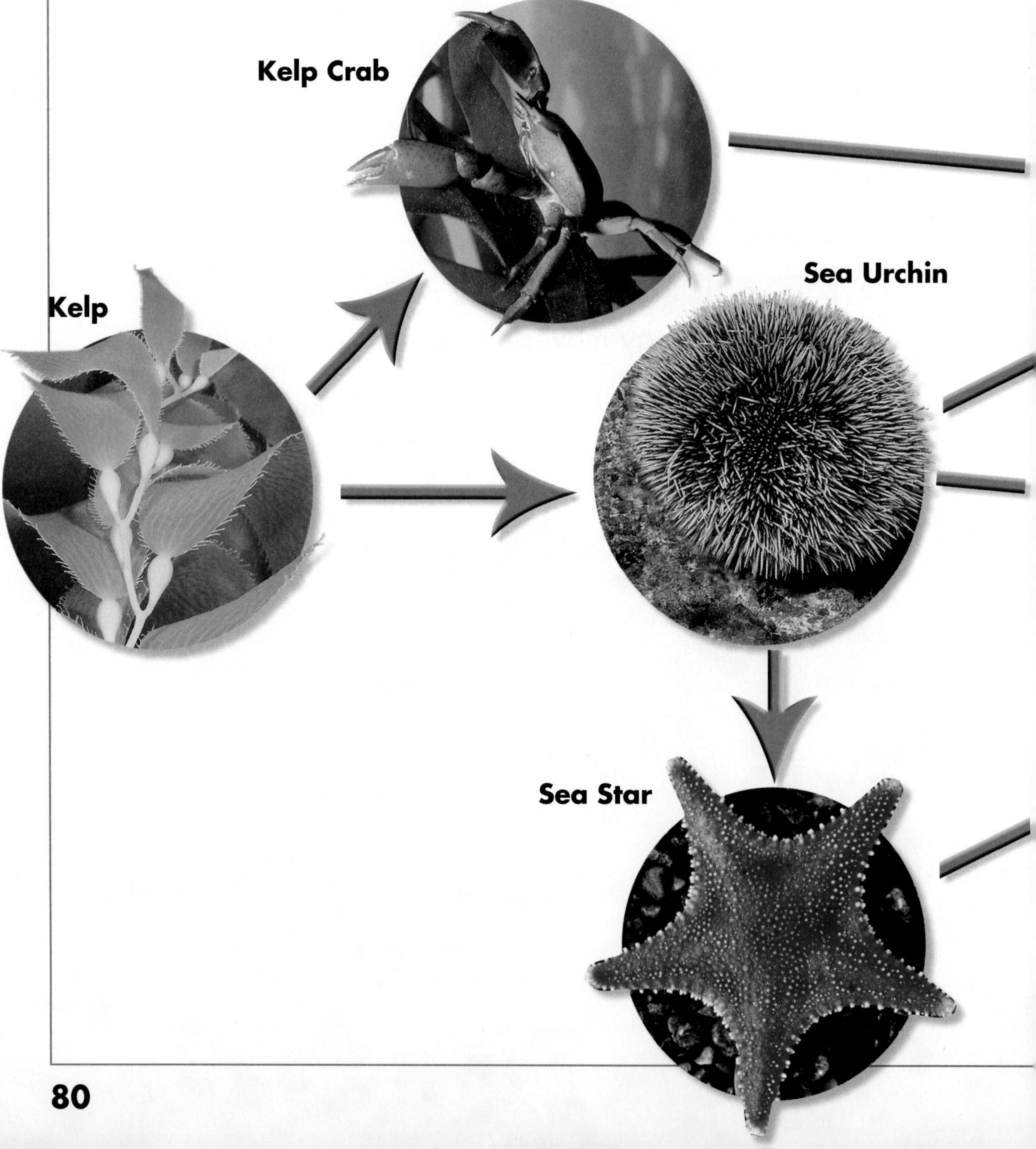

Lesson Checkpoint

1. What eats kelp in this food web?
2. **Writing in Science** Write one sentence in your journal. Describe one food chain in this ocean food web.

These otters were covered with oil from the oil spill.

Lesson 4

What can cause a food web to change?

This ship had an accident. Oil spilled from the ship into the ocean.

Many things can cause changes in a food web. Some changes may make it hard for plants and animals to survive. Parts of the food web may be harmed or even die.

People can cause a food web to change. The picture shows an oil spill. Many plants and animals were covered with oil.

People washed the oil off of this otter's fur.

People worked together to wash the oil off the animals. People helped to clean the water. People made the water safe again for the plants and animals that live there.

Lesson Checkpoint

1. How did people help after the oil spill?
2. **Cause and Effect** What is one effect of an oil spill?

Lesson 5

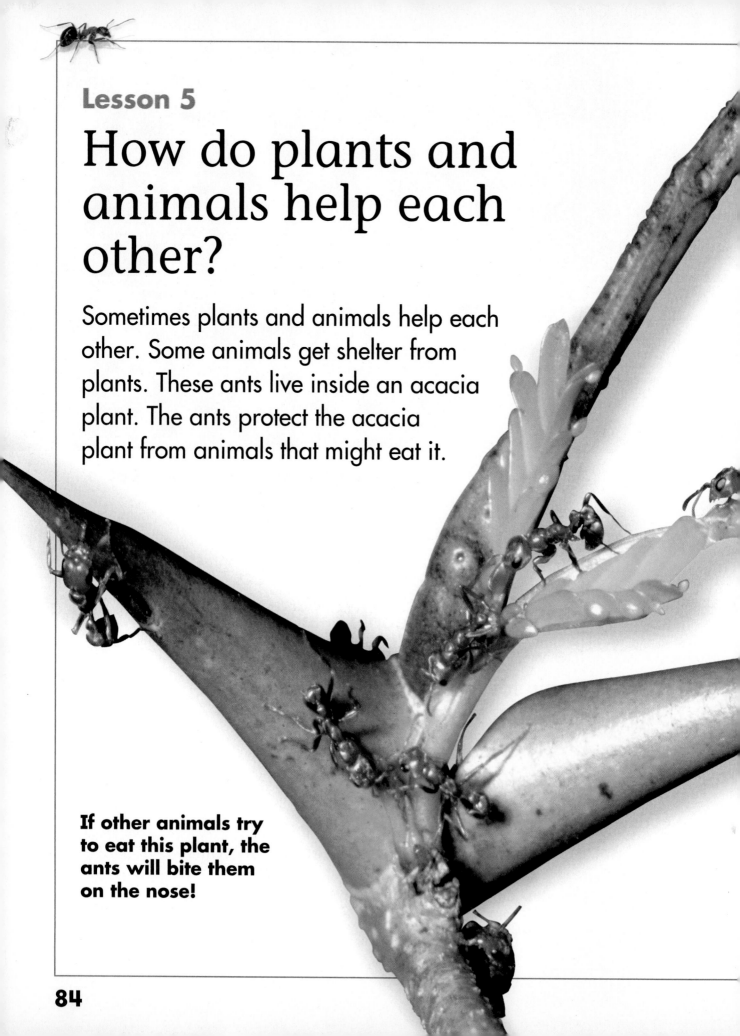

How do plants and animals help each other?

Sometimes plants and animals help each other. Some animals get shelter from plants. These ants live inside an acacia plant. The ants protect the acacia plant from animals that might eat it.

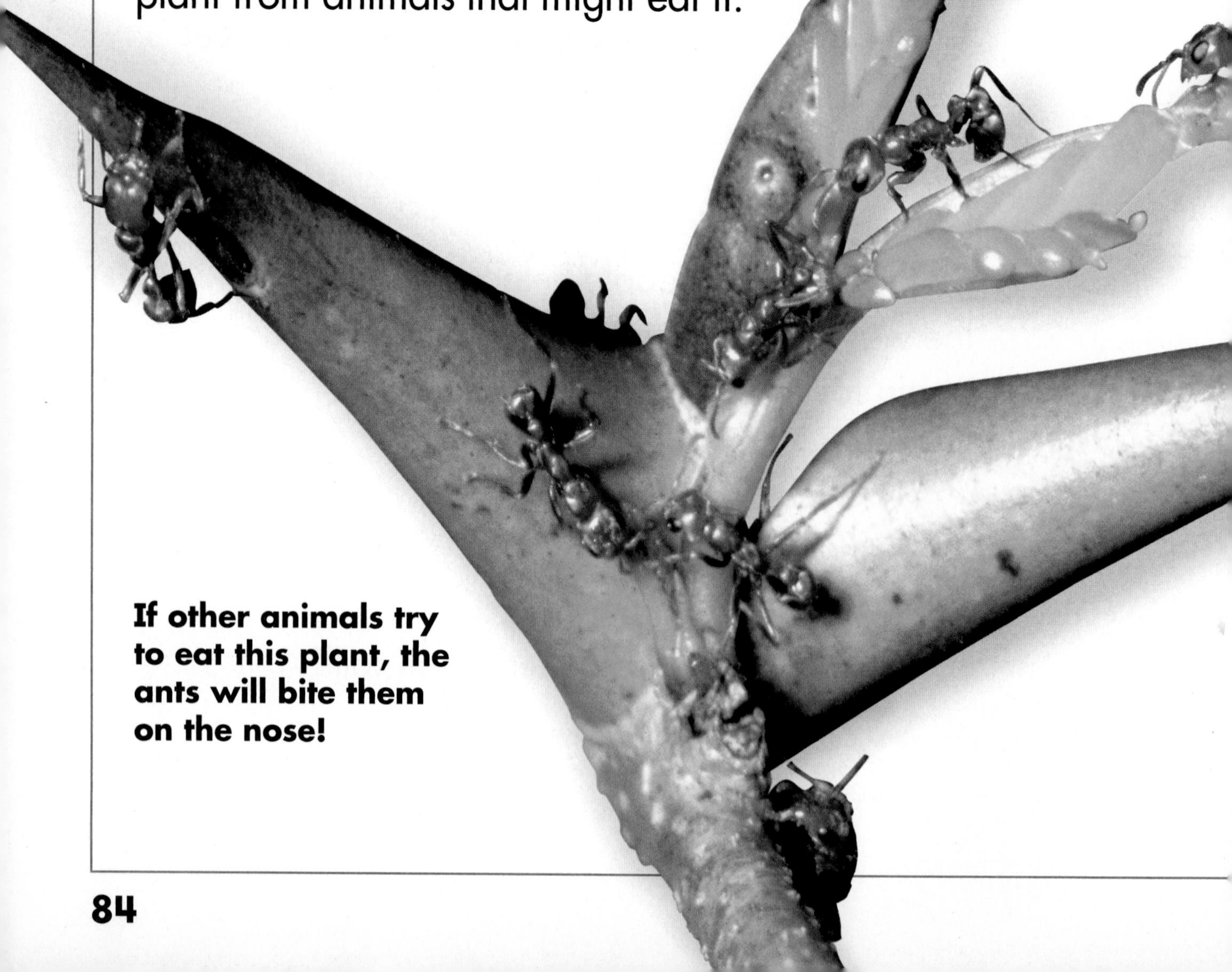

If other animals try to eat this plant, the ants will bite them on the nose!

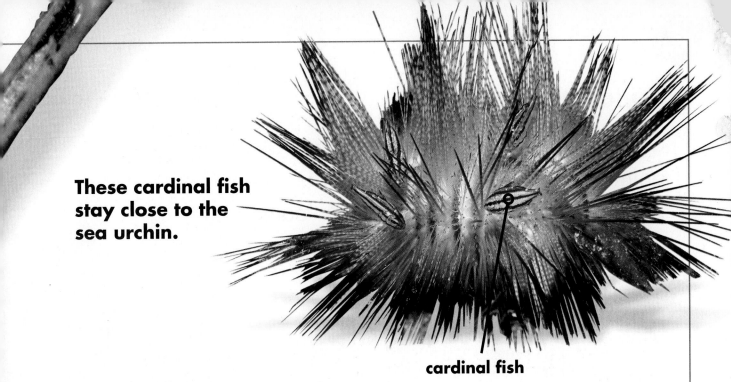

These cardinal fish stay close to the sea urchin.

cardinal fish

Some animals get protection from other animals. Find the cardinal fish in the picture above. Cardinal fish live near sea urchins. The sharp spines of the sea urchin protect the fish. The fish do not help or hurt the sea urchin.

1. **Checkpoint** How do ants protect an acacia plant?
2. **Social Studies in Science** Acacia plants live in Costa Rica. Find Costa Rica on a map. You can find it south of Florida.

Building Nests

Some animals depend on plants and other animals to build nests. Some animals use parts of plants. Some animals use feathers or fur from other animals to build their nests.

Look at the picture of the squirrel's nest. Twigs and leaves are on the outside of the nest. Dried grass, bark, feathers, and wool are on the inside of the nest.

The masked weaver makes a nest from plant parts.

Some owls that live in the desert build their nests in a cactus.

1. ✓Checkpoint What animal parts does the squirrel use to make its nest?

2. Writing in Science Write 2 or 3 sentences in your **science journal.** Tell what you learned about animals that build nests.

Animals Need Each Other

Animals need each other for many reasons. The remora fish in the picture below takes a ride with a blue shark. When the shark eats, the remora fish eats the leftovers! The remora does not hurt or help the shark.

The big blue shark scares predators away from the little remora.

A bird called an egret sits on top of a rhinoceros. The egret eats flies that might hurt the rhino.

Boxer crabs can hold an anemone in each claw. They use the anemones to sting predators. An anemone is a sea animal.

Lesson Checkpoint

1. How does a shark help a remora fish?
2. **Math in Science** Which is the best estimate of the weight of a rhinoceros: 35 pounds or 3,500 pounds?

Lab zone

Guided Inquiry

Investigate How can you model a food web?

Many different living things make up a food web. All of the animals you see are part of a food web.

Materials

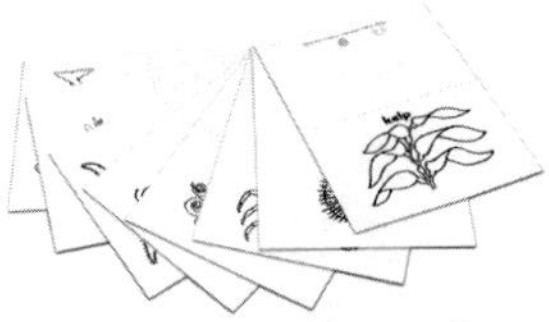

food web cards

tape

yarn

crayons or markers

Process Skills

When you act something out, you **model** it.

What to Do

1. Choose a card. Tape it on your shirt. Stand in a circle with your group.

2. Look for living things that you eat or that eat you. Toss the ball of yarn to one of them.

3. Take turns until everyone is connected. Lay down the yarn and the cards.

4 Draw your food web and write the names of the living things.

My Food Web

Explain Your Results

1. **Infer** What do the web lines mean?
2. How did you **model** a real food web?

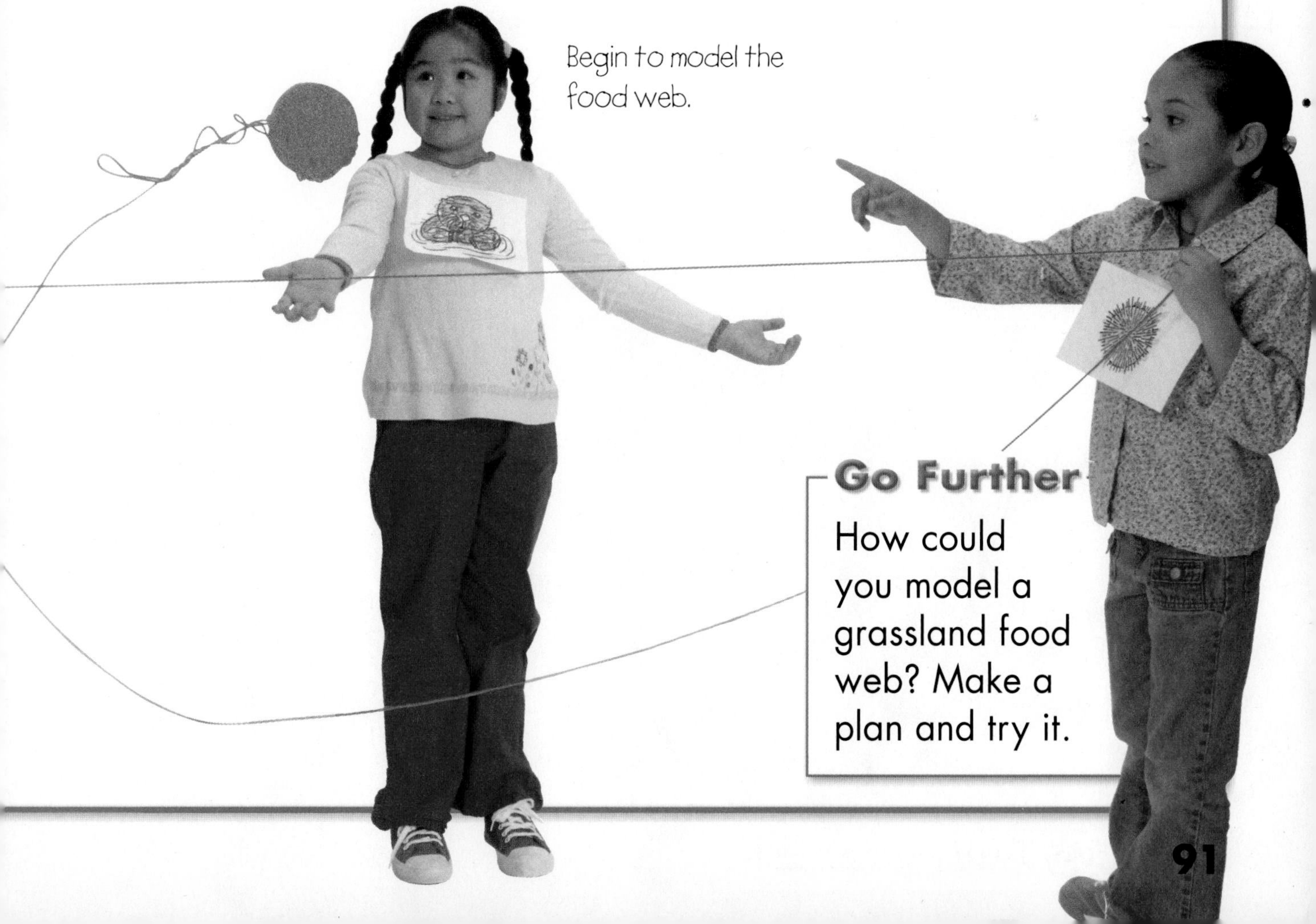

Begin to model the food web.

Go Further

How could you model a grassland food web? Make a plan and try it.

Math in Science

Measuring Length

These animals are from this chapter. They are some of the predators and prey in a grassland food web.

Read the table. Find out how long some of the animals can grow to be.

Animal	Length in cm
Raccoon	100 cm
Vole	20 cm
Fox	80 cm
Hawk	60 cm

1. Which animal is the shortest?
2. Which animal is the longest?
3. How much longer is the fox than the vole?
4. Put the animals in order from shortest to longest.

Lab zone Take-Home Activity

Use a ruler. Find objects at home that match the length of each animal in the table. List the objects. Share your list with your family.

Chapter 3 Review and Test Prep

Vocabulary

Which picture goes with each word?

1. producer
2. consumer
3. food chain

A

B

C
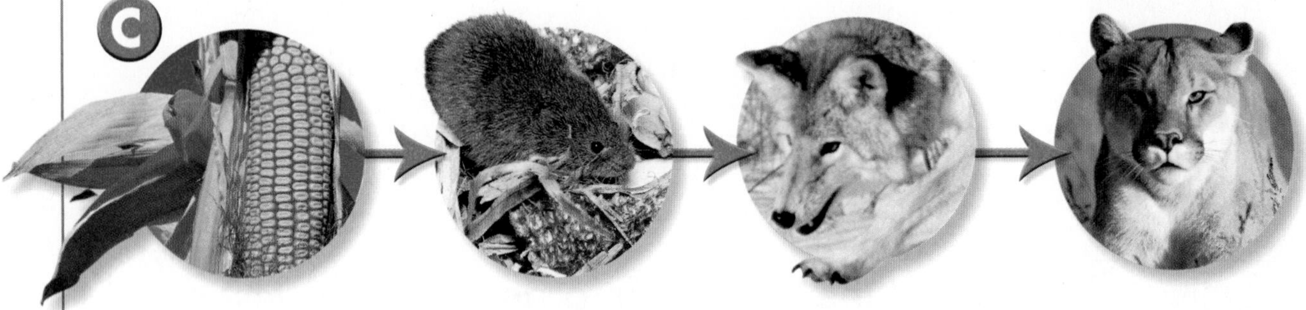

What did you learn?

4. What do all animals need to live?
5. Name a predator from this chapter. What is its prey?
6. What are some ways animals help each other?

Process Skills

7. Infer What would happen to an ocean food web if there were no more kelp?

Cause and Effect

8. Read the captions.

It rained all day in this forest.

The mountain lion found shelter from the rain in a cave.

What **caused** the mountain lion to go into the cave?

Test Prep

Fill in the circle next to the correct answer.

9. Which animal finds shelter in an acacia plant?

Ⓐ masked weaver
Ⓑ egret
Ⓒ cardinal fish
Ⓓ ant

10. Writing in Science Describe a food chain from the chapter. Tell how energy passes through it.

Career Farmer

Read Together

Farmers have an important job! Some farmers work on farms that grow grains, fruits, and vegetables for food. Some farmers raise animals that give people milk, eggs, and meat.

When fruits and vegetables are ready, farmers pick them. They ship the fruits and vegetables off to factories or markets. Farmers milk cows. Farmers gather eggs from chickens. Many people depend on farmers for food.

Lab zone Take-Home Activity

Draw a picture of plants and animals on a farm. Tell how a farmer cares for the plants and animals in your picture.

EC CRU 10 9 8 7 6 5 4 3 2 1

You Will Discover

- ways that living things are like their parents.
- how plants and animals change as they grow.

Chapter 4

How Living Things Grow and Change

online Student Edition
pearsonsuccessnet.com

Discovery Channel School Student DVD

Build Background

How do living things grow in different ways?

Chapter 4 Vocabulary

life cycle page 106

nymph page 108

seed coat page 114

germinate page 114

seedling page 114

germinate

Germinate means to begin to grow into a young plant.

seedling

Lab zone Directed Inquiry

Explore Which hand do different children use to write?

Materials

paper

crayon

scissors

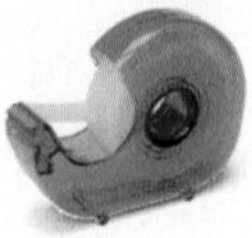
tape

chart paper

What to Do

1. Trace the hand you use to write.
2. Write your name in the middle. Cut out the hand.
3. **Collect data** Tape your hand to the graph.

Be careful!

Scissors are sharp!

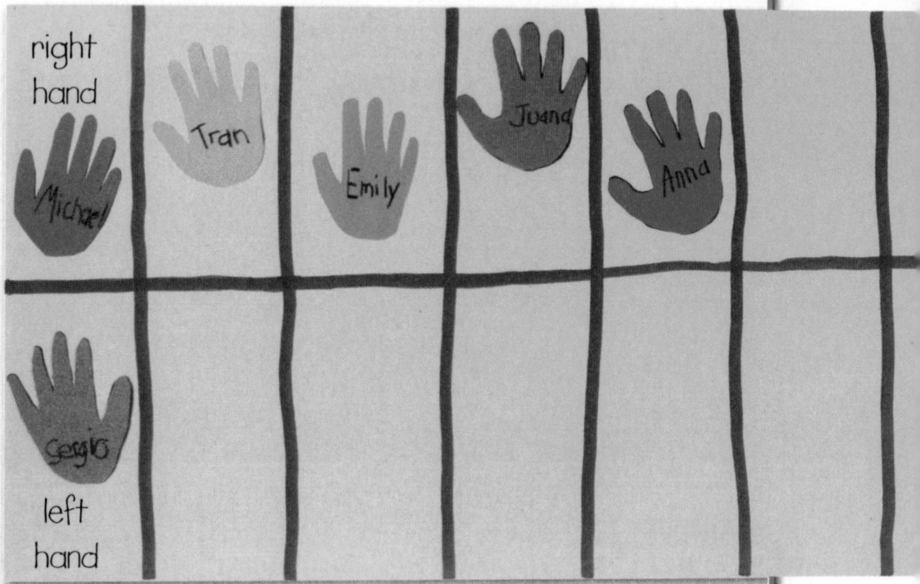

Process Skills

You **infer** when you get ideas from what you know.

Explain Your Results

Infer What does the graph show?

How to Read Science

Reading Skills

Target Skill: Infer

Infer means to use what you know to answer a question.

Science Article

Carol is right-handed. She uses her right hand for writing and to drink from a glass. She uses both hands to button her coat. Ben is left-handed.

Apply It!

Infer Which hand do you think Ben would use to cut paper or throw a ball?

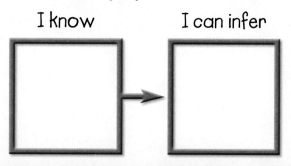

I know → I can infer

You Are There

Hi Little Turtle!

Sung to the tune of "Itsy Bitsy Spider"
Lyrics by Gerri Brioso & Richard Freitas/The Dovetail Group, Inc.

Look at the sea turtle coming from the sea.
Crawling on the sand, looking right at me.
Hey, little sea turtle, I would like to know,
How did you start out and how did you grow?

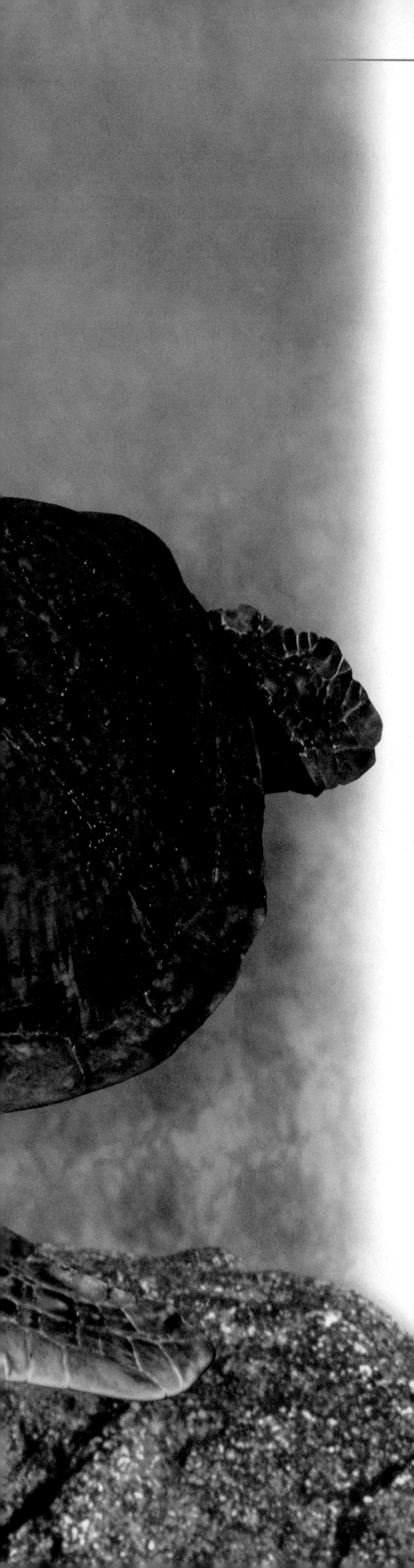

Lesson 1

How do sea turtles grow and change?

Living things need food and water. Living things grow and change. Living things can be parents. Plants and animals are living things.

The sea turtle is an animal. You will learn how a sea turtle grows and changes.

This toy turtle is a nonliving thing. It does not need food and water. It cannot grow and change. It cannot be a parent.

Sea Turtle Eggs

A sea turtle lives in the ocean. A sea turtle crawls onto a beach to lay eggs. A sea turtle uses its flippers to dig a hole in the sand. It lays eggs in the hole. Then the sea turtle covers the eggs with sand.

Sea turtles can lay many eggs at one time.

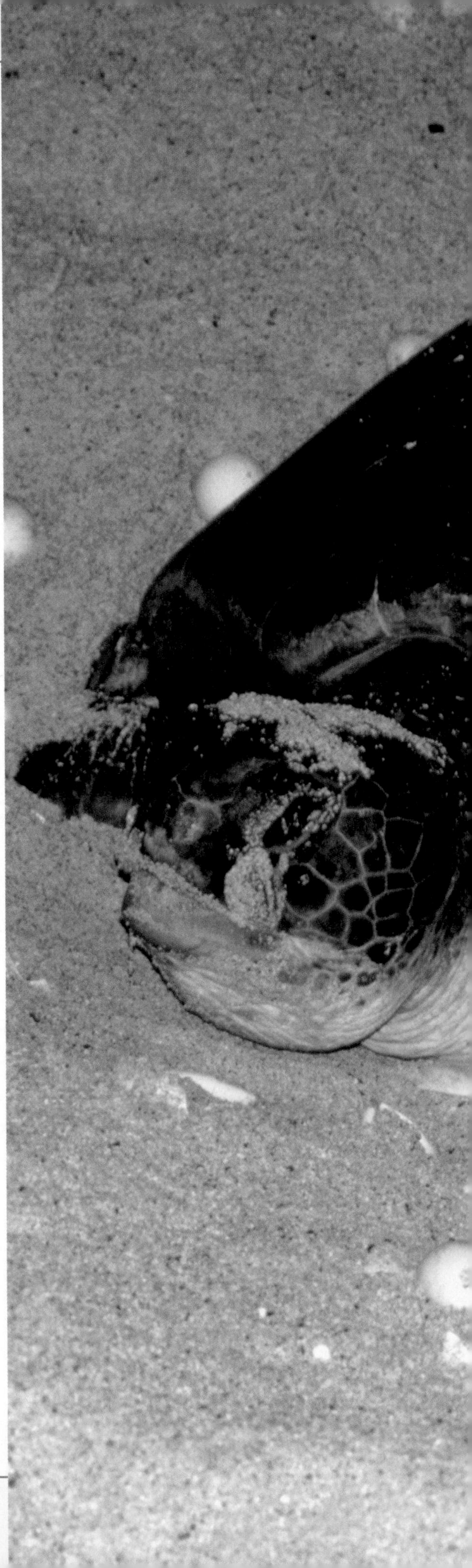

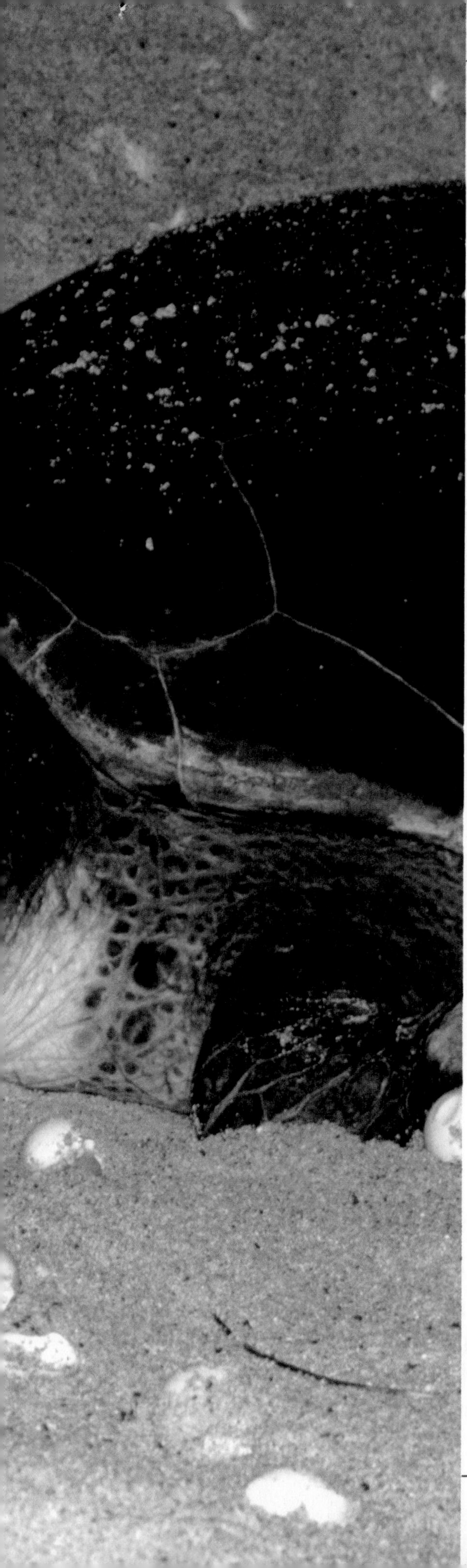

The eggs lay in the sand for about two months. Then the eggs are ready to hatch.

Baby turtles have a special tooth. The tooth helps them break open the egg's shell. Later, the tooth falls out.

A baby sea turtle hatches from its egg.

1. Checkpoint How do baby sea turtles get out of the egg?
2. Math in Science Suppose 3 sea turtles each laid 100 eggs. How many eggs were laid all together?

The Life Cycle of a Sea Turtle

The way a living thing grows and changes is called its **life cycle.** Follow the arrows to see the life cycle of a sea turtle.

The sea turtle starts life as an egg.
A young sea turtle comes out of the egg. Young sea turtles look like their parents.

One day, the sea turtle may have young of its own. A new life cycle begins.

Lesson Checkpoint

1. How do sea turtles start life?
2. **Social Studies** in Science Look at a map of the United States. Find some places where sea turtles might lay eggs.

Lesson 2

What is the life cycle of a dragonfly?

The life cycles of insects are different from the life cycles of other animals. Many young insects are called **nymphs.** Nymphs look a lot like their parents, but their wings are still growing. Nymphs shed their outside covering many times as they grow.

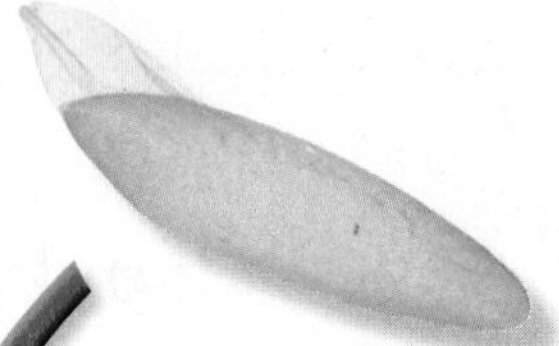

Dragonflies often lay eggs in the water.

A nymph hatches from the dragonfly egg. First, the nymph lives in the water. Then, the nymph crawls to the land.

The nymph has shed its covering one last time. Now it is an adult dragonfly with wings to fly. It may lay eggs.

Lesson Checkpoint

1. Tell the stages of a dragonfly life cycle in order.
2. **Infer** Why doesn't a nymph need wings?

Lesson 3

What is the life cycle of a horse?

A horse is a mammal. Most young mammals grow inside their mothers. Young mammals drink milk from their mother.

A young horse is called a foal.

The foal grows and grows. It looks like its parents.

The foal has become an adult horse. The adult horse is old enough to have foals of its own.

Lesson Checkpoint

1. **Infer** What is food for a foal?
2. **Writing in Science** Tell what you know about the life cycle of a horse.

Lesson 4

How are young animals like their parents?

Young animals often look like their parents in shape and color. Yet some young animals look different from their parents.

Young penguins are covered with fuzzy down feathers. The feathers become white and black as the penguin grows.

These kittens all have the same parents. Yet they look different from each other.

Giraffes have brown spots. Each giraffe has its own pattern of spots. No two patterns are the same.

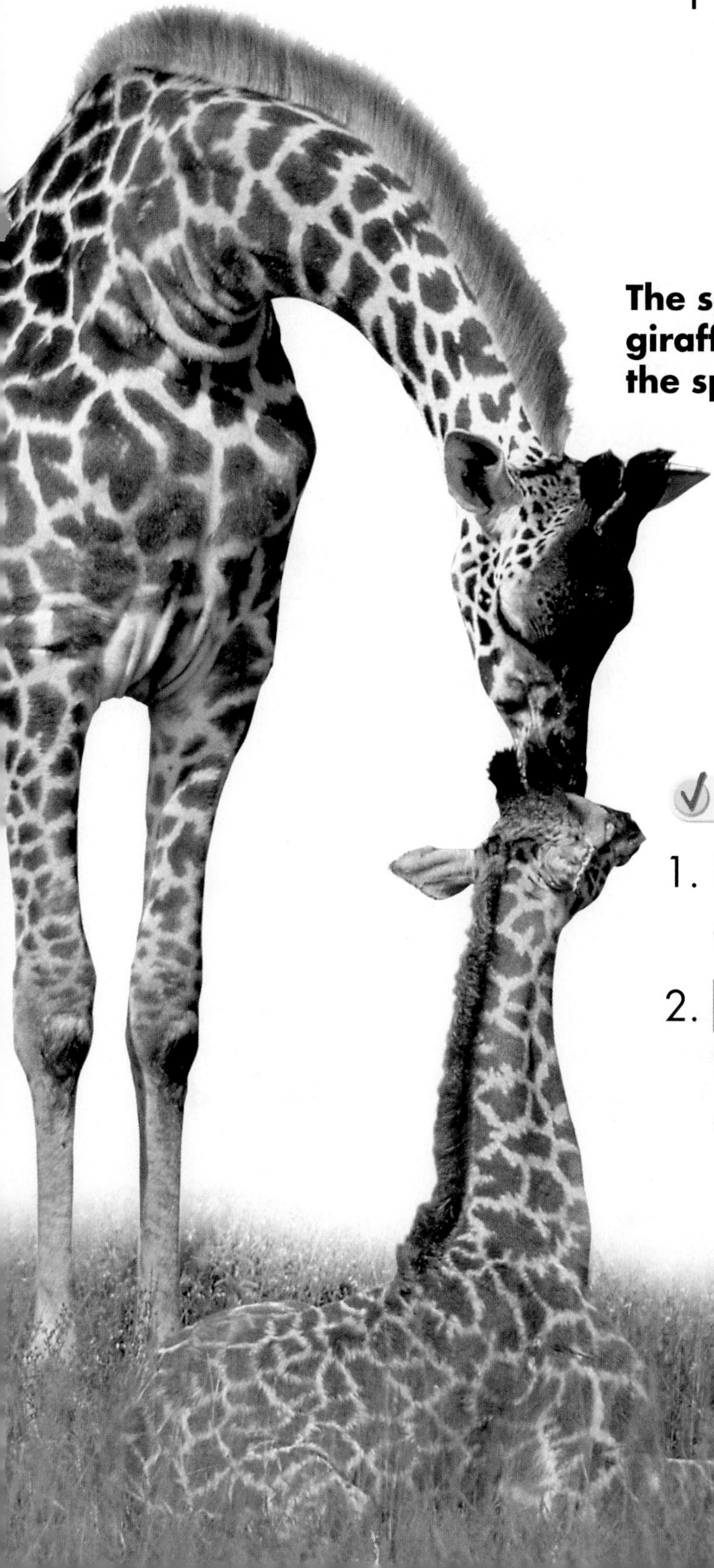

The spots on the adult giraffe are darker than the spots on its young.

Lesson Checkpoint

1. How are young penguins different from their parents?
2. **Writing** in Science Tell how you think the kittens are like their parents.

Lesson 5

What is the life cycle of a bean plant?

Most plants grow from seeds. A seed has a hard outer covering called a **seed coat.** A seed coat protects the seed.

Each seed contains a tiny plant and stored food. The tiny plant uses the stored food as it grows. A seed that gets enough water and air may **germinate,** or begin to grow. Roots from the germinated seed grow down into the ground. A stem grows up. A seedling grows out of the ground. A **seedling** is a young plant.

Seeds are the beginning of a bean plant life cycle.

The bean seed germinates and starts to grow.

Seed coat

A seedling grows from the seed.

SciLinks Take It to the Net pearsonsuccessnet.com keyword: seedling code: g2p114

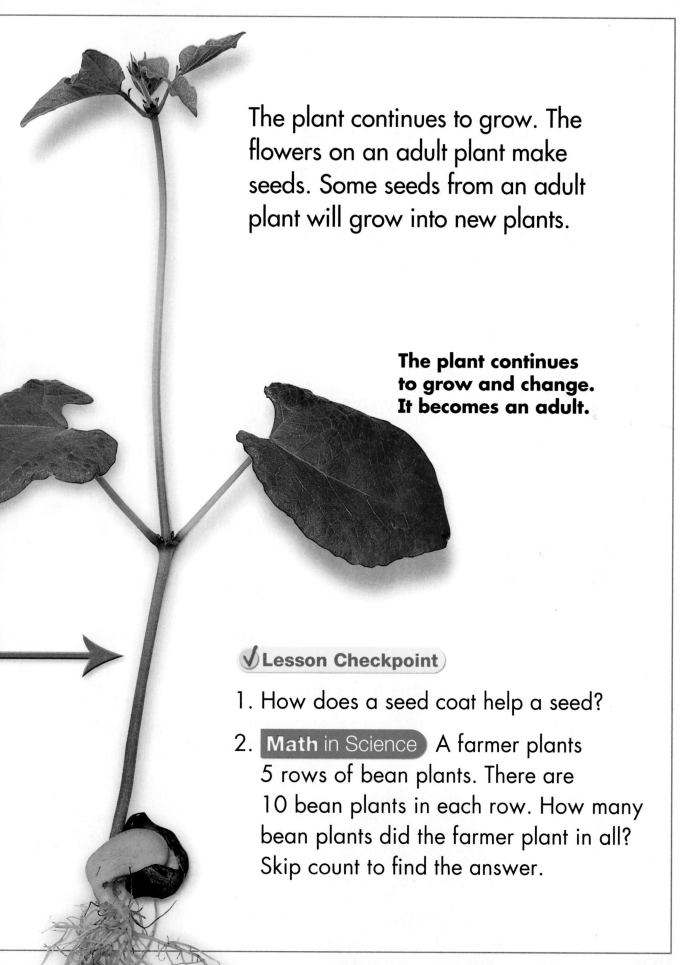

The plant continues to grow. The flowers on an adult plant make seeds. Some seeds from an adult plant will grow into new plants.

The plant continues to grow and change. It becomes an adult.

✓ Lesson Checkpoint

1. How does a seed coat help a seed?
2. **Math in Science** A farmer plants 5 rows of bean plants. There are 10 bean plants in each row. How many bean plants did the farmer plant in all? Skip count to find the answer.

Lesson 6

How are young plants like their parents?

Young plants are usually like the parent plant in color and shape. Young plants can be different from the parent plant in some ways too.

A young saguaro cactus has the same shape as an adult. It has the same color as an adult.

An adult saguaro cactus has arms.

A young saguaro cactus does not have arms.

Children in the same family might look like each other. They might look different from each other too. How might children in the same family look alike? How might they look different?

Parents and their children may look alike in some ways. They may look different in other ways. Look at the family in the picture on this page. How are the children like their parents? How are they different?

People in a family do not look exactly alike.

Lesson Checkpoint

1. What are some ways people can be different from each other?
2. **Infer** Where did the children in the picture get their dark eyes?

Lab zone

Guided Inquiry

Investigate How does a caterpillar grow and change?

Living things change as they grow. Some insects look different from their parents.

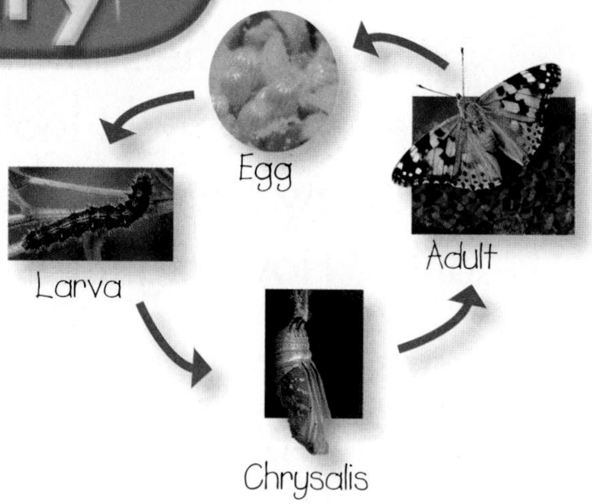

Materials

caterpillars

butterfly habitat

crayons and markers

What to Do

1. Observe your caterpillars every day. **Collect data** every day for 3 weeks.

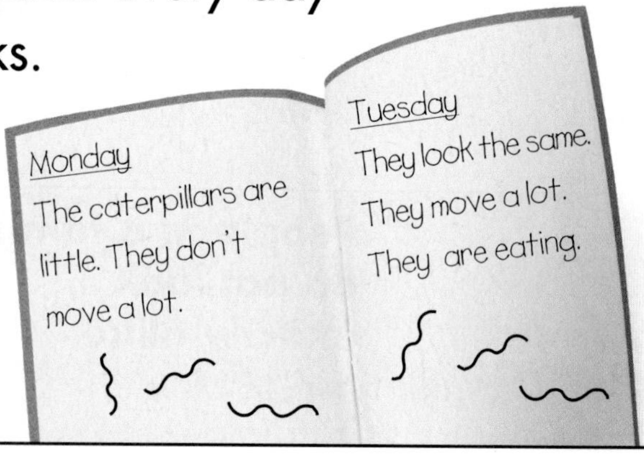

Monday
The caterpillars are little. They don't move a lot.
Tuesday
They look the same. They move a lot. They are eating.

2. Look for a chrysalis to form. Your teacher will put the chrysalis in the butterfly habitat.

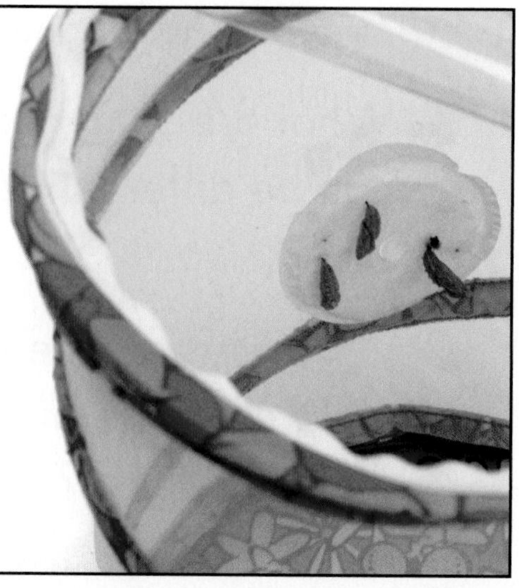

Process Skills

You **collect data** to help you remember information.

 More Lab zone Activities Take It to the Net pearsonsuccessnet.com

3 Continue to collect data. **Predict** what will happen next.

They're alive!
Handle with care.

4 Draw pictures that show how the caterpillars changed.

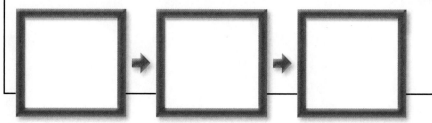

Explain Your Results

1. How did the caterpillars change?
2. **Infer** What happens inside a chrysalis?

Go Further

Can you make a model of how a caterpillar grows and changes? Try it.

Measuring Time

These pictures show the life cycle of a butterfly and the life cycle of a frog. They show the amount of time between each step in the life cycles.

A butterfly life cycle

1. How many days does it take a butterfly egg to hatch into a caterpillar?
2. How many days does it take for a butterfly egg to become a butterfly? Write a number sentence.
3. It takes 2 weeks for frog eggs to hatch into tadpoles. How many days is this? Write a number sentence.

A frog life cycle

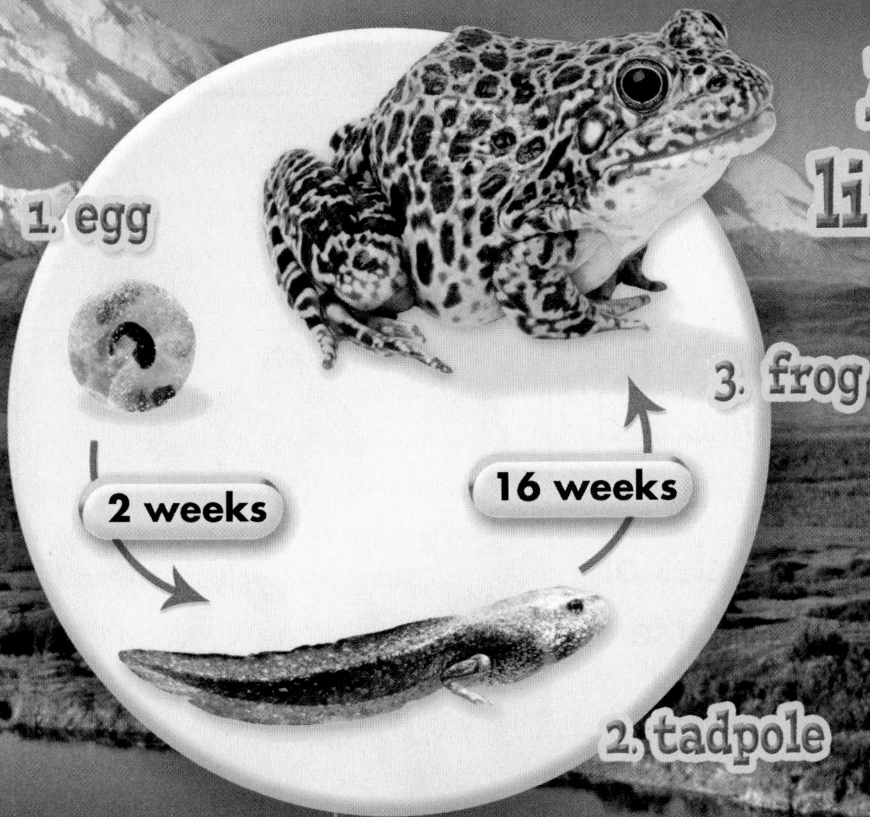

Lab zone Take-Home Activity

A caterpillar grows to be about 5 centimeters long. What other things might be 5 centimeters long? Measure to find out.

Vocabulary

Which picture goes with each word?

1. seed coat
2. life cycle
3. nymph
4. seedling

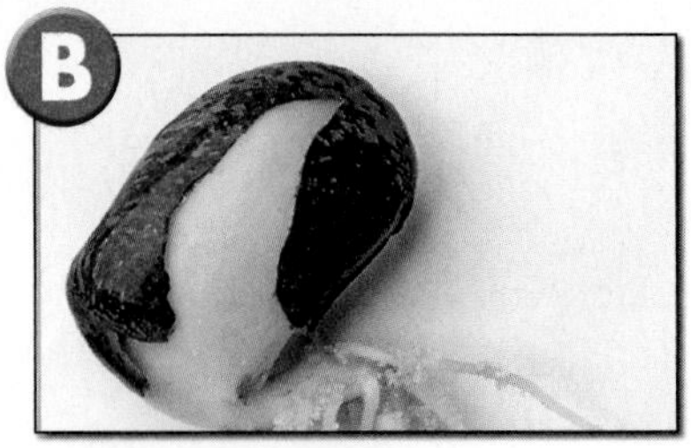

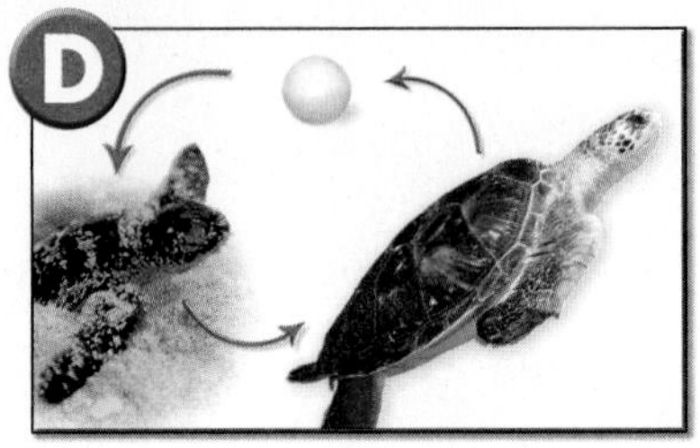

What did you learn?

5. How are people alike and different?
6. Compare the life cycles of a dragonfly and a horse. How are they alike and different?
7. What does germinate mean?

Process Skills

8. **Infer** Why does a baby turtle's special tooth fall out after it hatches from the egg?

Infer

9. People are wearing heavy coats and hats outside. They are wearing gloves and scarves. What can you **infer** about the weather?

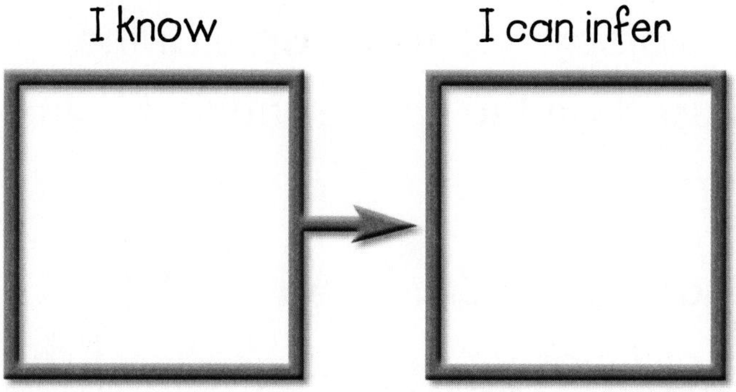

Test Prep

Fill in the circle next to the correct answer.

10. What kind of animal changes from an egg to a nymph?

Ⓐ mammal
Ⓑ insect
Ⓒ reptile
Ⓓ bird

11. Writing in Science How might living things be like their parents? Make a list.

NASA

Biography

SAVE the Sea Turtles

Meet Mario J. Mota

Read Together

Dr. Mota

Dr. Mario Mota is a marine biologist. He works at NASA. Dr. Mota studies turtle biology. He uses some of the tools used on the space shuttle to study the turtles.

Dr. Mota was born in Africa. When Dr. Mota was young, he liked to fish. Dr. Mota always loved the ocean. He knew he wanted to work by the ocean.

Sea turtles lay their eggs on or near the same beach where they hatched. They lay more than 100 eggs in each nest!

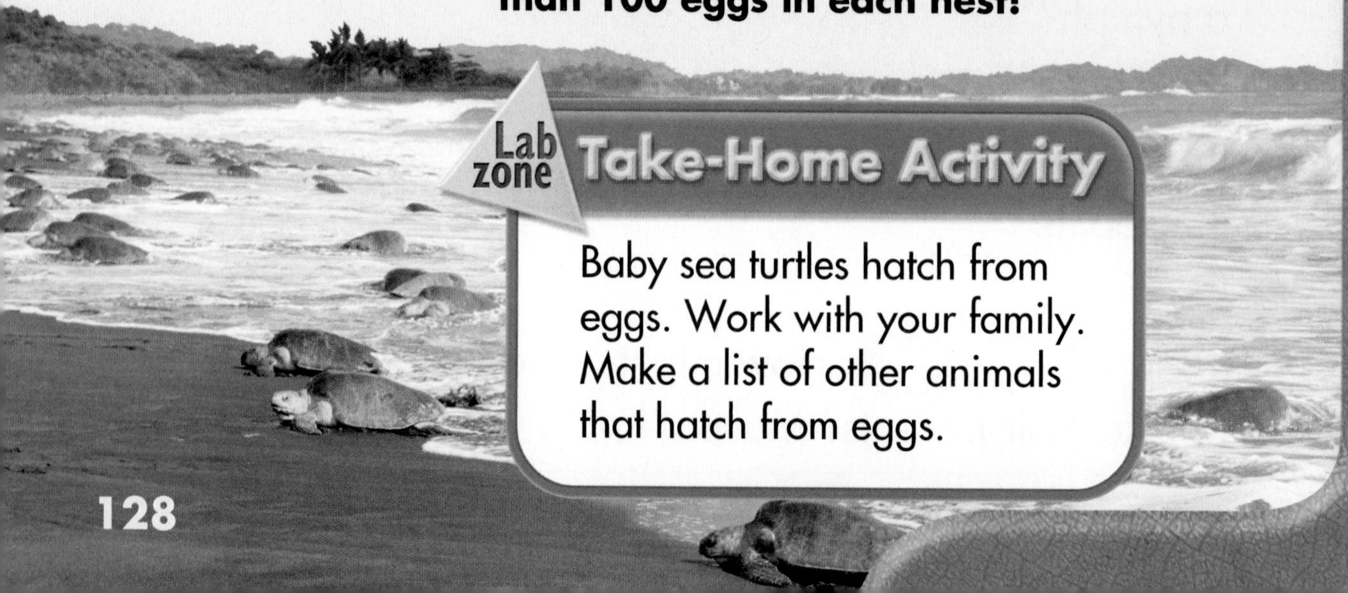

Lab zone Take-Home Activity

Baby sea turtles hatch from eggs. Work with your family. Make a list of other animals that hatch from eggs.

Unit A Test Talk

Test-Taking Strategies
- Find Important Words
- Choose the Right Answer
- Use Information from Text and Graphics
- Write Your Answer

Find Important Words

There are important words in science questions. These words help you understand the questions.

Megan lives near a big pond where lots of frogs live. One day, Megan sat on the grass by the pond. She liked watching the frogs. Megan saw one frog sitting very still. The frog's tongue zipped out. It caught a tasty insect to eat.

Read the question.

What is one thing that frogs eat?

Ⓐ ponds
Ⓑ sandwiches
Ⓒ grass
Ⓓ insects

First, find important words in the question. The most important words are **frogs** and **eat.** Next, find important words in the text that match the important words in the question. Use the words to answer the question.

Unit A Wrap-Up

Chapter 1

How do plants live in their habitats?

- Plants have adaptations that help them live in different environments.

Chapter 2

How are animals different from each other?

- Animals can be put into two groups. One group of animals has backbones. The other group of animals does not have backbones.

Chapter 3

How do living things help each other?

- Living things help each other in different ways. Animals and plants that need each other for food are part of a food chain.

Chapter 4

How do living things grow in different ways?

- Living things have different life cycles. A life cycle is the way a living thing grows and changes. Plants and animals have life cycles.

Performance Assessment

How Can You Sort Animals?

- Cut out pictures of different animals that live on the land, in water, and in the air.
- Put the animals into groups.
- Tell which animals have backbones and which animals do not have backbones.

Read More About Life Science!

Look for books like these in your library.

Lab zone Full Inquiry

Experiment Which bird beak can crush seeds?

Look at the heron's beak. Look at the cardinal's beak. How are the beaks alike? How are they different?

Materials

2 clothespins

2 craft sticks

glue

straw pieces

Process Skills

You **control variables** when you change only one thing.

Ask a question.

Which bird uses its beak to crush seeds? **Use models** to learn more.

Make a hypothesis.

Which crushes better, a model of a heron's beak, or a model of a cardinal's beak? Tell what you think.

Plan a fair test.

Be sure to use the same kind of clothespins.

Do your test.

1. Make a model of a heron's beak. Glue 2 craft sticks to a clothespin. Let the glue dry. Use the other clothespin as a model of a cardinal's beak. Use a piece of straw as a model of a seed.

2 Use the heron's beak.
Pick up a seed. Try it again.

3 Use the cardinal's beak.
Pick up a seed. Try it again.

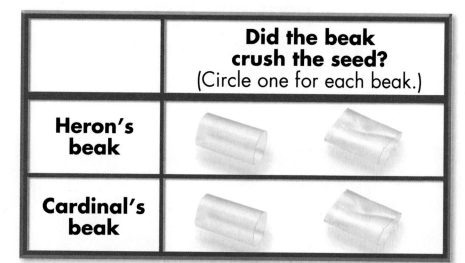

4 **Observe**. Which beak crushes the seeds?

Collect and record data.

	Did the beak crush the seed? (Circle one for each beak.)	
Heron's beak	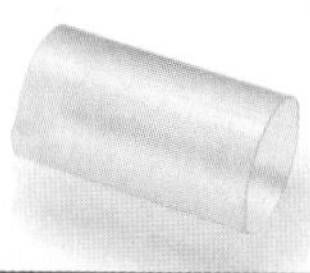	
Cardinal's beak		

Tell your conclusion.
Which model crushes a straw?
Infer Which bird uses its beak to crush seeds?

Go Further
Which beak will pick up seeds faster? Try it and find out.

Little Seeds

by Else Holmelund Minarik

Little seeds we sow in spring,
growing while the robins sing,
give us carrots, peas and beans,
tomatoes, pumpkin, squash and greens.

And we pick them,
one and all,
through the summer,
through the fall.

Winter comes, then spring, and then
little seeds we grow again.

Science Fair Projects

Full Inquiry

Using Scientific Methods

1. Ask a question.
2. Make a hypothesis.
3. Plan a fair test.
4. Do your test.
5. Collect and record data.
6. Tell your conclusion.
7. Go further.

Idea 1
Temperature and Seeds

Plan a project. Find out if seeds will grow faster in a warm place or a cold place.

Idea 2
Jumping Insects

Plan a project. Find out if crickets or grasshoppers are better jumpers.

EC CRU 10987654321

Unit B
Earth Science in Illinois

Did you know that you can see Sue, the world's largest *Tyrannosaurus rex* skeleton, in Chicago? Sue is at the Field Museum of Natural History.

Earth Science in Illinois

How are minerals, wild weather, and dinosaur fossils alike? They can all be found in Illinois. You will learn more about the science behind them in Unit B.

Rocks and Minerals

Fluorite is the state mineral in Illinois. It has many colors. It glows too. You will learn more about rocks and minerals in Chapter 5.

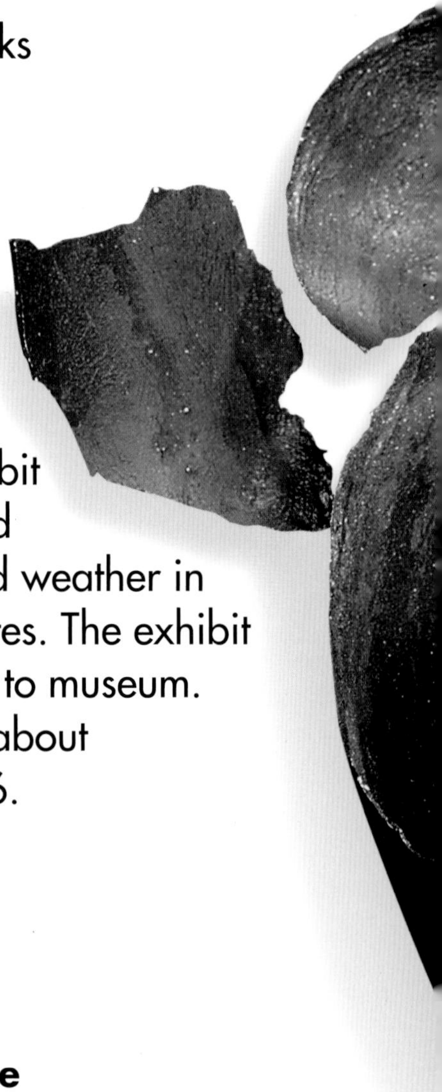

Wild Weather

Illinois can have thunderstorms, tornadoes, and snowstorms. An exhibit called "Midwest Wild Weather" shows wild weather in Illinois and other states. The exhibit moves from museum to museum. You will learn more about weather in Chapter 6.

Illinois Tornadoes from 1997 to 2000

Year	Number
2000	55
1999	64
1998	99
1997	29

The table shows the number of tornadoes in Illinois from 1997 to 2000.

Illinois Dinosaurs and Fossils

Dinosaurs lived a long time ago. The Hadrosaur lived in what is now Illinois. A group called B.I.G. looks for dinosaur fossils in Illinois. B.I.G. stands for Basics in Geology. You will learn more about dinosaurs and fossils in Chapter 7.

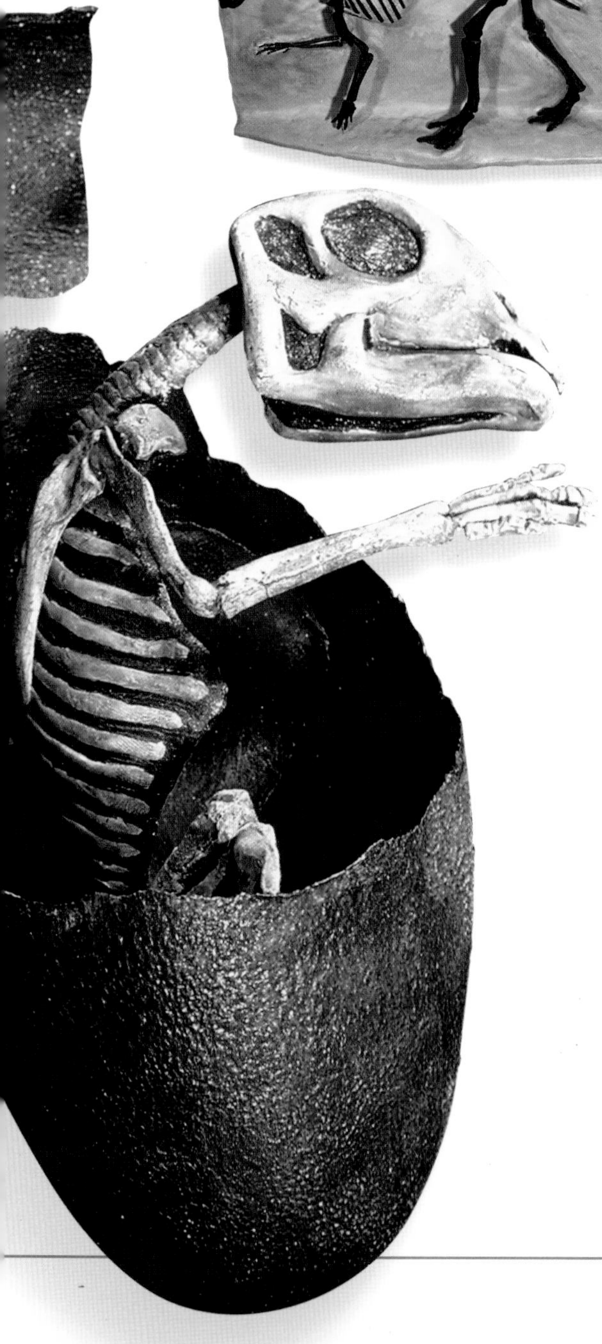

ISAT Prep

Answer the questions below. Write your answers on a separate sheet of paper.

Multiple-Choice Questions

1 What is the state mineral of Illinois?

A. fossil
B. tornado
C. Hadrosaur
D. fluorite

2 Which is an example of wild weather?

A. clouds
B. sunshine
C. fog
D. tornadoes

3 Which are two dinosaurs?

A. *Tyrannosaurus rex* and hadrosaur
B. *Tyrannosaurus rex* and fluorite
C. Fluorite and fluorescent
D. Hadrosaur and fluorite

Short-Response Questions

4 What does the group B.I.G. do in Illinois?

5 Were there more tornadoes in Illinois in 2000 or 1998?

ILLINOIS

Field Trip

The Field Museum of Natural History

The Field Museum of Natural History in Chicago has many exhibits about rocks and fossils. It has rocks that fell from space. There are big fossils and little fossils. You can even see how people learn about fossils.

Find out more:

Research to find out more about fossils.

- Make a fossil model. Make some clay into a block. Push a leaf into the block. Take away the leaf.
- What can you learn about fossils from your model?
- What do you know about dinosaurs from fossils?

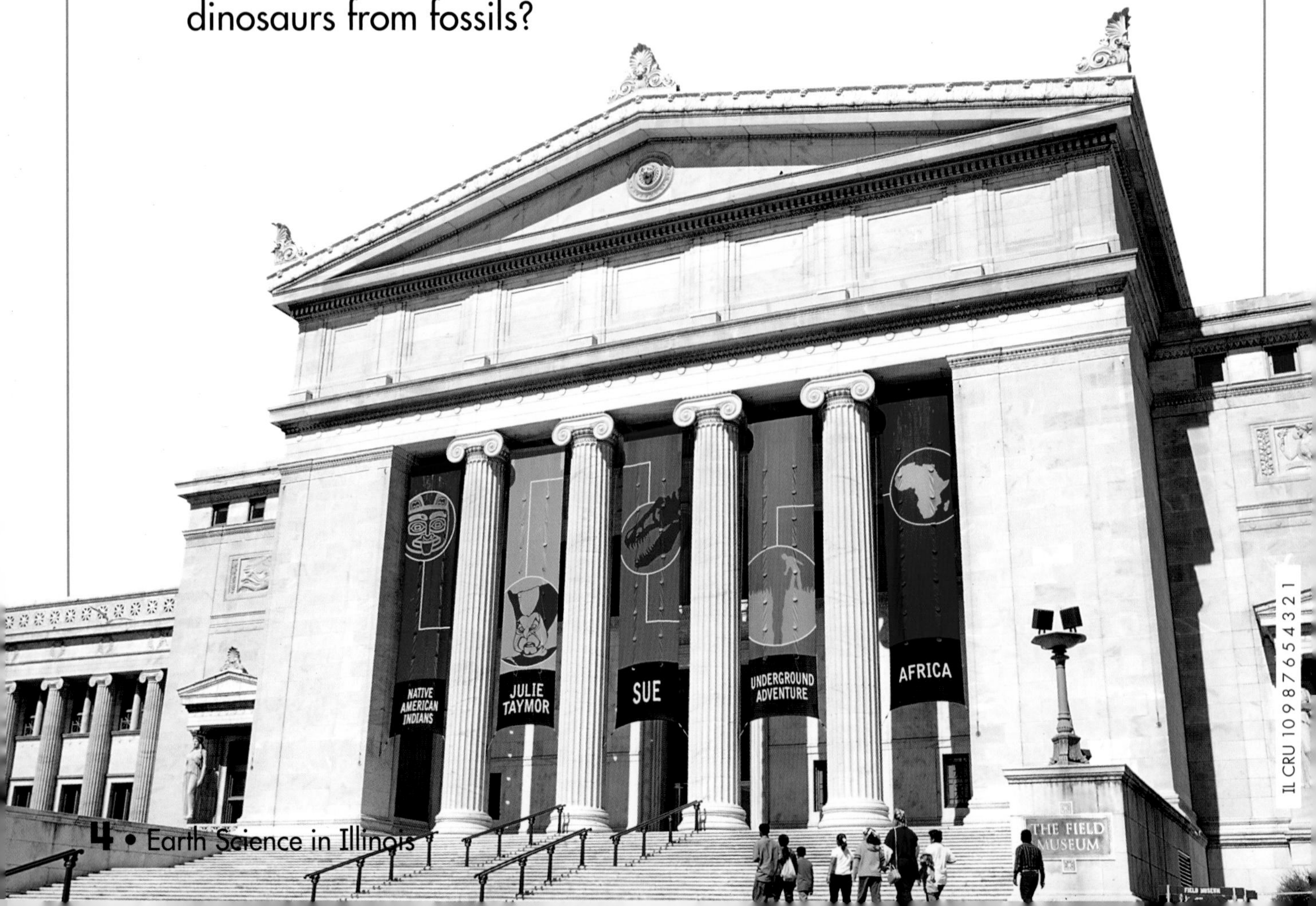

IL CRU 10 9 8 7 6 5 4 3 2 1

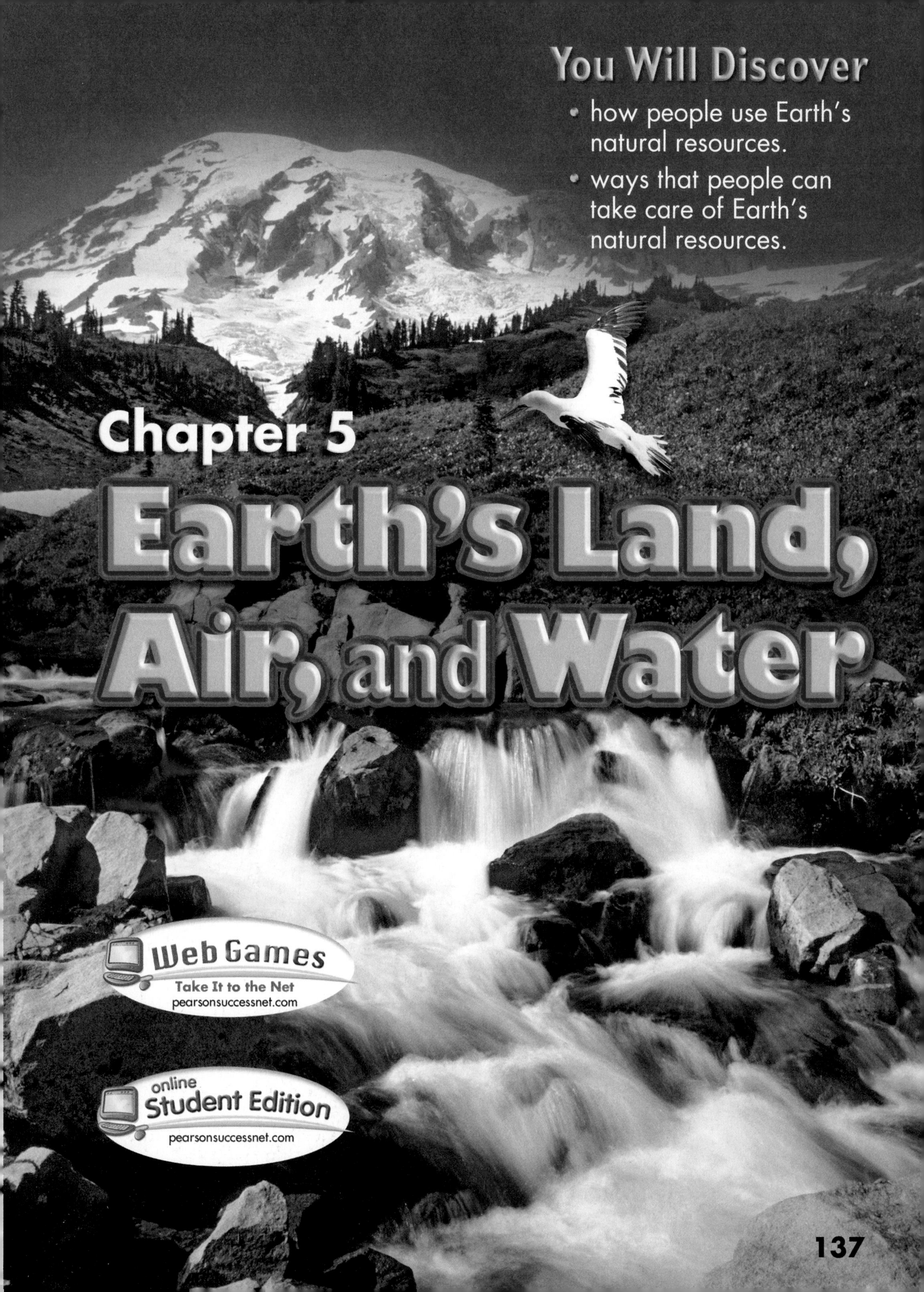

You Will Discover

- how people use Earth's natural resources.
- ways that people can take care of Earth's natural resources.

Chapter 5

Earth's Land, Air, and Water

Web Games
Take It to the Net
pearsonsuccessnet.com

online Student Edition
pearsonsuccessnet.com

Build Background

What are Earth's natural resources?

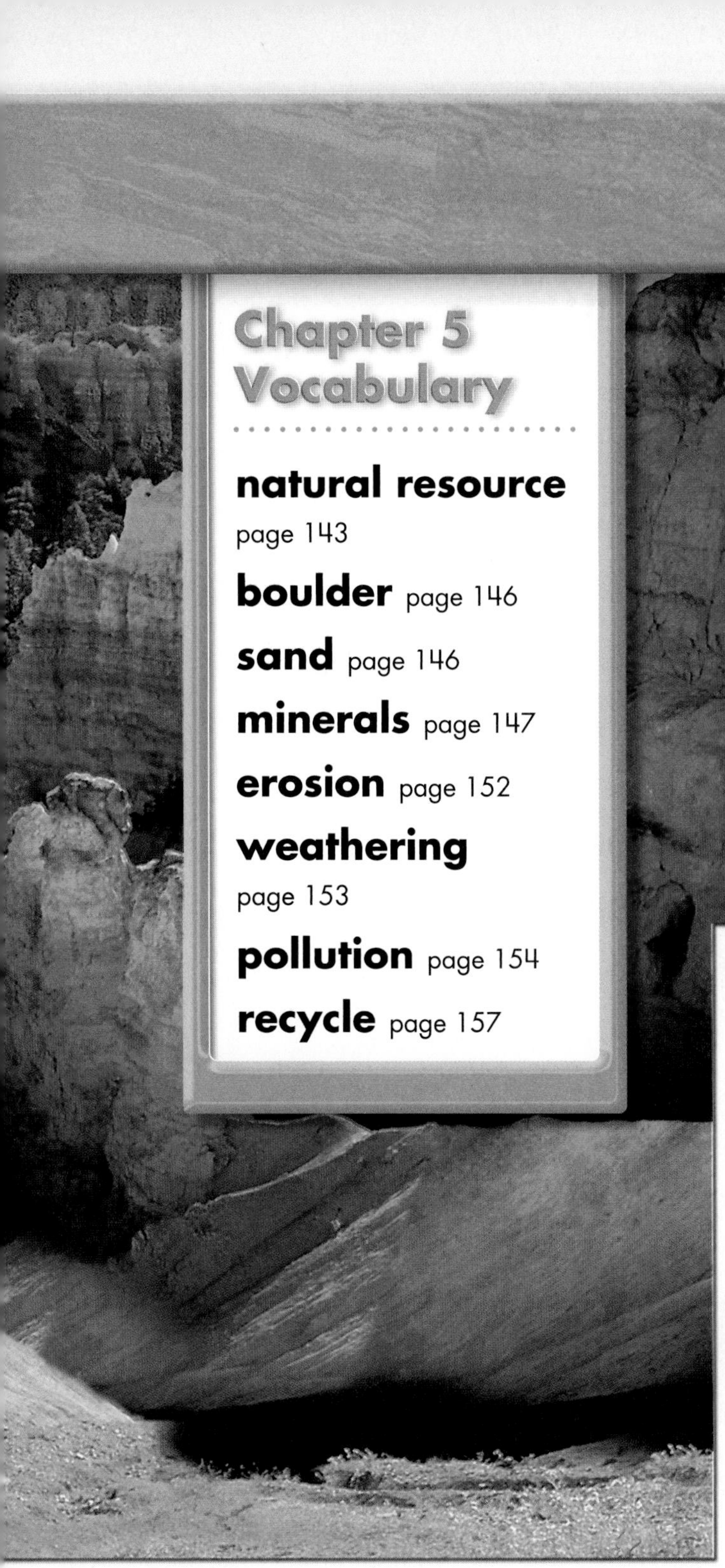

Chapter 5 Vocabulary

natural resource page 143

boulder page 146

sand page 146

minerals page 147

erosion page 152

weathering page 153

pollution page 154

recycle page 157

Lab zone **Directed Inquiry**

Explore How are soils different?

Materials

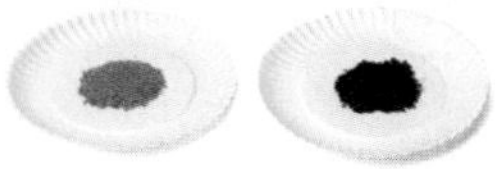
plates with soils

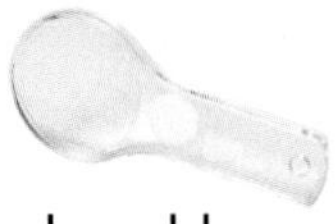
hand lens

dropper

cup with water

What to Do

1. Observe the soils. Look, smell, and touch.
2. Use the hand lens. Observe the smallest bits of soil.
3. Add water. Observe how the soils soak up the water.

Process Skills

You **observe** when you look, smell, and touch.

Explain Your Results

Observe How are the soils alike? How are they different?

How to Read Science

Reading Skills

Target Skill: Picture Clues

Pictures can give you clues about what you read.

Science Article

Soil

There are many kinds of living things in soil. Plants live in soil. Worms and other animals live in soil too.

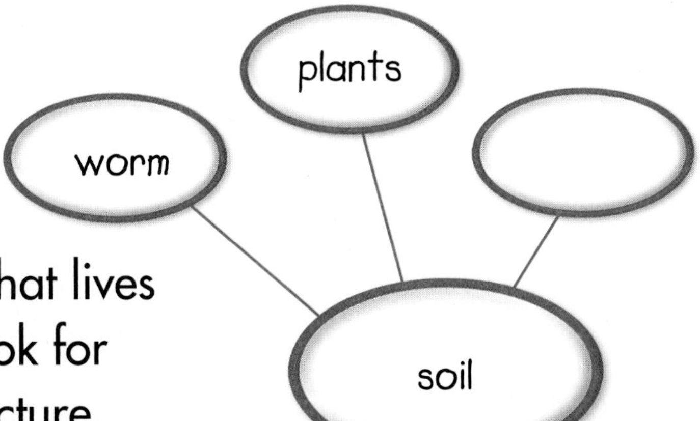

Apply It!
Observe What lives in the soil? Look for clues in the picture.

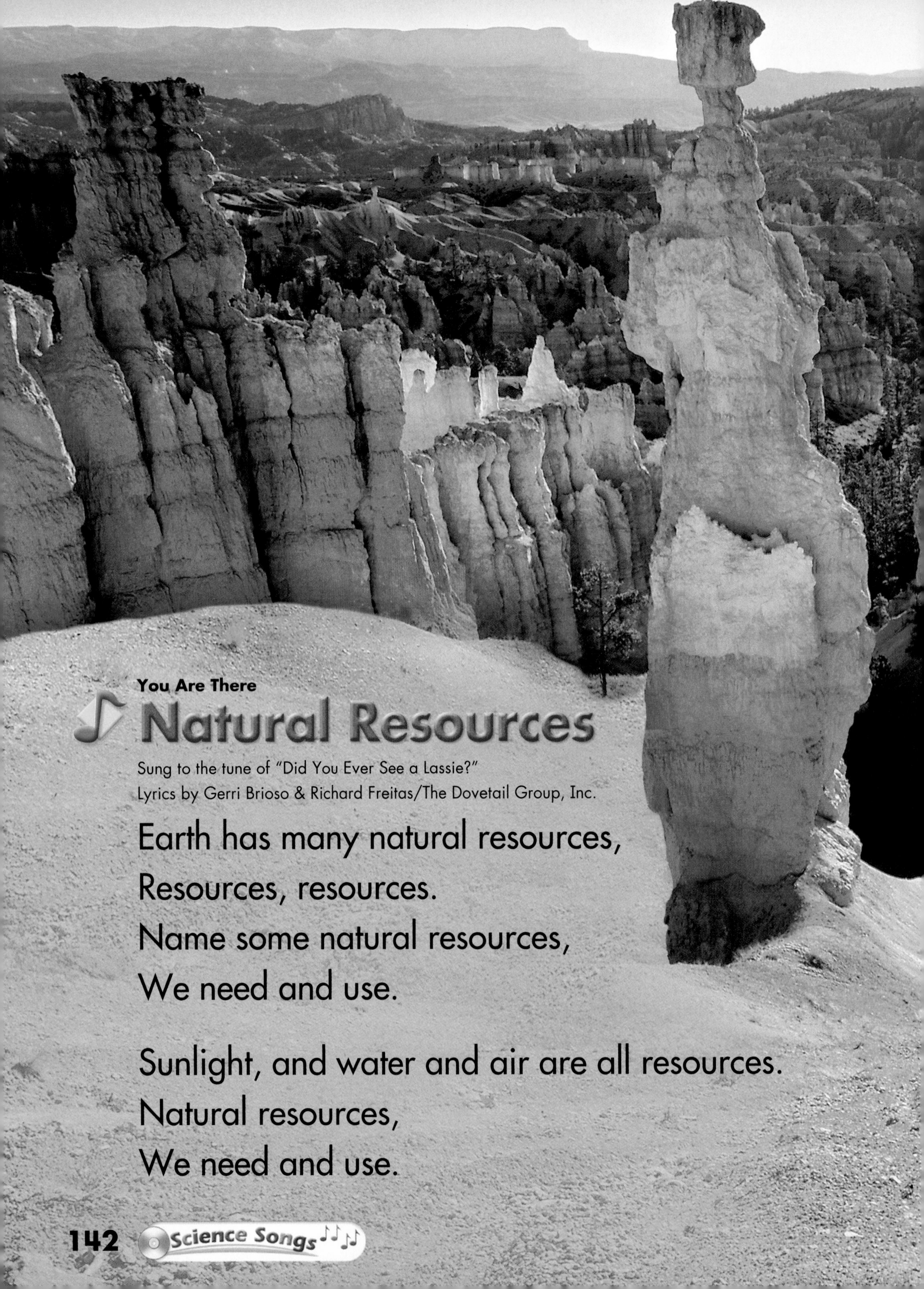

You Are There

Natural Resources

Sung to the tune of "Did You Ever See a Lassie?"
Lyrics by Gerri Brioso & Richard Freitas/The Dovetail Group, Inc.

Earth has many natural resources,
Resources, resources.
Name some natural resources,
We need and use.

Sunlight, and water and air are all resources.
Natural resources,
We need and use.

Lesson 1

What are natural resources?

Sunlight, water, and forests are natural resources. A **natural resource** is a useful thing that comes from nature. Oil and coal are natural resources too.

Some natural resources cannot be replaced after they are used up. Oil and coal cannot be replaced.

Some natural resources can be replaced after they are used. New trees can be planted to replace trees that are cut down for wood.

Some natural resources can never be used up. Sunlight, water, and air will never be used up.

Water and Air

Water is a natural resource. Plants, animals, and people need water to live. Ponds, rivers, streams, and lakes have fresh water. Oceans have salt water.

People use water in many ways. People drink water. People use water to cook and clean.

Air is a natural resource. Plants, animals, and people need air to live. Air is all around us. Wind is moving air.

✓ Lesson Checkpoint

1. Name some natural resources.
2. **Writing in Science** Make a list. What are some ways you use water every day?

Plants need water to live.

Air is used to fill this soccer ball.

This fishing boat brings fish from the ocean for people to eat.

Hot air fills this balloon.

Lesson 2

What are rocks and soil like?

Rocks are natural resources. Rocks come in many shapes, colors, and sizes. A very big rock is called a **boulder.** People use rocks to build houses.

Wind, rain, and ice can break rocks into smaller pieces. **Sand** is made of tiny pieces of rock. Some rocks can be smaller than grains of sand. People use sand to build roads.

Minerals are a natural resource. **Minerals** are nonliving materials that come from Earth. Rocks are made of minerals. Gold, iron, and silver are minerals.

Quartz is a mineral used to make glass.

Copper is a mineral. Some pots are made from copper.

1. **Checkpoint** Name four minerals.
2. **Math in Science** Think about a boulder. Is the length of a boulder closer to 10 inches or 10 feet? Explain your answer.

Soil

Soil is a natural resource. Soil covers most of Earth's land. Many soils are a mixture of clay, sand, and humus. Soil contains air and water. Most plants grow in soil.

Soil can be different colors. Soil can be hard or soft. Soil can feel wet or dry.

Clay soil has very small pieces. Clay soil feels smooth. It feels soft and sticky.

Sandy soil is loose. It feels dry and rough.

Humus is a part of soil that comes from living things.

Different kinds of plants grow best in different kinds of soil. Plants may grow well in one kind of soil. They may not grow as well in another kind of soil.

Lesson Checkpoint

1. Describe sandy soil, clay soil, and humus.
2. Use **picture clues.** Tell how sandy soil, clay soil, and humus are different.

Lesson 3

How do people use plants?

Plants are a natural resource. People use plants in many ways. Plants can be used to make food, shelter, and clothing. The pictures show some things you use every day that are made from plants.

People use cotton to make clothes. This T-shirt is made from cotton.

People use wood from pine trees to build houses.

Lesson Checkpoint

1. What is one way that people use cotton plants?
2. Use **picture clues.** What things are made from trees?

People use wheat to make food. This bread is made from wheat.

People use trees to make paper. What are some ways people use paper?

Lesson 4

How does Earth change?

Earth is always changing. Erosion can change Earth. **Erosion** happens when rocks or soil are moved by water or wind.

Plants can help prevent erosion. The roots on plants hold the soil in place.

Look at what erosion can do to a field!

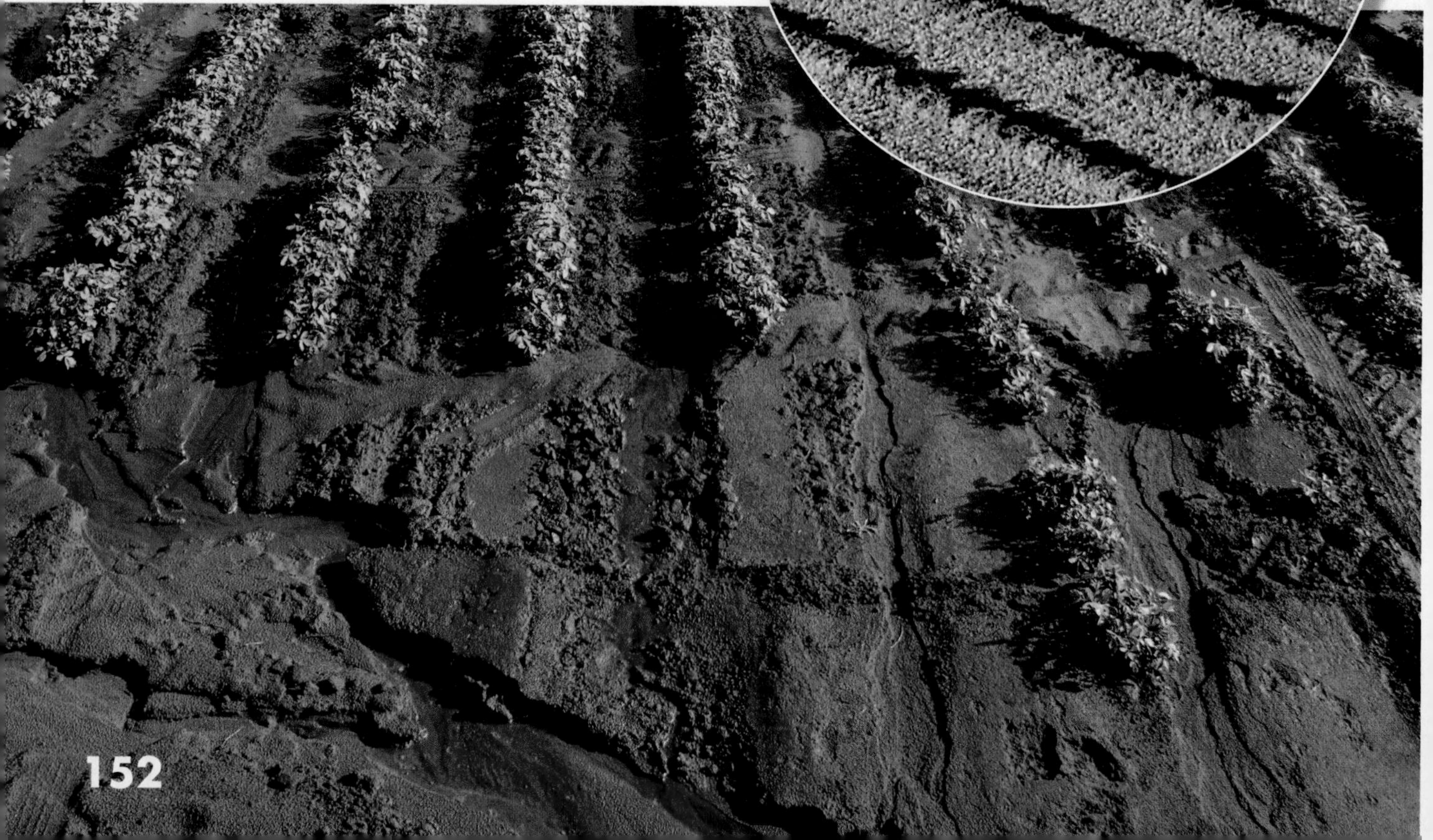

Weathering can change Earth too. **Weathering** is the breaking apart and changing of rocks. Water can cause weathering. Changes in temperature can cause weathering.

Lesson Checkpoint

1. How does weathering change Earth?
2. **Writing in Science** Look for erosion near where you live. Write about what you see.

Animals that dig homes in soil can change Earth too. Gophers change the shape of the land.

Lesson 5

How can people help protect Earth?

People change the Earth by causing pollution. **Pollution** happens when something harmful is added to the land, air, or water. Pollution can cause some plants and animals to get sick or die.

Many people have started working together to help reduce pollution. They want to make sure plants and animals stay safe. They want to take care of the Earth.

This lake was once polluted.

People worked to clean up this lake. It is now safe for plants and animals.

1. **Checkpoint** What is pollution?
2. **Health** in Science What are some ways clean water is important to people?

Reduce, Reuse, Recycle

What are some ways people can take care of Earth? People can pick up litter on the ground. People can reduce the amount of what they use. *Reduce* means to use less. How can you reduce the amount of water you use each day?

People can reuse things. *Reuse* means to use again. How could you reuse a shoe box?

Plastic milk cartons can be recycled to make new objects.

People can recycle. **Recycle** means to change something so it can be used again. Cans, glass, paper, plastic, and metal can all be recycled. Some parts of this playground were made from recycled plastic milk bottles!

1. ✓ **Checkpoint** What can you do to help take care of Earth?
2. **Art** in Science Collect empty containers and other trash. Use them to make art.

Protecting Plants and Animals

Chop! People cut down trees. Some animals live in trees. People plant new trees. Animals can make their homes in the new trees.

Campfires can turn into forest fires. Always put out campfires.

Wind and fire can kill trees. New trees start to grow back after a forest fire. These new trees might grow big and tall.

People build homes and factories on land. Plants and animals that lived on the land may have no place to go. People take plants and animals to a refuge. A refuge is a safe place to live. People cannot build on a refuge.

This bird lives in a refuge in Florida. People can see plants and animals at the refuge.

Lesson Checkpoint

1. What are some ways people can help protect plants and animals?
2. **Technology** in Science
   Read an article about wildfires on the Internet.

Lab zone

Guided Inquiry

Investigate How do worms change the soil?

Compost is a mixture of soil with other things like leaves and grass. How will worms change compost?

Materials

plastic gloves

bags with soil

leaves

worms

What to Do

1. Wear gloves. Put leaves in both bags.
2. Put worms in one bag.

Be sure to close the bags.

Process Skills

Filling in a chart can help you **collect data**.

3 **Observe** the bags for 3 weeks.

The worms are alive! Handle with care.

4 **Collect Data** Draw a chart like the one below to show what happens inside the bags.

Compost Bags		
	With Worms	**Without Worms**
Week 1		
Week 2		
Week 3		

Explain Your Results

1. Which bag had more leaves after 3 weeks?
2. **Infer** What happened to the leaves?

Go Further

What will happen if you use more worms? Investigate to find out.

Math in Science

Recycling Bar Graph

Nelson School wants to help keep the environment clean. The second graders decided to recycle cans.

Read the bar graph to find out how many cans each second-grade class recycled in one week.

1. How many cans did Mr. Green's class recycle?
2. How many more cans did Mrs. Hill's class recycle than Mr. Green's class? Write a number sentence.

 eTools Take It to the Net pearsonsuccessnet.com

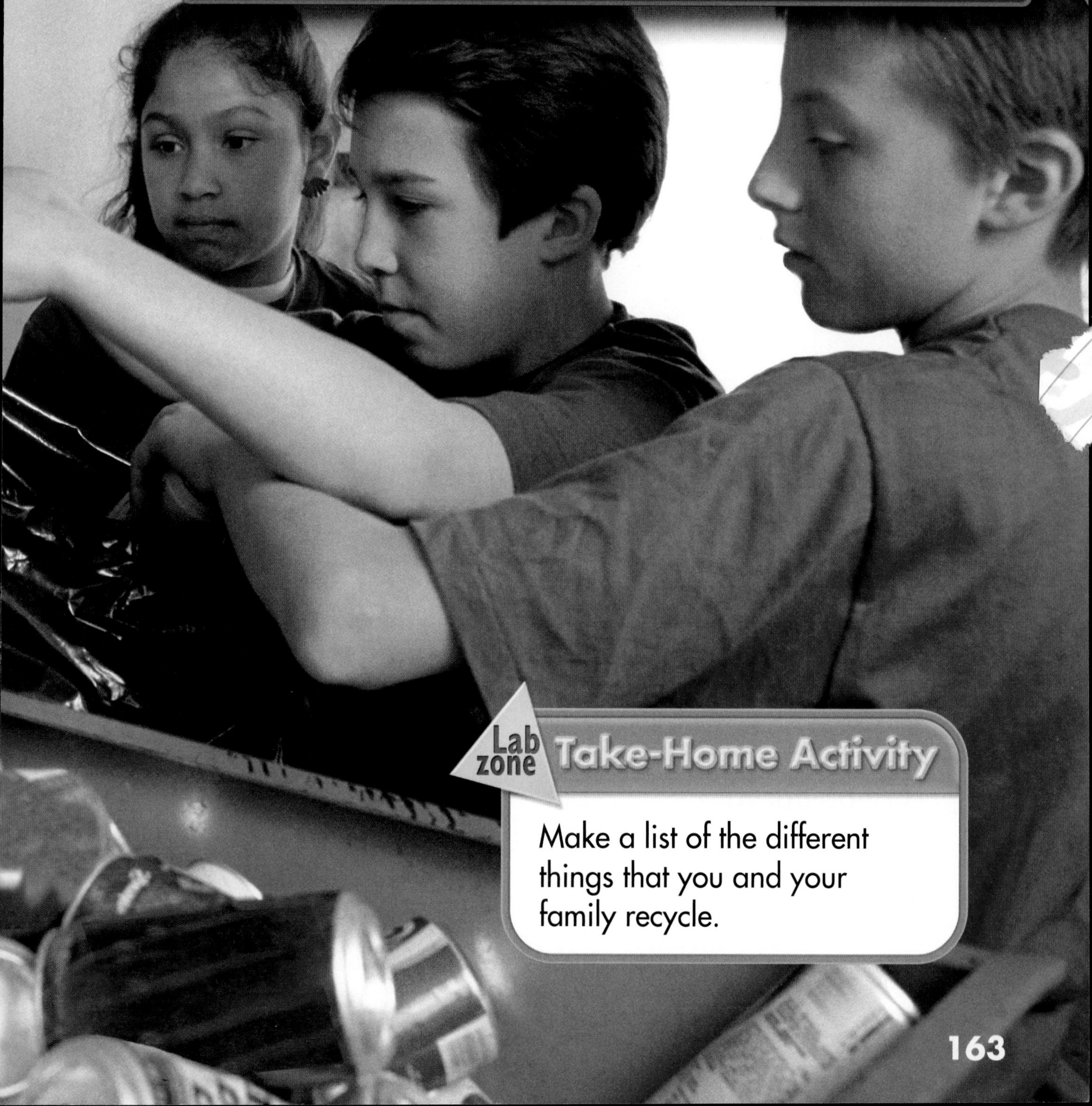

Lab zone Take-Home Activity

Make a list of the different things that you and your family recycle.

Chapter 5 Review and Test Prep

Vocabulary

Which picture goes with each word?

1. boulder

2. mineral

3. erosion

4. sand

5. recycle

6. pollution

What did you learn?

7. Name some of Earth's natural resources.

8. How does erosion change Earth?

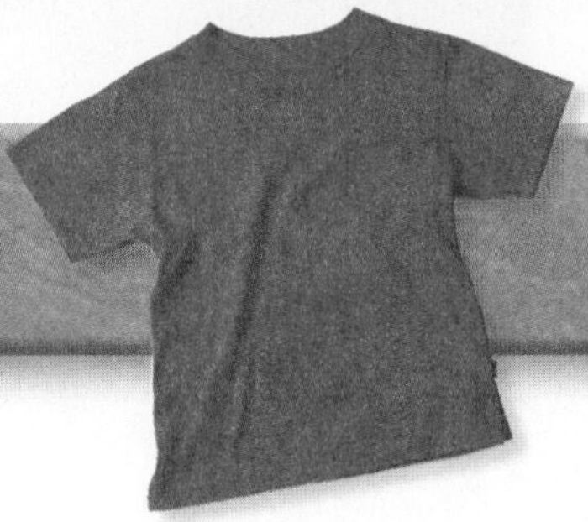

Process Skills

9. **Observe** Look at a plant outside. Describe the soil.

Picture Clues

10. **Use picture clues** Tell how people use air.

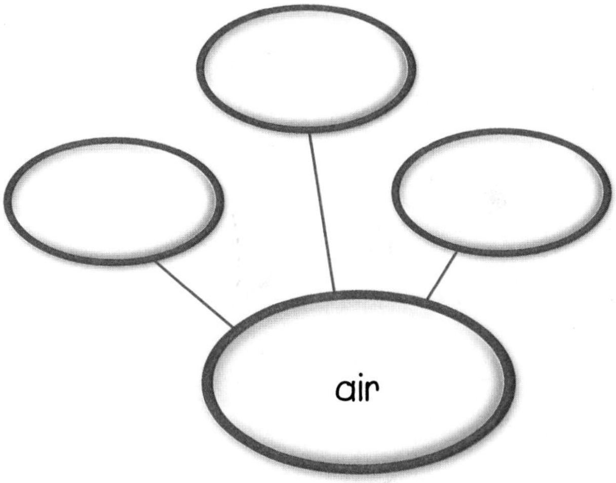

Test Prep

Fill in the circle next to the correct answer.

11. What do people make from cotton?

Ⓐ furniture
Ⓑ maple syrup
Ⓒ clothes
Ⓓ playgrounds

12. **Writing in Science** List some things people throw away. Tell how you could reuse one of those things.

Looking out for Earth

Many satellites move around Earth. NASA scientists send satellites to space. Scientists use satellites to take pictures of Earth's natural resources. Satellite pictures can show dirty air over cities. The satellite pictures can also show how well crops are growing. Spotting forest fires is easier from satellites too.

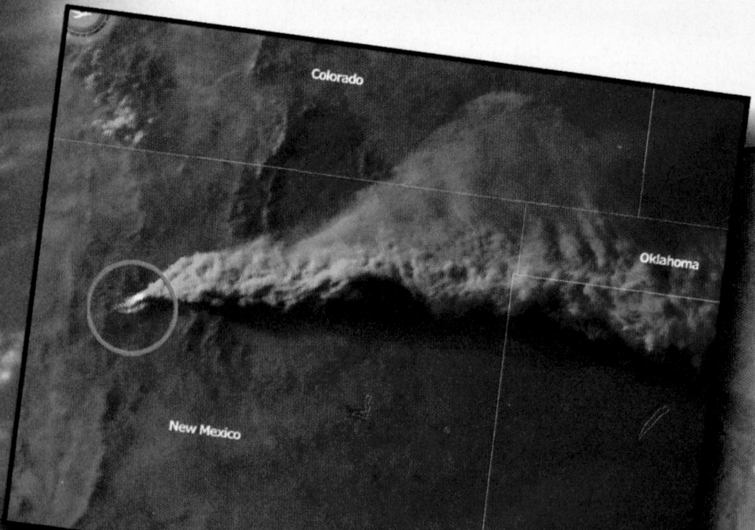

The smoky area shows a forest fire.

A satellite takes pictures of new plants.

Lab zone Take-Home Activity

NASA satellites take pictures of Earth. Draw a picture of what you think Earth looks like from space.

Forester

Read Together

Foresters have many jobs. They build roads in forests. They work to prevent forest fires. They decide how many trees can be cut. They plant new trees.

Foresters study forests and learn how to keep them healthy. They help protect plants and animals that live in forests. Foresters teach other people how to be safe in the forest.

Lab zone Take-Home Activity

Tell what job you would like to do if you were a forester. Tell your family about how your job would help the forest.

EC CRU 10 9 8 7 6 5 4 3 2 1

You Will Discover

- that there are patterns in the weather.
- how weather changes from season to season.

Chapter 6

Earth's Weather and Seasons

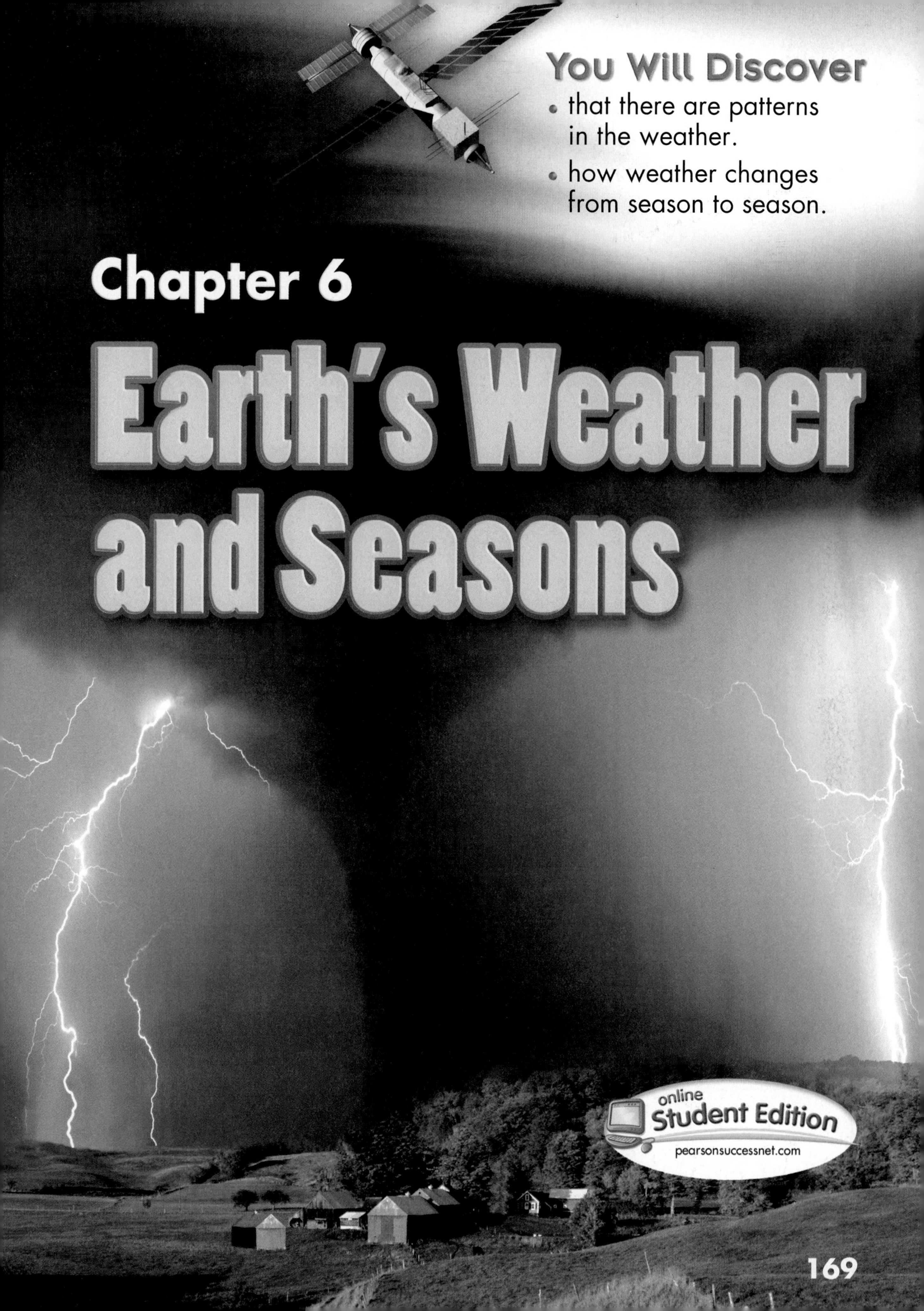

online Student Edition
pearsonsuccessnet.com

How does weather change?

Chapter 6 Vocabulary

water cycle page 178

evaporate page 179

condense page 179

migrate page 184

hibernate page 186

lightning page 188

tornado page 190

hurricane page 192

Lab zone Directed Inquiry

Explore How much rain falls?

Make a tool to measure how much rain falls.

Materials

jar

tape

ruler

black pencil

What to Do

1. Number each centimeter line up to 12. Start at the bottom of the tape.

2. Fasten tape to the jar.

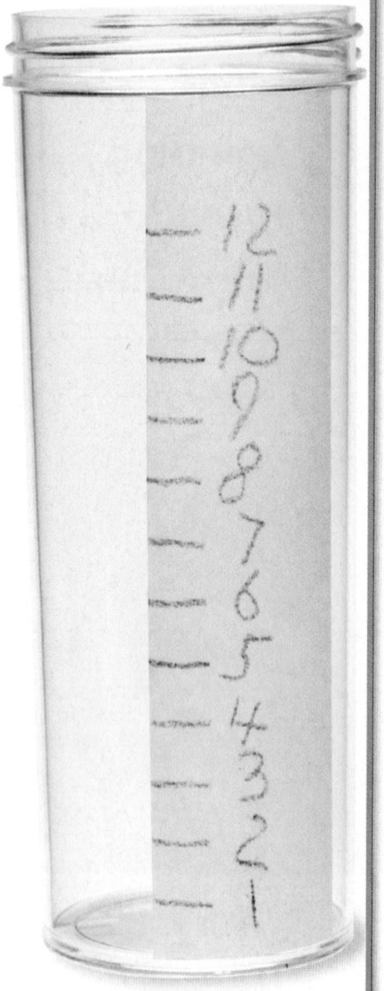

Process Skills

You can use what you know and what you have learned to **infer**.

Explain Your Results

Infer How could you use this tool to measure how much rain falls?

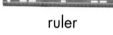

How to Read Science

Reading Skills

Draw Conclusions

You draw conclusions when you decide about something you see or read.

Science Picture

Apply It!

Look at the picture.
Infer What is the weather like outside?

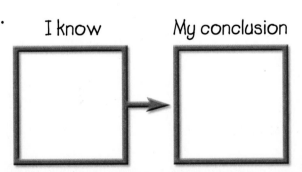

I know → My conclusion

You Are There

What's the Weather?

Sung to the tune of "Yankee Doodle"
Lyrics by Gerri Brioso & Richard Freitas/The Dovetail Group, Inc.

There's all kinds of weather and
Of that I'm really sure.
Just open up a window
Or peek out an open door.

Lesson 1

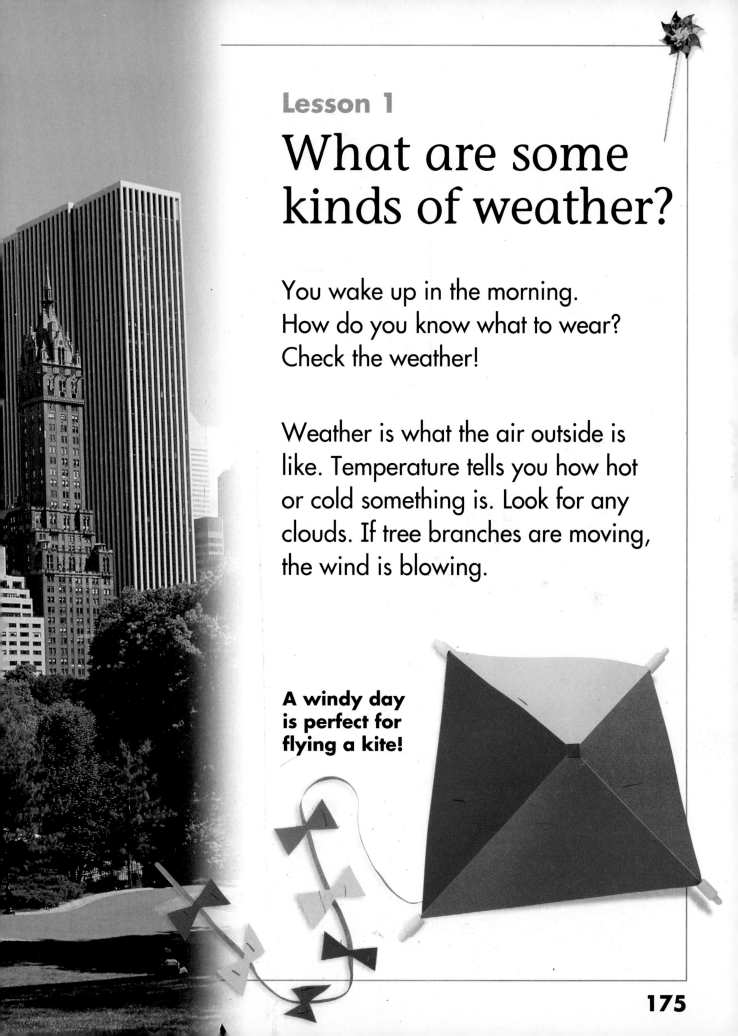

What are some kinds of weather?

You wake up in the morning. How do you know what to wear? Check the weather!

Weather is what the air outside is like. Temperature tells you how hot or cold something is. Look for any clouds. If tree branches are moving, the wind is blowing.

A windy day is perfect for flying a kite!

Heavy rains can fall in spring and summer.

Some places get snow in winter.

Hail is pieces of ice that fall from clouds.

Wet and Dry Weather

Clouds can help tell you what kind of weather is coming. Clouds are made up of drops of water and small pieces of ice. When the small pieces of ice join together, they start to fall.

Snowflakes fall in cold weather. Blizzards are snow storms with strong winds. In warm air, snow melts into rain as it falls. Sleet is rain that freezes as it falls. Snow, rain, and sleet are different kinds of wet weather.

The land is very dry in a drought.

A drought can happen when it does not rain for a long time. A drought is one kind of dry weather. There may not be enough water for many plants and animals during a drought.

Some plants may not be able to live in a drought.

✓ Lesson Checkpoint

1. What are three kinds of wet weather?
2. **Technology** in Science Go to www.nws.noaa.gov on the Internet. What will the weather be like tomorrow where you live?

Lesson 2

What is the water cycle?

The way water moves from the clouds to Earth and back to the clouds again is called the **water cycle.** Look at this picture. Follow the steps in the water cycle.

Water falls from the clouds. The water might be in the form of rain, snow, hail, or sleet.
Water flows into rivers, lakes, and oceans.

SciLinks Take It to the Net pearsonsuccessnet.com keyword: water cycle code: g2p178

When the water vapor in clouds gets cold, it condenses. Condense means to change into tiny drops of water. The tiny drops of water form clouds.

Energy from the Sun makes some of the water evaporate. Water evaporates when it changes into water vapor. *Water vapor* is water in the air. You cannot see water vapor.

Lesson Checkpoint

1. What are the steps in the water cycle?
2. **Draw Conclusions** How does energy from the Sun change water in water puddles?

Lesson 3

What is spring?

Weather in many places changes with the seasons. The four seasons are spring, summer, fall, and winter. The seasons repeat every year.

Some spring days are cool. Other spring days are warm. Spring days can be rainy. The rain helps plants grow. Many animals have babies in the spring.

This mother deer had her baby in the spring.

✓ Lesson Checkpoint

1. Tell about two things that can happen in spring.
2. **Writing in Science** Write two sentences. What are some things you like to do in spring?

Holland, Michigan is known for its beautiful tulips. Tulips bloom in the spring.

Spring can be very rainy.

New leaves start growing on trees in the spring.

Lesson 4

What is summer?

Summer comes after spring. Summer has more daylight hours than spring. Summer often has hot days and warm nights. In most places, summer is the hottest season of the year. Green leaves grow on many trees and other plants. Flowers, fruits, and vegetables grow.

✓ Lesson Checkpoint

1. How are daylight hours in spring and summer different?
2. **Art** in Science Draw a picture of your neighborhood in summer.

You can see many animal families in the summer.

Parks can be beautiful in the summer. This park is in Charleston, South Carolina.

Many people like to grow vegetables in the summer.

The adult duck is swimming with her babies on a summer day.

Lesson 5

What is fall?

Fall comes after summer. There are fewer hours of daylight in fall than in summer. The air begins to get cooler.

The leaves on some trees turn different colors in fall. Then the leaves fall to the ground.

Some animals, such as chipmunks and squirrels, begin to store food for the winter. Other animals **migrate,** or move to a different place.

✓ Lesson Checkpoint

1. What are two things animals might do in fall?
2. **Draw Conclusions** Suppose you see many groups of geese flying south in the fall. What do you think is happening?

In fall, some animals gather food for the winter.

Look at the trees in Bloomington, Indiana. The leaves have turned different colors.

Sandhill cranes migrate every fall.

In fall, farmers harvest crops.

Lesson 6

What is winter?

Winter comes after fall. In some places, winter can be very cold. It may even snow. Ponds and streams may turn to ice.

Winter has fewer daylight hours than fall. Many trees have no leaves.

Some animals hibernate in winter. **Hibernate** means to have a long, deep sleep. Animals that hibernate come out in spring to look for food.

Most bears hibernate in winter.

Lesson Checkpoint

1. What happens when an animal hibernates?
2. Writing in Science Write in your journal about winter where you live. What is the weather like?

There can be heavy snowstorms in Adirondack, New York.

You can see many trees and roofs covered with snow in winter.

It is fun to play in the snow. Be sure to wear coats and hats.

Lesson 7

What are some kinds of bad weather?

A thunderstorm is a kind of bad weather. A thunderstorm has heavy rain with thunder and lightning. **Lightning** is a flash of light in the sky. Thunder is the loud sound that you hear after lightning flashes. Sometimes thunderstorms have hail and strong winds.

1. Checkpoint What is lightning?
2. Art in Science Make a safety poster. Show how to stay safe during a thunderstorm.

A lot of rain can fall during a thunderstorm.

Thunderstorm Safety

- Find shelter in a building or car.
- Stay away from water.
- Stay away from metal objects.
- Do not stand under a tree.
- Do not use telephones.
- Keep away from objects that use electricity.

Tornadoes

Tornadoes can happen during thunderstorms. A **tornado** has very strong winds that come down from clouds in the shape of a funnel.

Tornadoes form quickly. It is hard to predict when a tornado will happen. A tornado that touches the ground can destroy things.

Tornadoes can happen in spring or summer.

1. **Checkpoint** What is one way to stay safe during a tornado?
2. **Writing in Science** Tell what a tornado is like.

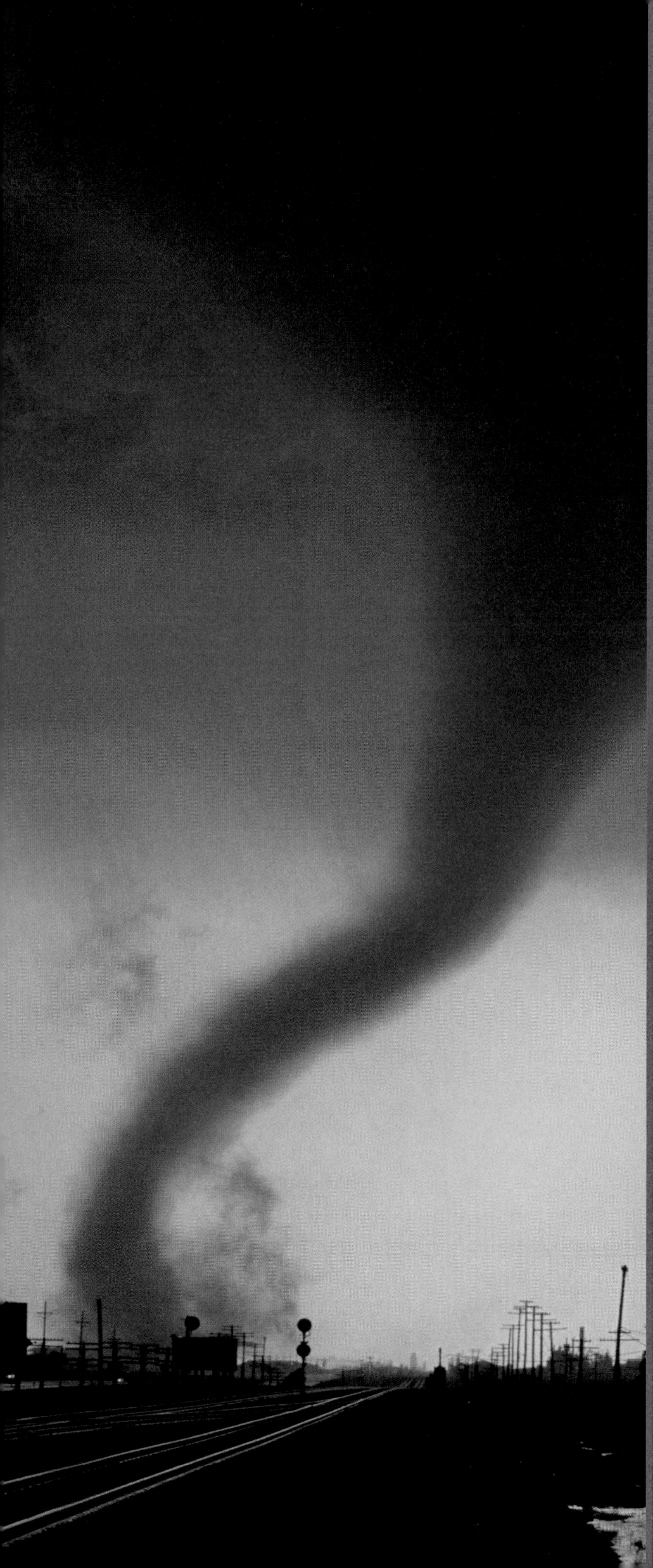

Tornado Safety

- Go to the basement or an inside hall, closet, or bathroom.
- Sit under the stairs or near an inner wall.
- Keep away from windows, water, metal, and objects that use electricity.
- Cover your head.
- If you cannot get to shelter, lie flat in a low place.

Hurricanes

A **hurricane** is a large storm that starts over warm ocean water. A hurricane has heavy rains. The rains can cause floods.

A hurricane has very strong winds. The winds can knock down trees and buildings.

Lesson Checkpoint

1. What is a hurricane?
2. **Draw Conclusions** What might happen to objects left outside during a hurricane?

This picture shows the eye of a hurricane. The eye is a calm area in the center of the storm.

Hurricane Safety

- Move away from the ocean if you can.
- Board up windows.
- Bring loose objects inside.
- Keep extra water on hand for drinking.
- Check the batteries in your flashlights and radio.
- During the storm, stay inside. Stay away from windows.

Lab zone Guided Inquiry

Investigate How can you measure weather changes?

There are many tools for measuring weather. A rain gauge measures rainfall. A thermometer measures temperature.

Materials

rain gauge

thermometer

What to Do

1. Put the weather tools outside.
2. Check them every day for one week.
3. Write how much rain fell each day. Write the temperature for each day.

Process Skills

You can use a chart to help **classify** weather.

Temperature and Rain for One Week		
Day of the Week	rain gauge	thermometer
Monday		
Tuesday		
Wednesday		
Thursday		
Friday		

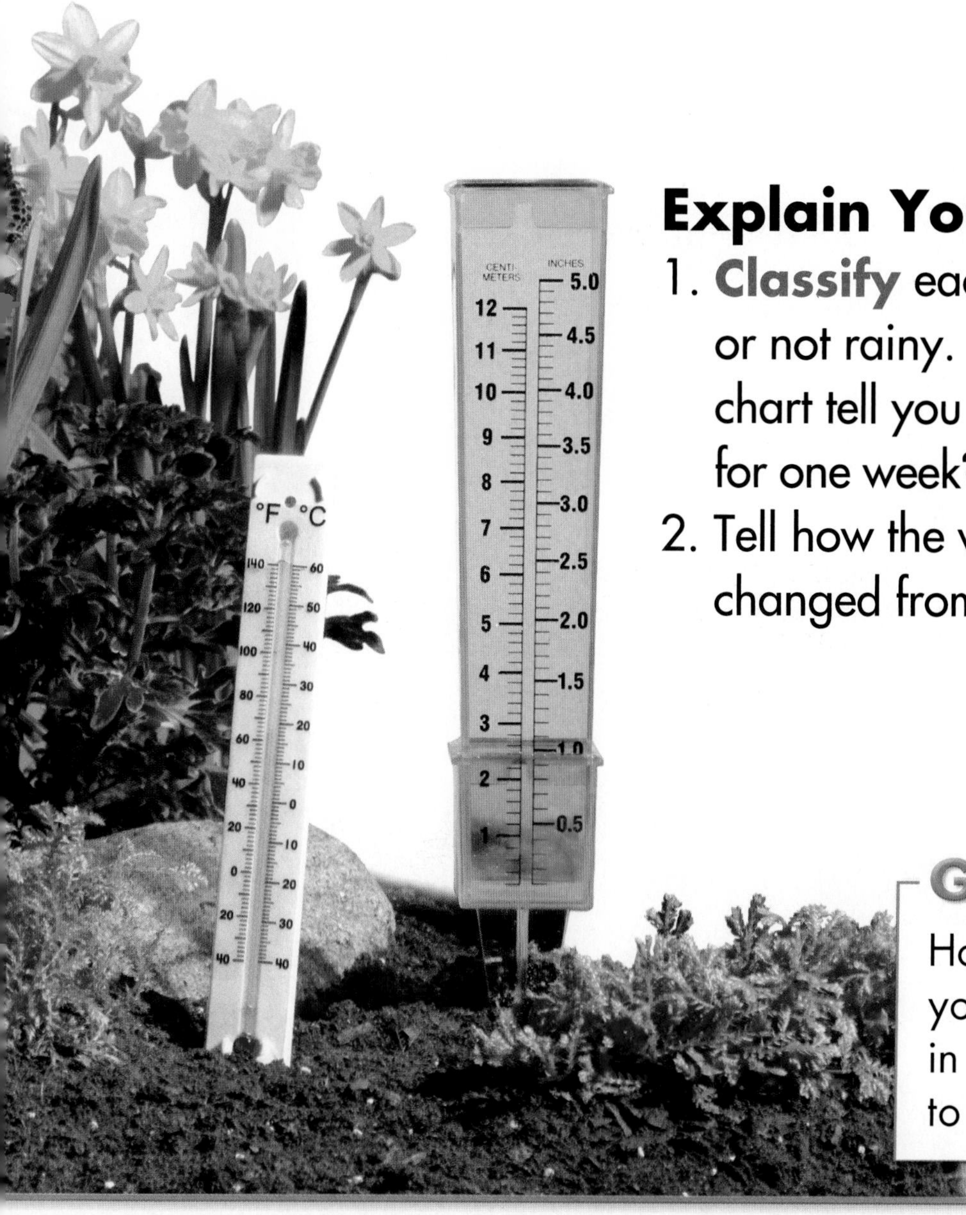

Explain Your Results

1. **Classify** each day as rainy or not rainy. What does your chart tell you about the weather for one week?
2. Tell how the weather changed from day to day.

Go Further

How much rain do you think might fall in 5 days? Measure to find out.

Math in Science

Charting Favorite Seasons

Nan wanted to find out what her classmates' favorite seasons were. She made a chart to show this information.

Look at the chart. Answer the questions.

1. How many children liked summer best?
2. Use <, >, or =. Compare how many children liked summer best to how many liked winter best.
3. How many more children liked fall than liked spring?

Lab zone Take-Home Activity

Ask six friends or family members what their favorite season is. Make a chart like Nan made. Which season do your friends and family like best?

Vocabulary

Which picture goes with each word?

1. hurricane
2. lightning
3. hibernate
4. migrate
5. tornado

A

B

C

D

E

What did you learn?

6. Tell what happens in each step of the water cycle.
7. Which season has the most daylight hours?

Process Skills

8. **Collect Data** Observe the weather for 10 days. Record the number of days that are sunny, cloudy, and rainy.

Draw Conclusions

9. Look at the picture. Which season do you think it is?

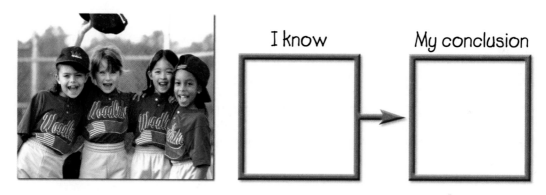

I know		My conclusion
	→	

Test Prep

Fill in the circle next to the correct answer.

10. When water vapor changes to liquid it ________.

Ⓐ evaporates
Ⓑ hibernates
Ⓒ condenses
Ⓓ migrates

11. **Writing in Science**

Write four sentences. Describe what the weather is like where you live in each of the four seasons.

Career

Robbie Hood works as an Atmospheric Scientist at NASA.

Atmospheric Scientist

Read Together

Atmospheric scientists study the weather. Some atmospheric scientists who work at NASA study hurricanes. They want to learn more about how hurricanes work and what is the best way to use satellites to observe them.

Studying hurricanes has helped NASA scientists learn how to predict when and where a hurricane is likely to occur. This way, warnings can be given sooner and more people can move to places where they can stay safe.

Lab zone Take-Home Activity

Talk with your family about hurricanes. Make a list of reasons why atmospheric scientists are important people.

EC CRU 10 9 8 7 6 5 4 3 2 1

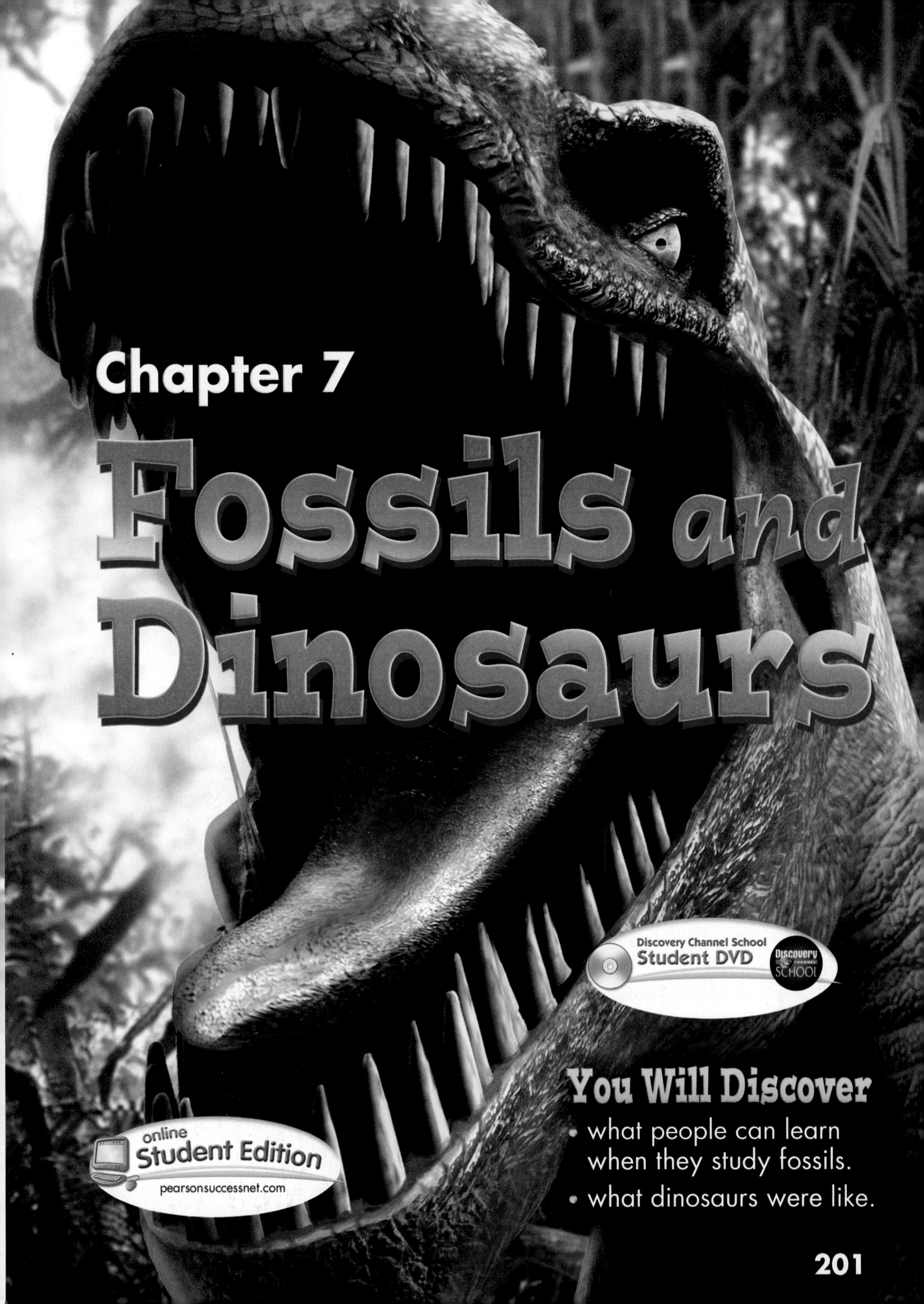

Chapter 7

Fossils and Dinosaurs

Discovery Channel School
Student DVD

You Will Discover

- what people can learn when they study fossils.
- what dinosaurs were like.

online
Student Edition
pearsonsuccessnet.com

Build Background

How can people learn about the Earth long ago?

How to Read Science

Reading Skills

Retell

Retell means to tell what you learned in your own words.

Science Story

Fossil Shell

Long ago, an animal lived in this huge fossil shell. The animal had long arms. Scientists think the arms had rows of suction cups just like an octopus.

Apply It!

Communicate

Tell what you learned about the animal in the fossil shell.

Retell

You Are There

Go Find a Fossil

Sung to the tune of "Take Me Out to the Ballgame"
Lyrics by Gerri Brioso & Richard Freitas/The Dovetail Group, Inc.

Take a shovel, go digging.
In the dirt you may find,
Rocks that have shapes printed right in them.
Shapes of a leaf or an animal!

If you find one, you have a fossil.
A special clue to the past.
See what plants and animals looked like
A long time ago!

Lesson 1

How can we learn about the past?

A **fossil** is a print or remains of a plant or animal that lived long ago. Some fossils are very old bones. Other fossils are shapes left in rocks.

Scientists who study fossils are called **paleontologists.** Paleontologists use fossils to learn what plants and animals looked like long ago.

How Fossils Form

A fossil of a lizard has been left in a rock. The pictures on the next page show how one kind of fossil formed. Look at the other kinds of fossils on these pages.

This fossil shows the shape of another lizard that lived long ago.

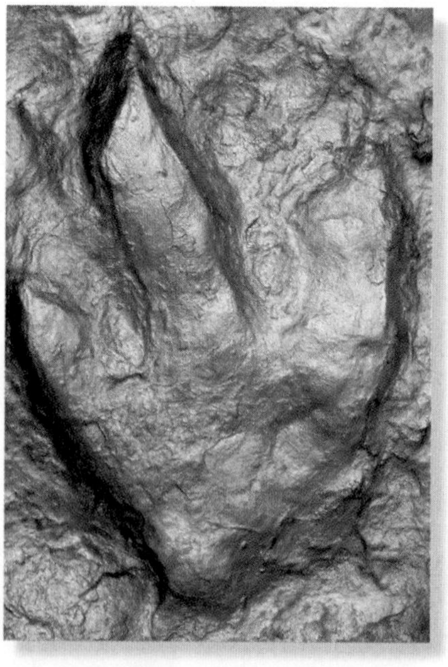

Long ago, an animal made this footprint in the mud. The mud turned to rock. The footprint is another kind of fossil.

This shell is a fossil.

This fossil is of a plant that lived long ago.

✓ Lesson Checkpoint

1. What are fossils?
2. **Retell** how fossils are formed.

A Fossil Is Formed

A lizard dies.

The lizard is covered by sand and mud.

The sand and mud become rock. The print of the lizard is a fossil.

Lesson 2

What can we learn from fossils?

Fossils show the size and shape of plants and animals that lived long ago. Some fossils are of plants and animals that are extinct. An **extinct** plant or animal no longer lives on Earth.

The Archaeopteris is an extinct plant that looked like a tree. This fossil shows the shape of its leaves.

Sometimes plants and animals no longer get what they need from their habitat. The plants and animals cannot live. They may disappear from Earth forever.

The Archaeopteryx is extinct. What animal today looks like this Archaeopteryx?

Lesson Checkpoint

1. What do paleontologists learn from fossils?
2. **Retell** What can happen to plants and animals when they no longer get what they need from their habitat?

Lesson 3

What were dinosaurs like?

Dinosaurs were animals that lived long ago. Some dinosaurs were very big. Other dinosaurs were small. Some dinosaurs ate plants. Some dinosaurs ate other animals. All dinosaurs are extinct.

A Compsognathus was about the same size as a chicken.

The Barosaurus was very tall.

Crunch!
The Iguanodon's big, flat teeth helped it chew plants.

Gulp!
A Dilophosaurus caught and ate other dinosaurs.

1. **Checkpoint** What did an Iguanodon eat?
2. **Writing in Science** Write about some ways dinosaurs were different. Tell how they are the same.

Learning About Dinosaurs

Paleontologists study fossils of dinosaur bones. They want to know what dinosaurs looked like. The Stegosaurus had a large body. Its head and mouth were small. Paleontologists think this dinosaur ate plants. A Stegosaurus needed an environment with lots of plants.

A Triceratops had three horns on its head! The horns may have helped stop other animals from attacking.

What big teeth! A Tyrannosaurus rex probably used its sharp teeth to eat meat.

Look at the skeleton of a Stegosaurus. Scientists used the skeleton to make a model of how the Stegosaurus may have looked.

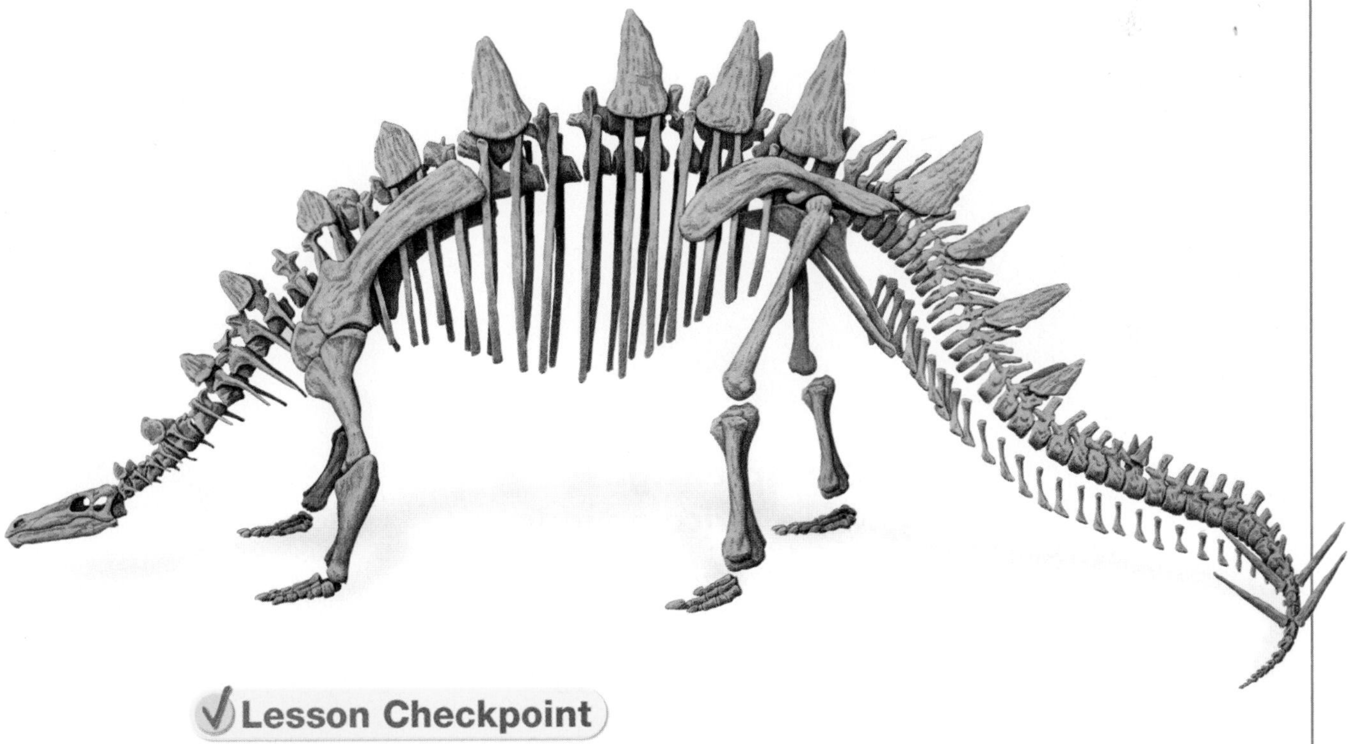

Lesson Checkpoint

1. What did paleontologists learn about a Stegosaurus by looking at its bones?
2. **Writing** in Science Write one sentence. Tell which dinosaur is your favorite and why.

Lesson 4

What are some new discoveries?

An Oviraptor was a small dinosaur. Paleontologists found fossils of an Oviraptor near some eggs. They thought the Oviraptor was stealing the eggs to eat them.

Oviraptor eggs were twice as long as chicken eggs.

Later, another Oviraptor fossil was found. It was sitting on the same kind of eggs. Now paleontologists think that the Oviraptor was not stealing the eggs. They think the Oviraptor was keeping its own eggs safe.

Paleontologists now think that Oviraptors kept their eggs safe from other animals.

Lesson Checkpoint

1. What did paleontologists learn about the Oviraptor?
2. **Math** in Science Oviraptor eggs were about 20 centimeters long. Find something in your classroom that you think is about 20 centimeters long. Measure it.

Lab zone

Guided Inquiry

Investigate How can you make a model of a fossil?

Materials

shell

clay

2 classroom objects

What to Do

1. **Make a model** of a fossil. Press a shell into clay.

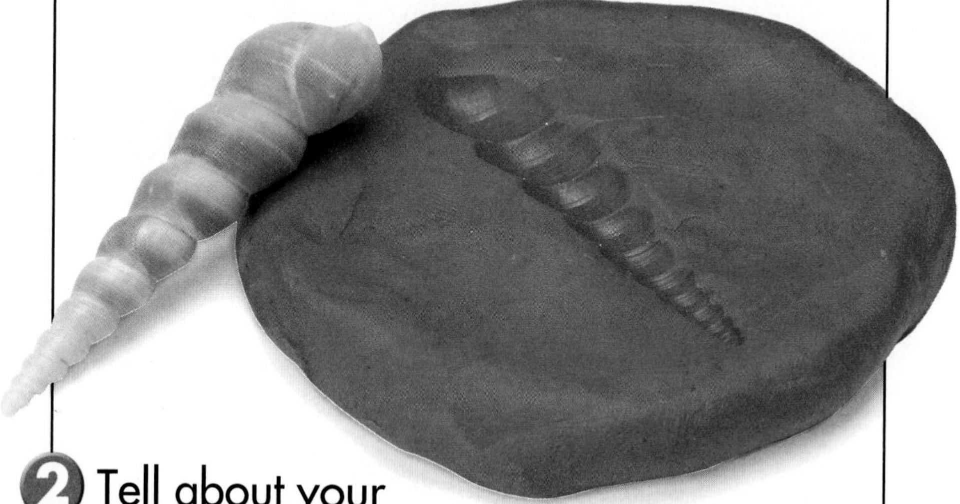

2. Tell about your fossil model and the shell.

How the Fossil Model and the Shell Are Alike and Different	
How are they alike?	**How are they different?**

Process Skills

You can **make models** to understand how things happen.

More Lab zone Activities Take It to the Net pearsonsuccessnet.com

3. Now pick an object in your classroom. Make a fossil model of the object.

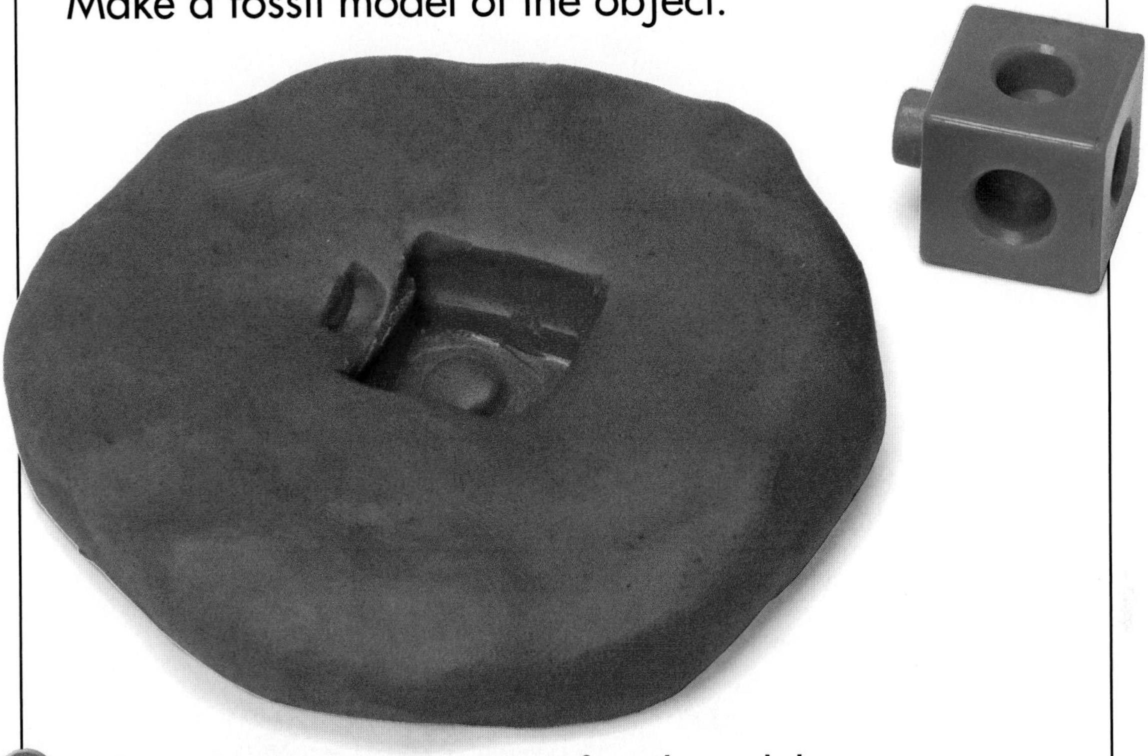

4. **Observe** your partner's fossil model. Guess what it is.

Explain Your Results

1. How did you **infer** what your partner's fossil model was?
2. How do fossils give clues about living things?

Go Further

What else could you do to make models of fossils? Make a plan and try it.

Math in Science

Measuring Fossil Leaves

Look at the fossils of 3 leaves. Estimate how long each leaf is in centimeters. Measure the leaves.

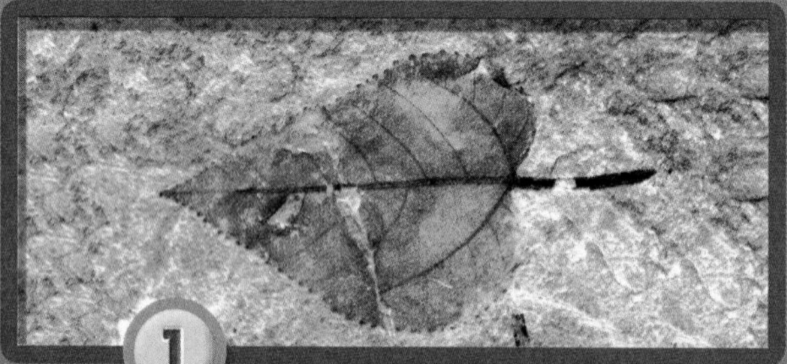

1

2

3

Make a bar graph like this one. Fill in the graph to show how long each leaf is. Use your bar graph to answer the questions.

1. Which leaf is the longest?
2. Which leaf is the shortest?
3. How much longer is the longest leaf than the shortest leaf?

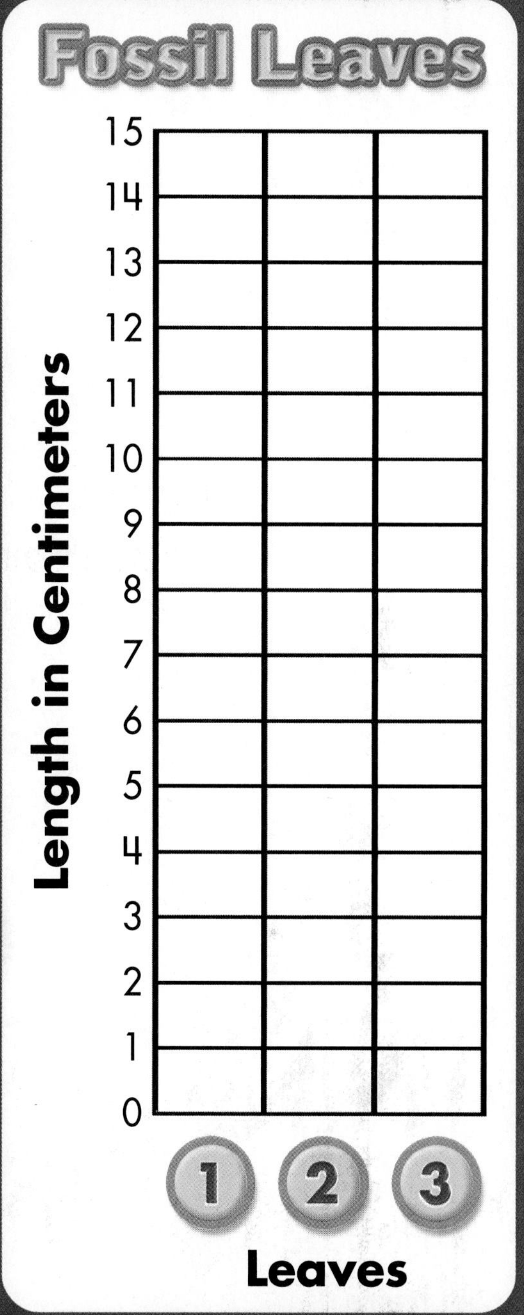

Lab zone Take-Home Activity

Find 3 leaves in your neighborhood. Measure the leaves. Make a bar graph to show how long the leaves are.

Chapter 7 Review and Test Prep

Vocabulary

Which picture goes with each word?

1. paleontologist
2. fossil
3. dinosaur

A

B

C

What did you learn?

4. Why do some plants and animals become extinct?
5. How does a leaf fossil form?
6. How can people use fossils to learn about the past?

Process Skills

7. **Communicate** Tell how fossils help us learn what some dinosaurs were like.

Retell

8. 

A Triceratops' head could grow up to 7 feet long. It had a bird-like beak to help it eat plants.

Retell what you learned about the Triceratops.

Retell

Test Prep

Fill in the circle next to the correct answer.

9. Which dinosaur was as tall as a chicken?

Ⓐ Tyrannosaurus
Ⓑ Barosaurus
Ⓒ Compsognathus
Ⓓ Archaeopteryx

10. **Writing in Science** Write two sentences. Tell what you learned about paleontologists.

Biography

A Tyrannosaurus rex skeleton

Susan Hendrickson

Read Together

How would you like to have a dinosaur named after you? This Tyrannosaurus rex is named Sue. It is named after Susan Hendrickson. Susan Hendrickson is a paleontologist. She looks for extinct animals to show in museums.

Sue, the Tyrannosaurus rex skeleton

Susan Hendrickson found the fossil bones of this Tyrannosaurus rex. You can see Sue the Tyrannosaurus rex if you visit the Field Museum in Chicago.

Lab zone Take-Home Activity

Use pipe cleaners to make a model of a Tyrannosaurus rex skeleton. Share your model with your family.

Test-Taking Strategies

Find Important Words
Choose the Right Answer
Use Information from Text and Graphics
Write Your Answer

Use Information from Text and Graphics

You can use information from text and charts to help you answer science questions.

Month	Rainfall
March	1 inch
April	4 inches
May	3 inches

March had the least rain. The months of April and May had more rain than March.

Use the information from the text and the chart to answer the question.

Which month had the most rain?

Ⓐ March
Ⓑ April
Ⓒ May
Ⓓ June

The text tells that April and May had more rain than March. Look at the chart. Which month had the most rain?

Unit B Wrap-Up

Chapter 5

What are Earth's natural resources?

- Sunlight, air, and water are some of Earth's natural resources.

Chapter 6

How does weather change?

- Weather can change from day to day.
- Different seasons have different kinds of weather.

Chapter 7

How can people learn about Earth long ago?

- People study fossils to learn about plants and animals that lived on Earth long ago.

Performance Assessment

Make a model of water erosion.

- Put some sandbox sand on a cookie pan.
- Tilt the pan slightly.
- Slowly pour water from a cup at the top of the pan.
- Watch the water erode the sand.
- Tell how you could keep the sand from eroding.

Read More about Earth Science!

Lab zone Full Inquiry

Experiment Does gravel, sand, or soil make the best imprint?

Sometimes sand can slowly change to rock. An imprint made by a plant or animal can become a fossil in the rock.

Materials

safety goggles

3 paper plates

3 index cards

cup with gravel,
cup with sand,
cup with soil

shell

Process Skills

A **hypothesis** answers a question that you can test.

Ask a question.

Which will make the best imprint?

Make your hypothesis.

Is the best imprint made in gravel, sand, or soil? Tell what you think.

Plan a fair test.

Use the same amount on each plate.

Do your test.

1. Put gravel, sand or soil on each plate.

Label each plate.

2 Press the shell into the gravel, sand, or soil.

Wash your hands when you are finished.

3 **Observe** the imprint in each pile.

Collect and record data.

Fill in the chart. Use an **X.**

Which is the best imprint?			
	Best Imprint	**Some Imprint**	**No Imprint**
Gravel			
Sand			
Soil			

Tell your conclusion.

Does gravel, sand, or soil make the best imprint? Which would make the best imprint fossil?

Go Further

What might happen if you use wet sand, soil, and gravel? Try it and find out.

The Spring Wind

by Charlotte Zolotow

The summer wind
is soft and sweet
the winter wind is strong
the autumn wind is mischievous
and sweeps the leaves along.

The wind I love the best
comes gently after rain
smelling of spring and growing things
brushing the world with feathery wings
while everything glistens, and
    everything sings
in the spring wind
after the rain.

Discovery Channel School

Science Fair Projects

Full Inquiry

Using Scientific Methods

1. Ask a question.
2. Make a hypothesis.
3. Plan a fair test.
4. Do your test.
5. Collect and record data.
6. Tell your conclusions.
7. Go further.

Idea 1
How Fast Water Evaporates

Plan a project. Find out if water evaporates faster in a cold place or a warm place.

Idea 2
Measuring Temperature

Plan a project. Find out how the temperature outside changes during the day.

EC CRU 10 9 8 7 6 5 4 3 2 1

Unit C

Physical Science in Illinois

Did you know that a symphony orchestra has four main groups of instruments? There are strings, brass, woodwinds, and percussion. The instruments are grouped by the way they make sound. Over 100 boys and girls play instruments in the Chicago Youth Symphony.

Physical Science in Illinois

How are ice fishing, nuclear energy, and farm animals alike? They can all be found in Illinois. You will learn more about the science behind them in Unit C.

Swimming and Ice Fishing

Water can be a solid, a liquid, or a gas. Lake Michigan is liquid in summer. People can go swimming. The surface of the lake is solid in winter. People can go ice fishing. You will learn more about how matter changes in Chapter 8.

Low Temperatures in Chicago

Month	Average Daily Low Temperature
January	–8°C (17°F)
February	–7°C (20°F)
March	–2°C (29°F)
April	4°C (39°F)
May	9°C (49°F)
June	15°C (59°F)

Henry Moore's sculpture *Nuclear Energy*

Nuclear Energy

People at the University of Chicago learn about nuclear energy. Nuclear energy can be used to make electricity. About half of the electricity used in Illinois comes from nuclear energy. You will learn more about energy and electricity in Chapter 9.

State Fair Sounds

Many different farm animals are at the Illinois State Fair every year. Different animals make different sounds. You will learn more about sound in Chapter 11.

ISAT Prep

Answer the questions below. Write your answers on a separate sheet of paper.

Multiple-Choice Questions

1 In Illinois, people do NOT ice fish in the summer because

A. fish sleep in summer.

B. days are too long.

C. fish are not hungry.

D. the water is liquid.

2 Which month is the warmest in Illinois?

A. January

B. May

C. February

D. June

3 What can nuclear energy make?

A. instruments

B. gasoline

C. electricity

D. animal sounds

Short-Response Questions

4 Where could you go to learn about different farm animals in Illinois?

5 How does the water in Lake Michigan change during the year?

ILLINOIS

Field Trip

Orchestra Hall at Symphony Center

Orchestra Hall at Symphony Center was 100 years old in 2004. Orchestra Hall has many concerts every year. The Chicago Youth Symphony Orchestra plays concerts at Orchestra Hall each year.

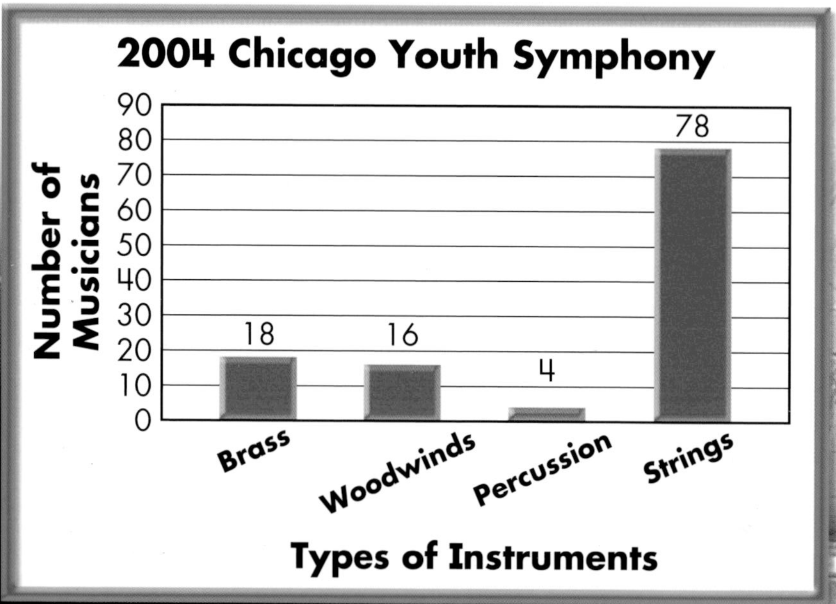

Find out more:

Research to find out more about orchestra instruments.

- Draw a picture of two different instruments.
- Explain how each instrument makes its sound. Describe the sounds.

II CRU 10 9 8 7 6 5 4 3 2 1

Chapter 8

Properties of Matter

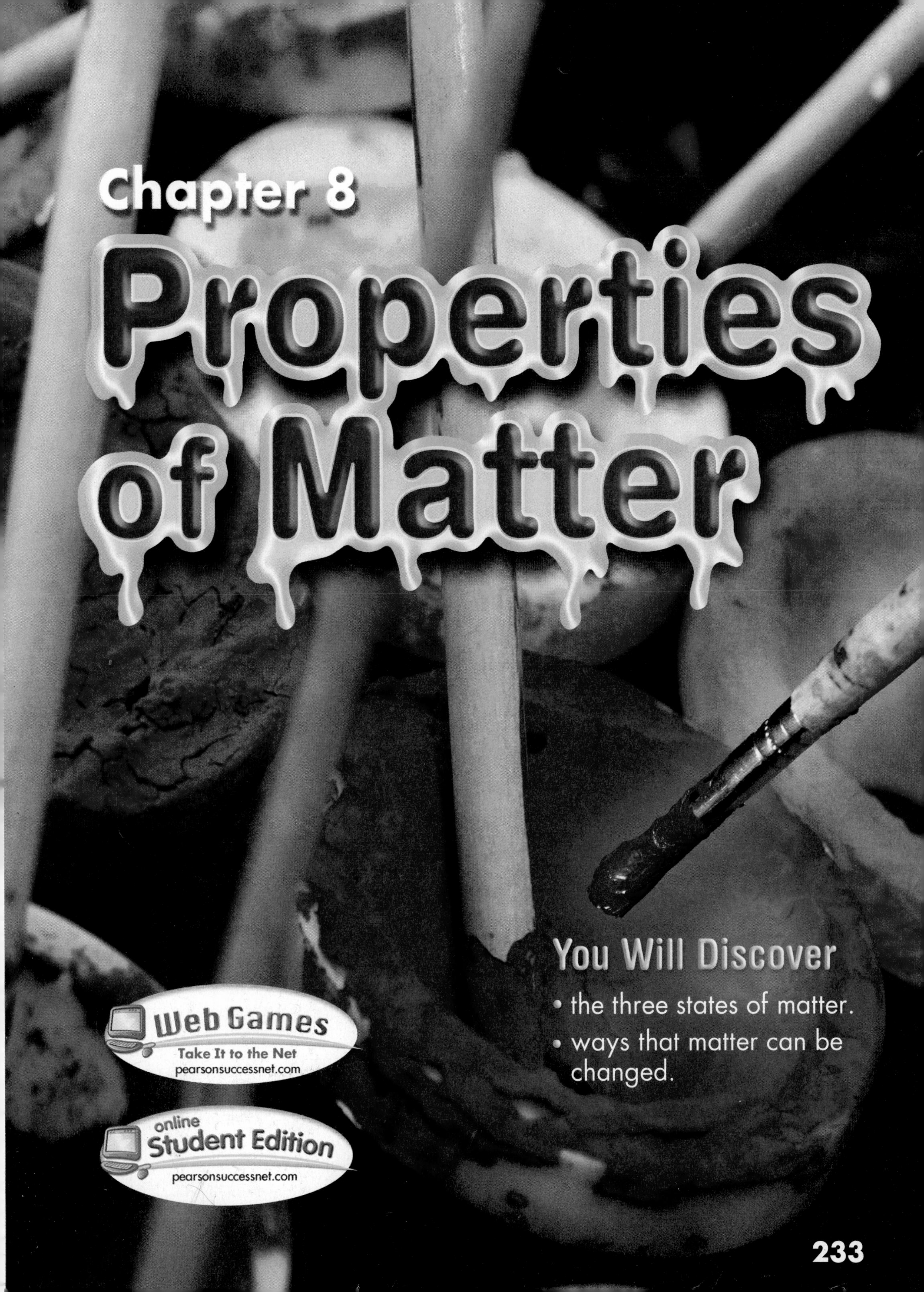

You Will Discover

- the three states of matter.
- ways that matter can be changed.

Web Games
Take It to the Net
pearsonsuccessnet.com

online Student Edition
pearsonsuccessnet.com

Build Background

What are some properties of matter?

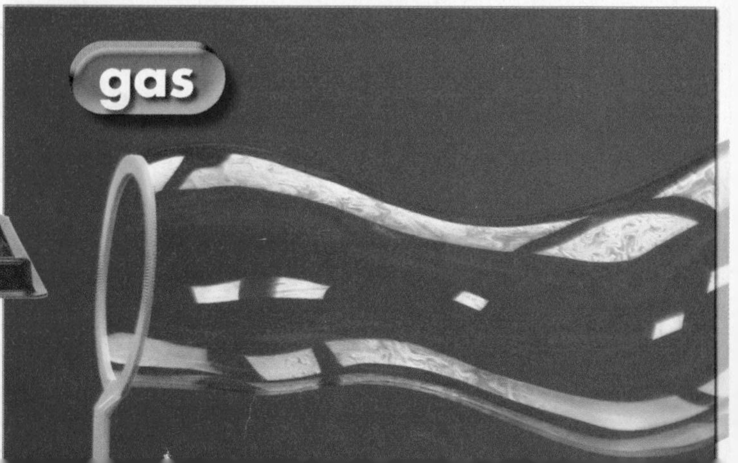

Chapter 8 Vocabulary

mass page 239

property page 240

states of matter page 242

solid page 242

liquid page 244

gas page 246

mixture page 250

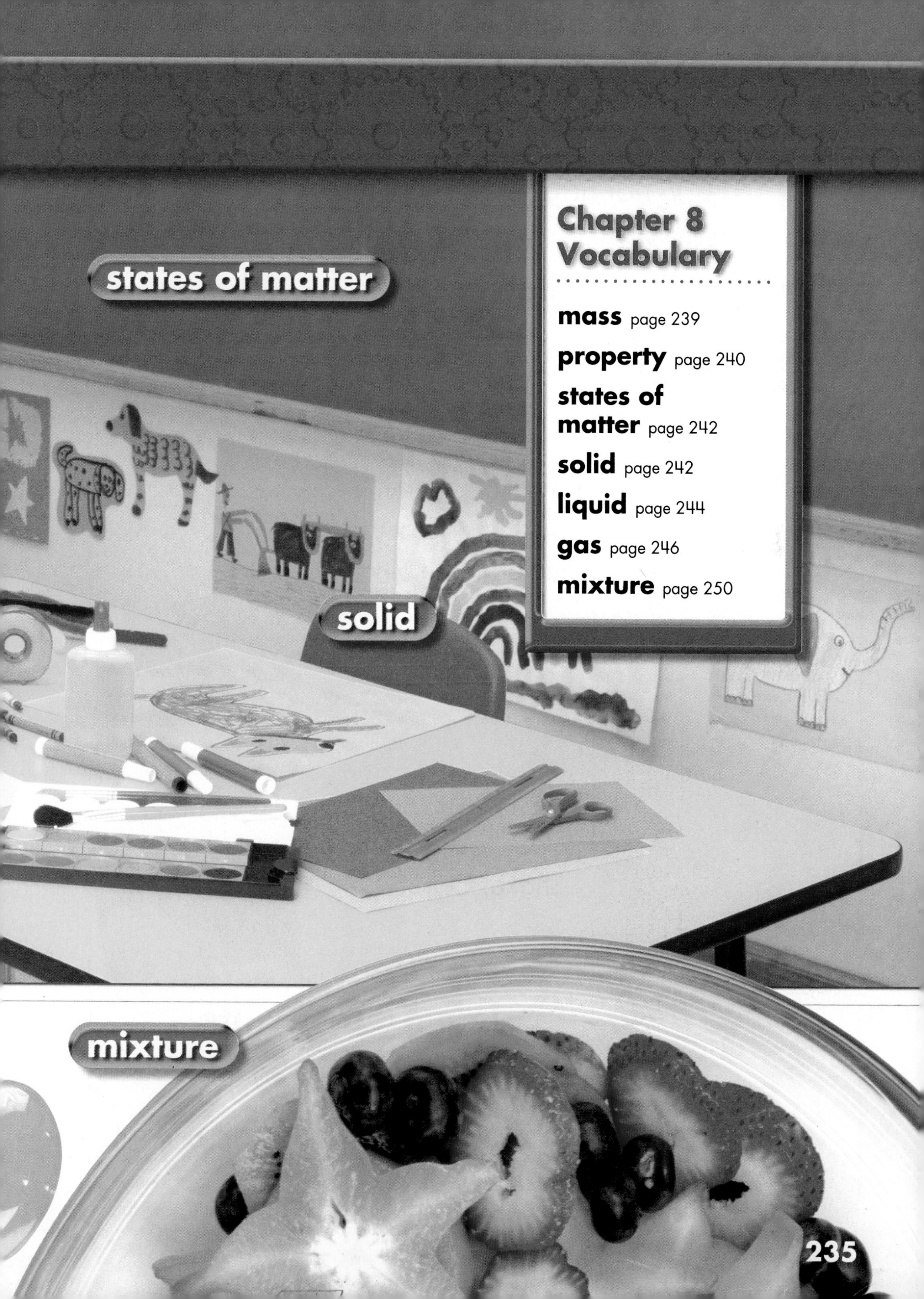

Lab zone

Directed Inquiry

Explore What happens when oil is mixed with water?

Materials

safety goggles

cup with oil, cup with colored water

measuring cups

jar with lid

What to Do

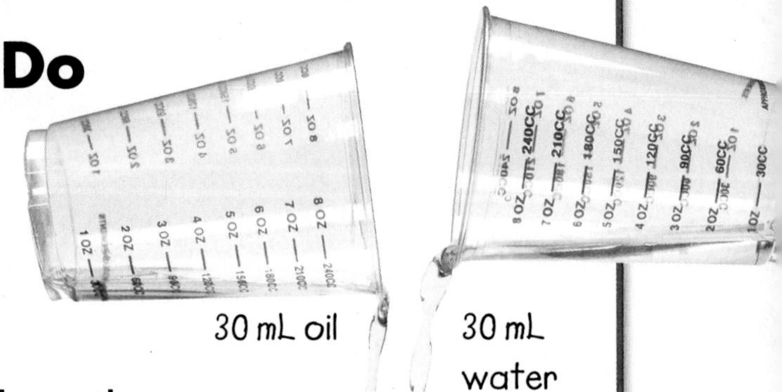

1. Measure the oil in one cup. Measure the water in the other cup.

2. Pour. Observe.

3. Shake. Observe.

Explain Your Results

1. What happened when you mixed the oil and the water?
2. **Infer** How could you separate oil from water?

Process Skills

You **infer** when you get ideas from what you know.

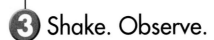

How to Read Science

Reading Skills

Target Skill: Draw Conclusions

You draw conclusions when you decide about something you see or read.

Science Activity

Work with a partner. You will need one cup with water and one cup with sand. Mix the sand into the water. Record the results in your science journal.

Apply It!

Infer What do you think will happen when you mix the sand and the water?

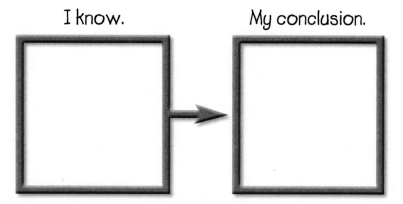

I know.		My conclusion.
	→	

You Are There

They're All Matter!

Sung to the tune of "Old MacDonald"
Lyrics by Gerri Brioso & Richard Freitas/The Dovetail Group, Inc.

Anything that takes up space
Is made up of matter.
Anything that has some mass
Is made up of matter.
Teddy bears, a crayon box,
Watermelon, rocking chairs,
  every wall around you
All have mass and take up space.
That's why they're all matter.

Lesson 1

What is matter?

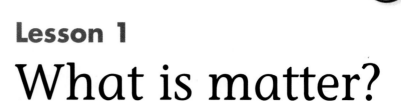

Matter is anything that takes up space and has mass. **Mass** is the amount of matter in an object.

Look around your classroom. Everything you see is made of matter.

Some things you cannot see are made of matter. The air around you has matter.

Matter is made of very small parts. You can use a hand lens to take a closer look at things.

Properties of Matter

All matter has properties. A **property** is something that you can observe with your senses. Some properties of matter are color, shape, and size. Mass is a property of matter. How something feels is a property of matter.

Is the brush hard or soft? Is the cup smooth or rough?

What colors are the pipe cleaners?

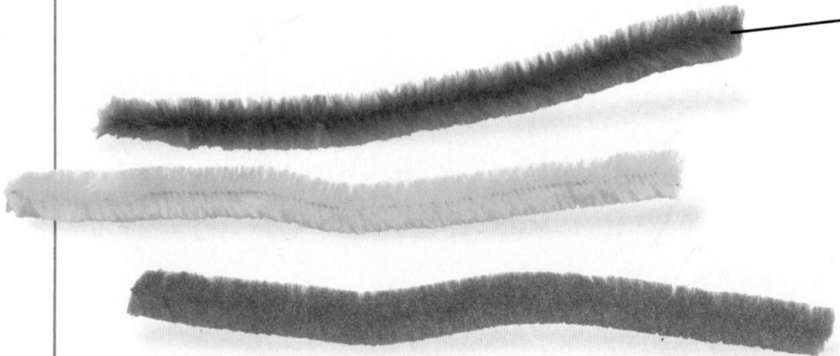

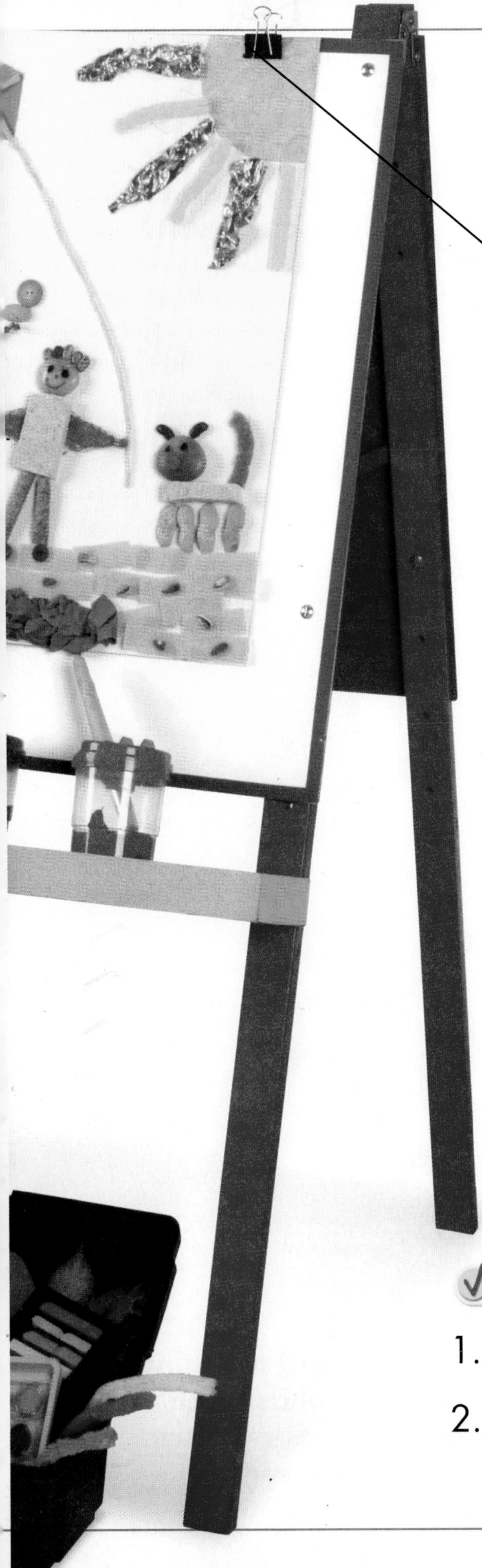

This clip is blue and silver. This clip feels smooth.

Do you think the sponge is heavy or light? Does it float or sink? Whether an object sinks or floats is a property.

✓ Lesson Checkpoint

1. What are some properties of matter?
2. **Math** in Science Tell four ways you can sort objects using properties.

Lesson 2

What are the states of matter?

Paintbrushes are solids. What are some properties of this paintbrush?

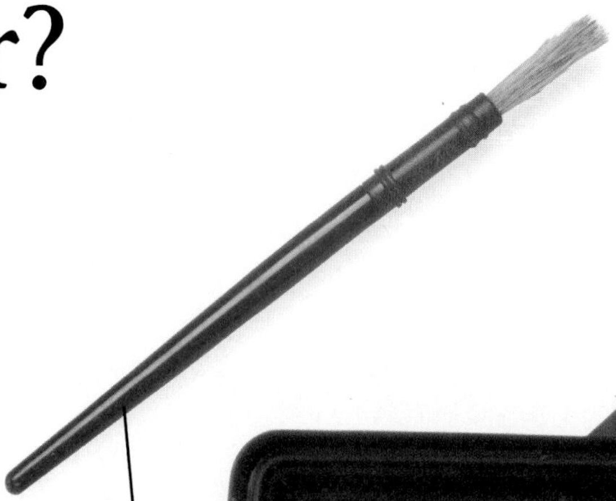

You know that everything around you is made of matter. The three **states of matter** are solids, liquids, and gases.

A **solid** is matter that has its own size and shape. Solids take up space and have mass.

You can use a balance to measure the mass of a solid.

The box and the things in it are solids. Each thing has its own size, shape, and mass.

Crayons are solids. What are some properties of the crayons?

You can use a ruler to measure solids.

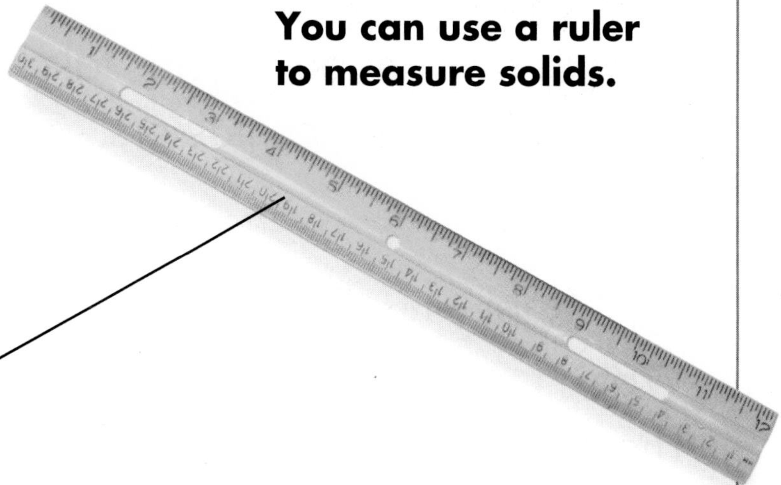

Notebooks are solids.

1. ✓Checkpoint What is a solid?

2. Math in Science Use a ruler to measure a solid in your classroom. Write how long, tall, and wide the solid is.

Liquids

A **liquid** is matter that does not have its own shape. Liquids take the shape of their containers.

Liquids take up space and have mass. Water is a liquid. Pour water into a jar. The water takes the same shape as the jar.

One way to measure liquids is to use a measuring cup. The amount of space a liquid takes up is called *volume*.

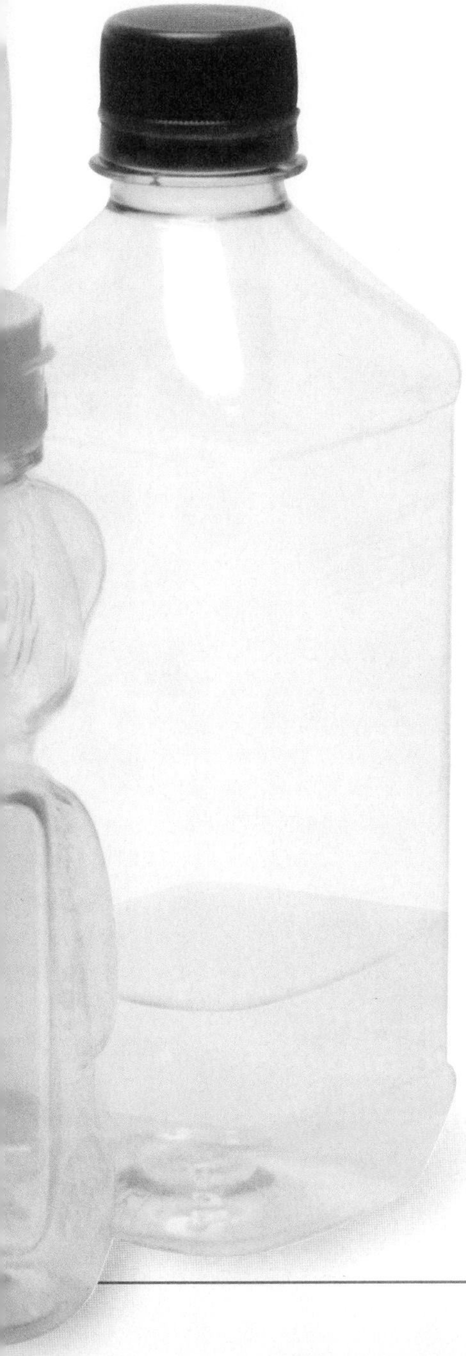

1. ✓Checkpoint What is a liquid?
2. Writing in Science Write 2 sentences about solids and liquids in your **science journal.** Tell how solids and liquids are alike and different.

Gases

A **gas** is matter that does not have its own shape or size. Gas takes the size and shape of its container. Gas always takes up all the space inside its container. Gas can change size and shape. Gas has mass.

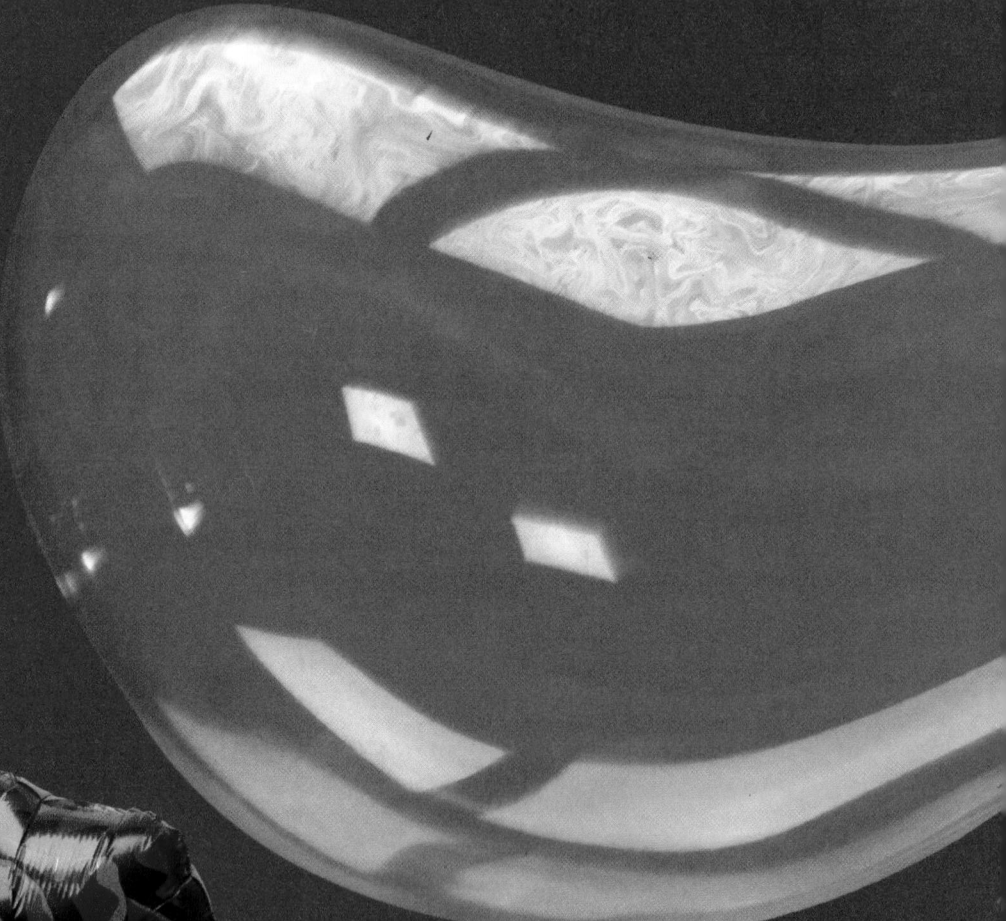

The bubble is filled with gas. Gas takes the size and shape of the bubble.

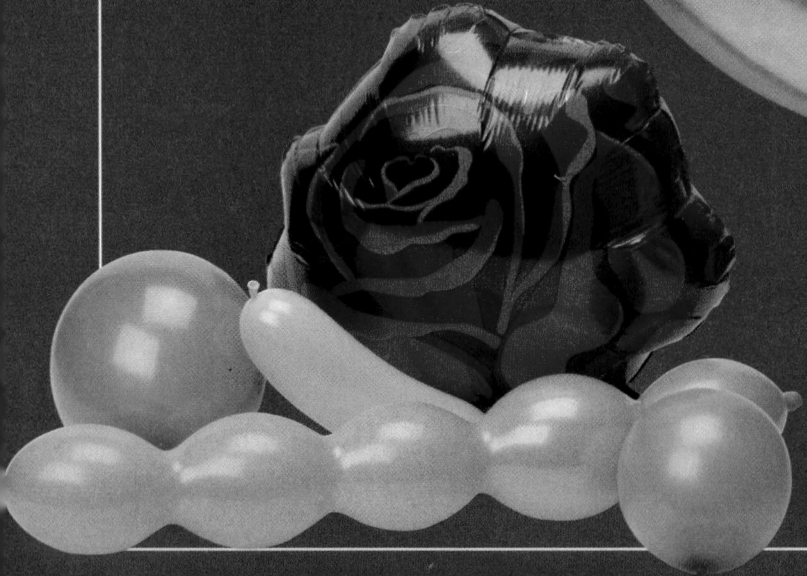

These balloons are filled with gas. Gas takes the size and shape of the balloons.

Breathe in. Breathe out. The air you breathe is made of gases.

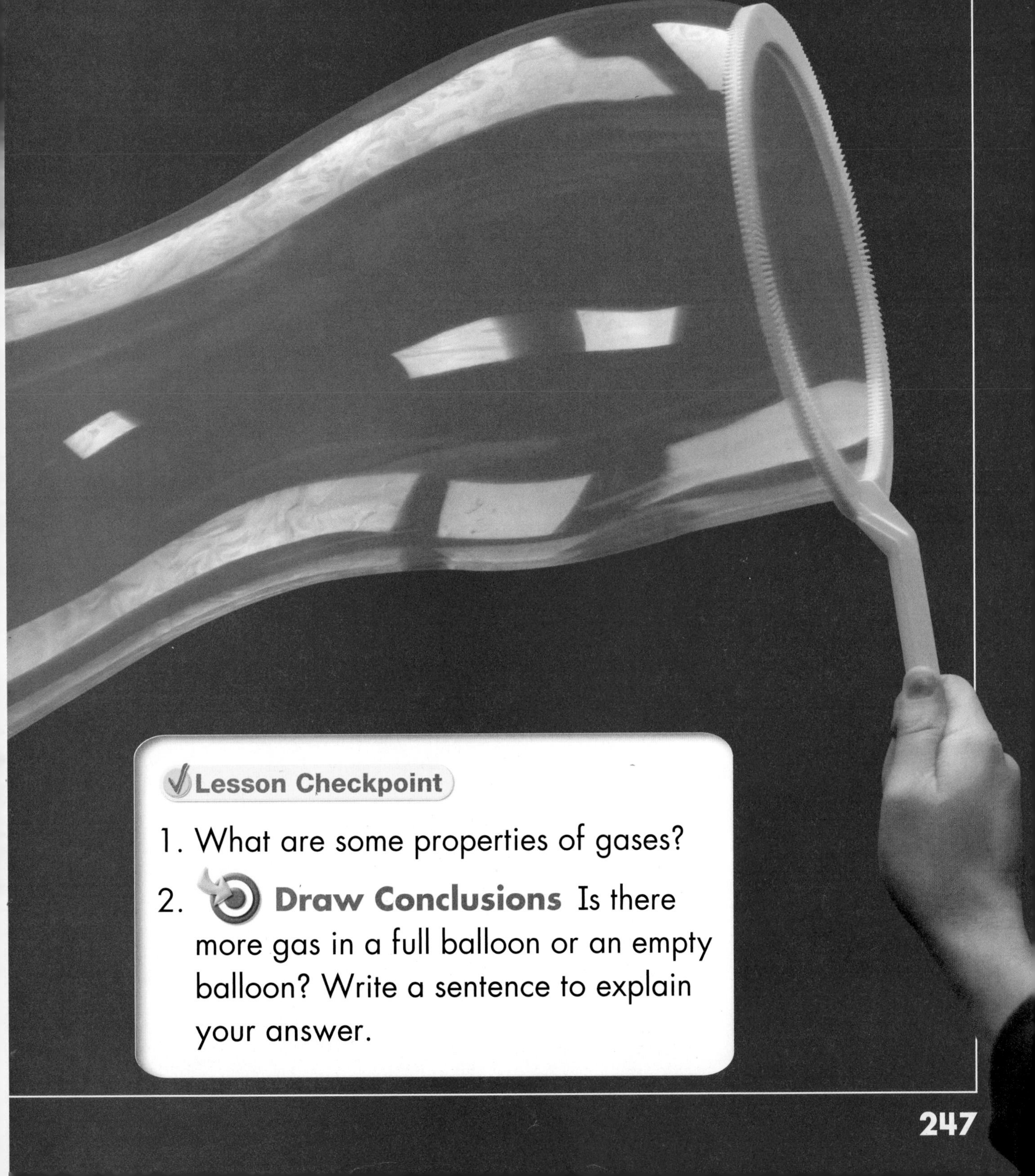

Lesson Checkpoint

1. What are some properties of gases?
2. **Draw Conclusions** Is there more gas in a full balloon or an empty balloon? Write a sentence to explain your answer.

Lesson 3

How can matter be changed?

Matter can be changed. Different matter changes in different ways. You can change the size of matter. You can change the shape of matter.

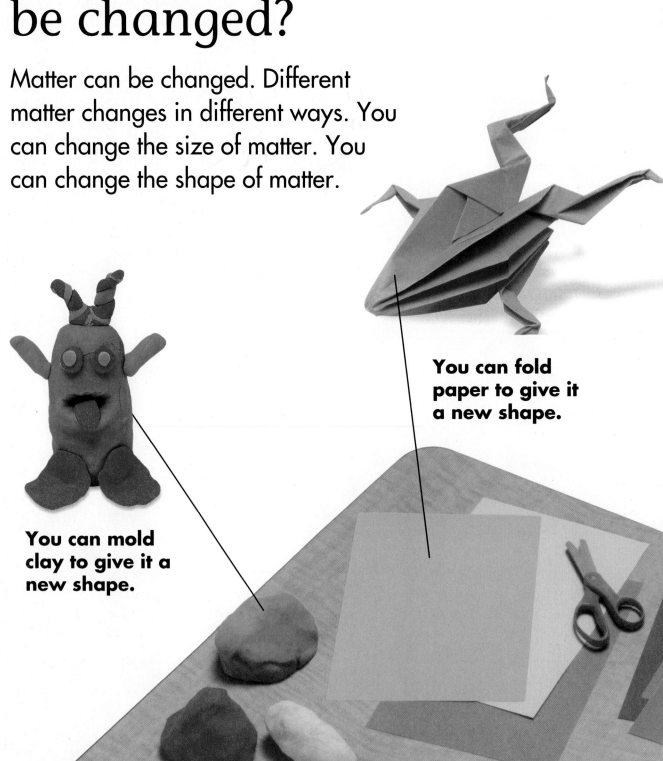

You can fold paper to give it a new shape.

You can mold clay to give it a new shape.

1. **✓Checkpoint** Name 3 ways that you can change the size or shape of matter.

2. **Draw Conclusions** What might happen to wood if you cut it? How might it change?

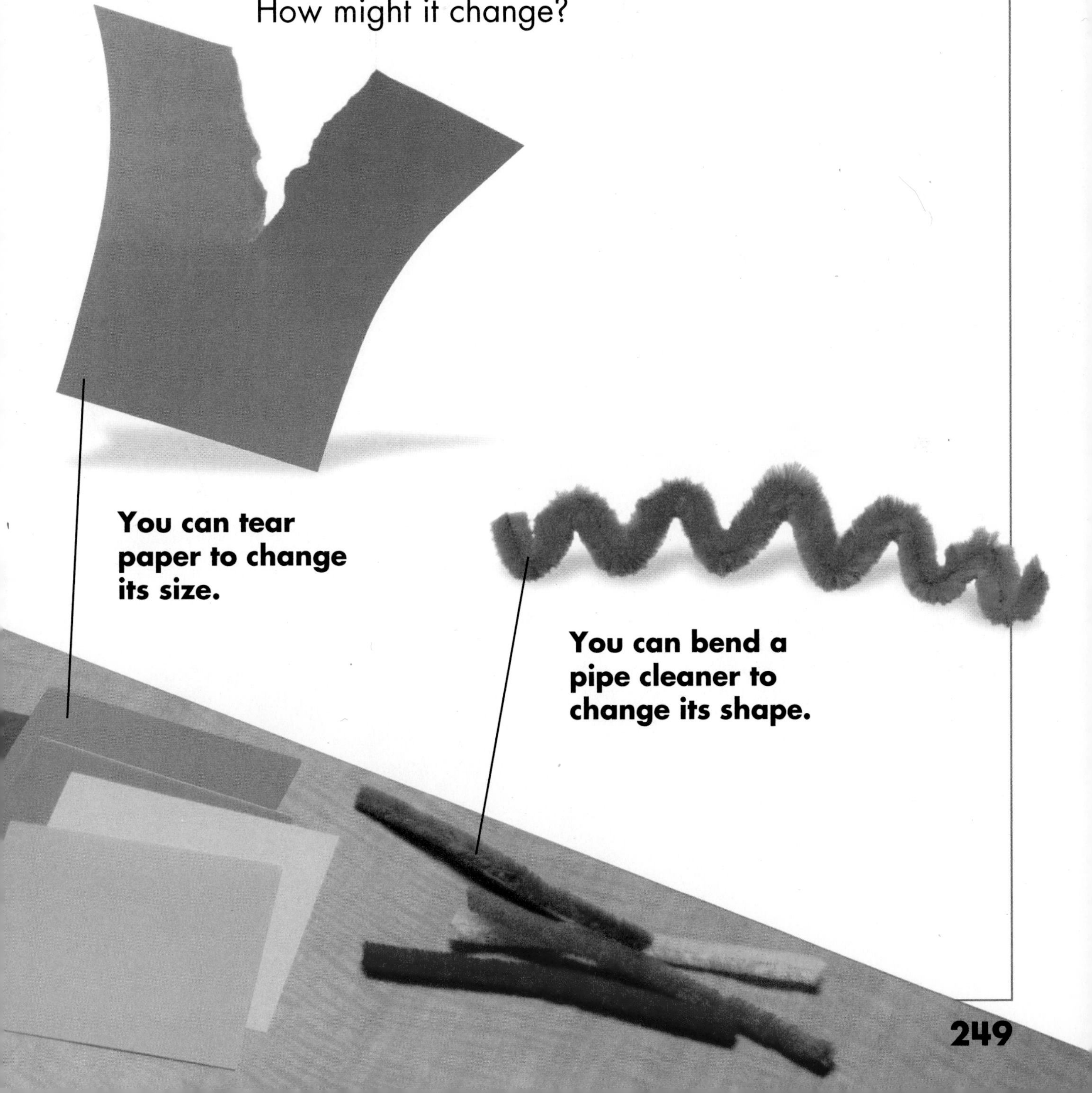

You can tear paper to change its size.

You can bend a pipe cleaner to change its shape.

Mixing and Separating Matter

A **mixture** is something made up of two or more kinds of matter. Matter in a mixture does not change. This fruit salad is a mixture.

You can separate a mixture to see its parts. Suppose you separate the fruits in the salad. Each piece of fruit will stay the same.

Look at the pictures. One mixture is made with sand and water. One mixture is made with salt and water. There are different ways to separate these mixtures. You can let the matter sink. You can let the water evaporate.

Mixing with Water

Look at this mixture. It is easy to see the sand and the water.

Look at the cup on the left. It has a mixture of salt and water. Look at the cup on the right. What happened after the water evaporated?

✓ Lesson Checkpoint

1. What are 2 ways to separate a mixture?
2. **Art in Science** Draw 2 things being mixed. How could you separate the mixture? Draw it.

Liquid water is poured into a plastic tray. The tray is put in a freezer. The water will change to ice.

Lesson 4

How can cooling and heating change matter?

Water is matter. Water can change. Suppose the temperature of water is below 0° Celsius. The water will freeze. The water will change to ice. Ice is solid water.

Water can change from a gas to a liquid. Water as a gas is called water vapor.

Water vapor in the air touches the cold glass. The water vapor changes from a gas to liquid. Tiny drops of water form on the glass.

Rain will freeze if the air temperature is very cold. Water on these leaves changed from a liquid to a solid.

1. **Checkpoint** How can you change water from a liquid to a solid?
2. **Math in Science** At what temperature does water become a solid?

Heating Matter

Heating can change the state of matter. Heat can change solids to liquids. Heat can change liquids to gases.

Ice and snow melt when the air warms. Solid water becomes liquid.

Heat from sunlight evaporates water. The liquid water changes to a gas.

When you boil water, the liquid water becomes a gas. This gas is called water vapor.

Heat changes other matter from solids to liquids. Butter melts when you heat it. What are some ways that you can use melted butter?

Lesson Checkpoint

1. How can heat change water?
2. Writing in Science Write 3 sentences in your **science journal.** Describe water as a solid, a liquid, and a gas.

Lab zone Guided Inquiry

Investigate How can water change?

You can see water in many forms. Rain is liquid water. Ice is solid water.

Materials

cup with water

thermometer

What to Do

1. **Observe** Describe the liquid water. **Measure** the temperature.

Your teacher will put the water in the freezer.

Process Skills

You tell what you expect to happen when you **predict**.

2. Take the cup out of the freezer. Describe the water. Measure the temperature.

3. Record the temperature. Did it go up or down? What happened to the outside of the cup?

4. **Predict** What will happen in a few hours? Test it and find out. Record the temperature.

How does the temperature change?	
Time	**Temperature °C**
After 30 minutes	
After 1 hour	
After 2 hours	
After 3 hours	

Explain Your Results

1. Compare solid water to liquid water.
2. **Predict** How long would it take for the liquid water to evaporate? Try it and find out.

Go Further

What other kinds of matter change when they are frozen? Investigate to find out.

Math in Science

How Can You Measure Matter?

Collect these tools for measuring.

Collect each pair of objects.

Estimate the length of each book. Use a ruler to measure the length of each book in centimeters.

Estimate the volume of each cup. Use a measuring cup to measure the water in each glass. Use milliliters.

Estimate the mass of each balloon. Use a balance to measure the mass of each balloon in grams.

Measure each pair of objects.
Record your data in a chart.

My Measurements

Length	Volume	Mass
1. ___ cm	1. ___ ml	1. ___ g
2. ___ cm	2. ___ ml	2. ___ g

Lab zone Take-Home Activity

Measure things at home. Use paper clips to measure length. Use a drinking glass to measure volume. Use your hands like a balance to estimate mass.

Chapter 8 Review and Test Prep

Vocabulary

Which picture goes with each word?

1. solid

2. gas

3. mixture

4. liquid

A
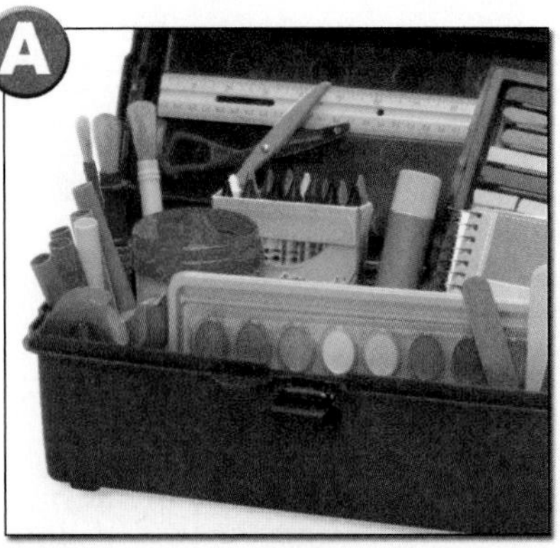

B
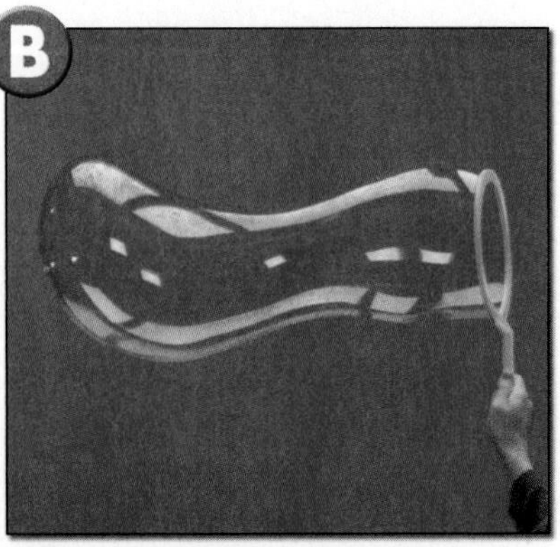

C
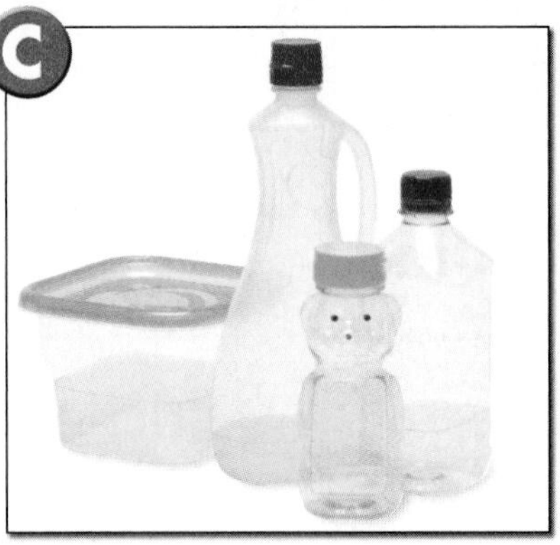

D
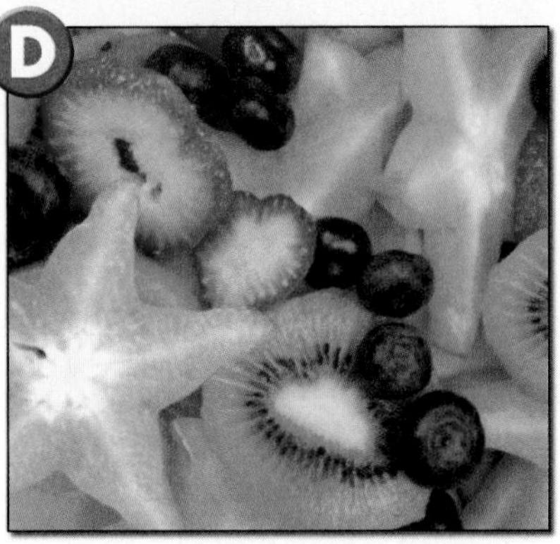

What did you learn?

5. What are three states of matter?

6. Name two ways to change properties of paper.

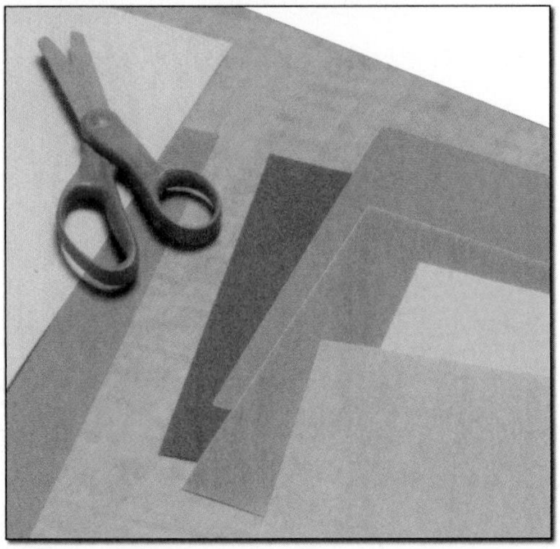

Process Skills

7. **Observe** Look around your classroom. Tell one way that matter in your classroom can be changed.

Draw Conclusions

8. **Draw Conclusions** What made the candle change? Fill in the graphic organizer.

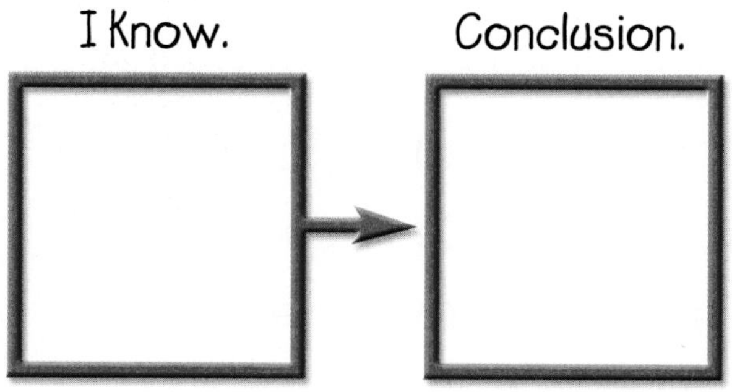

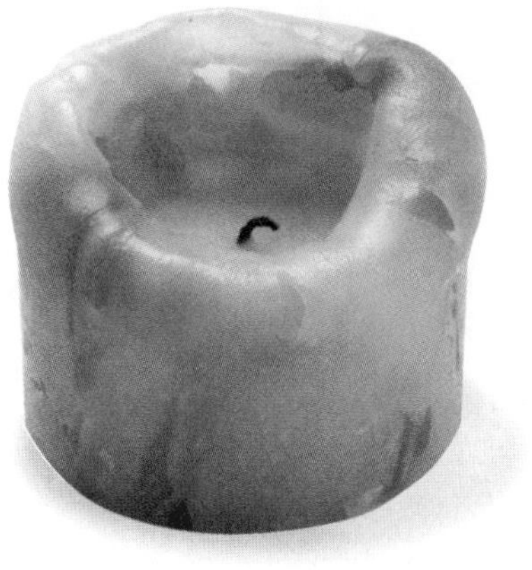

Test Prep

Fill in the circle next to the correct answer.

9. Which state of matter has its own shape and size?

Ⓐ solid
Ⓑ liquid
Ⓒ gas
Ⓓ property

10. **Writing in Science** Choose a solid in your classroom. Describe its properties.

Space Food

Astronauts in space need to take their food with them. Scientists have found a way to make taking food in space easier. Many foods contain water. Taking the water out of foods helps in space travel. Foods with no water have less mass.

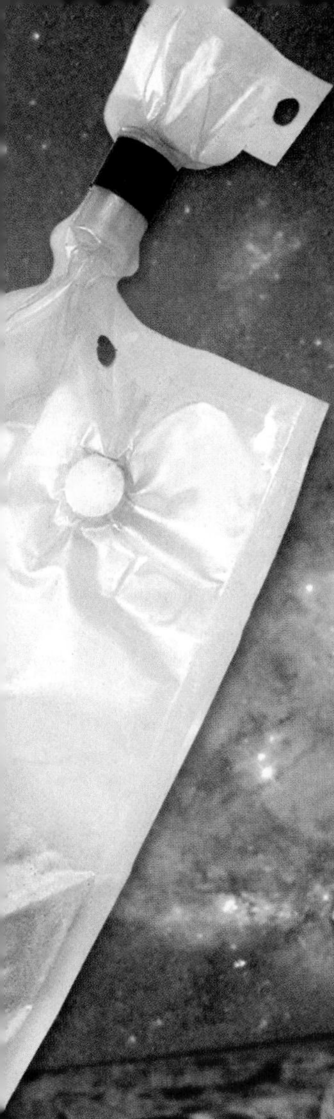

Taking the water out of foods means the food takes up less space. Some examples of food astronauts take into space are soup, macaroni and cheese, and scrambled eggs. Before astronauts eat this food, they have to put the water back in. When the water is mixed back in, the foods taste good.

Lab zone **Take-Home Activity**

What are some kinds of food or drink you make at home by adding water? How do you change the matter?

NASA Career

Material Scientist

Read Together

Material scientists study the properties of different kinds of matter. Some material scientists work at NASA.

Material scientists work to make things that can hold matter that is very hot. Material scientists at NASA also work to make things that will not break in space.

Narrottam Bansal is a material scientist. He works at NASA.

Lab zone Take-Home Activity

Which kind of matter can hold a spoon when it is wet? Try a tissue, a paper towel, and a piece of cloth. Tell your family what you learned.

EC CRU 10 9 8 7 6 5 4 3 2 1

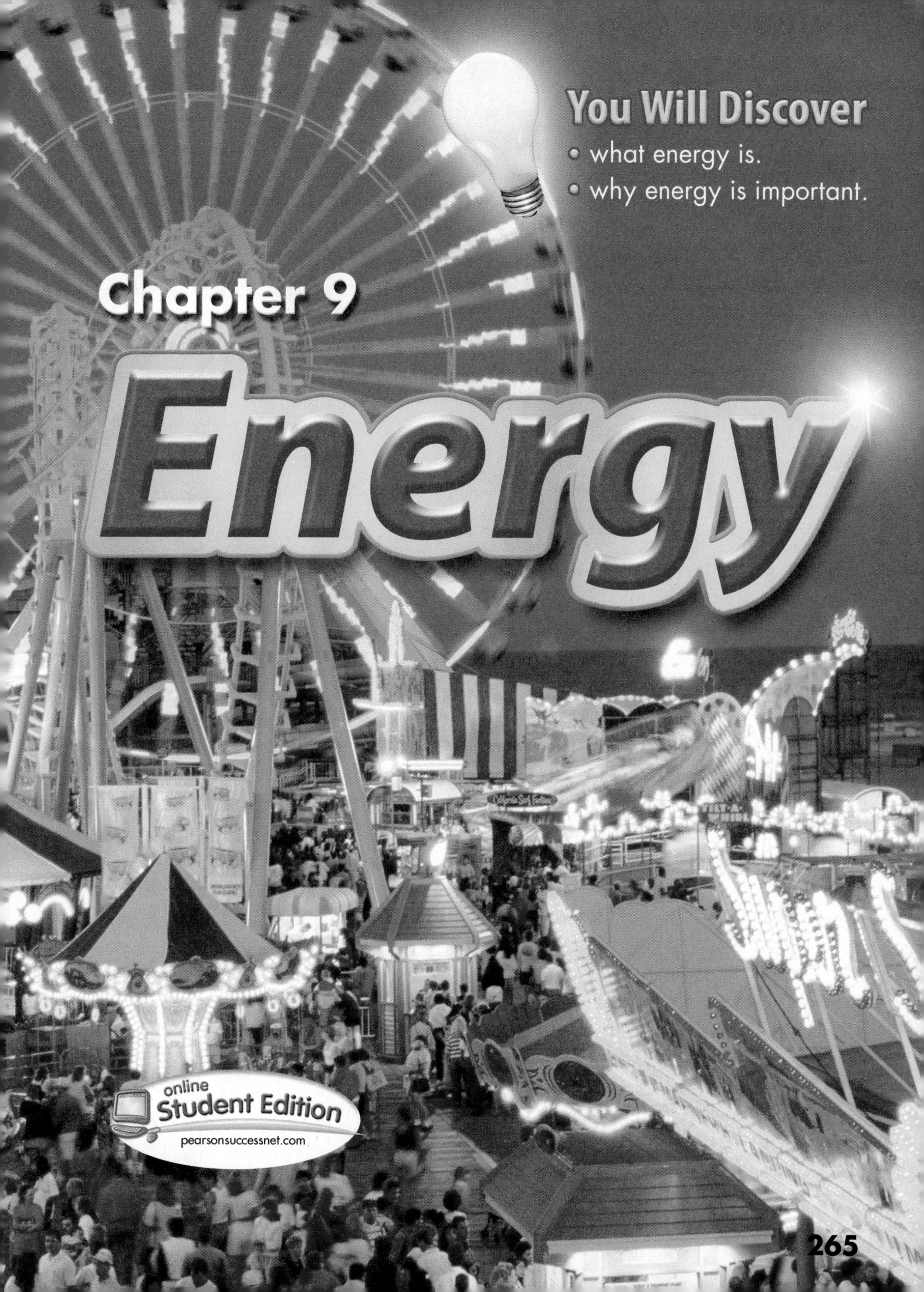

Chapter 9

Energy

You Will Discover

- what energy is.
- why energy is important.

online Student Edition
pearsonsuccessnet.com

Build Background

What are some kinds of energy?

Chapter 9 Vocabulary

energy page 271

solar energy page 272

source page 278

fuel page 279

conductor page 281

reflect page 282

shadow page 284

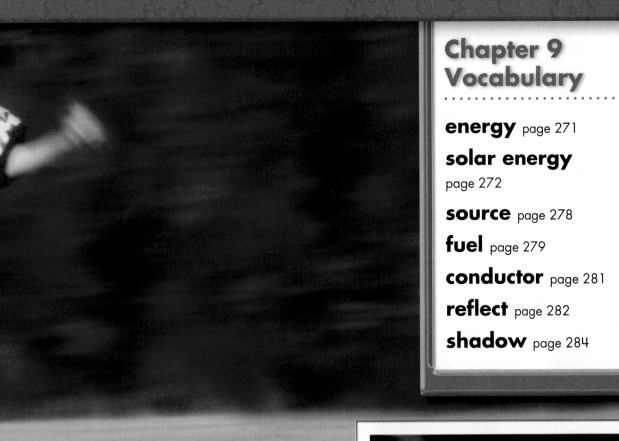

Lab zone Directed Inquiry

Explore Which color heats faster?

Materials

2 thermometers

black and white paper

tape

What to Do

1 Wrap thermometers.

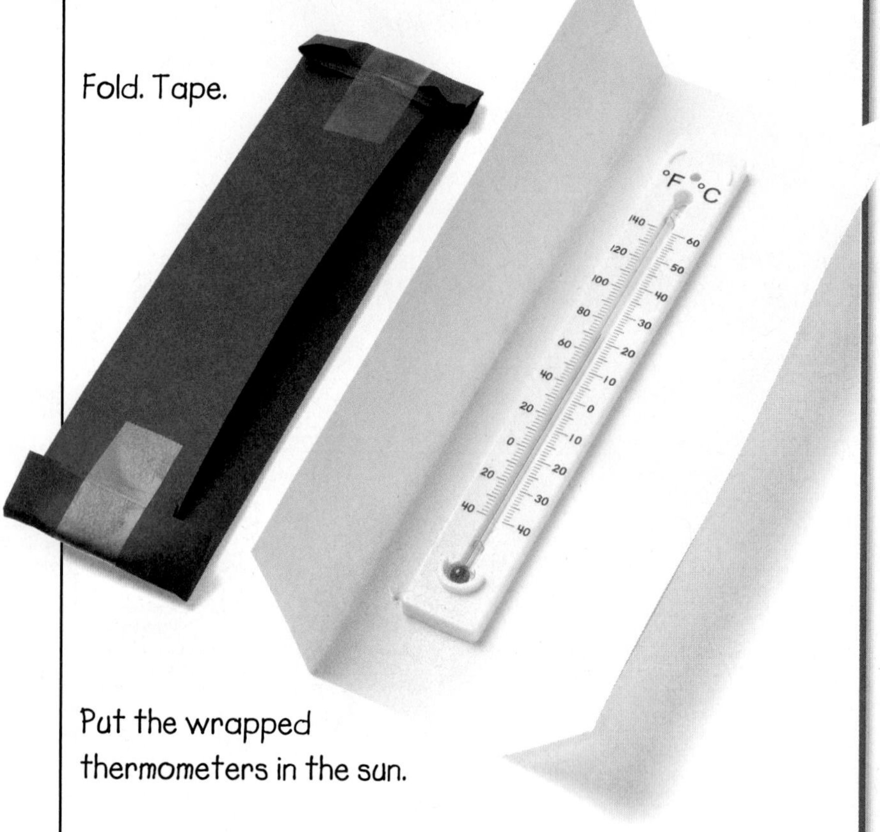

Fold. Tape.

Put the wrapped thermometers in the sun.

2 Wait 1 hour. Read the temperatures.

Process Skills

When you **infer**, you use what you observe to answer a question.

Explain Your Results

Infer How did color make a difference in temperature?

How to Read Science

Reading Skills

Target Skill: Infer

Infer means to use what you know to answer a question.

Science Story

Tom and Ramon play after school every day. Today they are playing football. It is a hot and sunny day.

Apply It!

Infer Which child will feel warmer?

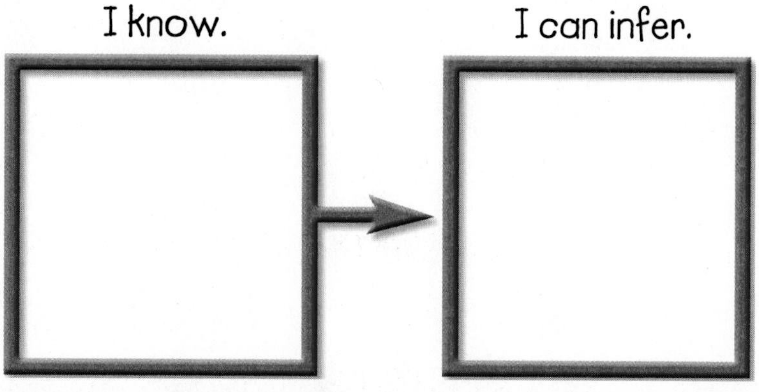

Where Do We Get Energy?

Sung to the tune of "Billy Boy"
Lyrics by Gerri Brioso & Richard Freitas/The Dovetail Group, Inc.

Oh, where do we get energy, energy?
Oh, where do we get energy?
We get most of it from the Sun.
So there's heat for everyone.
Yes we get lots of energy from the Sun.

Lesson 1

What is energy?

Anything that can do work and cause change has **energy.** You use energy when you do work or play. You use energy when you are awake. You use energy when you are asleep. You use energy when you walk, run, or breathe.

Energy from the Sun

Earth gets most of its energy from the Sun. Heat from the Sun warms the land, air, and water on Earth. **Solar energy** is heat and light from the Sun.

People and animals use sunlight to see in the daytime. Earth would stay dark without the Sun.

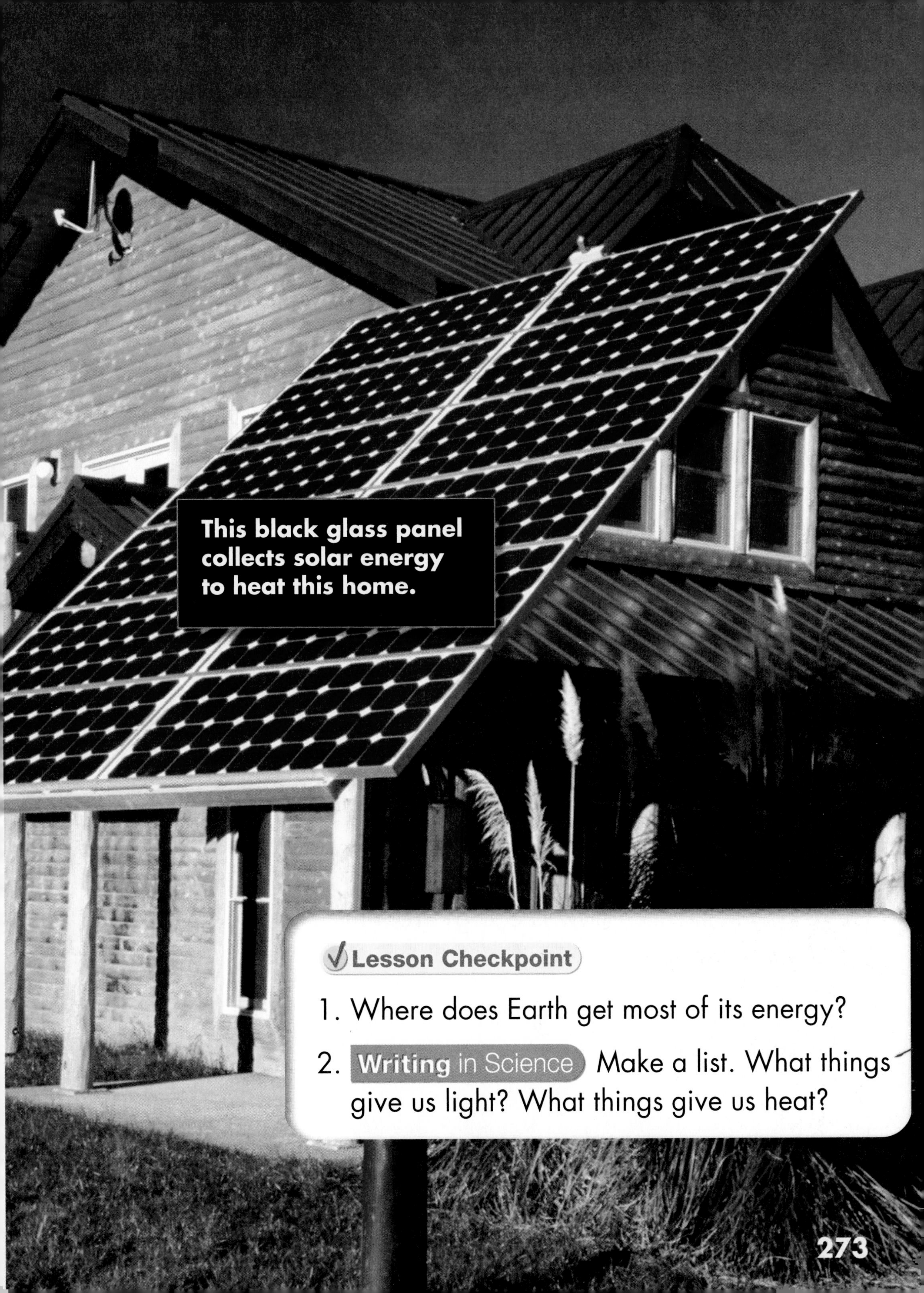

This black glass panel collects solar energy to heat this home.

Lesson Checkpoint

1. Where does Earth get most of its energy?
2. **Writing in Science** Make a list. What things give us light? What things give us heat?

Lesson 2

How do living things use energy?

Most living things need energy from the Sun. Green leaves on plants use sunlight, air, water, and nutrients to make food. Plants use the food to live and grow.

Animals use energy to live and grow. Animals get energy from the food they eat. The food comes from plants or from animals that eat plants. The plants get energy from the Sun. People need energy too.

1. **Checkpoint** How is energy from the Sun important to plants?
2. **Infer** How do you think people get and use energy?

4
5

How People Get Energy

Food gives you energy to work and play. Food gives you energy to grow.

The pictures show five food groups. You should eat foods from each food group every day. Eating food from these food groups can help you grow and stay healthy. Be careful not to eat too many sweets or foods with a lot of fat.

✓ Lesson Checkpoint

1. Name the five important food groups.
2. **Health** in Science Plan a healthful lunch. Be sure to choose something from each food group.

Vegetables

Vegetables have many vitamins your body needs.

Bread, Rice, Cereal, and Pasta

The foods in this group help give you energy.

Meat, Fish, Eggs, Dry Beans

The foods in this group have nutrients that help your body grow and stay strong.

Fruit

Fruit has many vitamins and minerals that can help you stay healthy.

Milk, Yogurt, Cheese

The foods in this group are important for healthy bones and teeth.

Lesson 3

What are some sources of heat?

Sunlight is one source of heat. A **source** is a place from which something comes. Sunlight warms Earth.

Heat comes from other sources too. What other sources of heat do you see in the pictures?

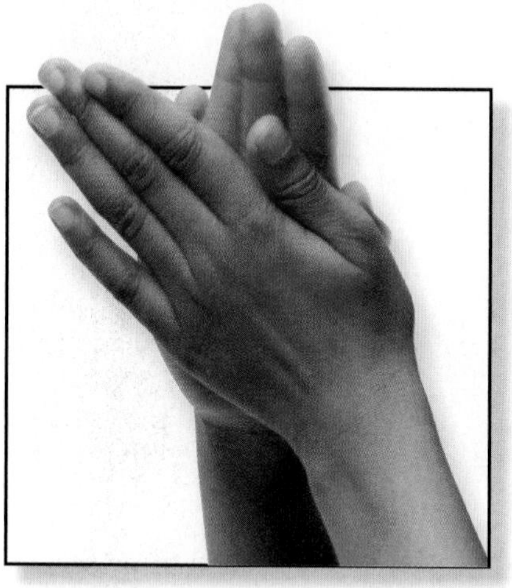

Rubbing your hands together can make your hands feel warmer.

You can feel heat from a candle.

The picture of the campfire shows wood burning. Wood is a kind of fuel. **Fuel** is something that is burned to make heat. Coal, gas, and oil are other kinds of fuels.

✓ Checkpoint

1. What are some sources of heat?
2. **Social Studies** in Science Look at a map of the United States. In which parts of the country do people need to use the most fuel to heat their homes?

Fire is a source of heat.

How Heat Moves

Heat moves from warmer objects and places to cooler ones. People can use heat to cook. Look at the picture. Heat moves from the hot burner on the stove to the pan. Then heat moves from the hot pan to the cold food.

The metal pan conducts heat.
Heat moves from the stove to the pan to the food.
This cooking mitt is made of cloth. It helps keep your hand safe from heat.

How do you boil water?

Fill a pot with water. The pot and the water are cool. Put the pot on the stove. Heat moves from the stove to the pot. Then the heat moves from the pot to the water. The heat makes the water hot enough to boil.

The pan in the picture is metal. Metal is a conductor. A **conductor** is something that lets heat easily move through it. Some materials are not good conductors. Wood and cloth are not good conductors. Heat does not move easily through wood and cloth.

Lesson Checkpoint

1. Why are many pans made of metal?
2. **Writing in Science** Make a list. What things conduct heat well? What things do not conduct heat well?

Lesson 4

How does light move?

Light is a form of energy. The Sun, a lamp, a flashlight, and a fire are sources of light. Most light sources give off heat too.
Light moves in straight lines. Light can move through some things such as clear glass.

Light **reflects** when it bounces off something. Light reflects well from smooth, shiny things such as a mirror. The picture shows how light reflects.

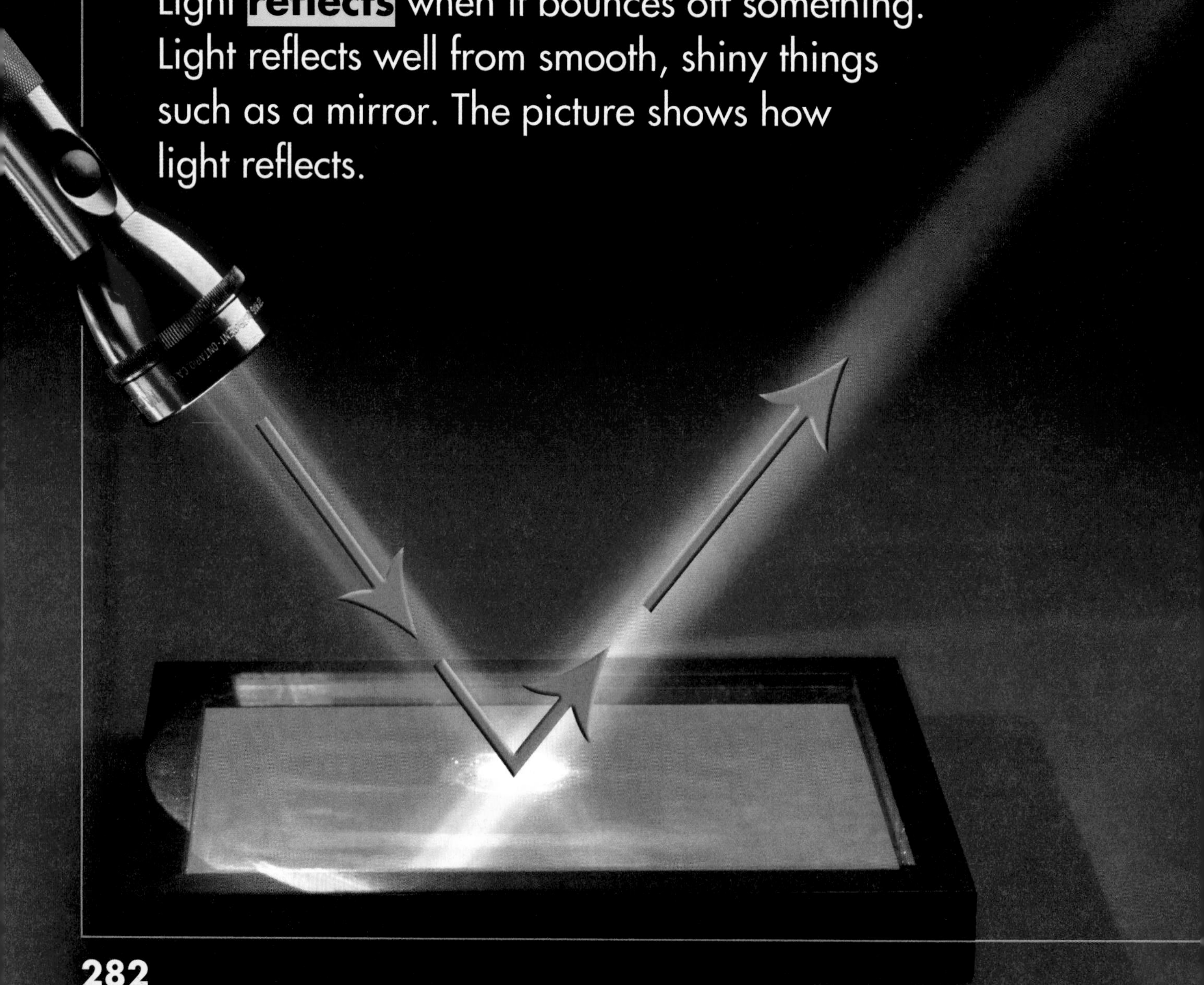

Most of the light you see is white light. The rainbow shows the colors that make up white light. Raindrops in the air can bend sunlight. Then the sunlight is separated into the colors in a rainbow.

Dark colors take in light. You might feel warm when you wear dark colors in the sunlight. Light colors reflect the sunlight. You can stay cooler when you wear light colors.

The colors in a rainbow are red, orange, yellow, green, blue, and violet.

Light colors help you stay cool in warm weather.

1. **Checkpoint** How is a rainbow made?
2. **Art in Science** Use crayons to show the six colors in a rainbow.

Shadows

A **shadow** is made when something blocks the light. You can see your shadow when your body blocks the sunlight.

Shadows change during the day. The Sun looks low in the sky in early morning. Shadows look long. The Sun looks high in the sky in the middle of the day. Shadows look short.

Shadows are long in the morning when the Sun rises. They get shorter until noon.

Shadows are shortest at noon. Then they grow longer until sunset.

You can use a flashlight to make shadows. Block the light with a shape cut from paper. Move the shape away from or toward the light. You can make the size of the shadow change.

✓ Lesson Checkpoint

1. Suppose you are standing outside on a sunny day. When would your shadow be the shortest?
2. **Math in Science** A shadow is 200 cm at breakfast, 100 cm at morning recess, and 50 cm at lunch. What pattern do you see?

Lesson 5

What are other kinds of energy?

You use different kinds of energy every day. Look at the picture of the grocery cart. You could push the cart to make it move. The moving cart would have energy of motion.

Wind is another kind of energy. Look at the picture of the boat. Wind energy can make the boat move.

Look at the musical instruments in the picture. What sounds do the instruments make? Sound is a kind of energy.

✓ Checkpoint

1. What are some other kinds of energy?
2. **Social Studies** in Science Look at a map of the United States. Where might you be able to sail a boat?

variety pack

526

Using Electricity Safely

What happens when you turn on a light? Electricity makes the light work. What other things in your home use electricity? What kinds of things at school use electricity?

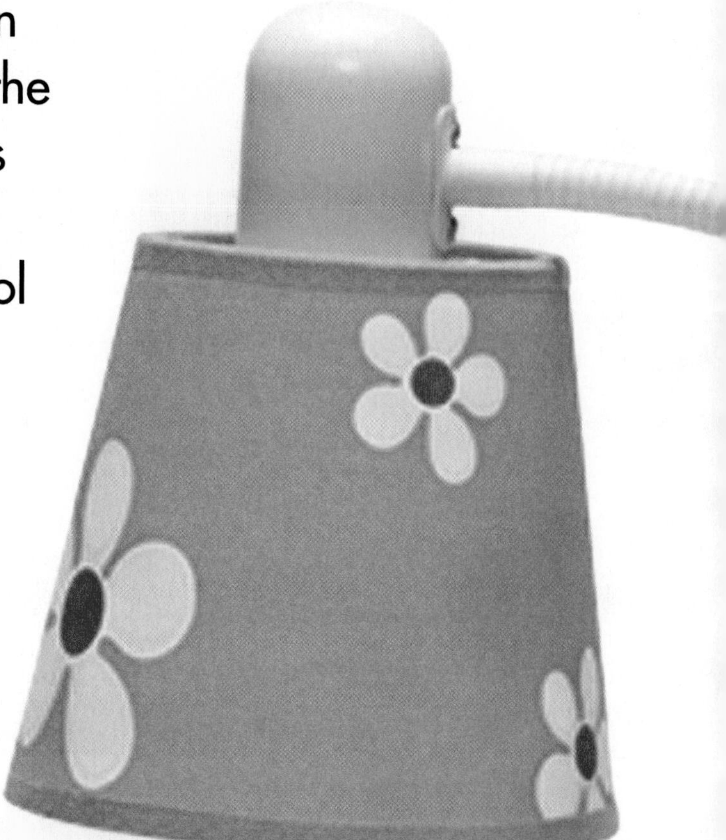

Batteries can help provide electricity.

A lamp and a clock use electricity.

Electricity Safety Tips

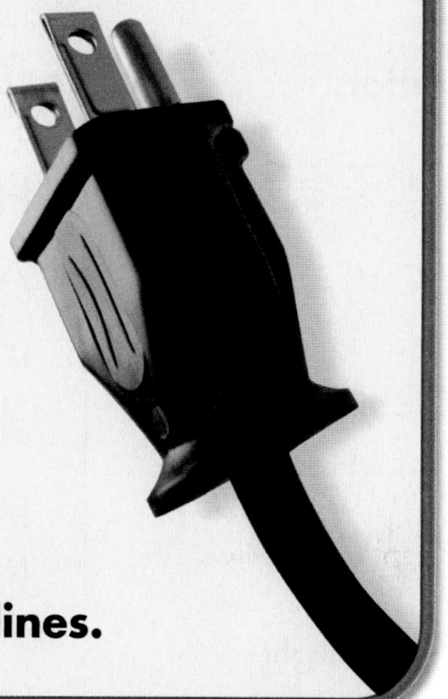

- **Keep things that use electricity away from water.**
- **Do not put too many plugs into outlets.**
- **Do not pull on cords to unplug things. Hold onto the plug.**
- **Do not touch cords that have wire showing.**
- **Do not play near power lines.**

It is important to use electricity safely. The chart tells you how to stay safe when using electricity.

Lesson Checkpoint

1. What is one way you can stay safe around electricity?
2. **Infer** Why shouldn't you use a hair dryer in the bathroom?

Lab zone Guided Inquiry

Investigate How can you change light?

Materials

mirror

tub with water

flashlight

posterboard

crayons or markers

What to Do

1. Hold a mirror on one side of the tub. Ask a partner to shine light on the mirror. Your partner should hold the posterboard behind the flashlight.

2. Tilt the mirror to shine the light on the posterboard.

3. **Observe.** Draw what you see.

Changing Light

Process Skills

You **observe** the colors that the light and water make.

Explain Your Results

1. What are some of the colors you saw?
2. **Infer** How does the light change when it passes through water?

Go Further

How would using colored paper change the colors you see? Try it and find out.

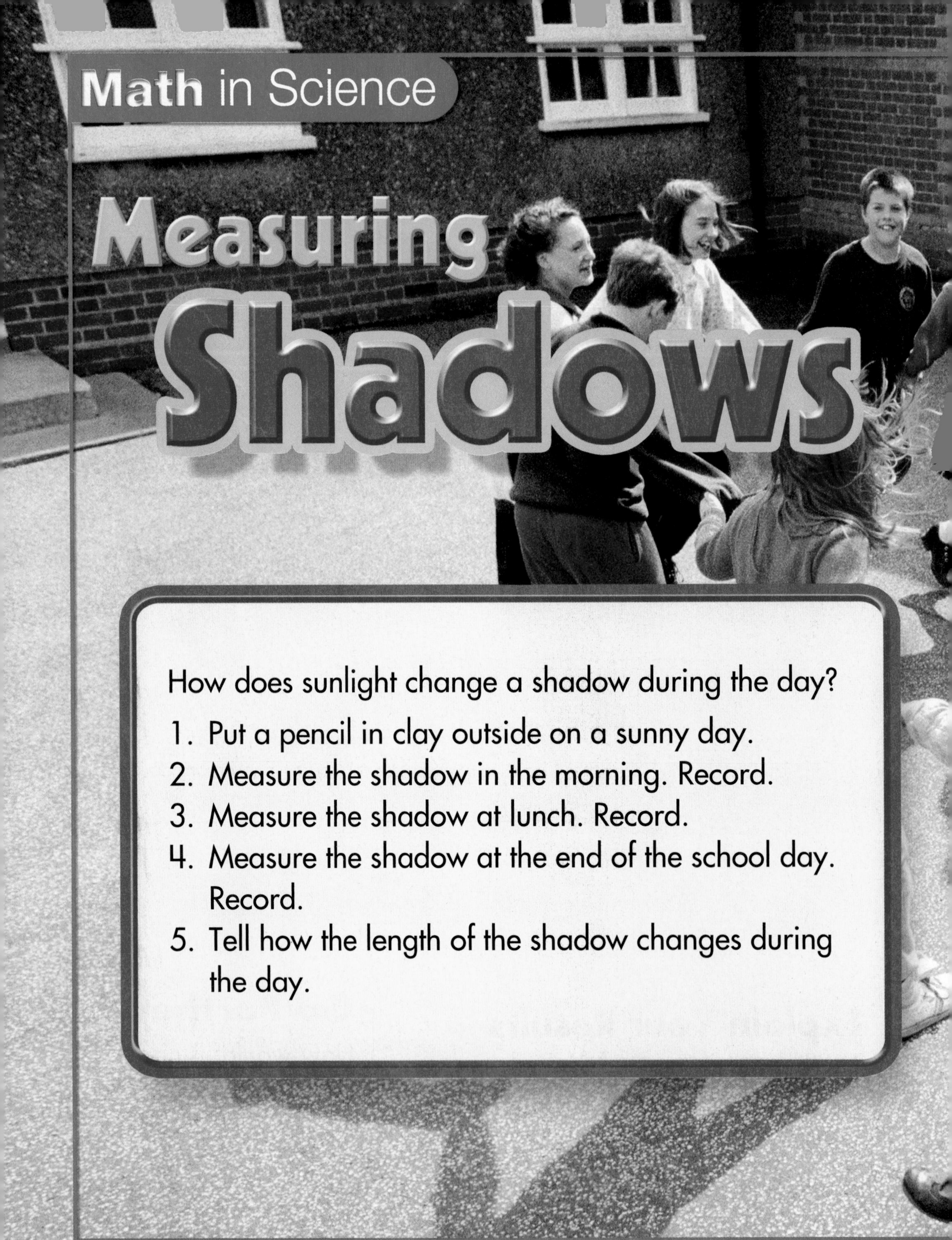

Math in Science

Measuring Shadows

How does sunlight change a shadow during the day?

1. Put a pencil in clay outside on a sunny day.
2. Measure the shadow in the morning. Record.
3. Measure the shadow at lunch. Record.
4. Measure the shadow at the end of the school day. Record.
5. Tell how the length of the shadow changes during the day.

eTools Take It to the Net pearsonsuccessnet.com

Changing Shadows

Time of day	morning	lunch	end of day
Shadow length			

Lab zone Take-Home Activity

Have someone measure your shadow at different times during the day. Write down what you find. Tell how your shadow changes as the Sun moves.

Chapter 9 Review and Test Prep

Vocabulary

Which picture goes with each word?

1. solar energy
2. fuel
3. reflect

A
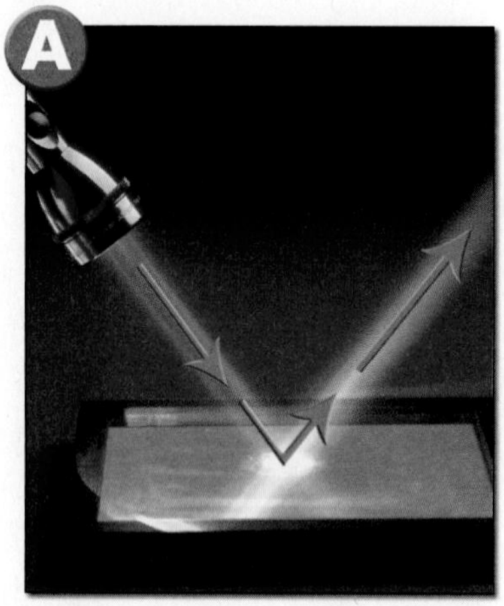

B

C

What did you learn?

4. How do people get energy?
5. Name four kinds of energy.
6. What conducts energy better, a metal pan or a wooden spoon?

Process Skills

7. **Observe** a shadow outside your classroom window. How does the shadow change during the day?

Infer

8. **Infer** Look at the shadow of the tree. What time of day do you think it is?

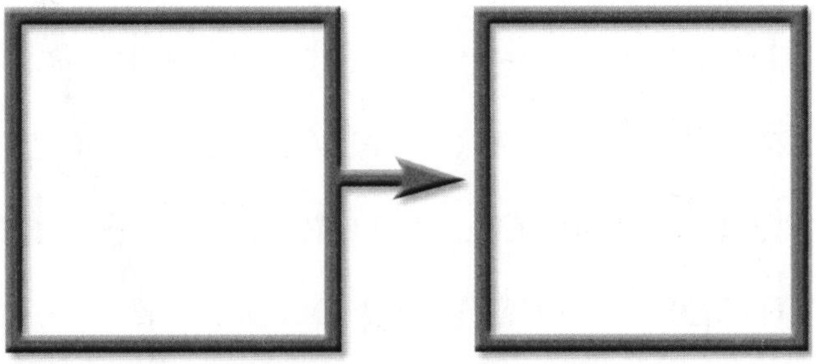

Test Prep

Fill in the circle that correctly answers the question.

9. Where does Earth get most of its energy?

   Ⓐ from food
   Ⓑ from the Moon
   Ⓒ from the Sun
   Ⓓ from wind

10. **Writing in Science** Describe two kinds of energy. Tell how they are important to you.

Career

Lights, Camera, Action!

Lighting Operator

Read Together

Do you know what a gaffer is? Have you heard of a best boy? They are people who work with the lights on a movie set. A gaffer is a lighting operator. A best boy helps the lighting operator.

Lighting operators use lights to make it look cloudy when it is sunny. They can also make it look bright when the sky is dark.

Lighting operators use lights to make it look very bright on the movie set.

Lab zone Take-Home Activity

You can use a lamp to help you see in the dark. Draw a picture of one more thing that you could use for light when it is dark.

EC CRU 10 9 8 7 6 5 4 3 2 1

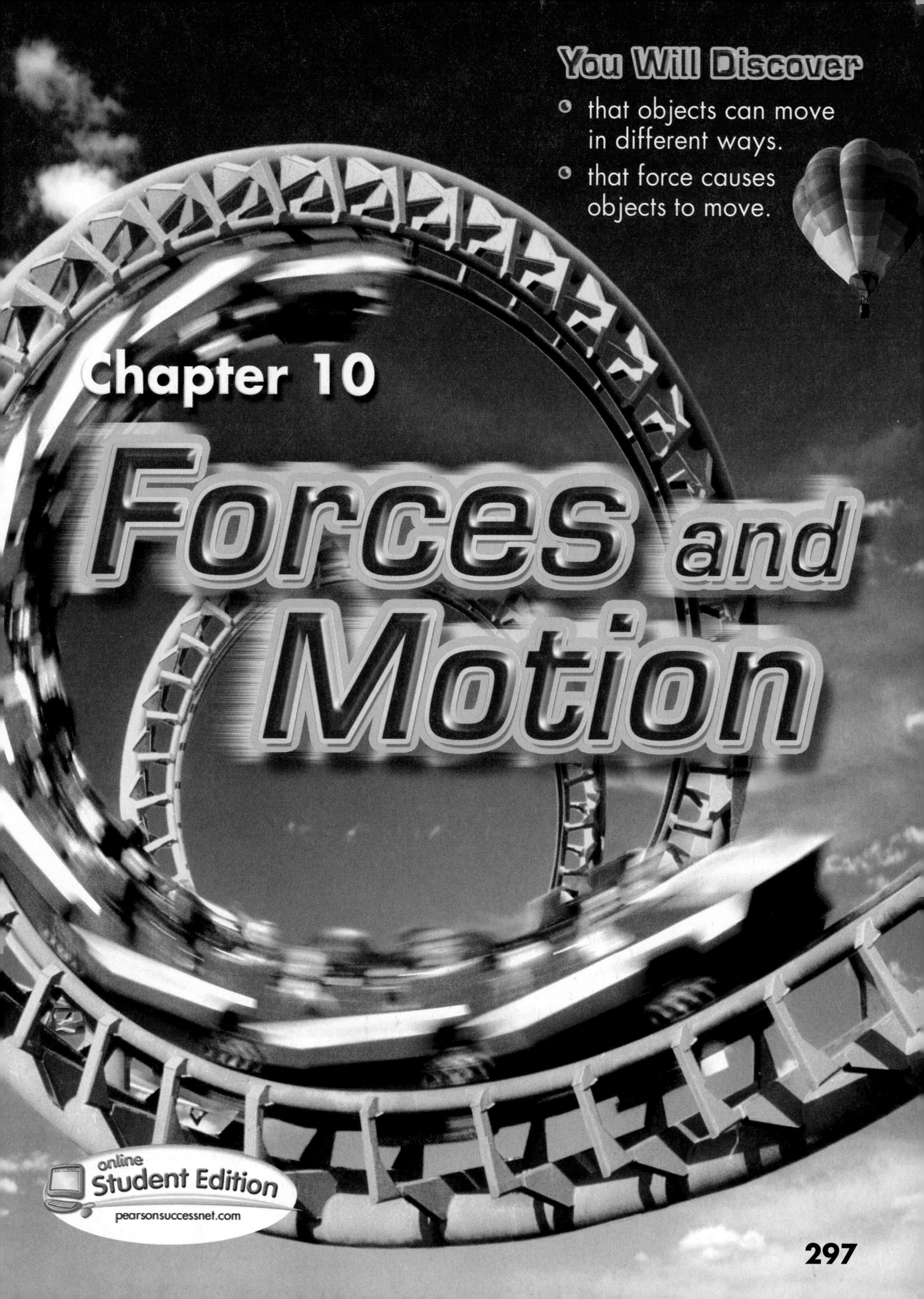

You Will Discover

- that objects can move in different ways.
- that force causes objects to move.

Chapter 10
Forces and Motion

online Student Edition
pearsonsuccessnet.com

How do forces cause objects to move?

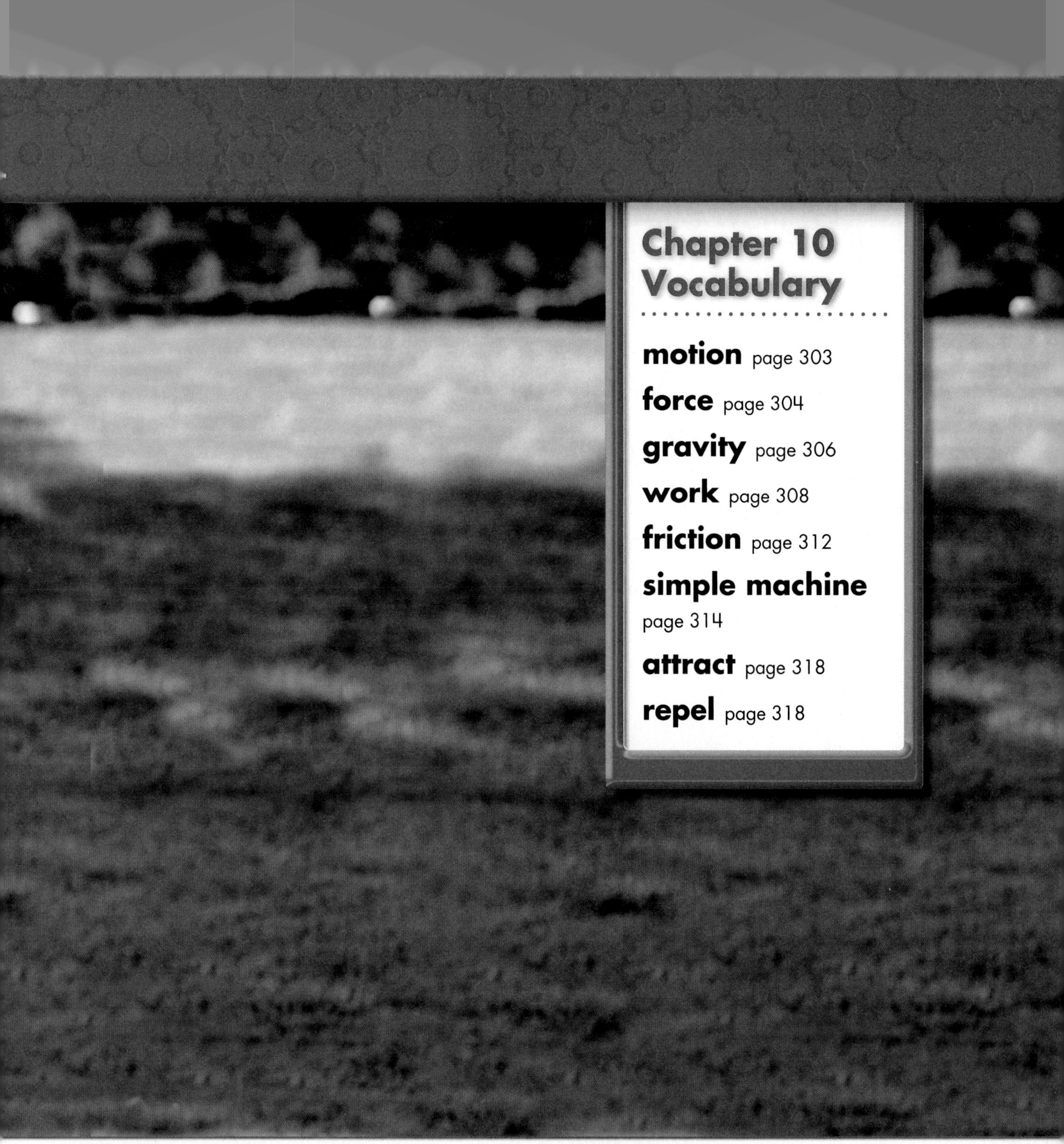

Chapter 10 Vocabulary

motion page 303

force page 304

gravity page 306

work page 308

friction page 312

simple machine page 314

attract page 318

repel page 318

Lab zone

Directed Inquiry

Explore How can you measure force?

You use force when you pull and push things.
Force can be measured.

Materials

safety goggles

rubber band and string

2 books

ruler

What to Do

1. Pull the rubber band to move the book. **Measure** how long the rubber band is when you pull it.

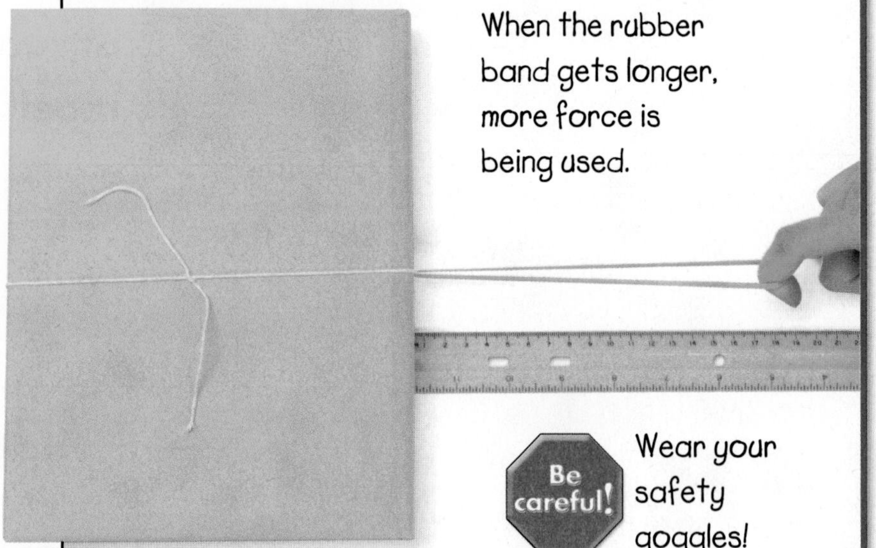

When the rubber band gets longer, more force is being used.

Be careful! Wear your safety goggles!

2. Add 1 more book. Pull and measure.

Process Skills

You share information with your classmates when you **communicate**.

Explain Your Results

Communicate How are the measurements different?

 More Lab zone Activities Take It to the Net pearsonsuccessnet.com

How to Read Science

Reading Skills

Put Things in Order

When you put things in order, you tell what happens first, next, and last.

Science Story

Books!

Tony went to a used book sale in his neighborhood.
He saw so many books he wanted to buy!
Tony used his wagon to take all of his books home.

Apply It!

Communicate Look at the pictures. Tell how to put the pictures in order to tell what happened first, next, and last. Use the story to help you.

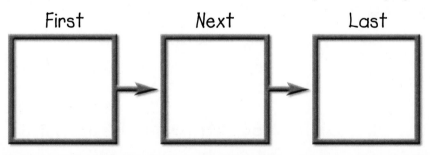

First → Next → Last

You Are There

Use Some Force!

Sung to the tune of "If You're Happy"
Lyrics by Gerri Brioso & Richard Freitas/The Dovetail Group, Inc.

If you want to move the ball,
Use some force.
If you want to move the ball,
Use some force.
If you want it to go far,
Kick it hard and there you are.
You just moved the ball by using lots of force.

Lesson 1

How do objects move?

Motion is the act of moving. Objects can move in different ways. Push a toy truck across the floor. The truck can move in a straight line. Move the truck in a zigzag motion. This means you push the truck in one direction and then another direction.

A swing moves back and forth. The merry-go-round in the picture moves around and around.

Force

You can move things in different ways. A push or a pull that makes something move is called a **force.** A force can change the way an object moves.

You use force to move a wagon.

An object will move in the direction it is pushed or pulled. Pull on the wagon. The wagon will move forward.

The boy gives the swing a push.

An object moves faster when you apply more force. The swing will move faster if you push it with more force.

You need to apply more force to move heavier objects than lighter ones. Would you need more force to move a book or a pencil?

1. ✓Checkpoint What is force?
2. Writing in Science Write a sentence in your **science journal.** Tell about something you need force to do.

Gravity

The children in the picture are throwing leaves into the air. What will happen to the leaves? Gravity will pull the leaves down. **Gravity** is a force. Gravity pulls things toward the center of Earth.

Suppose you jump up in the air. What will happen? Gravity will pull you down to Earth. If you let go of an object, gravity will pull it down to Earth too.

Throw a basketball up to the hoop. Gravity pulls it down. Swoosh!

✓ Lesson Checkpoint

1. Why do you come down after you jump up?
2. **Put Things in Order** Suppose you wanted to throw a basketball through a hoop. Put the steps you should follow in order.

Lesson 2

What is work?

Suppose you push a crayon across the desk. You use force to move the crayon. **Work** happens whenever a force makes an object move. You do work when you push the crayon across the desk.

The amount of work you do depends on how much force you use and how far the object moves. It does not take much work to move the crayon across the desk. It takes a lot of work to push this bobsled up the hill.

If an object does not move, no work is done. Push hard against a wall. You are not doing work because the wall does not move.

These people cannot move the rock. They are not doing work.

✓ Lesson Checkpoint

1. How can you tell if you are doing work?
2. Writing in Science Make a list in your **science journal.** Write down five kinds of work you do each day.

Lesson 3

How can you change the way things move?

You know that a force can change the way an object moves. A moving object that is pushed or pulled will speed up, slow down, or change direction.

How can you make a soccer ball roll just a little bit? How can you make it roll farther? It depends on how much force you use. Tap a soccer ball gently. It will not go far.

Kick a soccer ball harder. It will move farther. It takes more force to move objects farther.

Suppose you change the direction of the force. The soccer ball will move in a different direction. Someone kicks the soccer ball to you. The ball changes direction when you kick it back.

Bam!

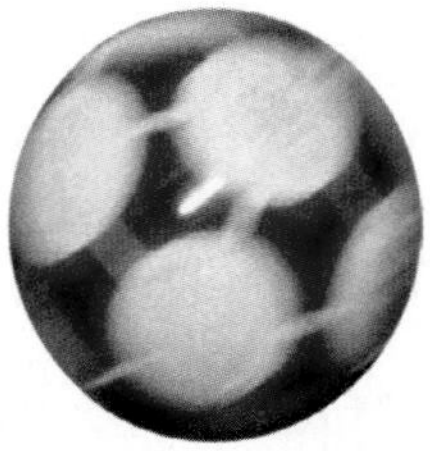

1. **Checkpoint** How can the amount of force used change the way an object moves?
2. **Math in Science** Push a book across the floor. Measure how far it goes. Push it harder. Measure how far it goes. Compare the results.

Friction

Think about rolling a ball across a field. Why does the ball stop moving? **Friction** is a force that makes moving objects slow down or stop moving.

Look at the bicycles in these pictures. A bicycle will move faster on a smooth road than it will on grass. The friction between the bicycle tires and the grass will make the bicycle slow down.

Rub your hands together. Your hands feel warm. Objects become warm when they rub together. Friction causes heat.

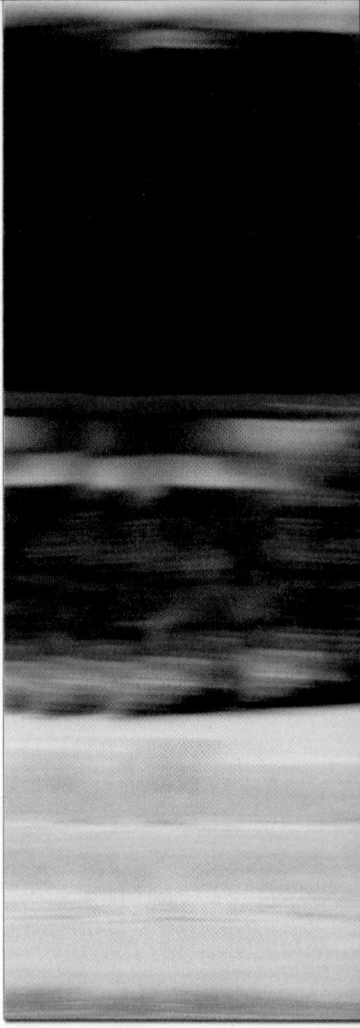

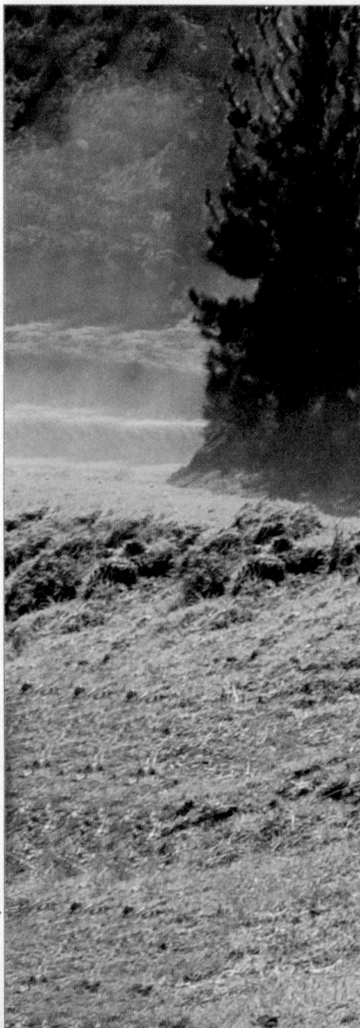

✓ Lesson Checkpoint

1. How does friction change the motion of an object?
2. **Put Things in Order** You want to ride your bike. Put the steps you should follow in order.

Lesson 4

How can simple machines help you do work?

Suppose you want to move an object. You might use a tool to help you. A machine is a tool that can make work easier. A **simple machine** is a tool with few or no moving parts.

A wheel and axle is a simple machine. A wheel and axle can help you move things.

A wedge is a simple machine that is used to push things apart.

A screw is a simple machine. A screw is used to hold things together.

A lever is a simple machine. It is used to move things. This screwdriver is used as a lever.

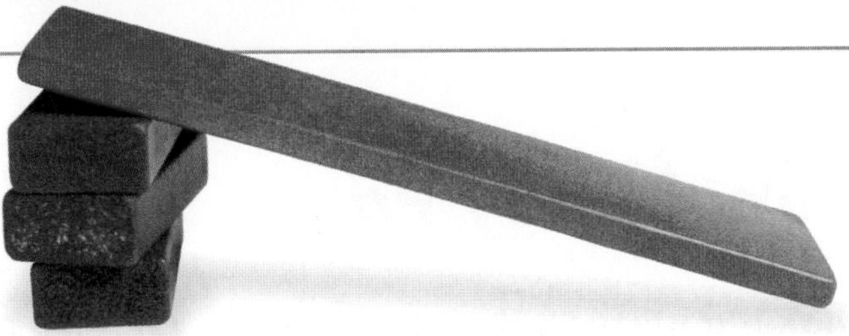

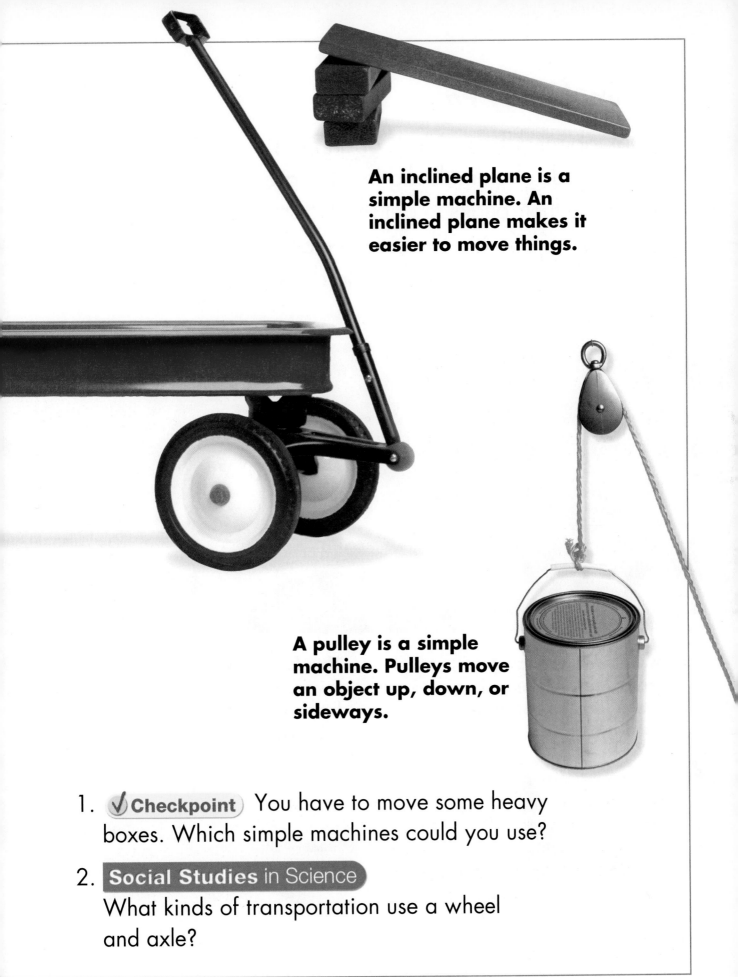

An inclined plane is a simple machine. An inclined plane makes it easier to move things.

A pulley is a simple machine. Pulleys move an object up, down, or sideways.

1. ✓Checkpoint You have to move some heavy boxes. Which simple machines could you use?

2. **Social Studies** in Science
   What kinds of transportation use a wheel and axle?

Animal Body Parts

Think about different kinds of animals. Some kinds of animals dig into the ground. Birds use their beaks to get food. Some body parts of animals are like simple machines. Animals use these body parts to do work.

A beaver has long front teeth. It uses its teeth like a wedge to cut into wood.

This bird's beak is like a lever. This bird uses its beak to scoop fish from the water.

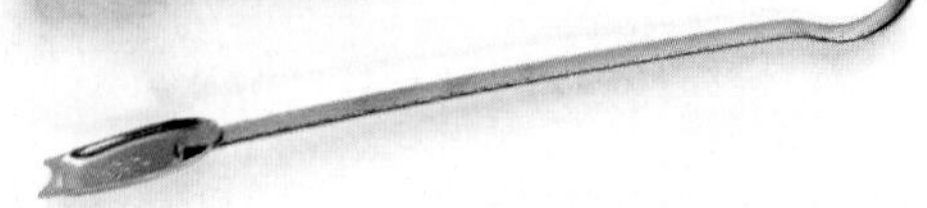

Lesson Checkpoint

1. How are a beaver's teeth like a simple machine?
2. **Technology** in Science Name some tools you use that are simple machines.

Badger claws are like wedges. The claws help the badger dig into the ground.

A rabbit can use its claws as wedges to dig into the ground. It can then use its claws and hind feet like shovels, or levers, to lift the dirt out.

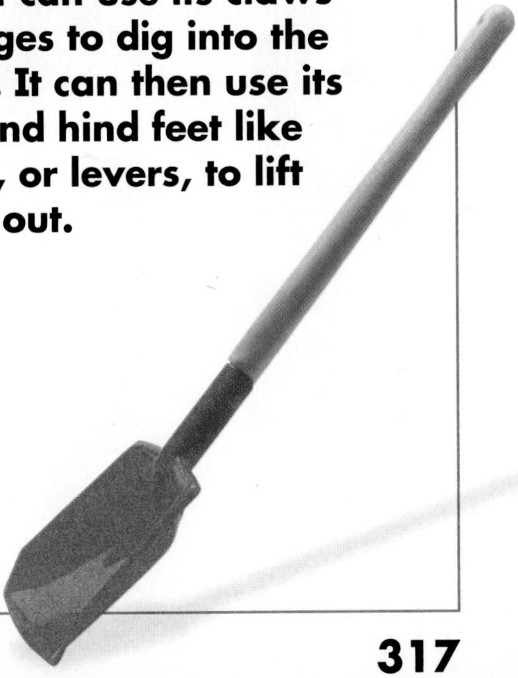

Lesson 5

What are magnets?

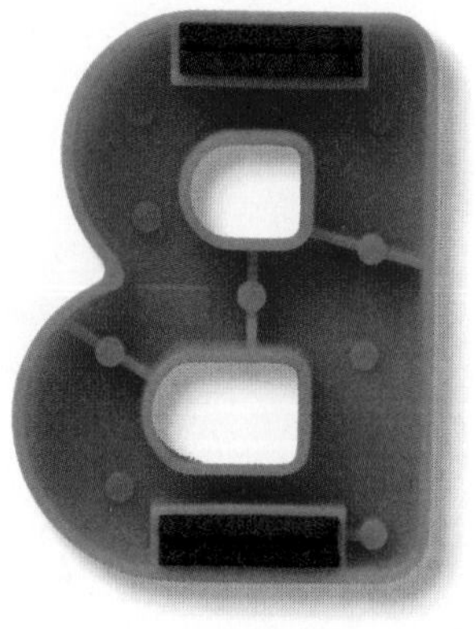

Magnets can push or pull certain metal objects. Magnets attract some metal objects. **Attract** means to pull toward. Magnets can repel other magnets. **Repel** means to push away.

Where have you seen magnets?

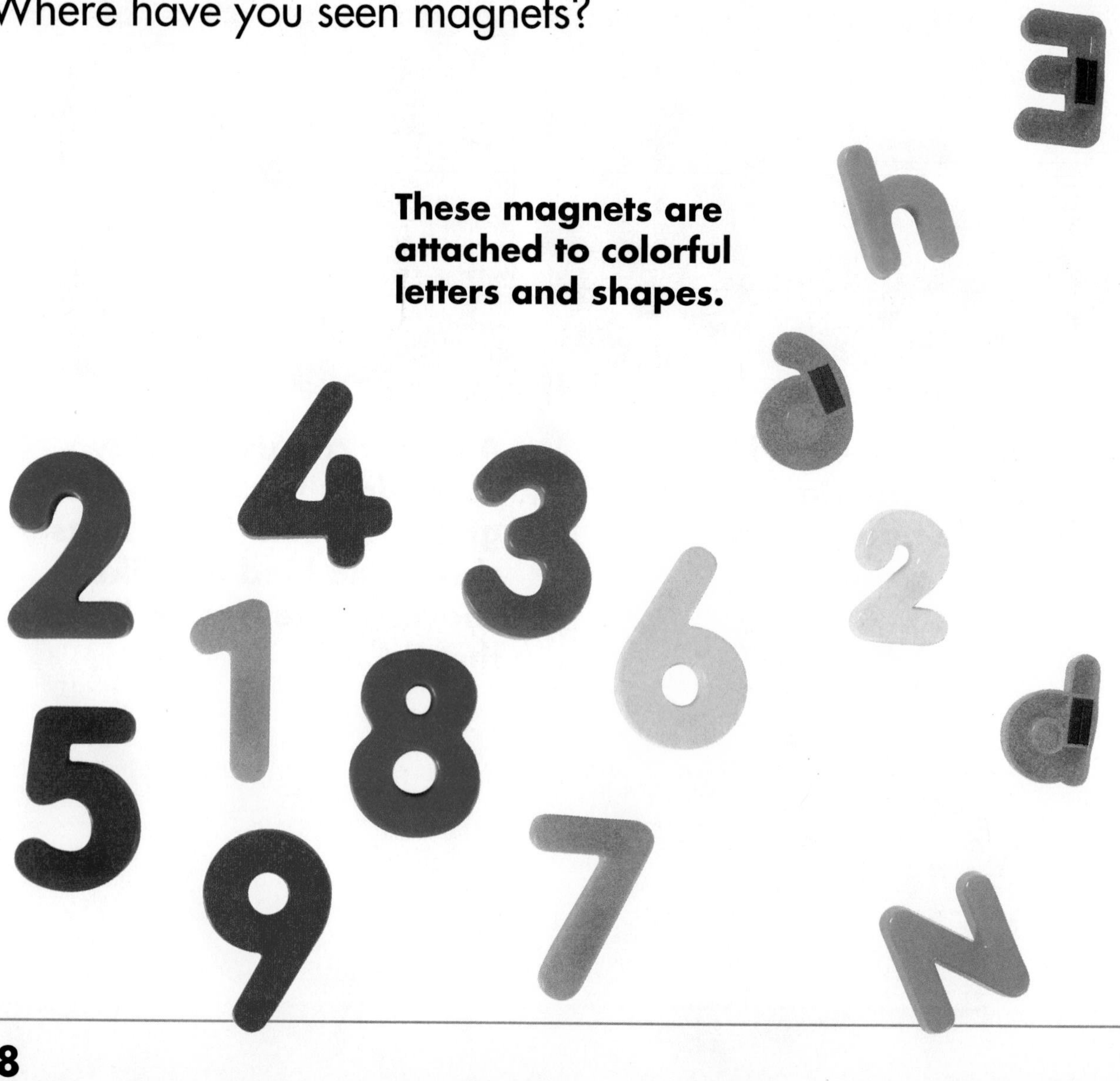

These magnets are attached to colorful letters and shapes.

Magnets have poles. The N stands for north pole. The S stands for south pole. A pole is the place on a magnet that has the strongest push or pull.

Like poles will repel when you put them together. The magnets will push away from each other. Opposite poles will attract when you put them together. The magnets will pull toward each other.

1. **Checkpoint** When do magnets repel each other?
2. **Art in Science** Draw a picture of how you can use a magnet. Label your picture.

What a Magnet Can Attract

You have learned that magnets attract some metal objects. Magnets will not attract all metal objects. A magnet will attract a nail. Some nails are made of iron. A magnet will not attract a penny. A penny is made of copper. Iron and copper are two kinds of metal.

You can use a magnet to find out which kinds of metal objects it will attract. Which objects in the picture do you think a magnet will attract?

Magnets do not attract marbles or a toothbrush.

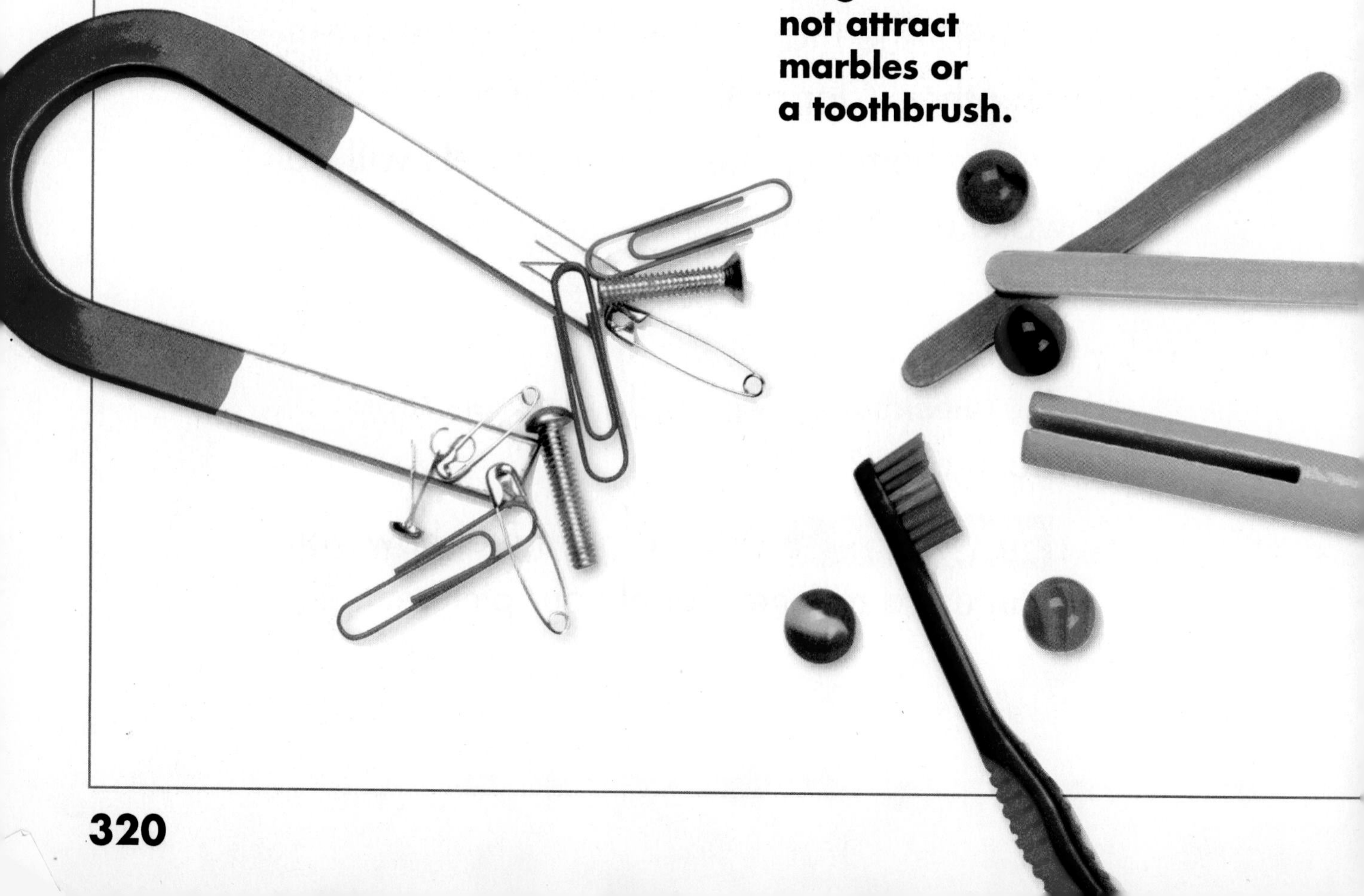

A magnet can move some things without even touching them. Look at the picture below. The force of the magnet moves this train.

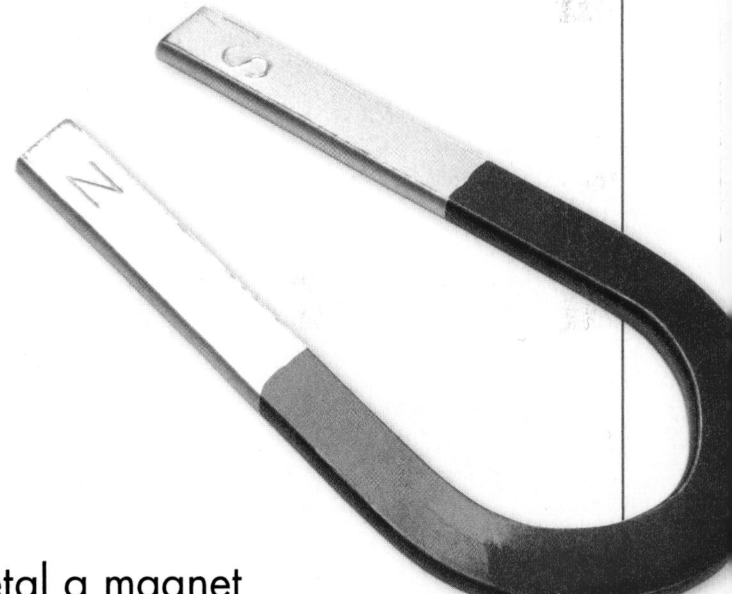

Lesson Checkpoint

1. What is one kind of metal a magnet will attract?
2. **Writing** in Science Make a list in your **science journal.** What are some objects a magnet will attract?

Lab zone **Guided Inquiry**

Investigate What can magnets do?

Materials

2 magnets

small objects

paper clip

plastic cup

cup with water

paper square

What to Do

1. Push the magnets together. What happens each time?

2. **Predict** which objects a magnet will pull. Try to pull each object.

Process Skills

When you **interpret data**, you use your chart to answer a question.

3 Try to pull a paper clip through things. Record what you **observe**.

Can a magnet pull through these things?

	Air	Plastic Cup	Water	Paper

	a gas	a solid	a liquid	a solid
yes				
no				

Explain Your Results

1. What objects did you predict a magnet would pull? Which objects did it pull?
2. **Interpret Data** What things could the magnet pull through?

Go Further

Can magnets pull objects through a piece of foil? Make a plan to find out.

Math in Science

Measuring Motion

You can measure how far something moves. The toy truck will roll farther with a higher ramp.

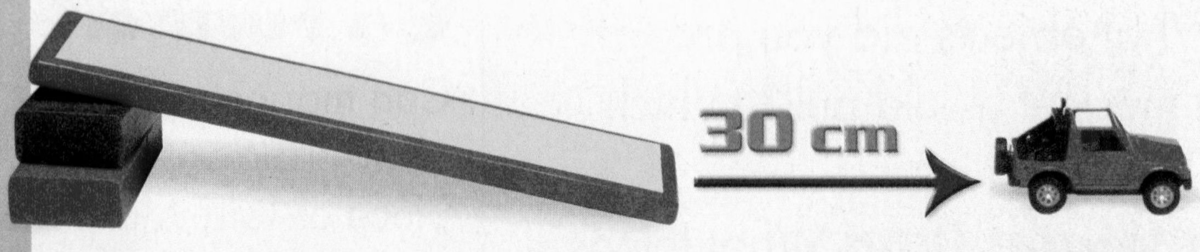

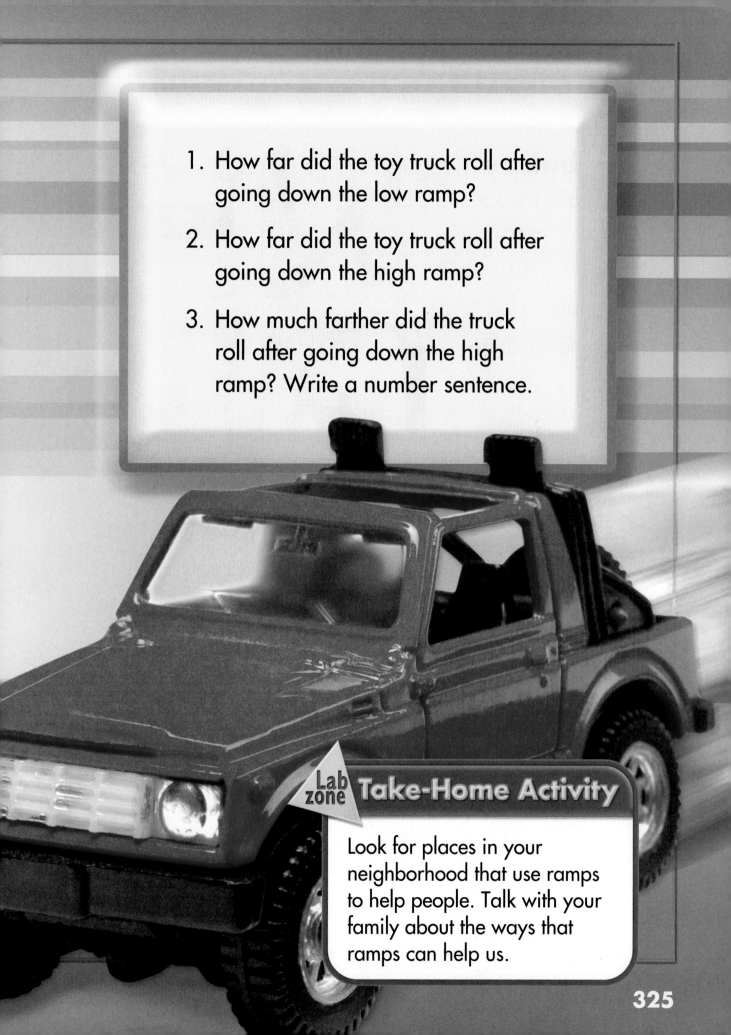

1. How far did the toy truck roll after going down the low ramp?
2. How far did the toy truck roll after going down the high ramp?
3. How much farther did the truck roll after going down the high ramp? Write a number sentence.

Lab zone **Take-Home Activity**

Look for places in your neighborhood that use ramps to help people. Talk with your family about the ways that ramps can help us.

Chapter 10 Review and Test Prep

Vocabulary

Which picture goes with each word?

1. force
2. motion
3. simple machine
4. attract
5. repel

A
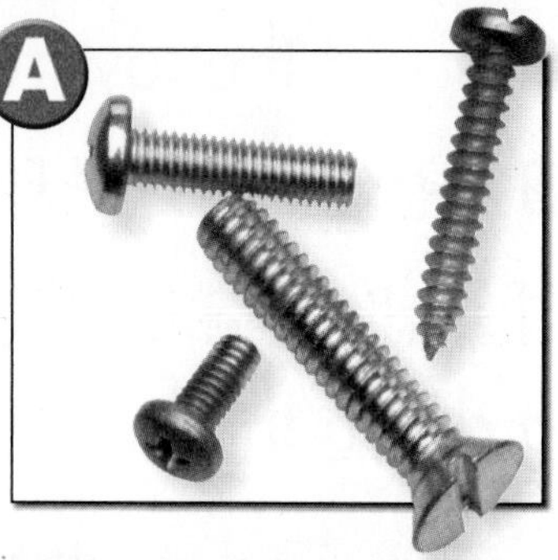

B

D

E

C

What did you learn?

6. Name two ways that objects can move.
7. What two things do you need for work to be done?
8. How does friction slow down a soccer ball on a grassy surface?

Process Skills

9. **Communicate** Does it take more force to pull a wagon full of books or an empty wagon? Tell why.

Put Things in Order

10. Tell how you could put the pictures in order.

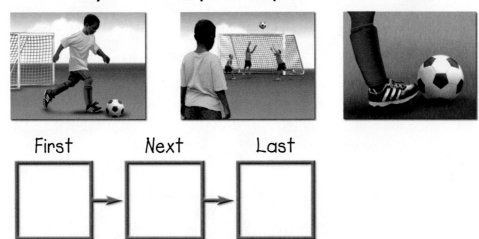

First → Next → Last

Test Prep

Fill in the circle next to the correct answer.

11. Which can be used as a lever?
 - Ⓐ a wagon
 - Ⓑ a slide
 - Ⓒ a screwdriver
 - Ⓓ a ramp

12. **Writing in Science** Write a sentence. Tell how you can make your friends move faster on a playground merry-go-round.

NASA Biography

Meet Luther Jenkins

Read Together

Luther Jenkins works at NASA. He is an Aerospace Engineer. He studies airplanes.

Math and science were Luther's favorite subjects in school. At first, Luther wanted to become a lawyer. He soon discovered that he liked to learn how things work. He decided to become an engineer.

At NASA, Luther uses math and science in his work. He uses wind tunnels to conduct experiments on airplanes. He works with special lasers to measure the speed of air.

Lab zone Take-Home Activity

Use the Internet or an encyclopedia to learn about the airplane flown by the Wright brothers in 1903. Draw a picture of their airplane.

EC CRU 10 9 8 7 6 5 4 3 2 1

You Will Discover

- how sounds can be different.
- how sound travels.

Chapter 11

Sound

Discovery Channel School
Student DVD

online
Student Edition
pearsonsuccessnet.com

Build Background

How is sound made?

Chapter 11 Vocabulary

vibrate page 335

loudness page 336

pitch page 338

Lab zone Directed Inquiry

Explore How can you make sound?

Materials

safety goggles

ruler

What to Do

1. Push down on one end of the ruler. Let go. **Observe**. What do you hear?

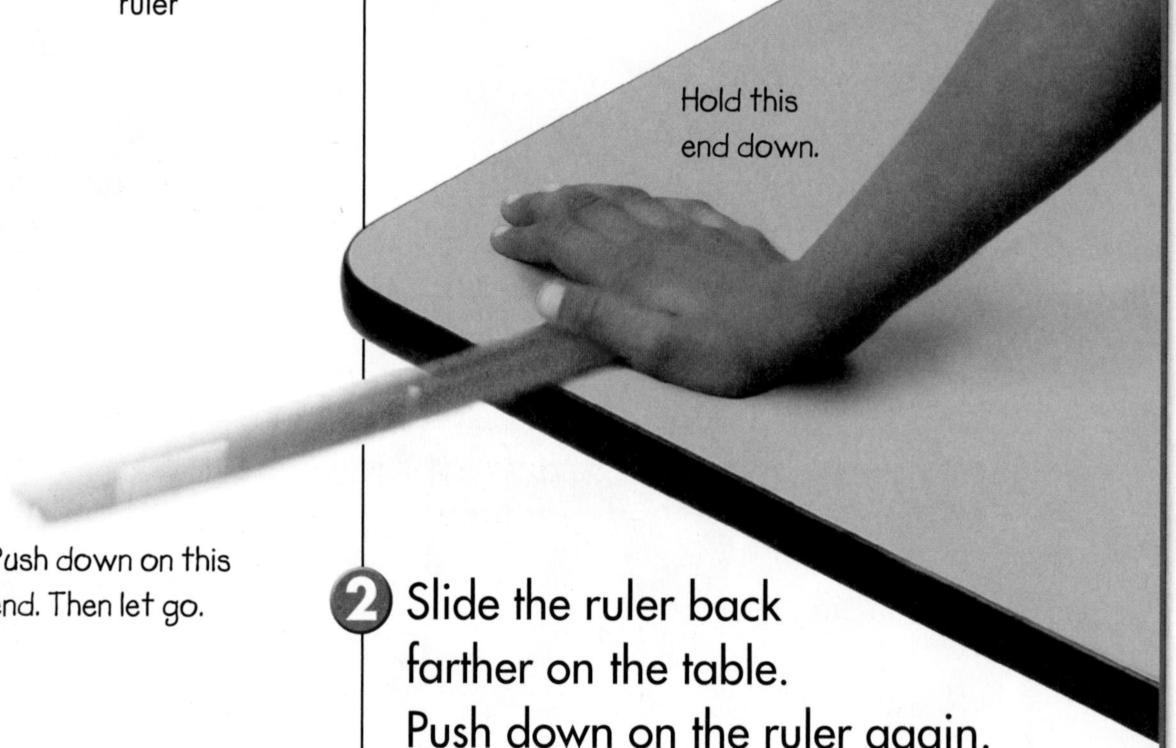

Push down on this end. Then let go.

2. Slide the ruler back farther on the table. Push down on the ruler again. What do you hear?

Explain Your Results

Observe Think about what your heard. How did the sound change when you moved the ruler back?

Process Skills

When you **observe**, you use one or more of your five senses.

How to Read Science

Reading Skills

Important Details

Important details are the words that tell you what you need to know.

Science Article

Sounds

Instruments can make soft sounds or loud sounds. Some instruments that make loud sounds are drums, cymbals, and tubas. Some instruments that make soft sounds are flutes, violins, and triangles.

Apply It!

Observe Read the article and look at the picture. What are some instruments that make soft sounds?

You Are There

Listen to the Sounds!

Sung to the tune of "Sidewalks of New York"
Lyrics by Gerri Brioso & Richard Freitas/The Dovetail Group, Inc.

Soft sounds, loud sounds,
High sounds and some low.
Listen for sounds all around you
Everywhere that you may go.

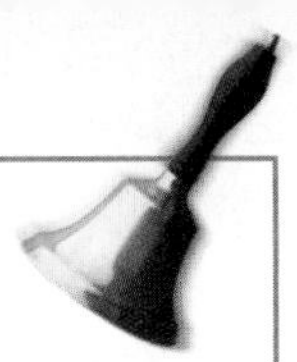

Lesson 1

What is sound?

There are many different instruments in a marching band. Each instrument makes a different sound when it is played.

How is sound made? Sound is made when an object vibrates. **Vibrate** means to move quickly back and forth. The instruments make the air vibrate to make sounds.

Loudness

One way to describe sound is by its loudness. **Loudness** means how loud or soft a sound is.

Suppose you hit a drum very hard. You would make a loud sound. The pictures on this page show things that can make loud sounds.

Suppose you lightly tapped a drum. You would make a soft sound. The pictures on this page show things that can make soft sounds.

Soft

✓ Lesson Checkpoint

1. What does *loudness* mean?
2. **Writing** in Science Think of one soft sound and one loud sound. Write two sentences in your **science journal** to explain how these sounds are different.

Lesson 2

What is pitch?

Pitch is another way to describe sound. **Pitch** means how high or low a sound is. Objects that vibrate quickly make a sound with a high pitch. Objects that vibrate slowly make a sound with a low pitch.

The air inside a bottle vibrates when you blow air across the bottle. Bottles with a lot of air make sounds with a low pitch. Bottles with less air make sounds with a higher pitch.

Lesson Checkpoint

1. What does *pitch* mean?
2. **Important Details** How does the way objects vibrate change pitch?

The bird makes sounds that have a high pitch. The bullfrog makes sounds that have a low pitch.

Which bottle makes the sound with the highest pitch?

Lesson 3

How does sound travel?

Sound travels through solids, liquids, and gases. Sound travels through gases such as air.

A woodpecker pecks at a tree. The sound moves through both the tree and the air.

A lion's roar travels through the air.

Sound travels faster through liquids, such as water, than it does through air. Sound travels fastest through solids such as wood or metal.

Dolphins whistle and click. Their sounds move through water.

Lesson Checkpoint

1. Does sound travel faster through air or water?
2. **Art in Science** Draw a picture of an animal that is making a sound. Write a sentence that tells about the sound.

Lesson 4

How do some animals make sounds?

Animals make sounds in many ways. The pictures show some ways animals use parts of their bodies to make sounds.

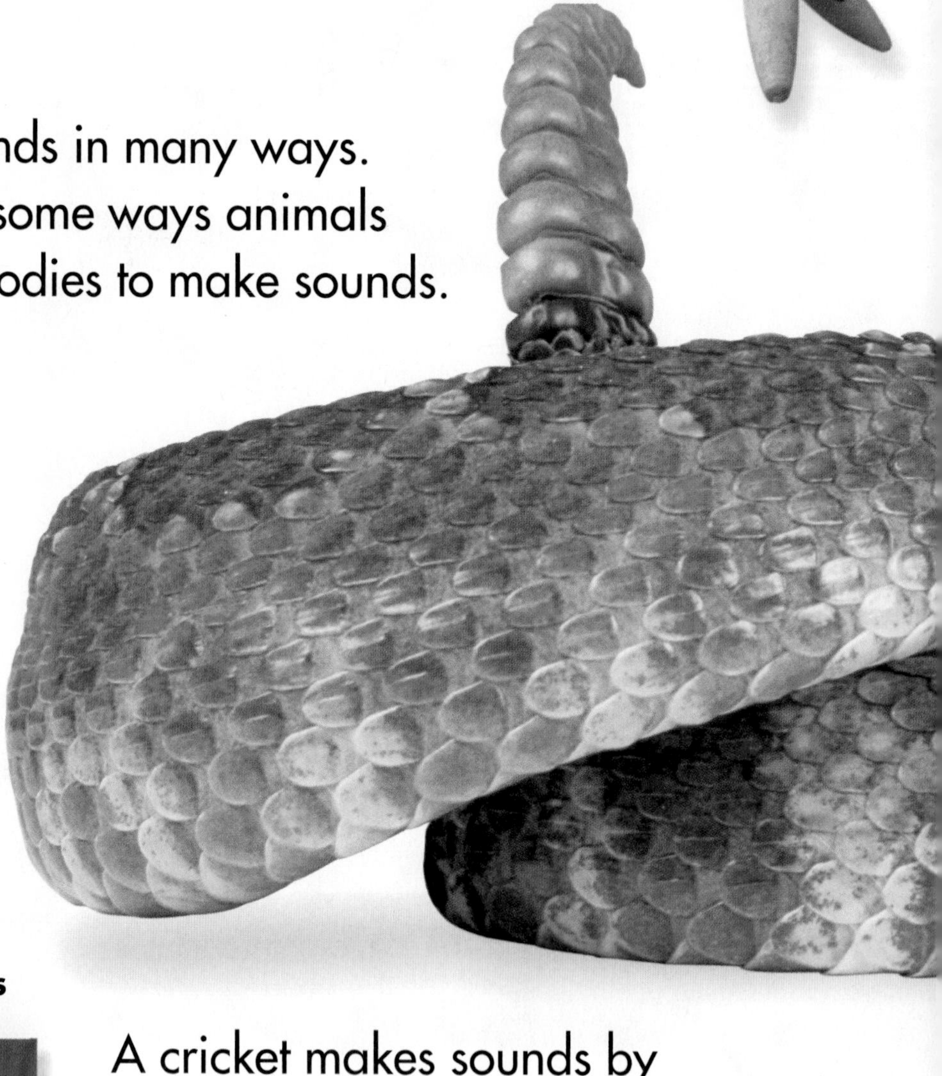

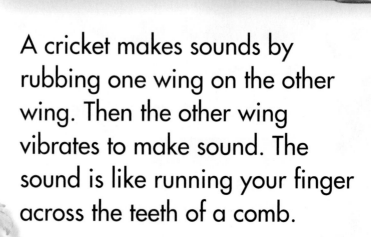

A cricket makes sounds by rubbing one wing on the other wing. Then the other wing vibrates to make sound. The sound is like running your finger across the teeth of a comb.

A rattlesnake makes sounds like maracas. The snake shakes the rattle in its tail.

A spiny lobster makes sounds like a violin. The violin is played by rubbing the bow against the strings. The lobster uses its antenna like a bow. It rubs its antenna along the side of its head.

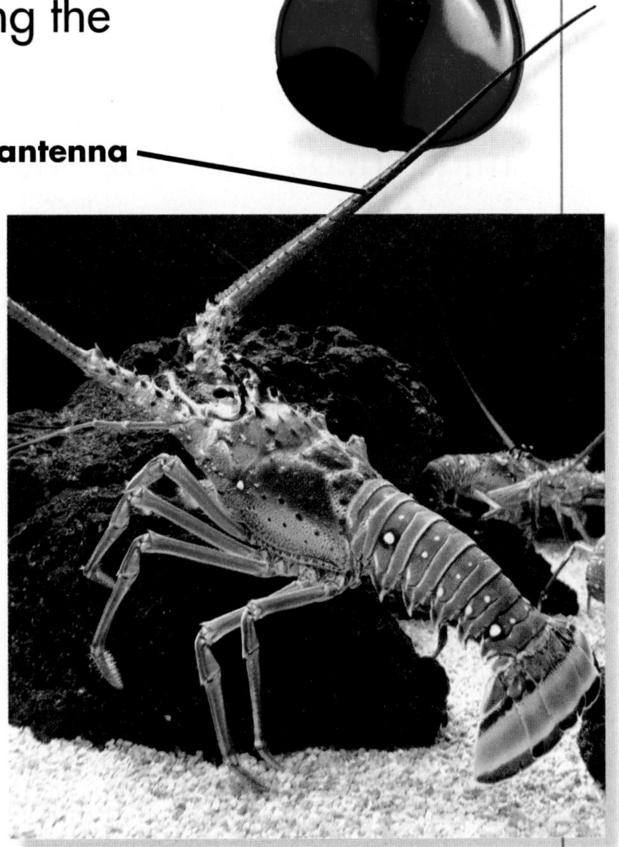

Lesson Checkpoint

1. What instrument does a spiny lobster sound like?
2. **Important Details** How does a cricket make sounds?

Lesson 5

What are some sounds around you?

Listen closely to the sounds around you. You might hear a siren or a group of children laughing. You might hear a fly buzz as it goes by. We hear many different sounds every day. Look at the picture. What sounds might the people and the objects in the picture make?

1. **Checkpoint** What kinds of sounds do you hear in your neighborhood?
2. **Writing in Science** Write one or two sentences in your **science journal.** Tell what sounds you might hear at your school.

RAIL ROAD
CROSSING
RAIL ROAD
CROSSING

Lab zone Guided Inquiry

Investigate How can you change sound?

Materials

safety goggles

rubber band

tissue box

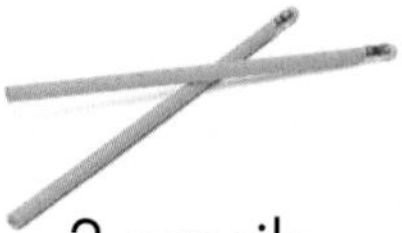
2 pencils

What to Do

1. Put the rubber band around the box. Put 2 pencils under the rubber band.

Be careful! Wear your safety goggles.

2. Pluck the rubber band hard. Then pluck gently.

3. Fill in the chart. **Infer**. What changes the sound?

	Is the sound loud or soft?
Hard plucks	
Gentle plucks	

Process Skills

When you **predict**, you tell what you think will happen.

4 Pluck the rubber band again. Move the pencils farther apart. **Predict** whether the sound will be higher or lower. Pluck the rubber band again.

5 Fill in the chart.

	Is the sound high or low?
Pencils close	
Pencils far apart	

Go Further

What other things can you do to change the sound? Investigate to find out.

Explain Your Results

1. What made the sound high? What made the sound loud?
2. **Infer** How could you make a soft, low sound?

Math in Science

Measuring Sounds

This bar graph compares the loudness of some sounds. A vacuum cleaner is much louder than a whisper.

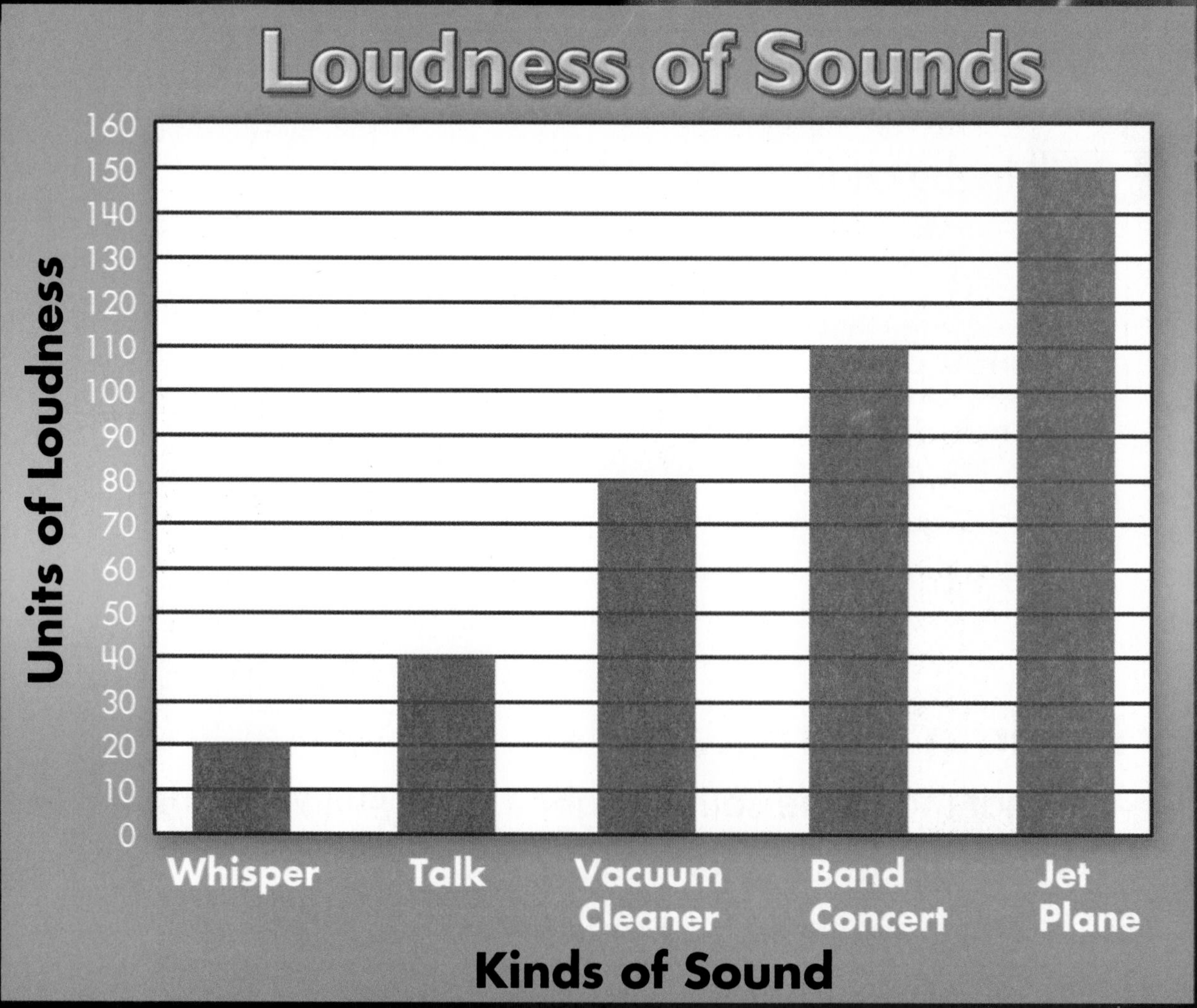

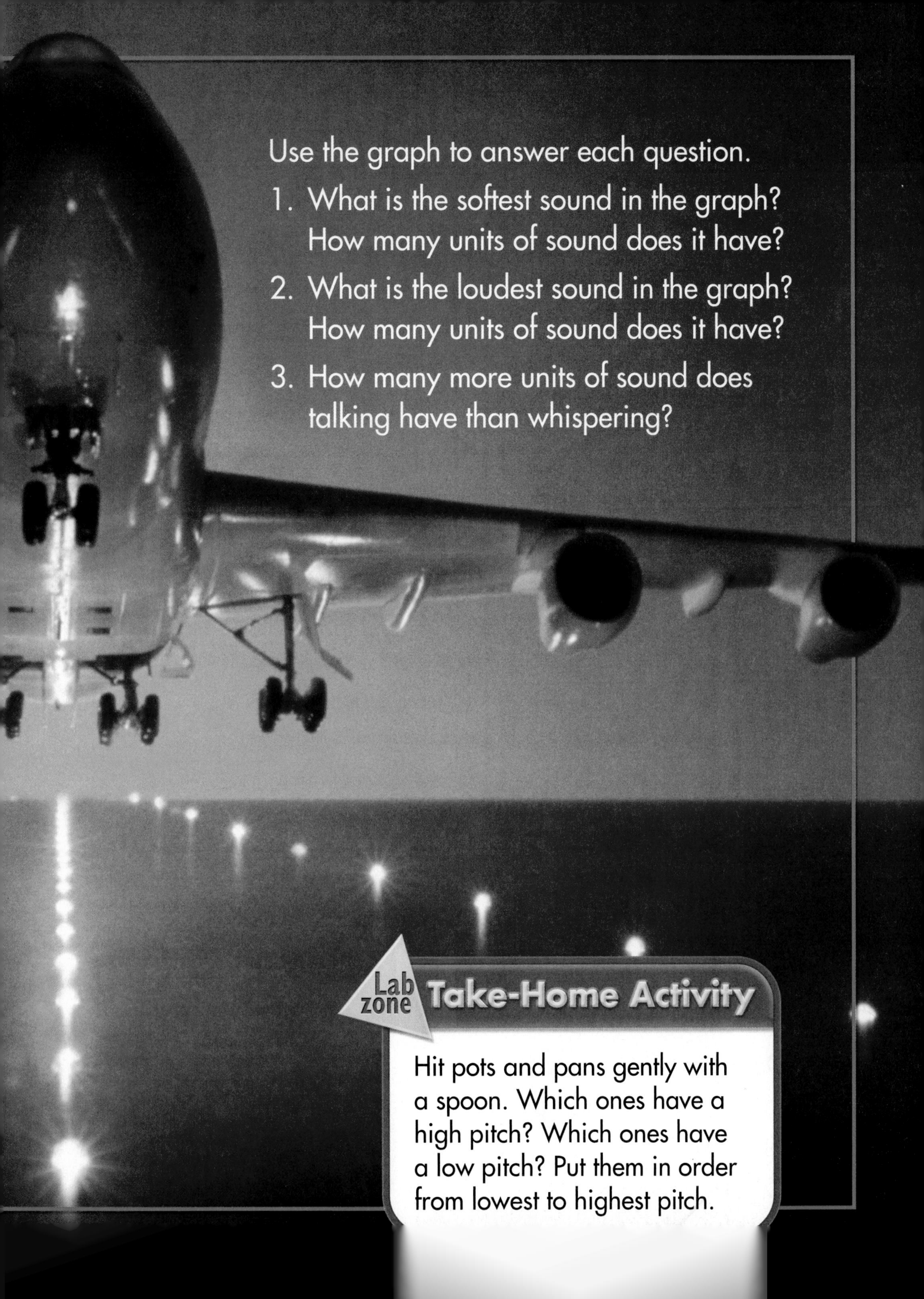

Use the graph to answer each question.

1. What is the softest sound in the graph? How many units of sound does it have?
2. What is the loudest sound in the graph? How many units of sound does it have?
3. How many more units of sound does talking have than whispering?

Lab zone Take-Home Activity

Hit pots and pans gently with a spoon. Which ones have a high pitch? Which ones have a low pitch? Put them in order from lowest to highest pitch.

Chapter 11 Review and Test Prep

Vocabulary

Which picture goes with each word?

1. pitch

2. vibrate

A

B

What did you learn?

3. What word describes how loud or soft a sound is?

4. What does *vibrate* mean?

5. Does sound travel fastest through solids, liquids, or gases?

Process Skills

6. **Observe** Think about lunch time at your school. What sounds might you hear?

Important Details

7. What are some words you can use to describe sound?

A

B

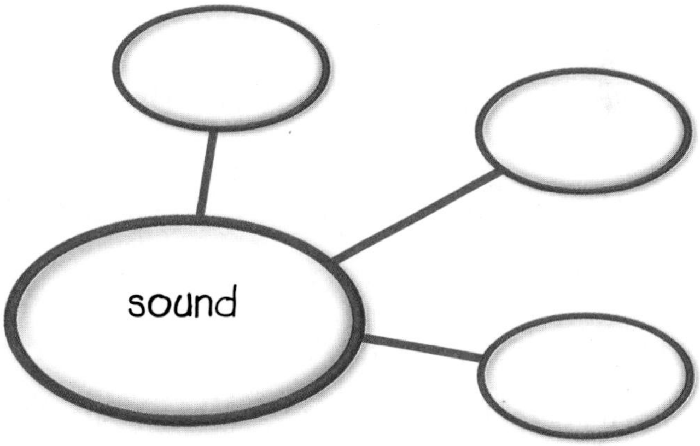

Test Prep

Fill in the circle next to the correct answer.

8. Which is made when an object vibrates quickly?

   Ⓐ low pitch sound
   Ⓑ high pitch sound
   Ⓒ soft sound
   Ⓓ loud sound

9. **Writing in Science** Choose an animal. Tell about how that animal makes sounds.

Biography

Alejandro Purgue

Dr. Purgue is an animal scientist.

Read Together

Alejandro Purgue studies animals and the sounds they make. People and many animals make sounds using vocal chords in their throats.

While Dr. Purgue was studying bullfrogs, he made an amazing discovery. Bullfrogs actually make most of their sound through their ears!

Like other animals, bullfrogs also use their ears for hearing. Think about this amazing fact the next time you hear a frog **ribbit!**

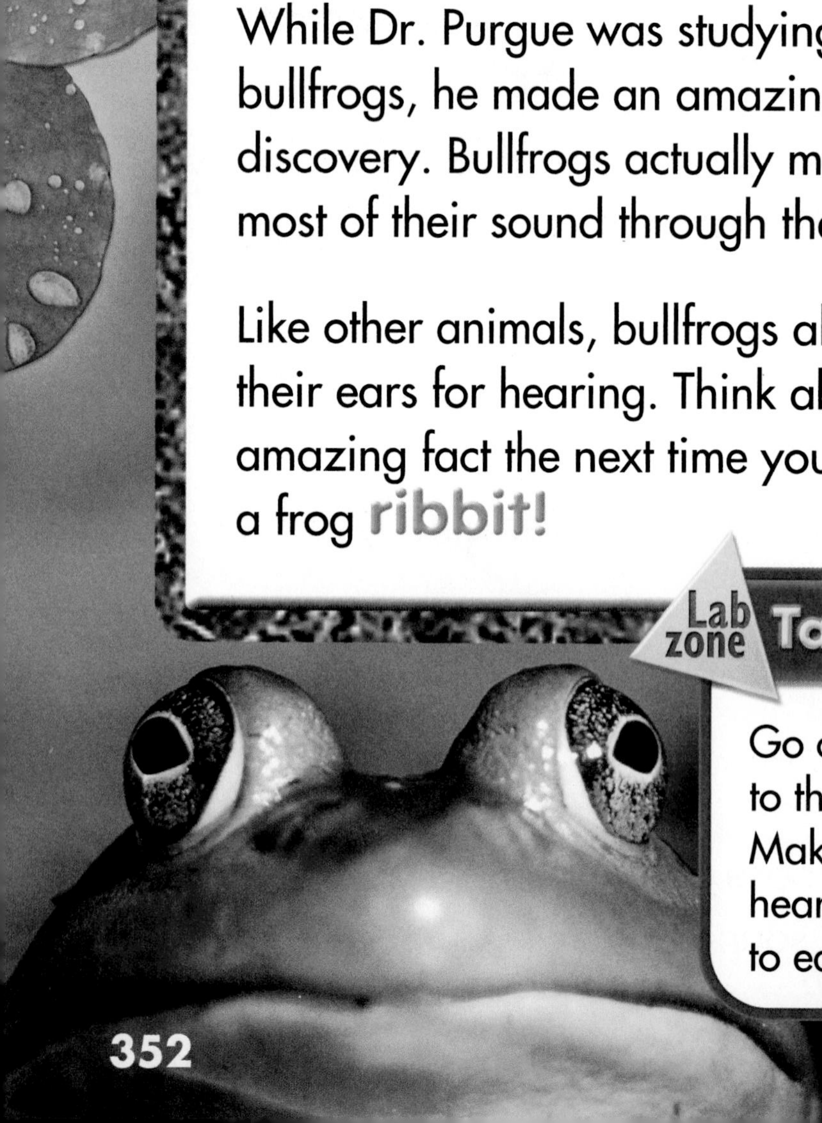

Lab zone Take-Home Activity

Go outside at home and listen to the sounds around you. Make a list of the sounds you hear. Write *quiet* or *loud* next to each sound.

Unit C Test Talk

Test-Taking Strategies

- Find Important Words
- ▷ Choose the Right Answer
- Use Information from Text and Graphics
- Write Your Answer

Choose the Right Answer

Remove wrong answer choices to help you choose the right answer.

Lunch

Emil made himself lunch. He used bread, peanut butter, and jelly to make a sandwich. Emil poured juice to drink.

Which state of matter is juice?

Ⓐ bread
Ⓑ solid
Ⓒ liquid
Ⓓ jelly

Your answer should be a state of matter. Find the two answers that are states of matter. Which one answers the question?

Unit C Wrap-Up

Chapter 8

What are some properties of matter?

- Some properties of matter are color, shape, and size. Mass and how it feels are also properties of matter.

Chapter 9

What are some kinds of energy?

- Solar energy, light, and electricity are some kinds of energy.

Chapter 10

How do forces cause objects to move?

- The amount of force used on an object affects how far and how fast the object moves.

Chapter 11

How is sound made?

- Sound is made when an object vibrates.
- Loudness is how loud or soft a sound is.
- Pitch is how high or low a sound is.

3 Test the other objects. Record. Do steps 1 and 2 again.

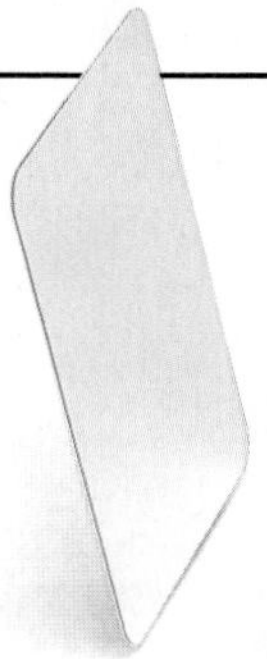
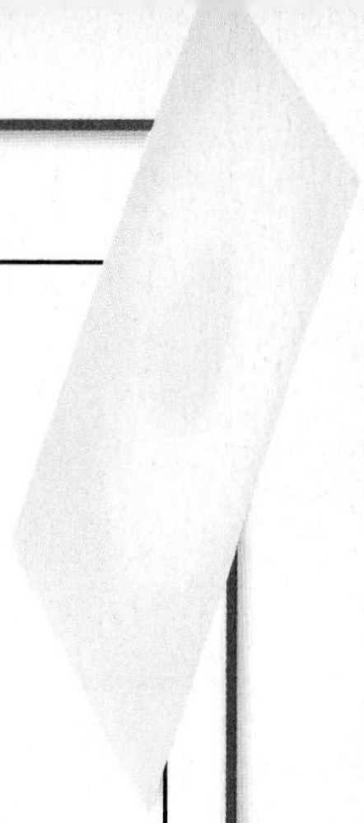

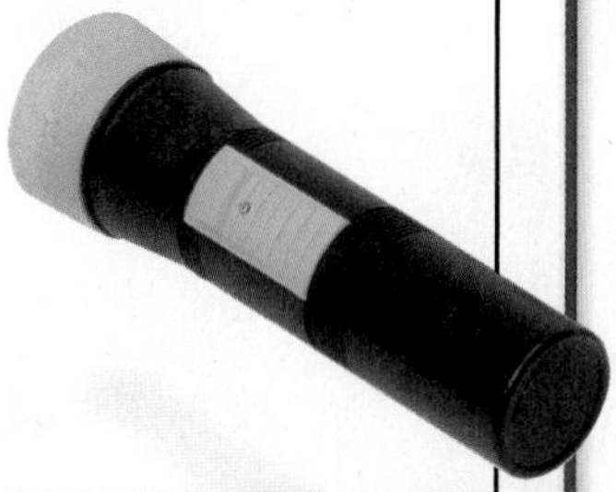

Collect and record data.

	Is it smooth? yes or no	**Is it shiny?** yes or no	**Does it reflect light clearly?** yes or no

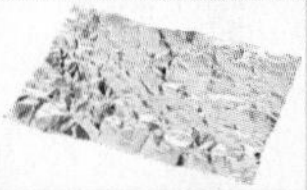			

Tell Your Conclusion.

Do smooth and shiny objects reflect light clearly? How do you know?

Go Further

What might happen if you test other classroom objects? Experiment to find out.

Apple Shadows

by Patricia Hubbell

Out in the orchard
what do I see?

Apples
and their shadows
high on every tree,

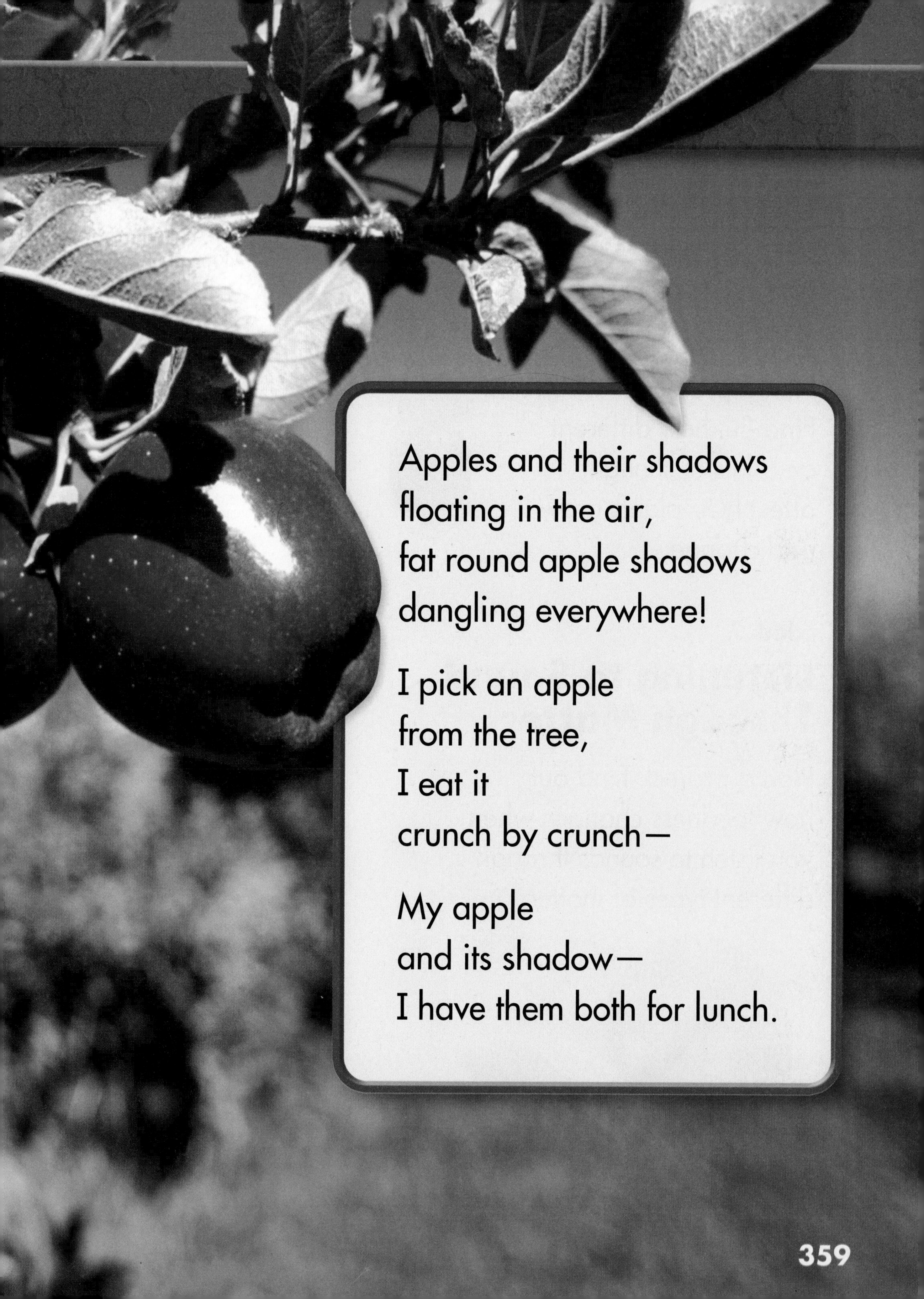

Apples and their shadows
floating in the air,
fat round apple shadows
dangling everywhere!

I pick an apple
from the tree,
I eat it
crunch by crunch—

My apple
and its shadow—
I have them both for lunch.

Science Fair Projects

Full Inquiry

Using Scientific Methods

1. Ask a question.
2. Make a hypothesis.
3. Plan a fair test.
4. Do your test.
5. Collect and record data.
6. Tell your conclusions.
7. Go further.

Idea 1

Energy in My Terrarium

Plan a project.
Find out how different amounts of sunlight affect how plants grow and change.

Idea 2

Listening to Sound Through Matter

Plan a project. Find out how loudness changes when you listen to sounds through different types of matter.

EC CRU 10 9 8 7 6 5 4 3 2 1

Unit D

Space and Technology in Illinois

Do you know that many trains go through Illinois? Technology has changed the trains. People can go to the Illinois Railway Museum to see how trains have changed.

Space and Technology in Illinois

How are the seasons, the stars, and Mae Jemison alike? They can all be found in Illinois. You will learn more about the science behind them in Unit D.

Seasons in Illinois

Each season is different in Illinois. The Earth moves around the Sun every year. The number of hours of daylight changes during the seasons. You will learn more about seasons in Chapter 12.

Amount of Daylight in Springfield

Season	Length of Daylight
First day of summer	About 15 hours
First day of fall	About 12 hours, 10 minutes
First day of winter	About 9 hours, 21 minutes
First day of spring	About 12 hours, 12 minutes

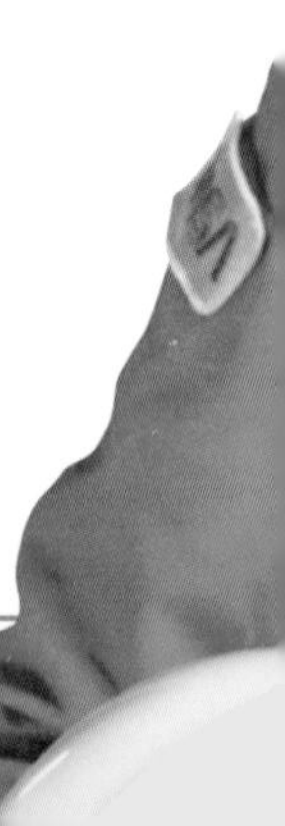

Staerkel Planetarium

The second largest planetarium in Illinois is in Champaign. People there like looking at stars and planets. You can see many stars when you look up at the dome of the planetarium. You will learn more about the night sky in Chapter 12.

Mae Jemison

Mae Jemison grew up in Chicago. She flew on the space shuttle *Endeavor* in 1992. Today, Jemison is using space technology to help sick people. You will learn more about space in Chapter 12.

You will learn more about technology in Chapter 13.

ISAT Prep

Answer the questions below. Write your answers on a separate sheet of paper.

Multiple-Choice Questions

1 During the winter, the days

A. get shorter.
B. stay the same.
C. get darker.
D. get longer.

2 How is Mae Jemison using space technology today?

A. to help sick people
B. to fly in space
C. to write letters home to Chicago
D. to do science experiments

Short-Response Questions

3 In what ways are the seasons different?

4 What can you see on the dome of Staerkel Planetarium?

5 Which day on the chart has the most hours of daylight?

ILLINOIS

Field Trip

Illinois Railway Museum

The Illinois Railway Museum is in Union. It is the largest railway museum in America. You can see how technology changed trains over time.

In the early 1800s, the first train traveled at a speed of about 8 kilometers per hour. The graph below shows the speeds of three trains today.

Find out more:

Research to find out more about trains in Illinois.

- Draw a picture of the train. Tell how fast your train goes.
- Plan a trip on a train. Make a schedule for your trip.

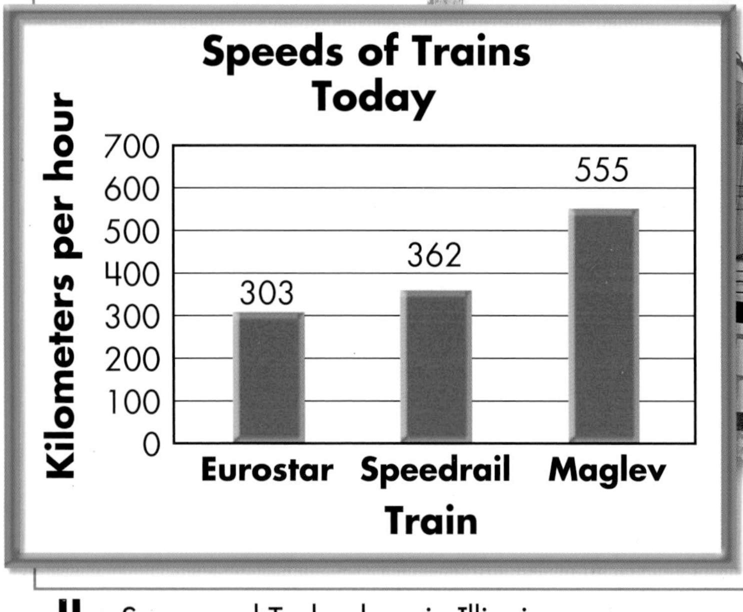

IL CRU 10 9 8 7 6 5 4 3 2 1

You Will Discover

- what is in the day and night sky.
- how Earth, the Sun, and the Moon move.

Chapter 12
Earth and Space

Discovery Channel School Student DVD

online Student Edition
pearsonsuccessnet.com

Build Background

What are some ways the Earth moves?

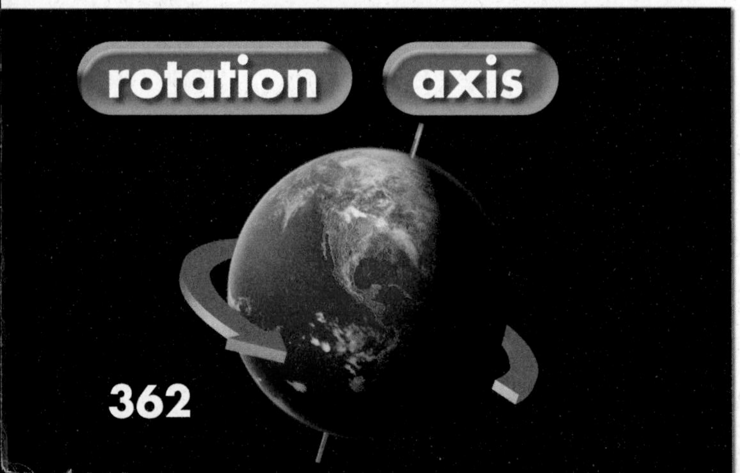

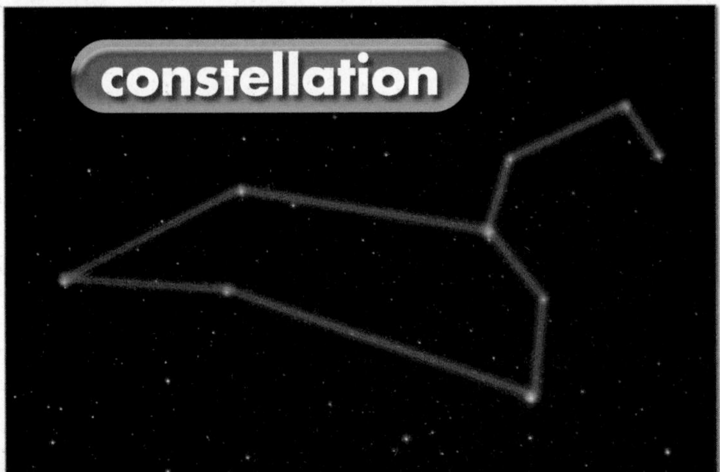

Chapter 12 Vocabulary

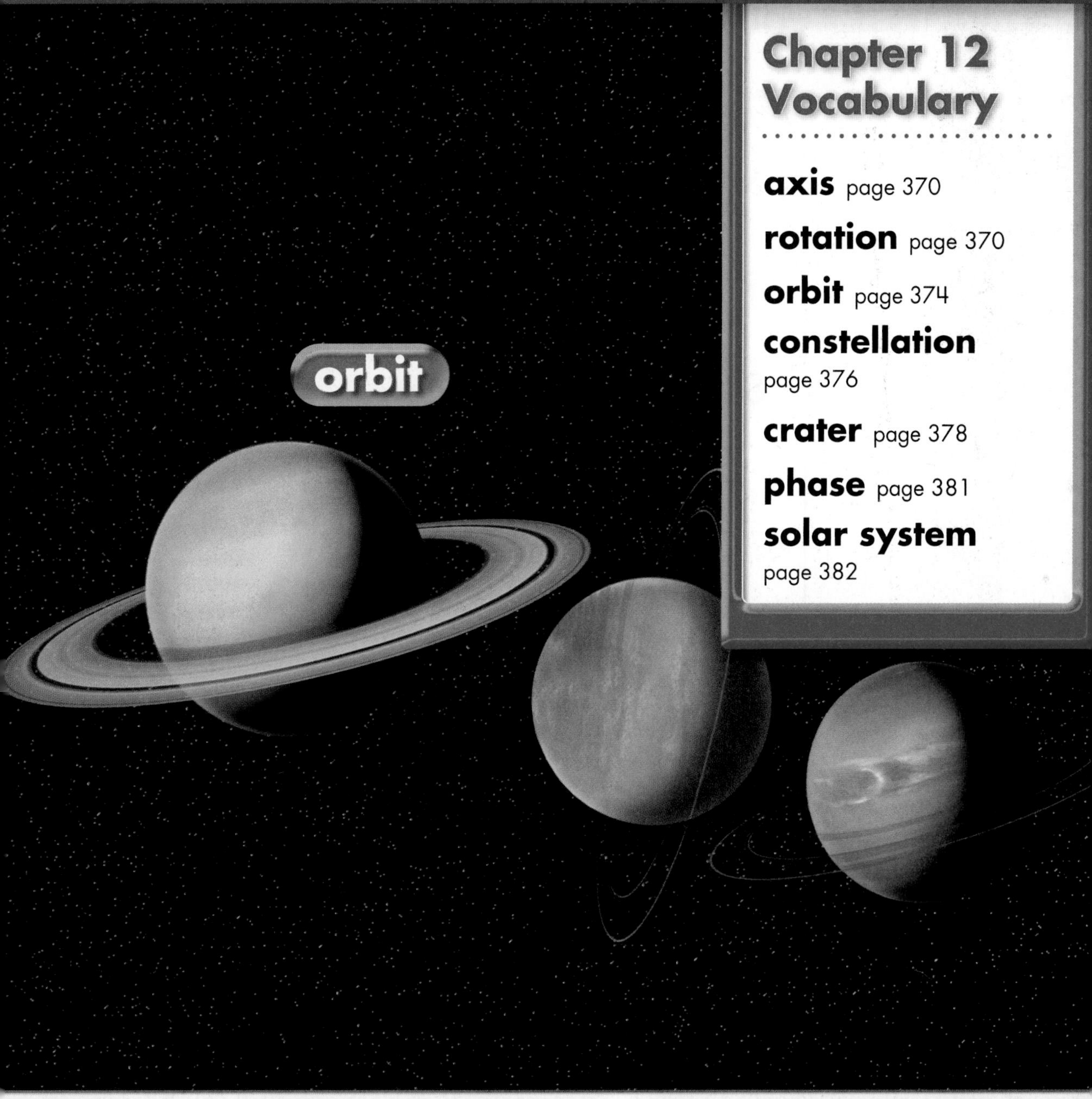

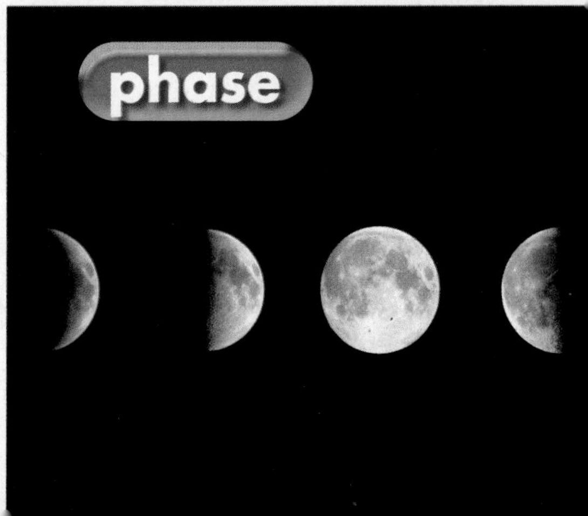

Lab zone Directed Inquiry

Explore What causes day and night?

Materials

foam ball

pencil

dot sticker

crayons or markers

flashlight

What to Do

1. **Make a model** of Earth.

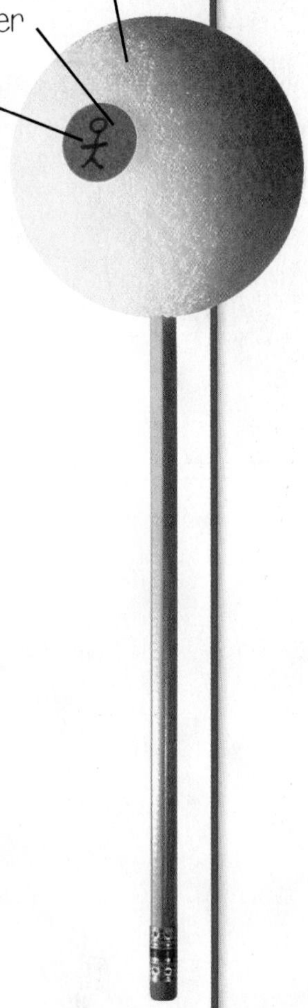

2. Shine a flashlight on your model.

The flashlight is like the Sun.

3. Turn your model of Earth. Watch the child.

Process Skills

You can use **models** of Earth and the Sun to understand what causes day and night.

Explain Your Results

How does your **model** show day and night?

How to Read Science

Reading Skills

Target Skill

Alike and Different

Alike means how things are the same.
Different means how things are not the same.

Science Pictures

Day and Night

Apply It!
Look at the pictures.
Tell how day and night are alike and different.
Think of your **model** to help you.

Alike	Different

You Are There

The Sun

Sung to the tune of "Twinkle Twinkle Little Star"
Lyrics by Gerri Brioso & Richard Freitas/The Dovetail Group, Inc.

In the sky's a great big star.
It's the Sun and it's real far!
The Sun lights up the sky so bright.
It also lights the Moon at night.
Heat and light come from the Sun
And that is needed by everyone!

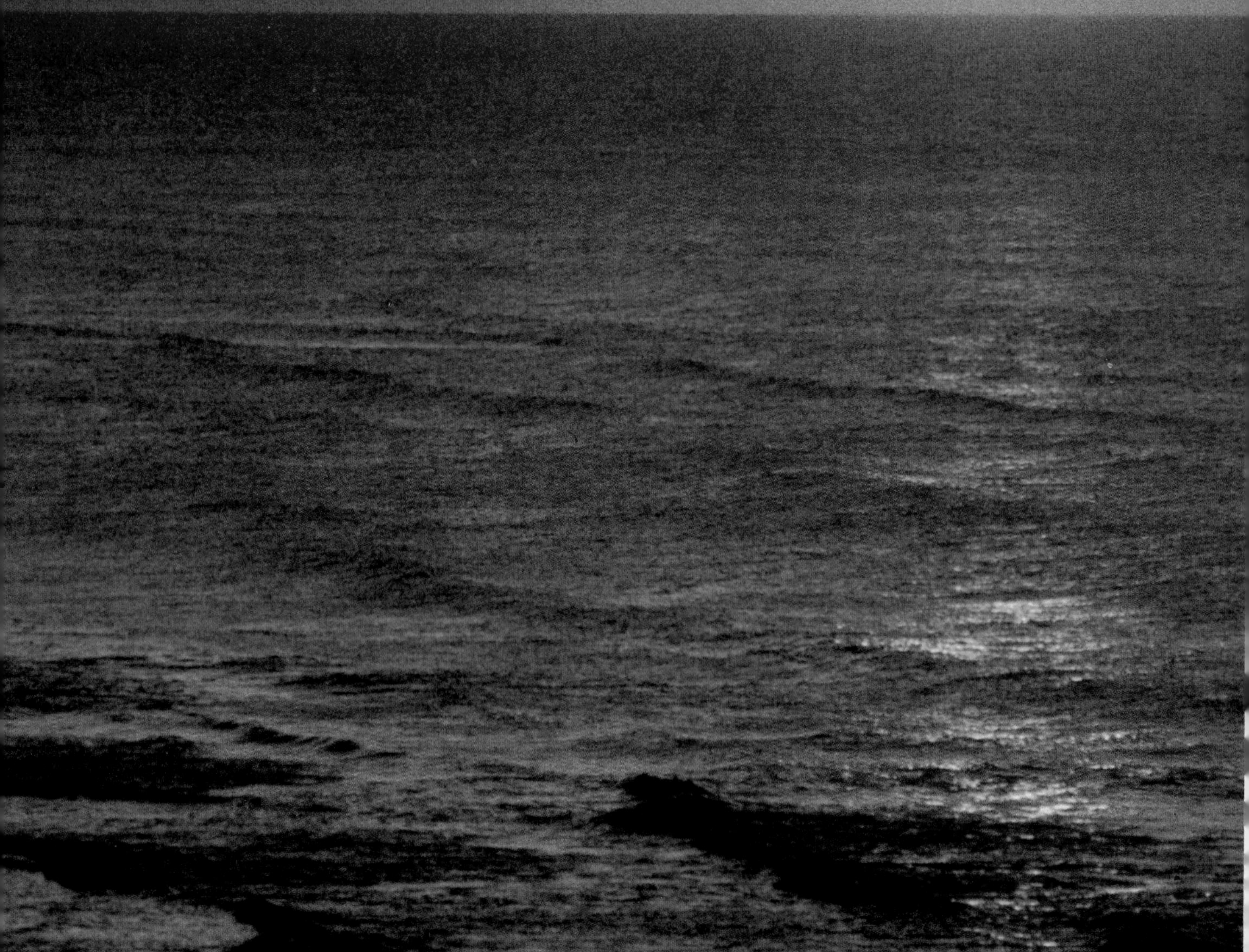

Lesson 1

What is the Sun?

Think of the stars you see in the sky at night. Stars are made of hot, glowing gases. The Sun is a star too. The Sun seems brighter and larger than the other stars. This is because the Sun is the closest star to Earth. The Sun is so bright that you cannot see other stars during the day.

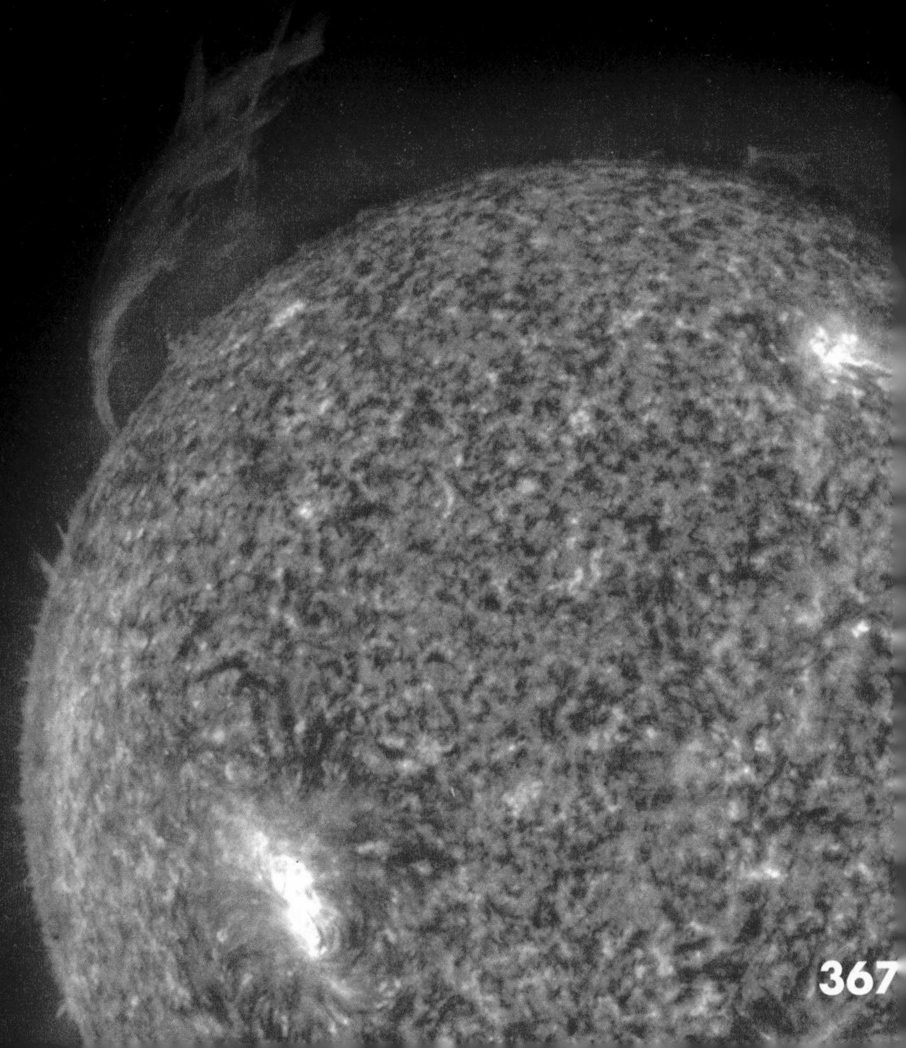

Why We Need the Sun

The Sun may look small, but it is really very big. The Sun is much bigger than Earth. The Sun looks small because it is so far away.

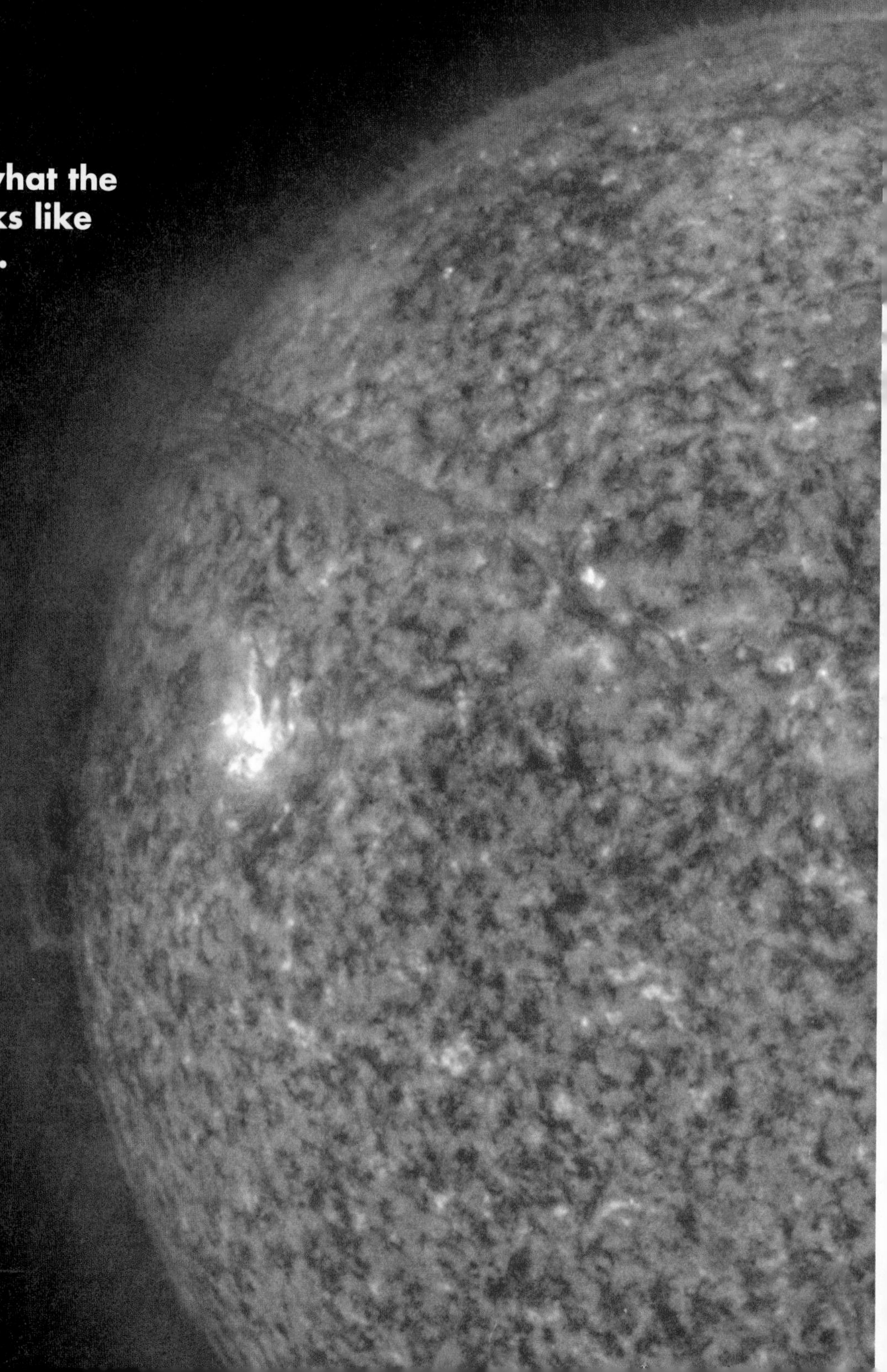

This is what the Sun looks like in space.

The Sun is important to Earth. Earth gets light and heat from the Sun. Living things on Earth need light and heat. People, plants, and animals can live on Earth because of the Sun.

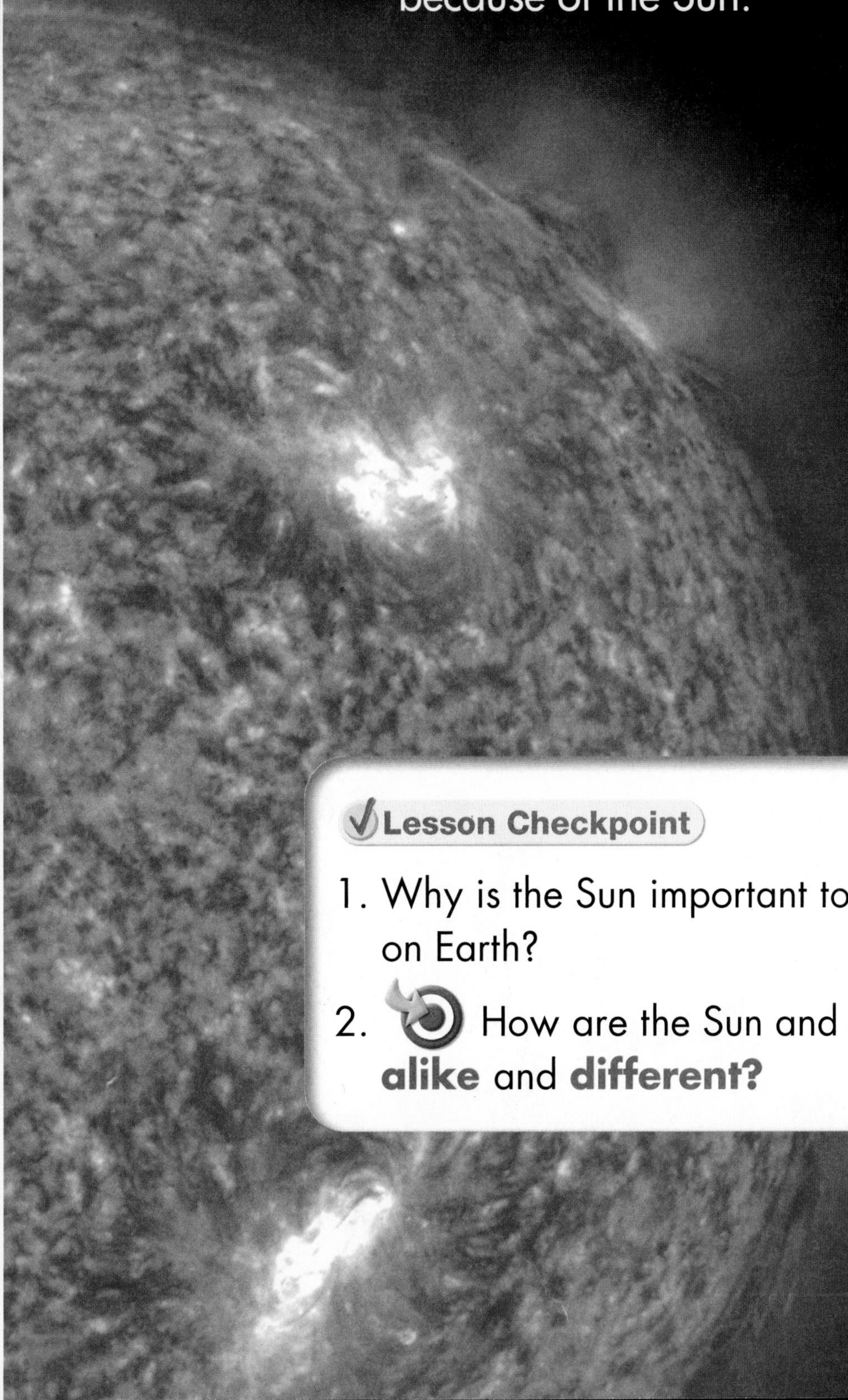

Lesson Checkpoint

1. Why is the Sun important to living things on Earth?
2. How are the Sun and other stars **alike** and **different?**

Lesson 2

What causes day and night?

The picture shows an imaginary line through the center of Earth. This line is called an **axis.** Earth is always spinning on its axis. This spinning on an axis is called a **rotation.** Earth makes one complete rotation each day.

Earth's rotation causes day and night. When your side of Earth is facing the Sun, you have day. When your side of Earth is facing away from the Sun, you have night.

Checkpoint

1. What is Earth's axis?
2. **Writing in Science** Write 2 sentences in your **science journal.** Tell why one side of Earth has day when the other side has night.

It takes about 24 hours for Earth to make one complete rotation.

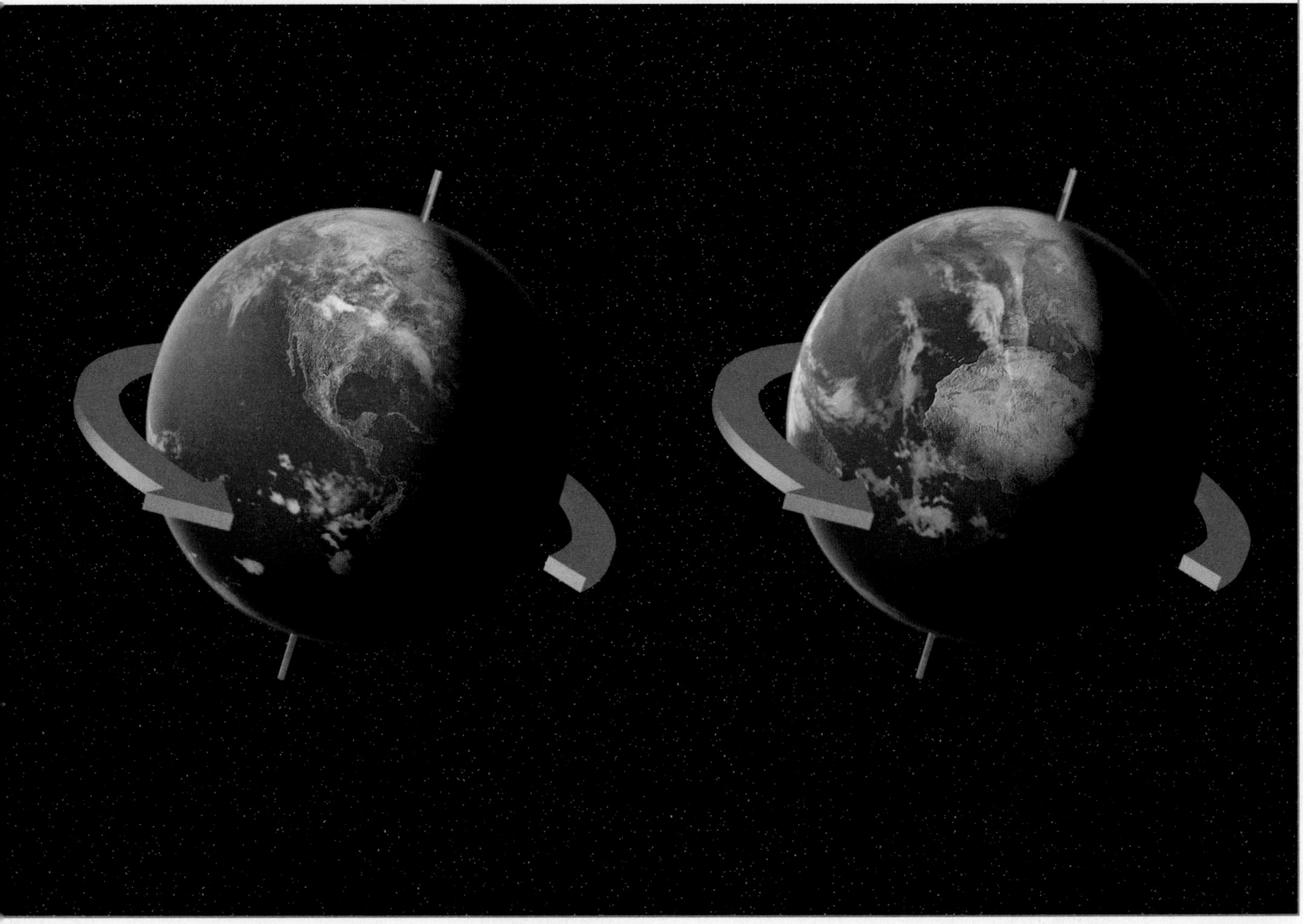

The Sun in the Sky

The Sun seems to move across the sky during the day. The Sun looks low in the sky early in the morning. By the middle of the day, the Sun is high in the sky. In the evening, the Sun is low in the sky again.

The Sun is always shining. The Sun is hard to see on some days.

The Sun is not really moving across the sky. The Sun only looks like it is moving. It is really the Earth that is moving.

sunset

✓ Lesson Checkpoint

1. Why does the Sun look like it is moving across the sky?
2. Writing in Science Write 2 sentences in your **science journal.** Tell what time sunrise and sunset are today where you live.

Lesson 3

What causes seasons to change?

Earth is tilted on its axis. Earth is always tilted in the same direction.

You know that Earth spins on its axis. Earth moves around the Sun in an orbit too. An **orbit** is a path around another object.

It takes Earth about one year to orbit the Sun one time. The tilt of Earth and its orbit cause the seasons.

Lesson Checkpoint

1. What causes the seasons?
2. **Social Studies** in Science Look at a calendar. When is the official first day of summer?

summer

In summer, the part of Earth where we live is tilted toward the Sun.

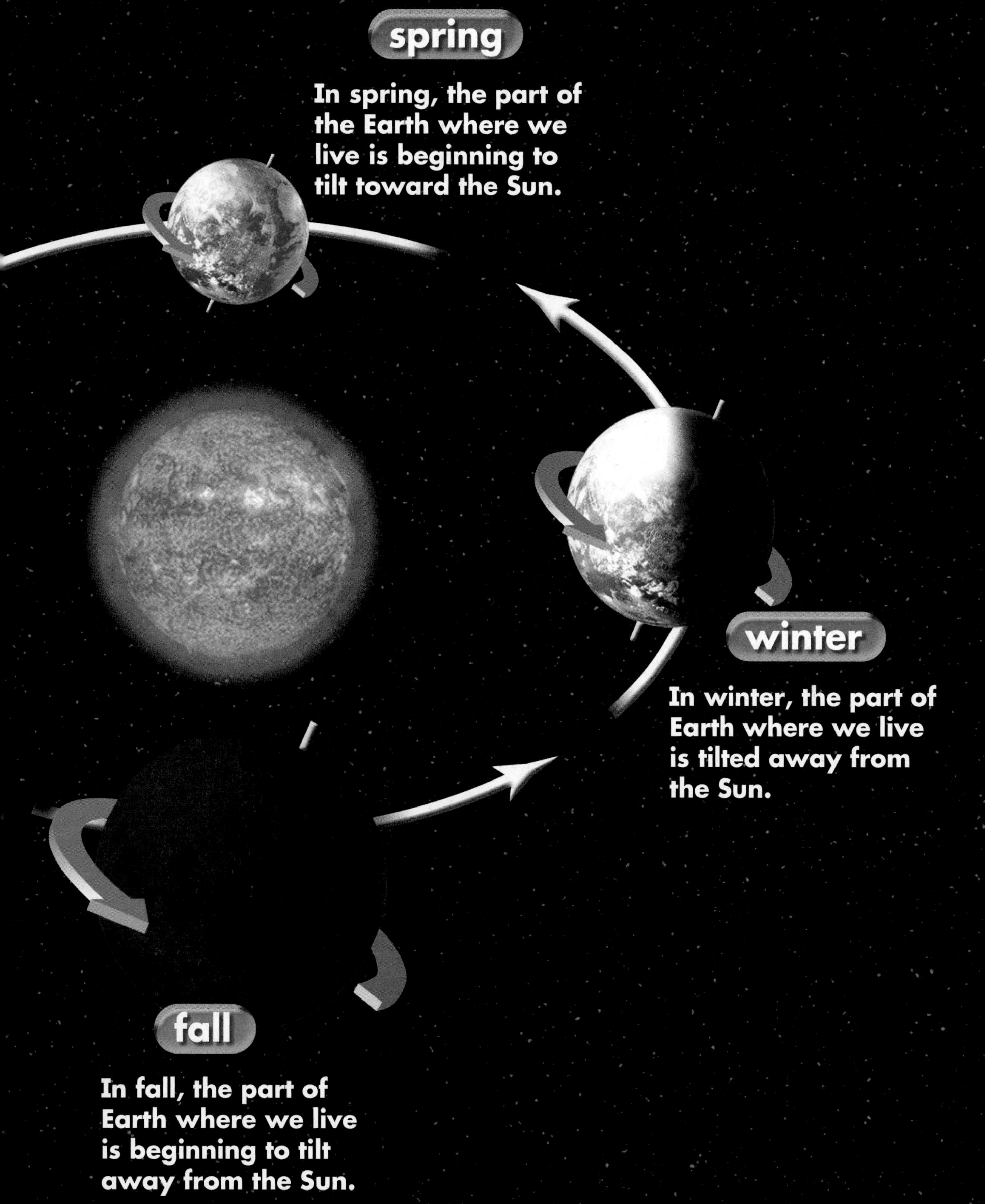
spring
In spring, the part of the Earth where we live is beginning to tilt toward the Sun.
winter
In winter, the part of Earth where we live is tilted away from the Sun.
fall
In fall, the part of Earth where we live is beginning to tilt away from the Sun.

Lesson 4

What can you see in the night sky?

You can see many other stars at night. Stars in the night sky look small because they are far away. Sometimes it looks like there are more stars than you can count!

Long ago, people thought they saw patterns in some groups of stars. They imagined lines that formed pictures. A group of stars that form a picture is called a **constellation.**

This constellation looks like a lion. It is called Leo.

1. Checkpoint What is a constellation?
2. Technology in Science What tools can you use to see the stars better at night?

Look at these two constellations. They are called the Big Dipper and the Little Dipper.

The Moon

You might see the Moon in the night sky too. The Moon is the largest and brightest object in the night sky.

The Moon has mountains and deep craters. A **crater** is a hole in the ground that is shaped like a bowl. A crater is formed when a large rock from space hits the Moon.

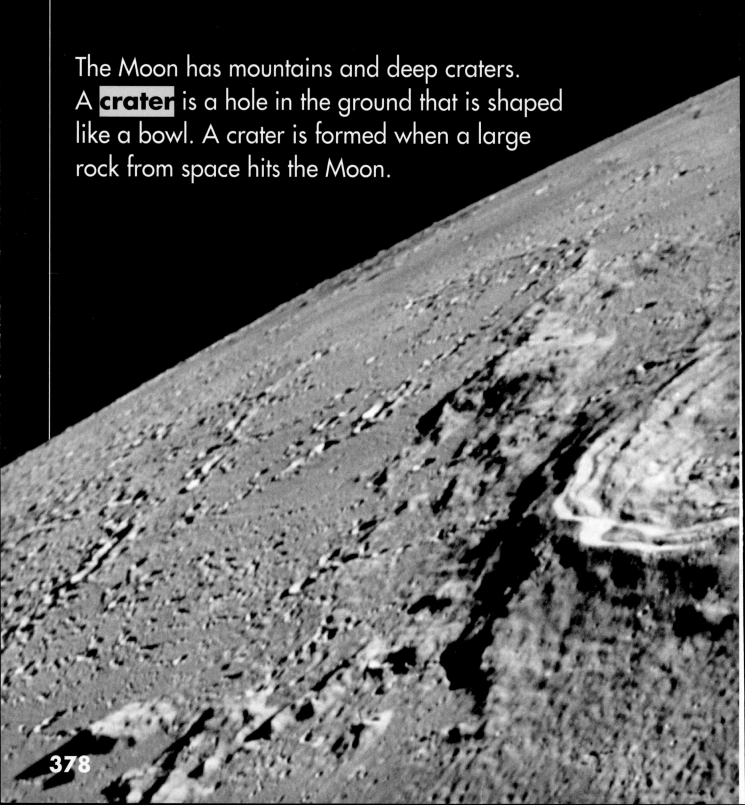

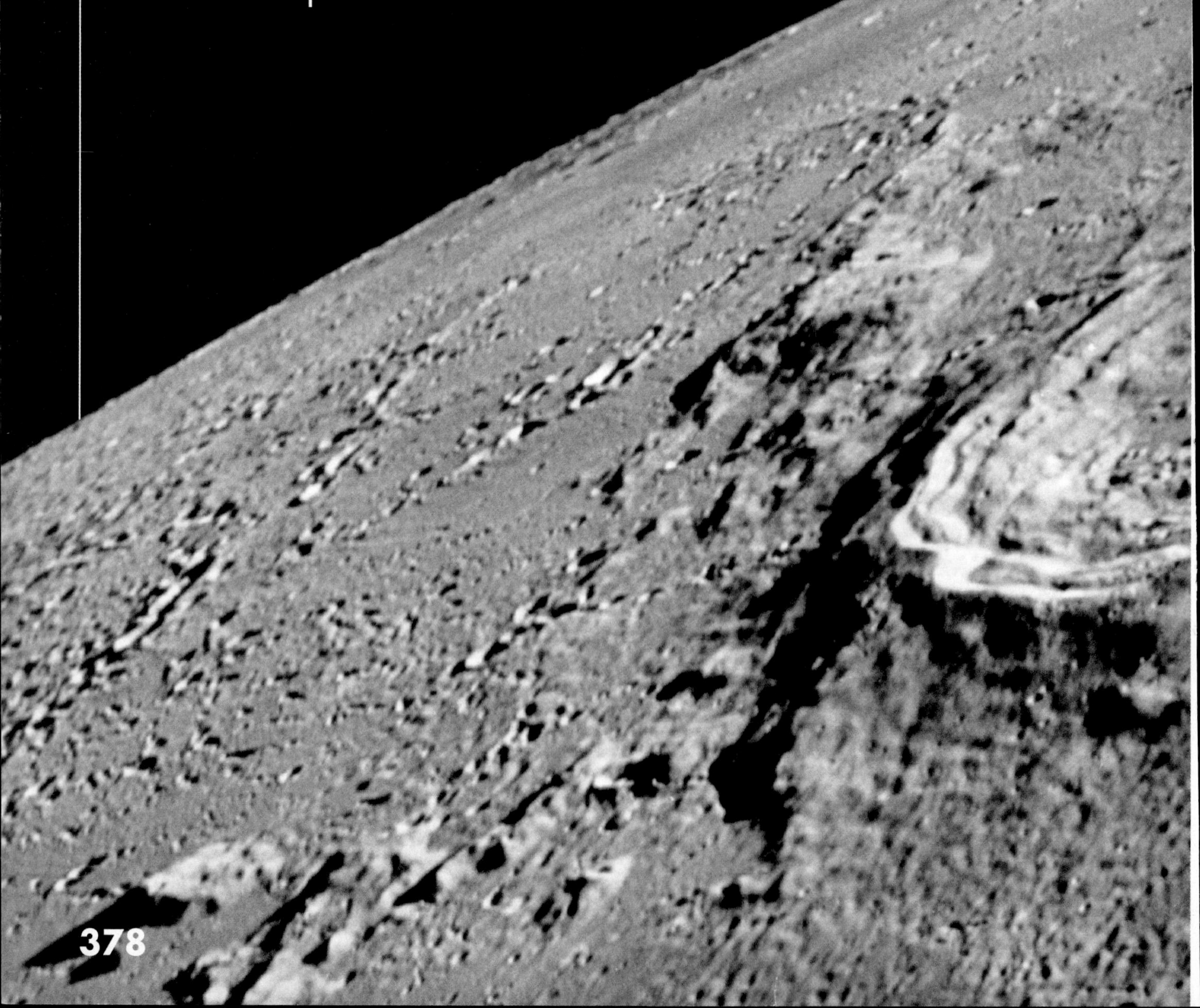

The Moon has many craters like this one.

Sometimes you can see the Moon in the daytime.

✓ Lesson Checkpoint

1. What causes craters on the Moon?
2. **Art** in Science Draw a picture of the clear night sky. Use chalk and dark paper.

Lesson 5

Why does the Moon seem to change?

The Moon rotates just like Earth. It moves in an orbit around Earth. The Moon orbits Earth while Earth orbits the Sun. It takes about four weeks for the Moon to orbit Earth one time.

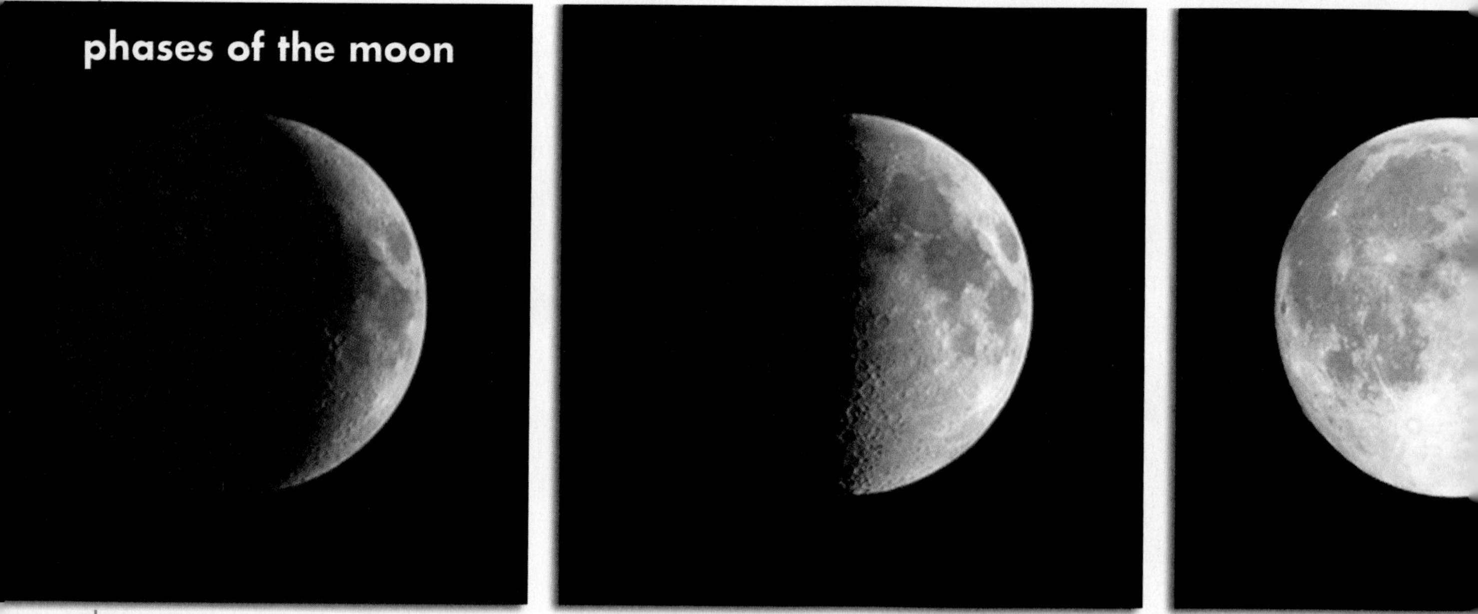
phases of the moon

The Moon does not make its own light. The Moon reflects light from the Sun. You only see the part of the Moon that has light shining on it.

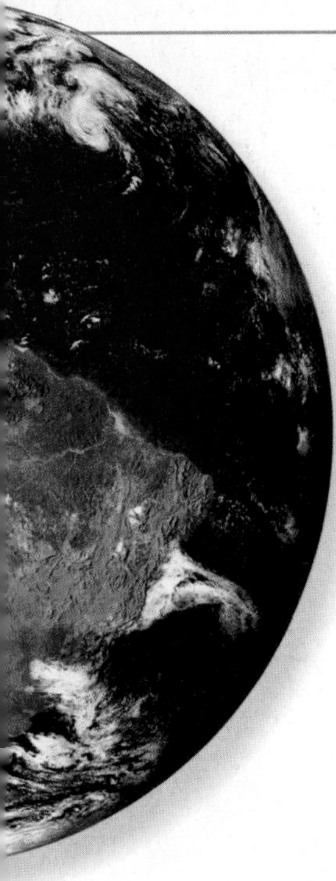

The Moon seems to change shape. Sometimes the Moon looks round. Sometimes you see smaller parts of the Moon. Sometimes you cannot see the Moon at all. The shape of the lighted part of the Moon is called a **phase.**

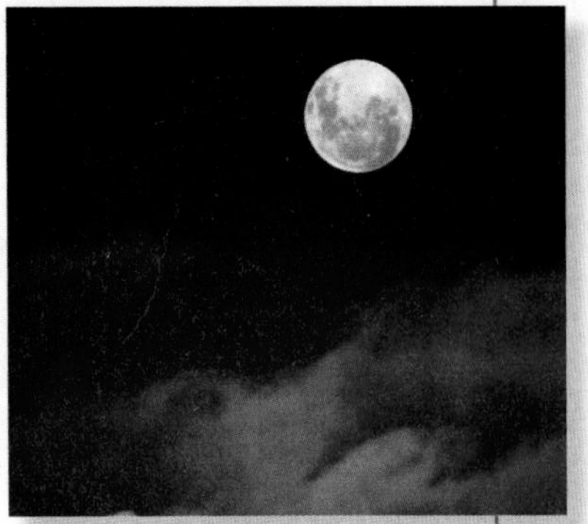

The Moon is the biggest and brightest object in the night sky.

Lesson Checkpoint

1. Why can we see the Moon?
2. **Math** in Science How long will it take for the Moon to move around the Earth 3 times?

Lesson 6

What is the solar system?

Earth is a planet. You know that Earth orbits around the Sun. Other planets orbit around the Sun too. The planets and their moons and other objects that move around the Sun are called the **solar system.**

The Sun is the center of our solar system. All of the objects in the solar system orbit the Sun. Count the other planets that orbit the Sun. How many planets do you count?

Lesson Checkpoint

1. What is at the center of Earth's solar system?
2. Look at the planets. Tell how they are **alike** and **different**.

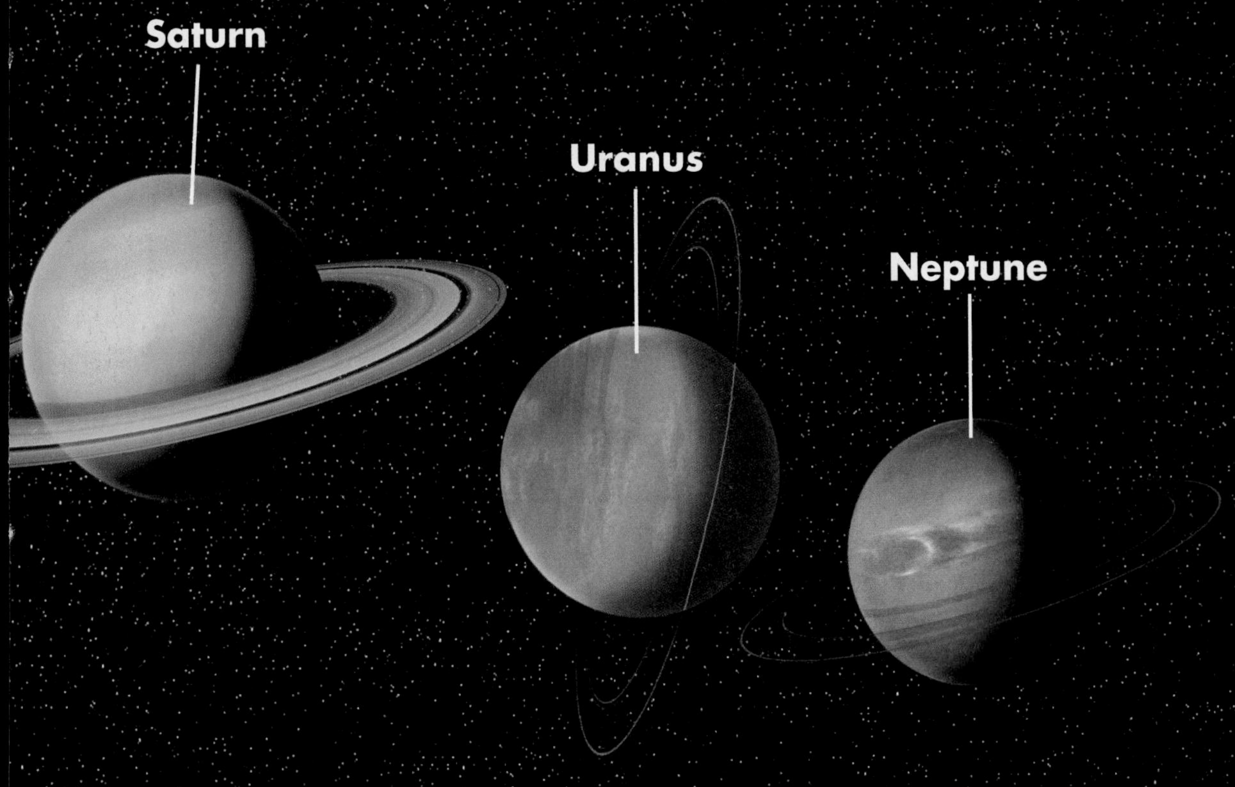

Lab zone Guided Inquiry

Investigate How can you make a model of a constellation?

Materials

safety goggles

pencil

black paper

flashlight

What to Do

1. Make a **model** constellation. Poke holes through the paper with a pencil.

2. Make the room dark. Hold the paper near a wall.

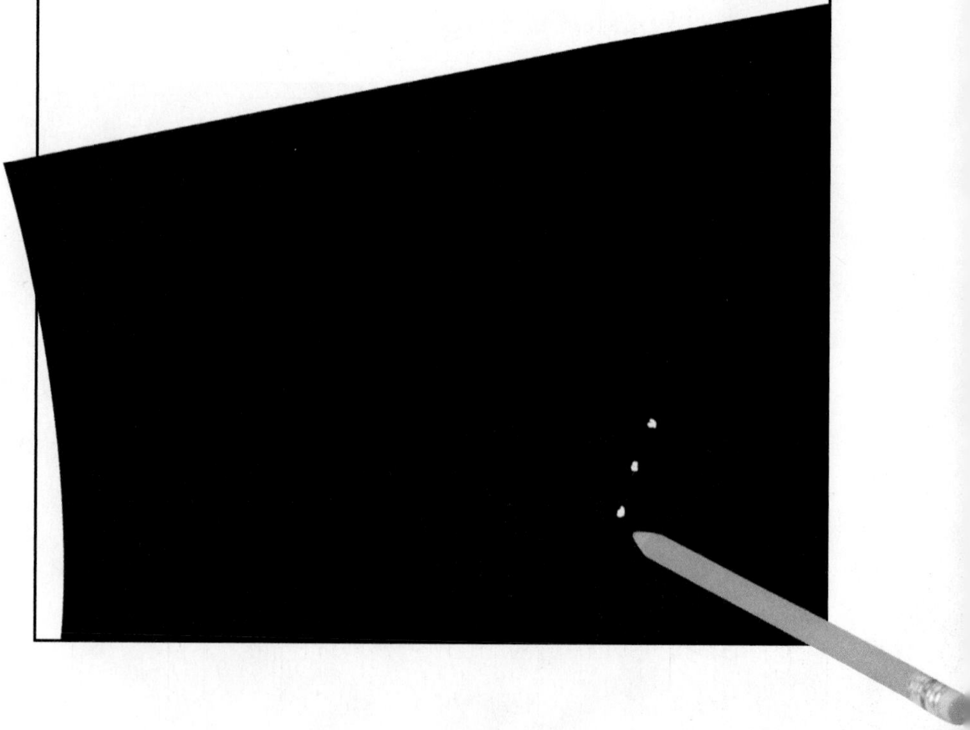

Process Skills

You use what you learn to **make a definition** of a constellation.

3. Have your partner shine a flashlight on the holes in the paper. **Observe** the picture the light makes. This is your constellation.

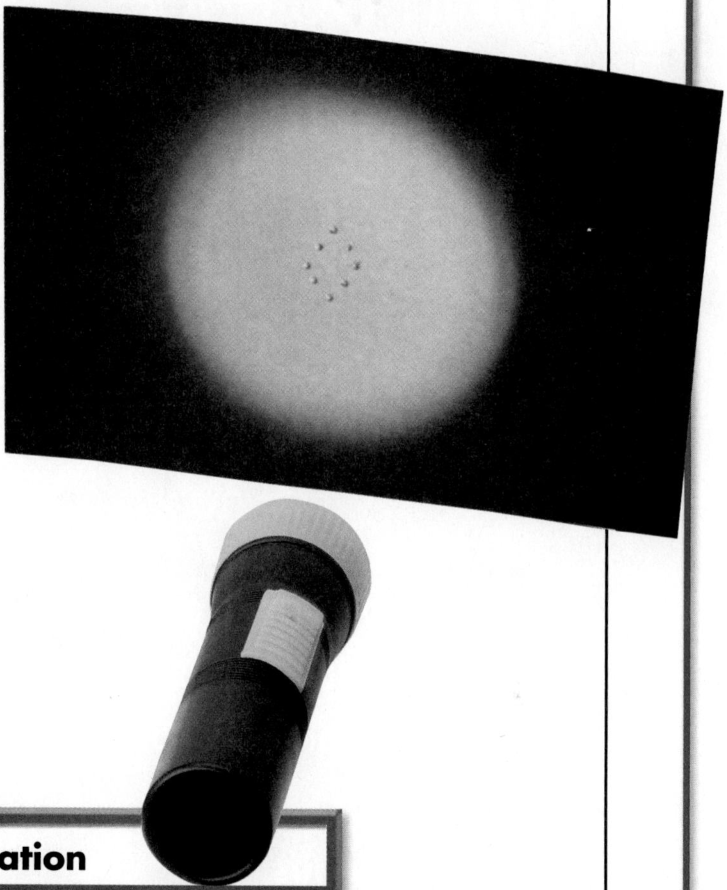

4. Draw and name your constellation.

My Constellation

Explain Your Results

1. Tell about your constellation. How is your model like a real constellation? How is it different?
2. **Make a definition** of a constellation.

Go Further

How else could you make a model of your constellation? Investigate to find out.

Planets in Orbit

Each planet takes a different number of days to orbit the Sun. This table shows how long the orbits are for some of the planets.

Planet	Orbit
Earth	365 days
Mercury	88 days
Venus	225 days
Mars	687 days

1. Which of these planets takes the most number of days to orbit the Sun?
2. Which of these planets takes the fewest number of days to orbit the Sun?
3. List these planets in order from the fewest to the most number of days to orbit the Sun.

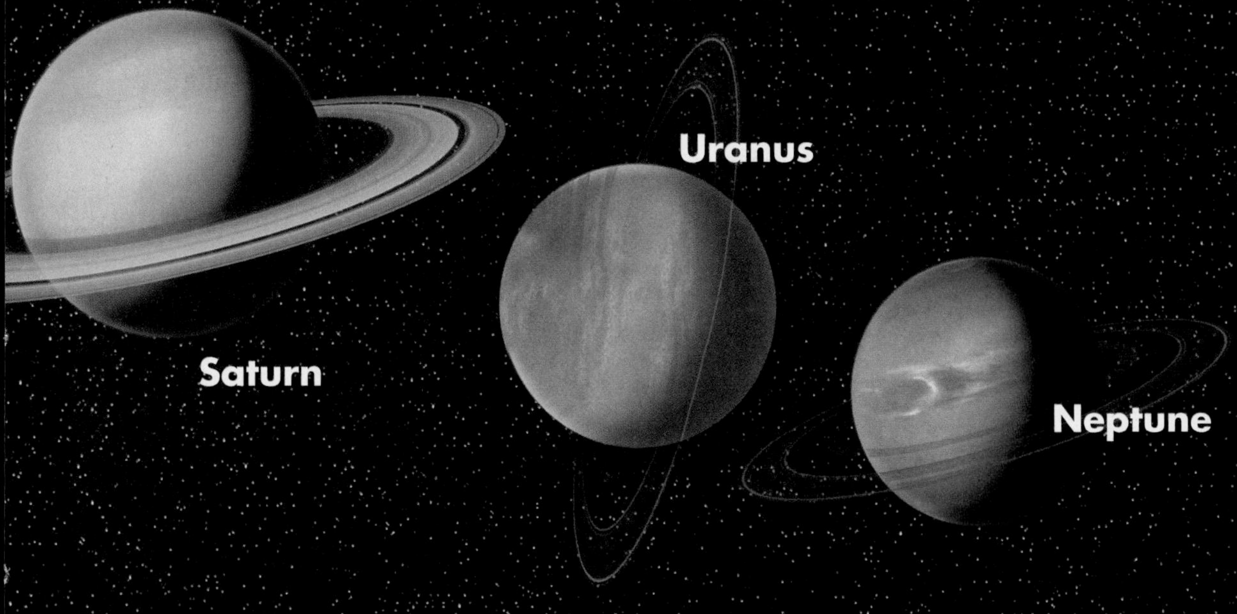

Lab zone Take-Home Activity

Work with your family to find out how many days it takes each of the planets to orbit the Sun. Use the Internet and other resources to help you.

Chapter 12 Review and Test Prep

Vocabulary

Which picture goes with each word?

1. axis
2. crater
3. constellation
4. orbit
5. phase
6. rotation
7. solar system

A

B
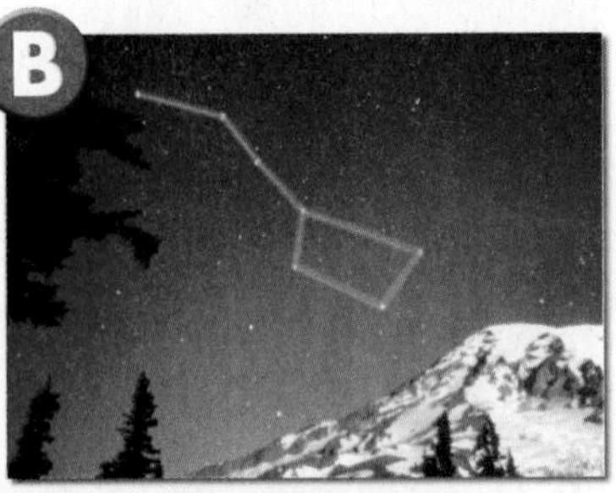
C

D
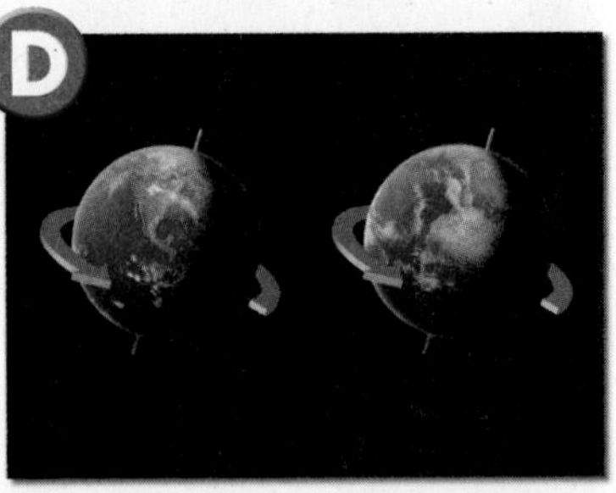
E

F
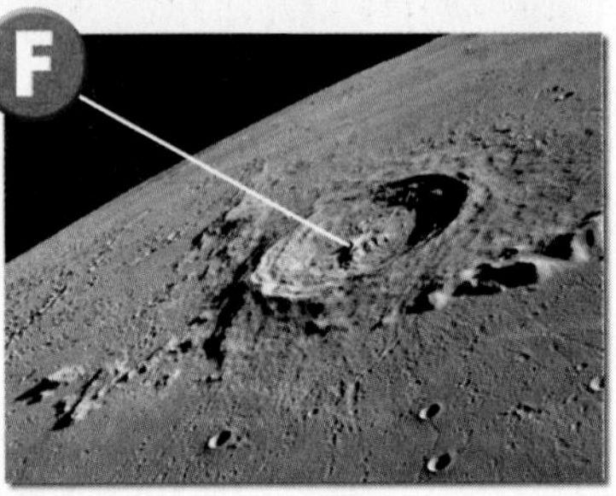
G
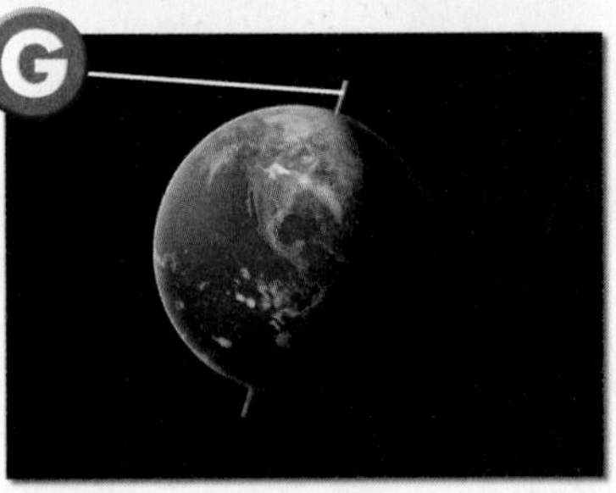

What did you learn?

8. What is caused by Earth's rotation?
9. Why is the Sun the only star you can see during the day?

Process Skills

10. **Communicate** Tell why we have light during the day.

Alike and Different

11. Tell how the Sun and the Moon are **alike** and **different.**

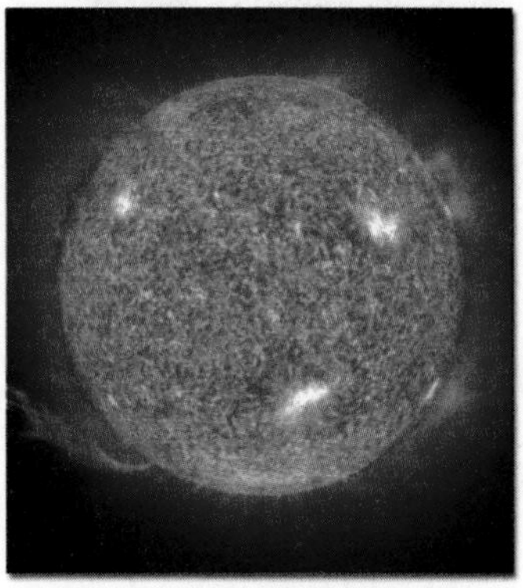

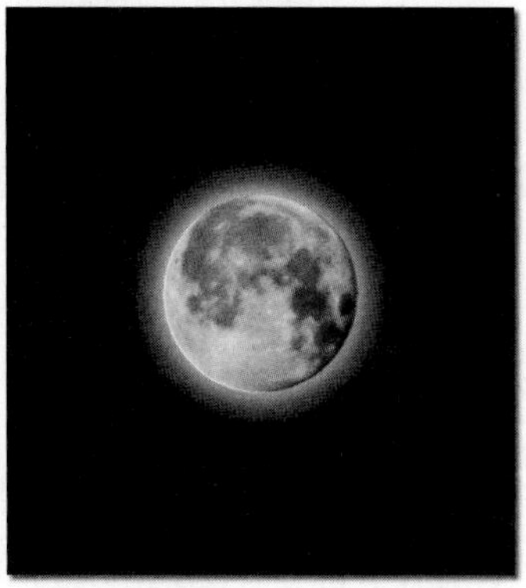

Alike	Different

Test Prep

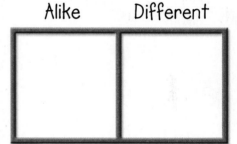

Fill in the circle next to the correct answer.

12. Which star is closest to Earth?

Ⓐ the Sun

Ⓑ the Big Dipper

Ⓒ the Moon

Ⓓ Leo

13. **Writing in Science** Describe what you might see if you traveled around the solar system.

Mission To Mars

NASA scientists want to learn more about the planet Mars. Mars is a planet that is close to Earth. Mars and Earth are alike in some ways. Water is needed for life on Earth. Scientists want to learn more about water on Mars.

NASA sent robots to Mars to learn about the planet. Some robots fly around Mars taking pictures. Some robots called rovers have landed on Mars. These rovers travel across the surface.

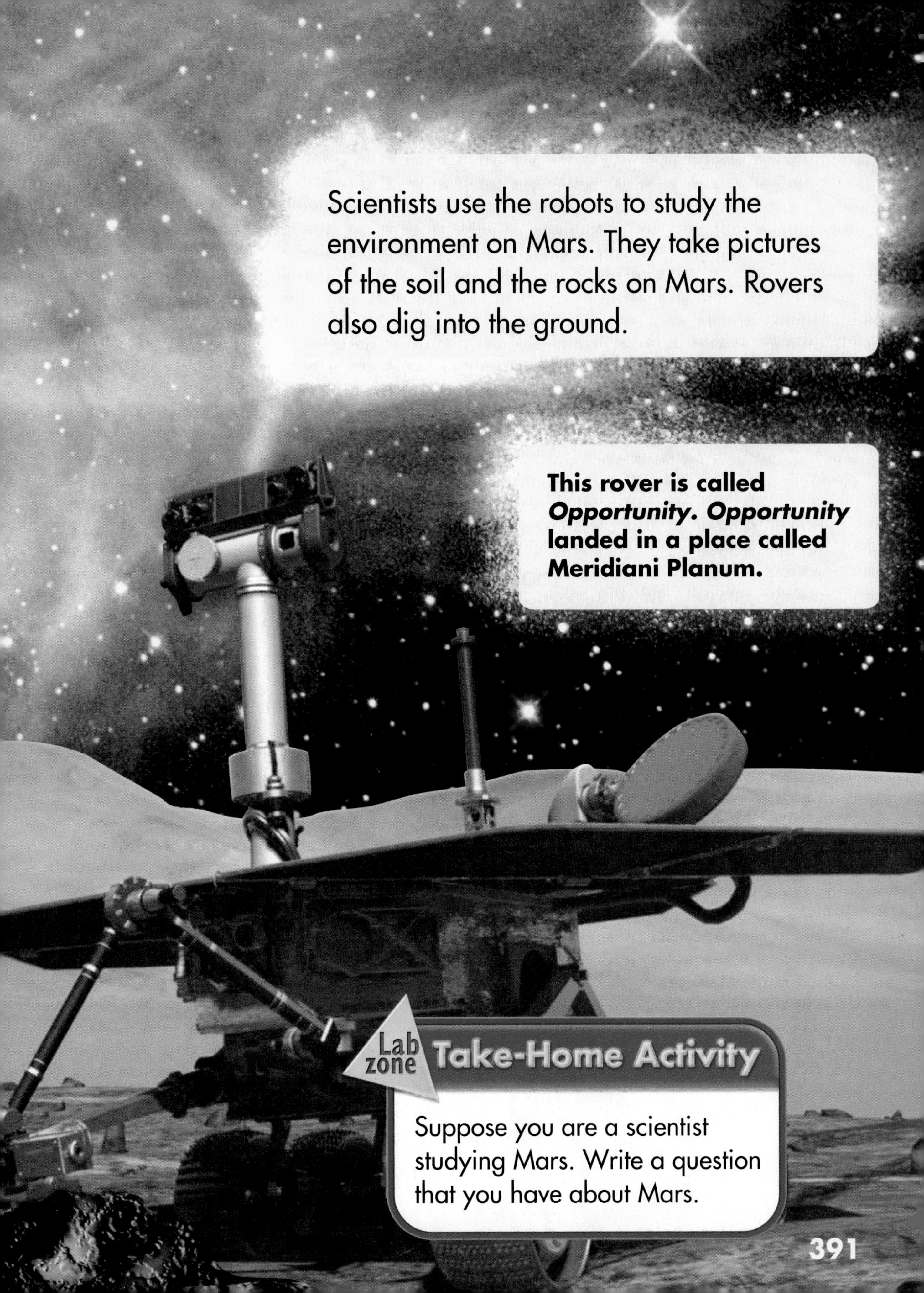

Scientists use the robots to study the environment on Mars. They take pictures of the soil and the rocks on Mars. Rovers also dig into the ground.

This rover is called *Opportunity*. *Opportunity* landed in a place called Meridiani Planum.

Lab zone Take-Home Activity

Suppose you are a scientist studying Mars. Write a question that you have about Mars.

NASA

Career

Astronomer

Laura Peticolas is an astronomer who works with NASA. She studies natural displays of light called *auroras*. Two examples of auroras are Northern lights and Southern lights.

Read Together

Have you ever looked at the stars at night? People who study the Sun, stars, planets, and other things far from Earth are called astronomers.

Many astronomers use special tools called telescopes to help them see far out into space. A telescope helps things that are far away look nearer, larger, and brighter.

To study the universe, scientists at NASA launch many telescopes. One such telescope is the Hubble Space Telescope. Every day this telescope sends information to astronomers all over the world.

Lab zone Take-Home Activity

Go outside on a clear night with your family. Look at the sky. Write about what you see.

EC CRU 10 9 8 7 6 5 4 3 2 1

You Will Discover

- how technology has changed the world we live in.
- ways we use technology every day.

Chapter 13

Technology in Our World

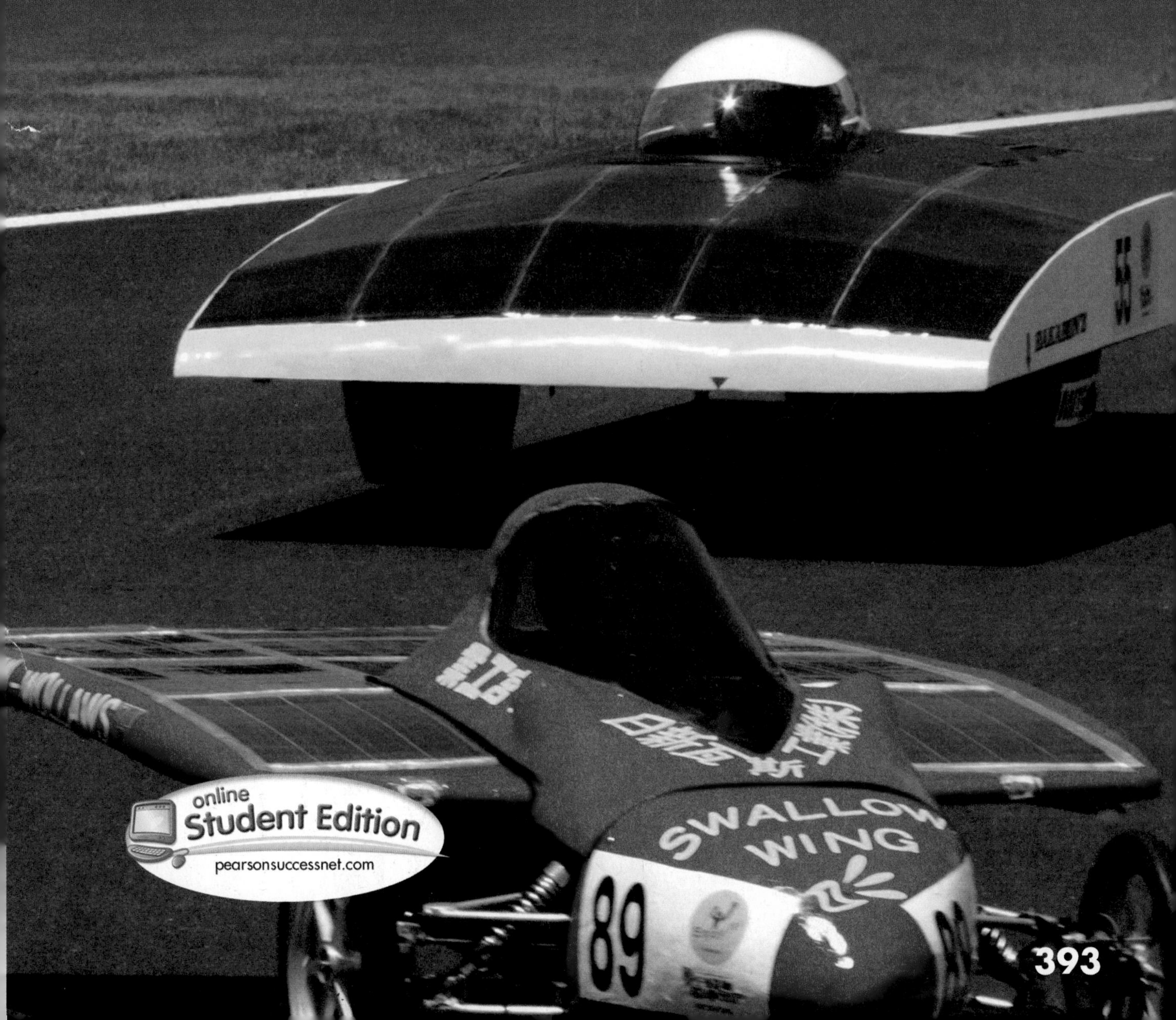

online Student Edition
pearsonsuccessnet.com

Build Background

What are some ways technology helps us?

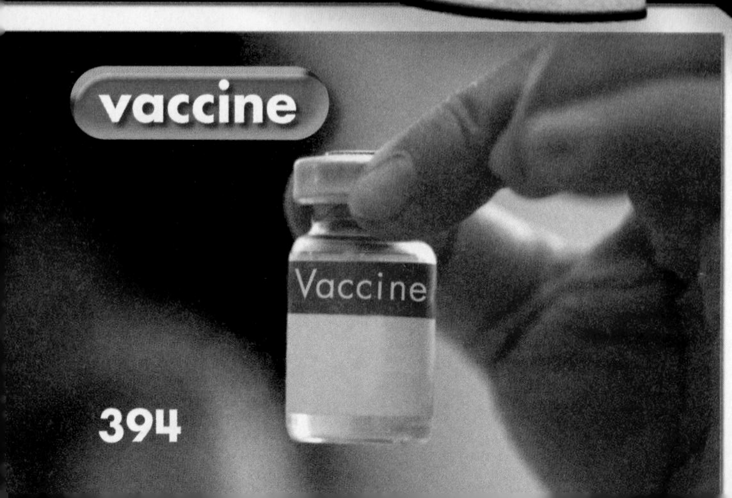

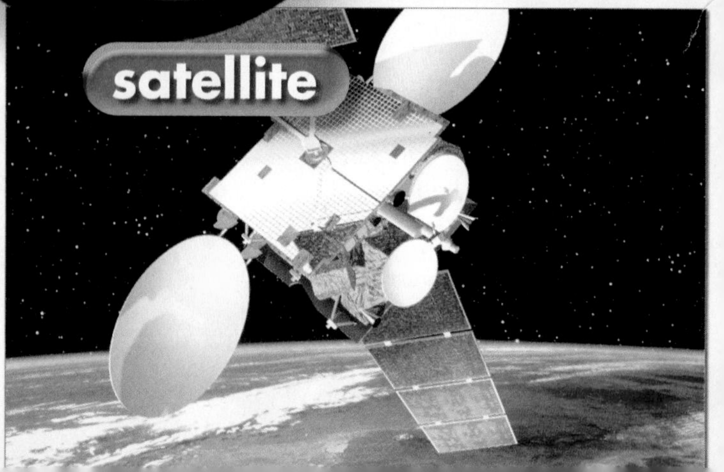

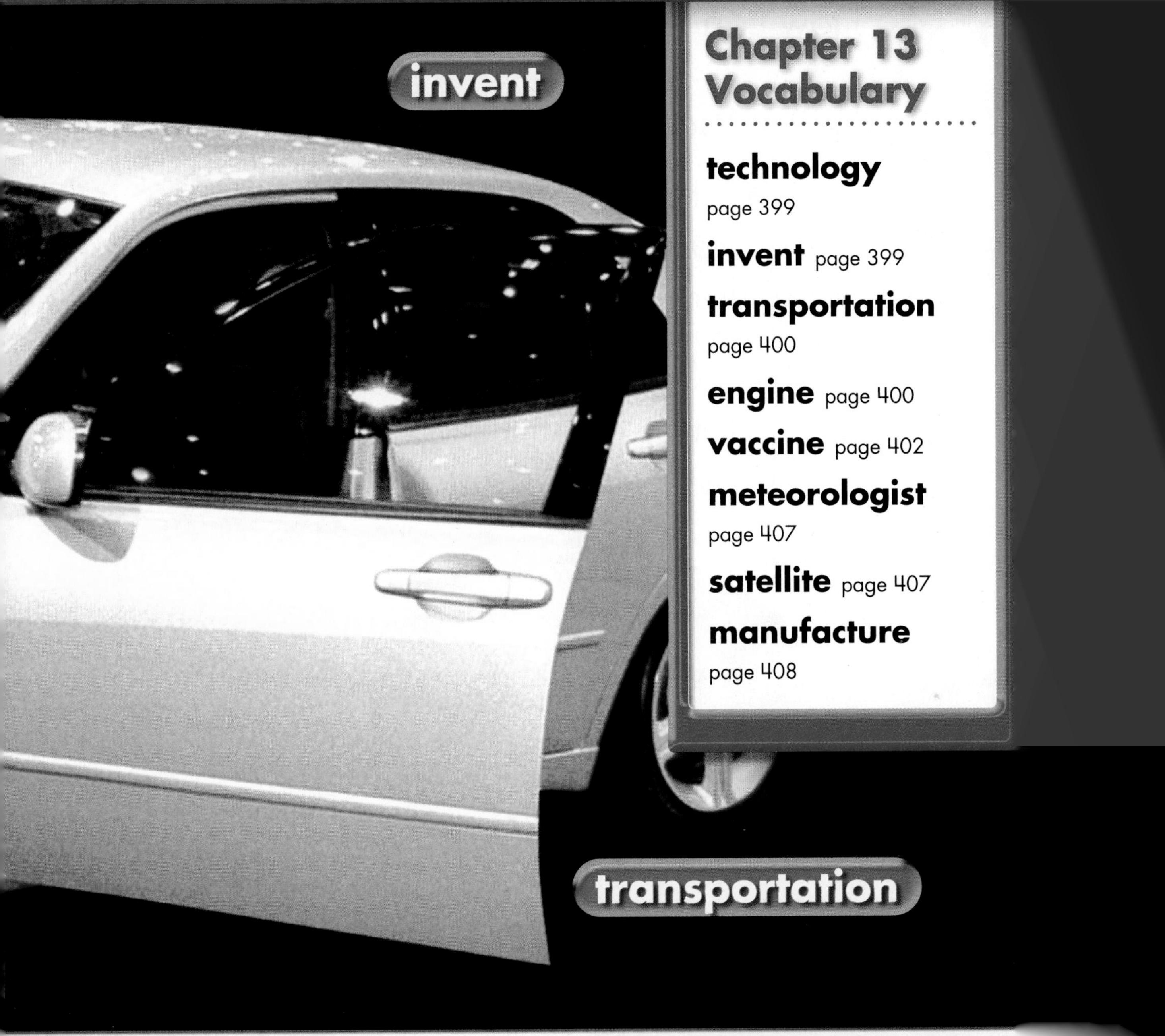

Chapter 13 Vocabulary

technology page 399

invent page 399

transportation page 400

engine page 400

vaccine page 402

meteorologist page 407

satellite page 407

manufacture page 408

manufacture

To make by hand or machine.

Lab zone **Directed Inquiry**

Explore How can you move the ball?

Materials

metal ball

books

cup

pencil

ruler

magnet

spoon

What to Do

1. Put the ball on the books. Place the cup 25 cm away from the books.

2. Solve this problem. Put the ball in the cup. Use tools.

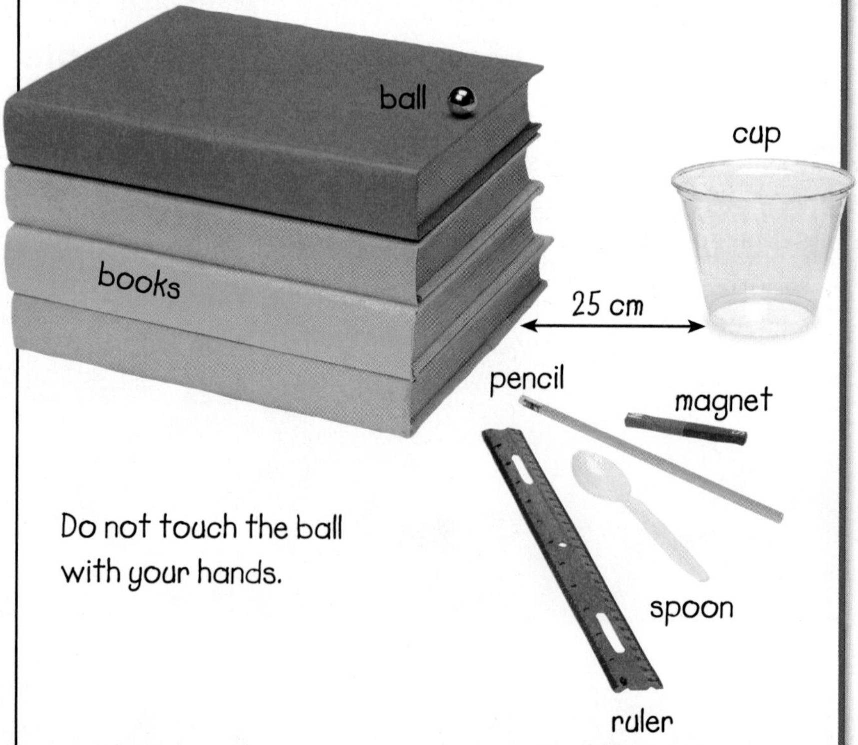

Process Skills

When you **communicate**, you tell how you moved the ball.

Explain Your Results

Communicate Tell how you solved the problem.

How to Read Science

Reading Skills

TARGET SKILL

Retell

Retell means to tell what you learned in your own words.

Science Article

Bicycles

The first bicycle was invented in 1817. Riders pushed their feet on the ground to make it move. Pedals were added in 1839. The pedals helped people ride bicycles with their feet off the ground.

Apply It!

Communicate

Tell what you learned about bicycles.

Retell

Technology Helps Us All

Sung to the tune of "Bingo"
Lyrics by Gerri Brioso & Richard Freitas/The Dovetail Group, Inc.

Technology now helps us all
In lots of different ways. It
Helps us travel fast,
Helps us travel far,
Helps us travel safe,
In cars, and trains and airplanes.

Lesson 1

What is technology?

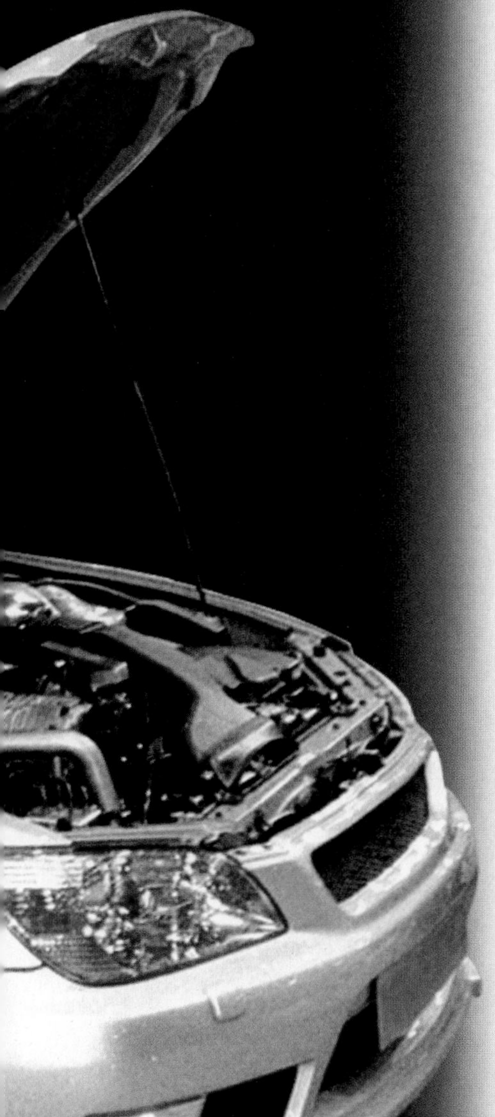

People ride in cars. People use computers. We can do these things because of technology. **Technology** means using science to help us solve problems.

Sometimes people use technology to invent things. **Invent** means to make something for the first time.

Inventions can be things we need or things we want. Many people need cars to travel long distances. Some people want computer games.

Changes in Transportation

Technology has changed transportation. **Transportation** moves people and things from place to place. Today people travel farther and faster than they did long ago.

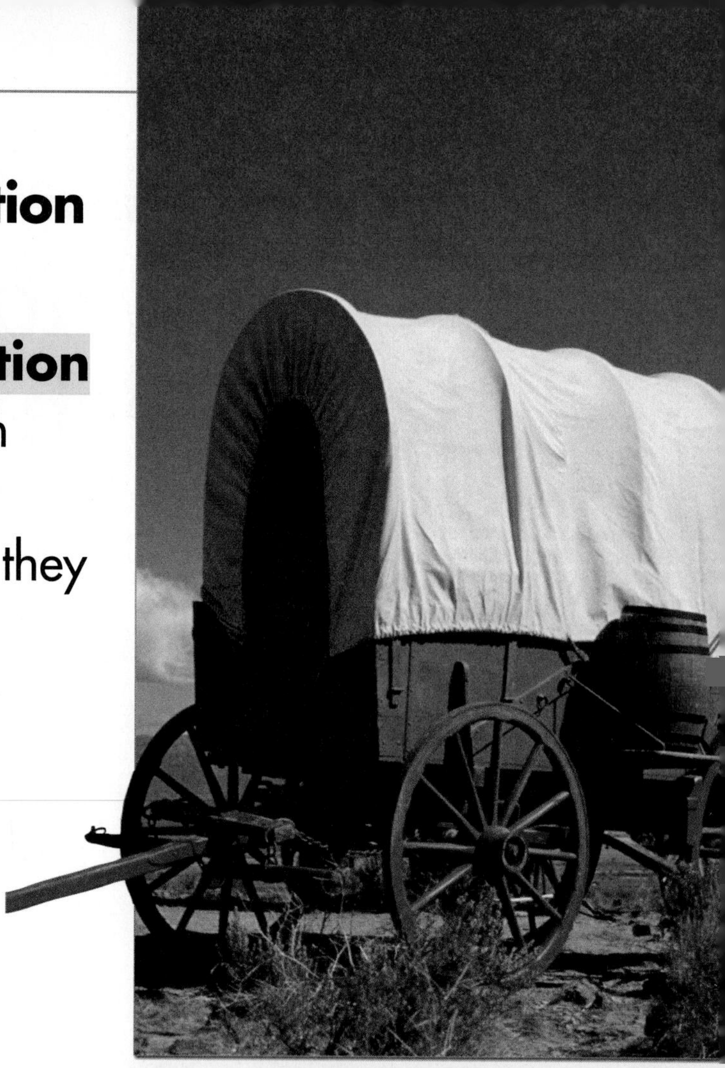

Some kinds of transportation have engines. An **engine** is a machine that does work or makes something move. Long ago, steam engines made trains and boats move. Today, cars, trains, and boats have gasoline or electric engines.

Technology helps people travel. Seat belts and air bags help make cars safe. Airplanes fly faster than ever before.

People use technology to help solve problems. Gasoline can cause pollution. New cars have been invented that use gasoline and electricity. These cars help reduce pollution.

Lesson Checkpoint

1. How has technology changed transportation?
2. **Writing** in Science Write a sentence in your **science journal.** Tell about some inventions that can help you.

Lesson 2

How does technology help us?

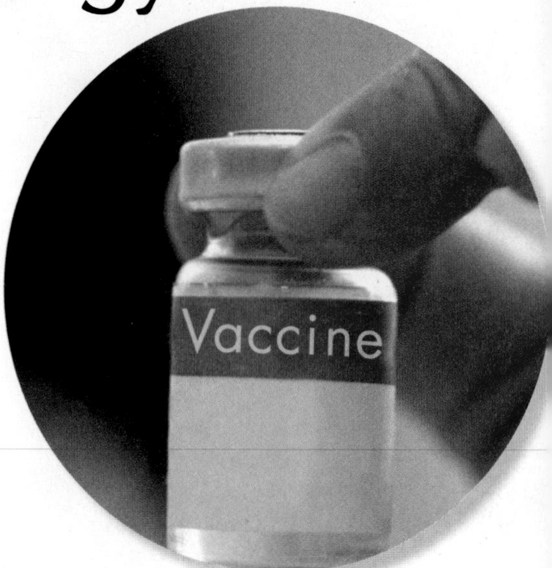

vaccine

Technology can help people stay healthy. People use technology to make vaccines. A **vaccine** is a medicine that can help prevent a disease.

Doctors use technology to help people. Glasses and contact lenses can help people to see. Hearing aids can help people to hear. Artificial legs can help some people to walk.

The doctor uses an x ray to help this boy get well.

This is a picture from an MRI.

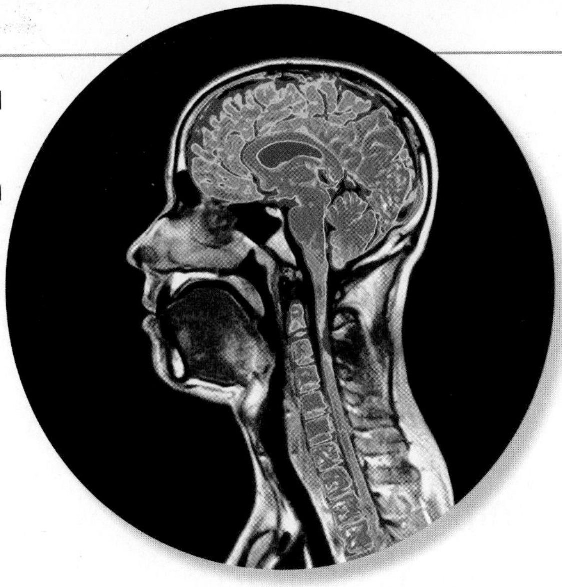

Technology can help doctors find out why people are sick. X rays, CAT scans, and MRIs are tools doctors can use to see inside people. When doctors know what is wrong, they can help people to get well.

This man can run with the help of his artificial leg.

Lesson Checkpoint

1. What are some ways that technology can help people?
2. **Retell** What are some tools that help doctors see inside people?

Lesson 3

How do we use technology to communicate?

What are some ways you communicate with your friends? The way technology is used to communicate has changed over the years.

Long ago, telephones were attached to a wall. Today you can carry a telephone with you. Telephones are much smaller today than they were years ago.

This telephone is from 1879!

The first computers were very big and very heavy. Today, computers are smaller, faster, and easier to use than the first computers.

The first computer was invented in 1946. It filled a whole room!

✓ Lesson Checkpoint

1. How has technology changed the way people communicate?
2. Math in Science Some early telephones were about 46 centimeters tall. Today, some phones are about 9 centimeters tall. How much taller were older telephones than newer telephones?

Lesson 4

What are some other ways we use technology?

MP3 players play music.

Technology has changed the way people have fun. People listen to music on compact discs. People use computers to play games.

Technology can also make our lives easier. People use Velcro® to close things. People use calculators to do math.

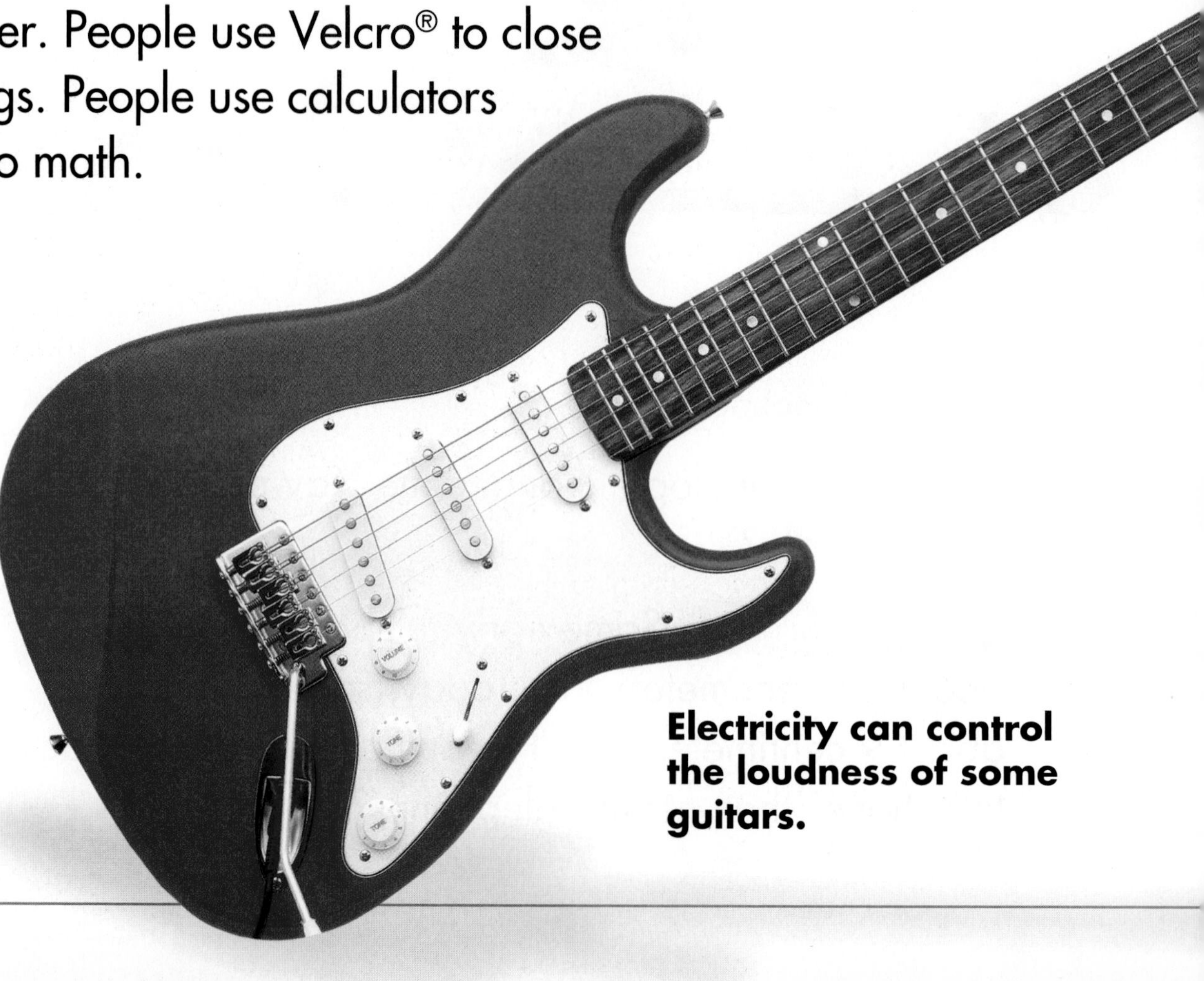

Electricity can control the loudness of some guitars.

Technology helps people in their jobs. A **meteorologist** is a person who studies weather. Meteorologists study pictures taken by satellites to predict weather. A **satellite** is an object that revolves around another object.

Satellites send information about the weather to Earth.

Meteorologists get information about the weather from satellites.

Lesson Checkpoint

1. How does a meteorologist use information from satellites?
2. Writing in Science Write a sentence in your **science journal.** Tell three ways you used technology today.

Lesson 5

How do people make things?

People manufacture things we use every day. **Manufacture** means to make by hand or by machines. Coats and bicycles are two things that are manufactured.

Natural materials were used to make parts of this coat.

Different types of materials are used to manufacture things. Some materials come from nature. This coat was made using wool from sheep. The buttons were made from wood.

Some materials are made by people. The seat of this bicycle is made from plastic. The tires are made from rubber. Plastic and rubber are materials made by people.

This bike uses materials made by people.

Lesson Checkpoint

1. What are some manufactured things you use in school?
2. **Retell** What are some materials used to make a bicycle?

Lab zone Guided Inquiry

Investigate How can you make a maze?

Materials

safety goggles

marble

cardboard

paper tubes

box

tape and scissors

What to Do

1. How can you make a maze that a marble can follow? Make a plan. Draw it.
2. Tape paper tubes to the cardboard.
3. **Predict** Will your maze work?
4. Test your maze. **Observe** the marble. Move the tubes to make the maze work better.

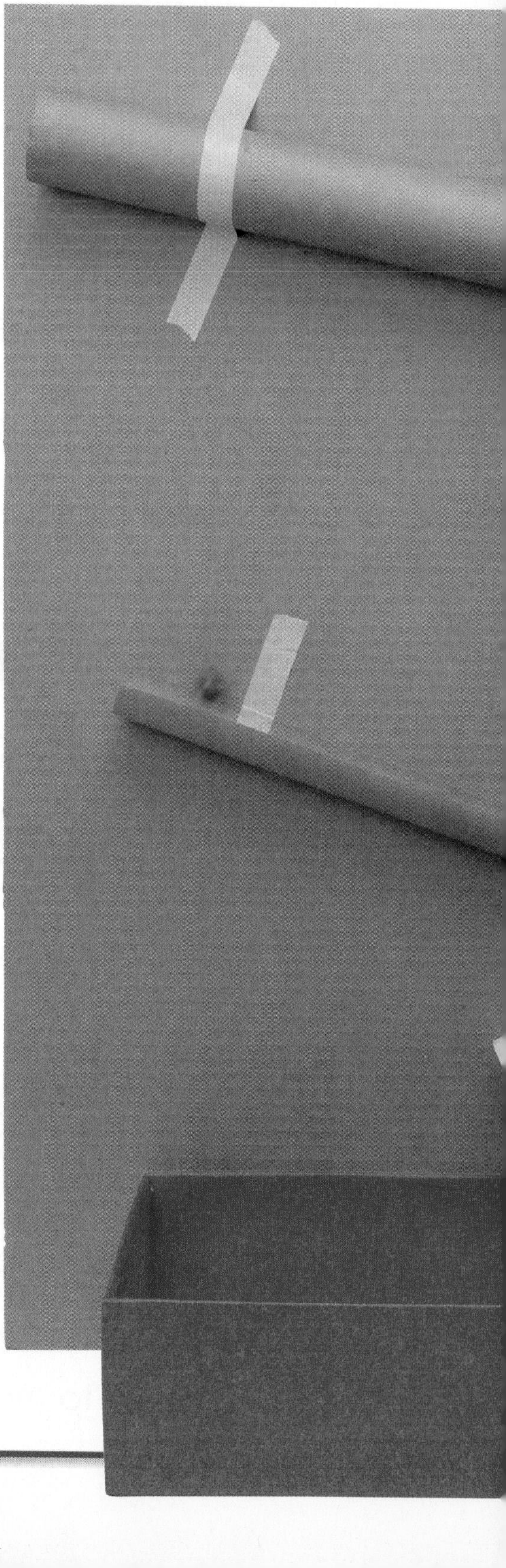

Process Skills

You **predict** when you tell what you think will happen.

5 Test your maze 2 more times.

Test your maze.	
Test	**Did the marble follow the maze?**
1	
2	
3	

Your maze might look like this one.

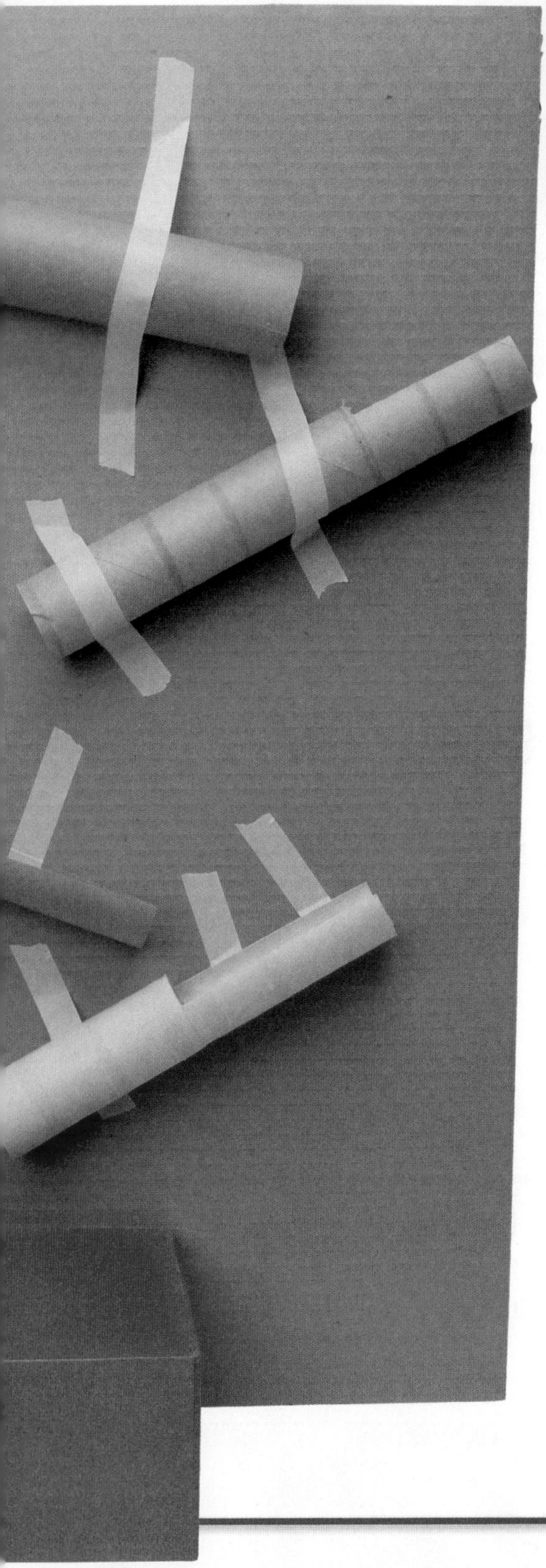

Be careful!

Be sure to wear your safety goggles.

Explain Your Results

Communicate Tell how the parts of your maze work together.

Go Further

How can you make your marble move in a different way? Investigate to find out.

Math in Science

Technology in Your School

Look around your school. How many things can you find that help people communicate? How many things can you find that help people move from place to place? Fill in your table with examples.

Technology in My School

Communication	Transportation

1. Count the examples you found for each column.
2. Compare the number of examples you found. Use <, >, or =.

Lab zone Take-Home Activity

Walk around your home. Look for ways you use technology. Make a table like the one you made for your school.

Chapter 13 Review and Test Prep

Vocabulary

Which picture goes with each word?

1. engine

2. vaccine

3. satellite

4. meteorologist

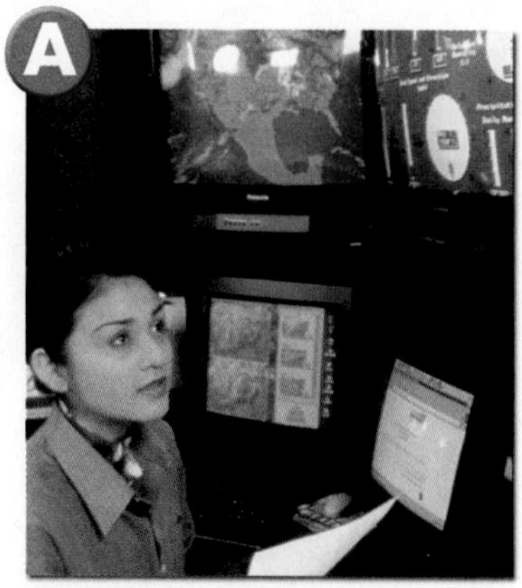

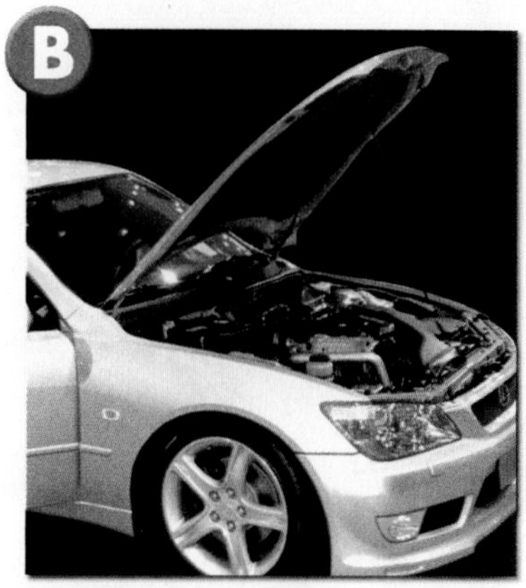

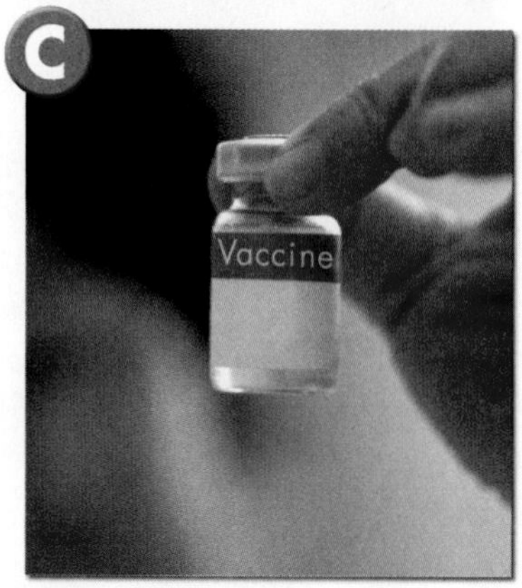

What did you learn?

5. What is technology?

6. Name two ways you use technology every day.

7. How has technology changed communication?

Process Skills

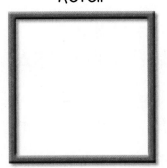

8. Infer Why do people invent new things?

Retell

9. Tell what you learned about toothbrushes.

Retell

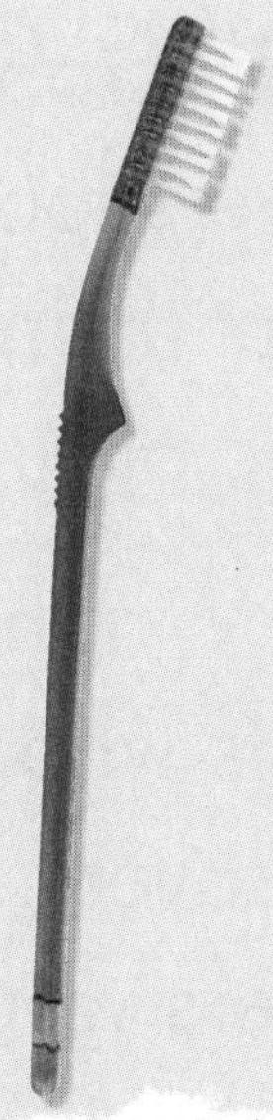

The first toothbrush was invented in China in the 1400s. The bristles were made from animal hair. The first electric toothbrush was invented in 1960. Today, bristles are made from nylon.

Test Prep

Fill in the circle next to the correct answer.

10. What is an object that travels around another object?

- Ⓐ engine
- Ⓑ vaccine
- Ⓒ satellite
- Ⓓ velcro

11. Writing in Science Make a list. Tell how people use technology.

Biography

Meet Shonte Wright

Shonte Wright traveled across the United States with five other scientists. They told people about the rovers that landed on Mars in 2004.

Read Together

In 2004 NASA sent two robots to Mars. The robots were called rovers. The rovers took pictures of Mars and sent them back to Earth. NASA used the pictures to study the planet.

Shonte Wright is one of the scientists who worked with NASA on the rovers. She helped make sure the rovers would still work after the long trip through space.

Ms. Wright knew she wanted to be a scientist and work at NASA when she was ten years old. She took many math and science classes to help her get ready for her job.

Lab zone Take-Home Activity

Suppose you are going to invent a robot to explore another planet. Draw what the robot would look like.

Unit D Test Talk

Test-Taking Strategies

Write Your Answer

You can write your answer to science questions. Remember that your answer should be short but complete.

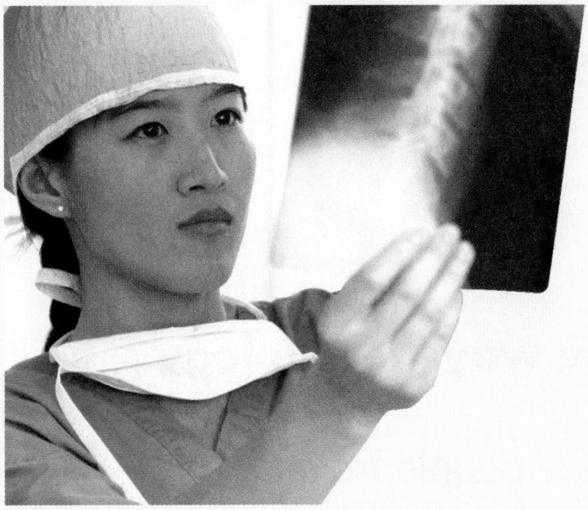

X-ray

Doctors use technology to help you when you are sick or hurt. They can use X-ray, CAT scan, or an MRI to see inside your body. Best of all, using these machines doesn't hurt!

Read the question. Look at the text.

Why does a doctor use X-ray or CAT scan technology?

Which words can you use to help write your answer? Write your answer.

Unit D Wrap-Up

Chapter 12

What are some ways the Earth moves?

- Earth is always spinning on its axis.
- Earth moves around the Sun in an orbit.

Chapter 13

What are some ways technology helps us?

- Technology helps people travel, communicate, and make things.
- Doctors use technology to help people get well.

Performance Assessment

Make a Technology Collage

- Find pictures of people using technology to communicate.
- Cut out the pictures.
- Make a collage.
- Tell about the pictures you found.

Read More About Space & Technology!

Look for books like these in your library.

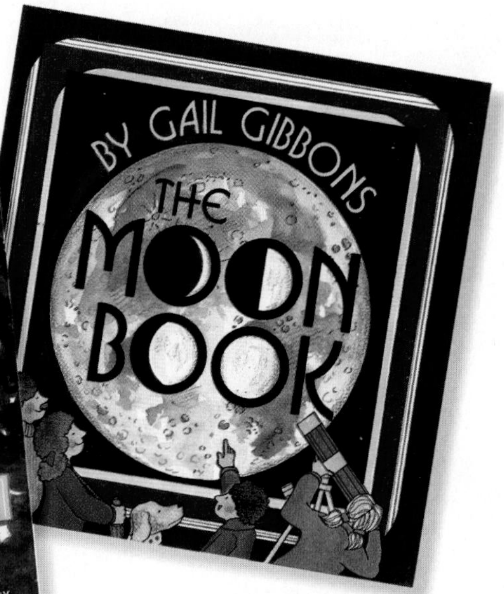

Lab zone **Full Inquiry**

Experiment Which tissue is the strongest?

Tissues can be strong or weak. Experiment to find out which tissue is the strongest. The tissue that holds the most water is the strongest.

Materials

3 tissues

jar and rubber band

dropper and cup with water

marbles

balance

gram cubes

Process Skills

You **collect data** when you use a chart to record your data.

Ask a question.

Are tissues that cost more stronger than tissues that cost less?

Make a hypothesis.

If a tissue costs the most, then it is the strongest.

Plan a fair test.

Use the same amount of water to wet each tissue. Use 3 different brands of tissue.

Do your test.

1. Put a tissue on the jar. Put a rubber band around it.
2. Wet the tissue drop by drop. Use 30 drops.

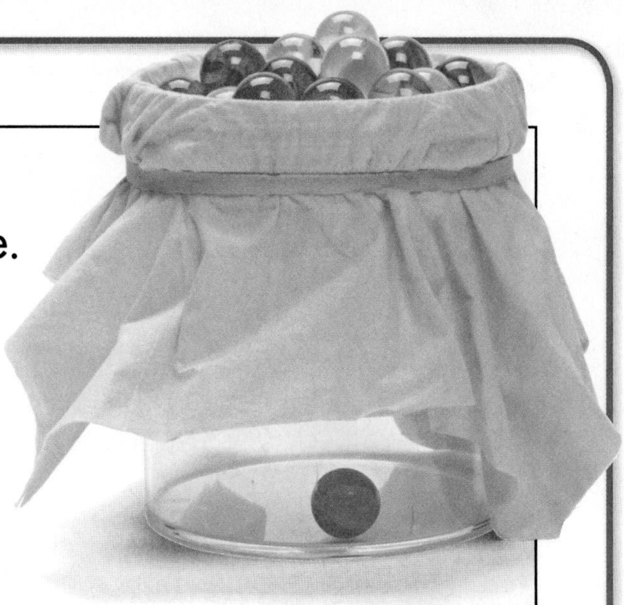

3. Carefully place one marble at a time on top of the tissue.

4. Count how many marbles it takes to break the tissue.

5. **Measure** the mass of the marbles.

6. Repeat with the other tissues.

Collect and record data.

Tissue Cost	How many marbles?	How many grams?
Most		
Middle		
Least		

Go Further

What if you used less water to wet each tissue? Try it and find out.

Tell your conclusion.
Which tissue is the strongest?

End with a Poem

This Happy Day

by Harry Behn

Every morning when the Sun
Comes smiling up on everyone,
It's lots of fun
To say good morning to the Sun.
    Good morning, Sun!

Every evening after play
When the sunshine goes away,
It's nice to say,
Thank you for this happy day,
    This happy day!

Discovery Channel School

Science Fair Projects

Full Inquiry

Using Scientific Methods

1. Ask a question.
2. Make a hypothesis.
3. Plan a fair test.
4. Do your test.
5. Collect and record data.
6. Tell your conclusion.
7. Go further.

Idea 1

Phases of the Moon

Plan a project. Find out what the Moon looks like every day for one month.

Idea 2

Flying Better

Make a plan. Find out if changing the size of a helicopter's blades will make it fly better.

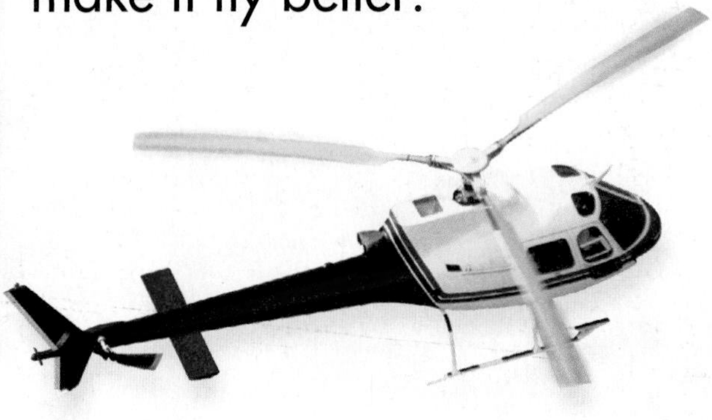

EC CRU 10 9 8 7 6 5 4 3 2 1

Metric and Customary Measurement

Science uses the metric system to measure things. Metric measurement is used around the world. Here is how different metric measurements compare to customary measurement.

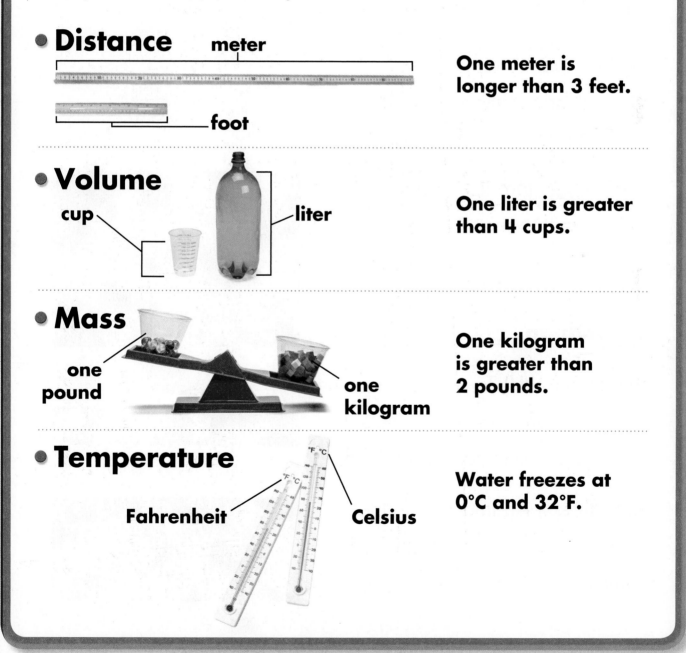

- **Distance**

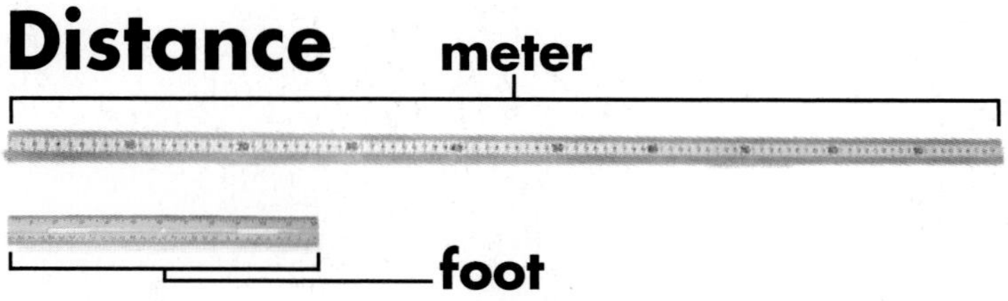

One meter is longer than 3 feet.

- **Volume**

One liter is greater than 4 cups.

- **Mass**

One kilogram is greater than 2 pounds.

- **Temperature**

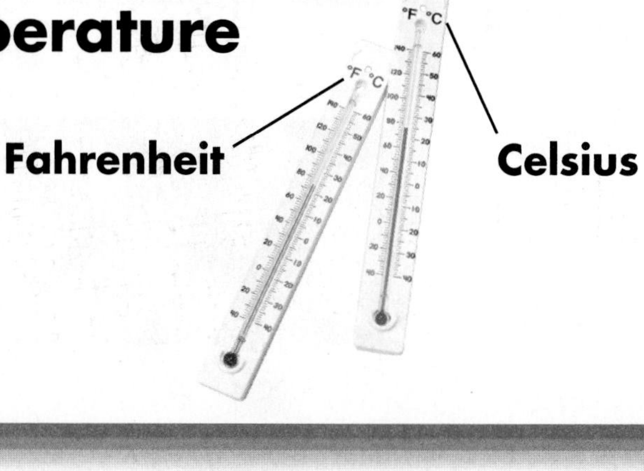

Water freezes at 0°C and 32°F.

Glossary

The glossary uses letters and signs to show how words are pronounced. The mark ′ is placed after a syllable with a primary or heavy accent. The mark ′ is placed after a syllable with a secondary or lighter accent.

To hear these words pronounced, listen to the AudioText CD.

Pronunciation Key

a	in hat	ō	in open	sh	in she
ā	in age	ȯ	in all	th	in thin
â	in care	ô	in order	ŦH	in then
ä	in far	oi	in oil	zh	in measure
e	in let	ou	in out	ə	= a in about
ē	in equal	u	in cup	ə	= e in taken
ėr	in term	u̇	in put	ə	= i in pencil
i	in it	ü	in rule	ə	= o in lemon
ī	in ice	ch	in child	ə	= u in circus
o	in hot	ng	in long		

A

adapt (ə dapt′) To change. Animals are **adapted** to live in their environment. (page 16)

amphibian (am fib′ē ən) An animal with bones that lives part of its life on land and part of its life in water. My pet frog is an **amphibian.** (page 41)

attract (ə trakt′) To pull toward. The opposite poles of two magnets will **attract** one another. (page 318)

axis (ak′sis) An imaginary line around which a planet turns. Earth spins on an **axis.** (page 370)

B

bird (bėrd) An animal with a backbone that has feathers, two legs, and wings. The **bird** flew from place to place searching for food. (page 40)

boulder (bōl′der) A very big rock. The **boulder** is by the water. (page 146)

C

camouflage (kam′ə fläzh) A color or shape that makes a plant or an animal hard to see. Some animals use **camouflage** to hide themselves from danger. (page 42)

condense (kən dens′) To change from a gas to a liquid. Water vapor **condenses** on the outside of my glass of juice. (page 179)

conductor (kən duk′tər) Something that lets heat easily move through it. Metal is a **conductor.** (page 281)

constellation (kon′sta lā′shen) A group of stars that form a picture. I like to search the night sky for **constellations.** (page 376)

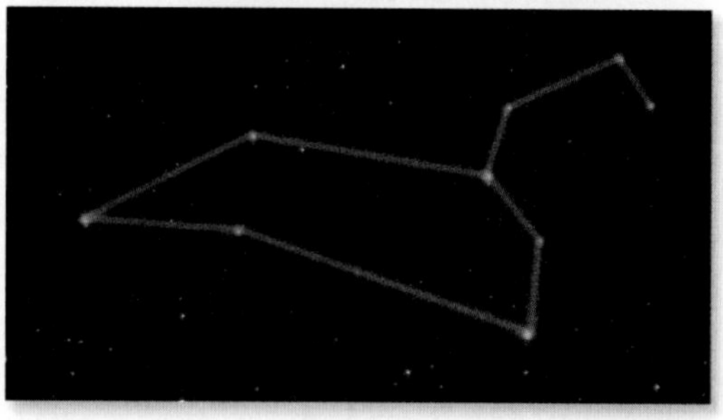

consumer (kən sü′mər) A living thing that cannot make its own food. Animals are **consumers.** (page 71)

crater (krā′tər) A hole that is shaped like a bowl. There are many **craters** on the surface of the Moon. (page 378)

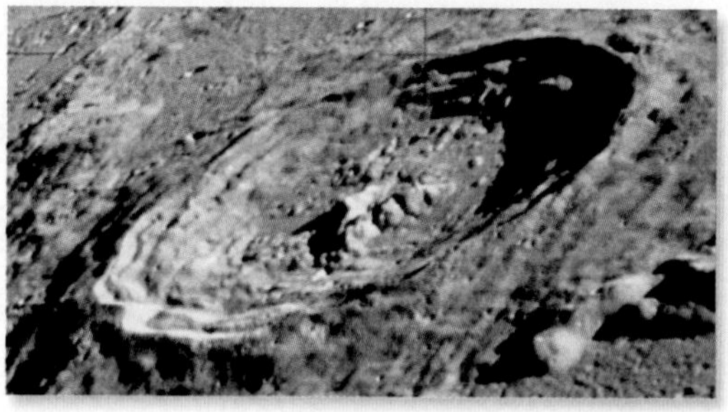

D

dinosaur (dī′nə sôr) An extinct animal that lived millions of years ago. **Dinosaurs** are large animals that lived on Earth long ago. (page 212)

E

energy (en′ər jē) The ability to do work or make change. You need **energy** to play soccer. (page 271)

engine (en′jən) A machine that changes energy into force or motion. Cars, trains, and airplanes have an **engine** that helps them run. (page 400)

environment (en vī′rən mənt) Everything that surrounds a living thing. A cactus is a plant that grows in a desert **environment.** (page 16)

erosion (i rō′zhən) Process by which rocks and soil are moved from one place to another. Heavy rains can cause **erosion.** (page 152)

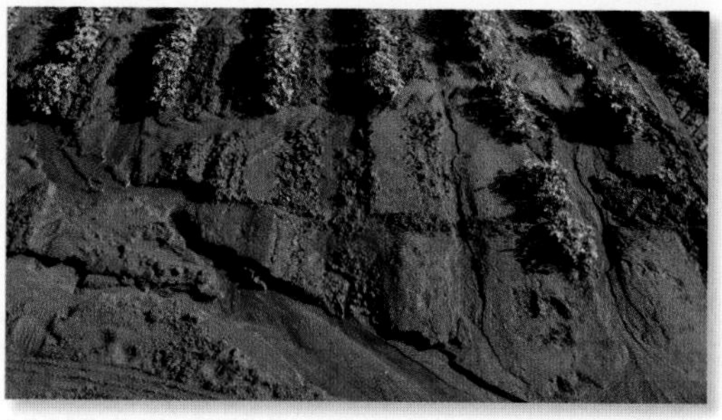

evaporate (i vap′ ə rāt) To change from a liquid to a gas. The puddle of water will **evaporate** and turn into water vapor. (page 179)

extinct (ek stingkt′) An animal or plant no longer living on Earth. Dinosaurs are **extinct.** (page 210)

F

fish (fish) An animal with bones that lives in water and has gills. Many types of **fish** live in an ocean. (page 40)

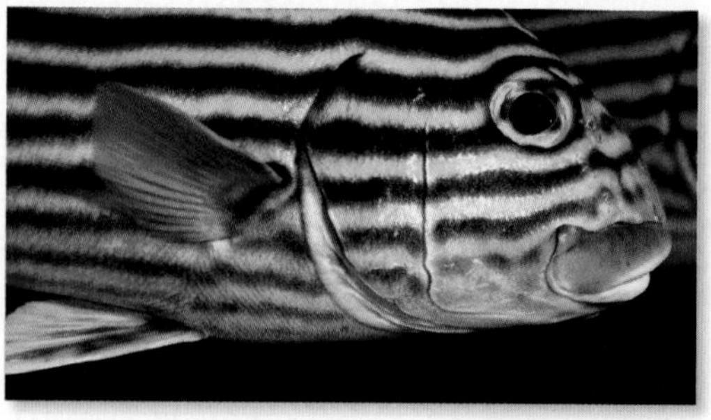

flower (flou′ər) The part of a plant that makes seeds. Some plants have many **flowers.** (page 9)

food chain (füd chān) Plants use sunlight, air, and water to make food. Animals eat the plants. Other animals eat those animals. This is called a food chain. A coyote and a mountain lion are part of a **food chain.** (page 74)

food web (füd web) A food web is made up of the food chains in a habitat. Corn, voles, and coyotes are part of a **food web.** (page 76)

force (fôrs) A push or pull that makes something move. You use **force** to move the wagon. (page 304)

fossil (fos′əl) A print or remains of a plant or animal that lived long ago. Dinosaur **fossils** are in the museum. (page 207)

friction (frik′shən) A force that slows down or stops moving objects. A bicycle's brakes use **friction** to slow down. (page 312)

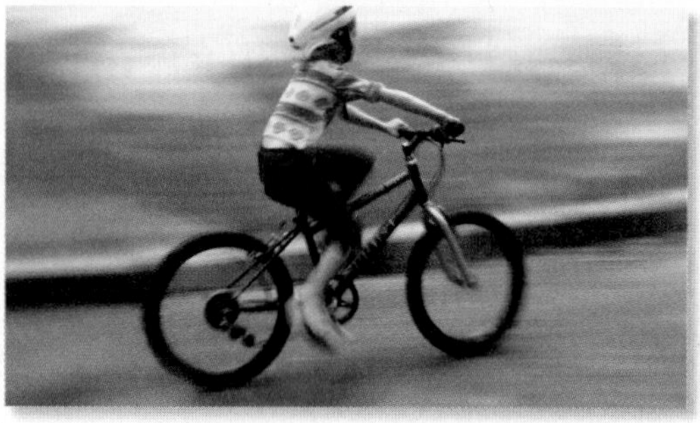

fuel (fyü′əl) Anything that is burned to make heat or power. We use wood as **fuel**. (page 279)

G

gas (gas) Matter that always takes the size and shape of its container. Bubbles are filled with **gas.** (page 246)

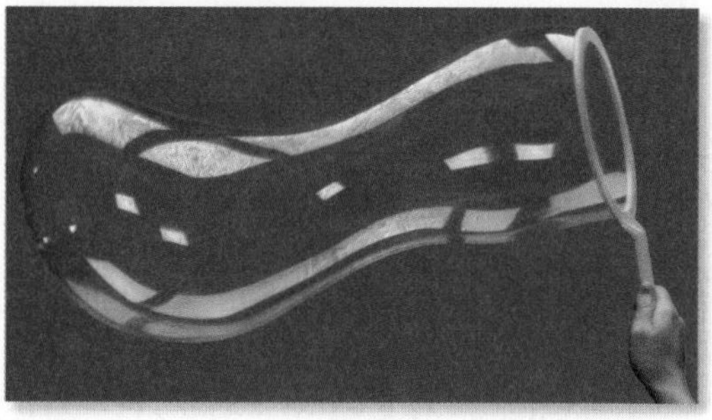

germinate (jėr′mə nāt) To begin to grow into a young plant. The plant seeds will soon **germinate.** (page 114)

gills (gilz) Special body parts that get oxygen from water. Fish have **gills**. (page 46)

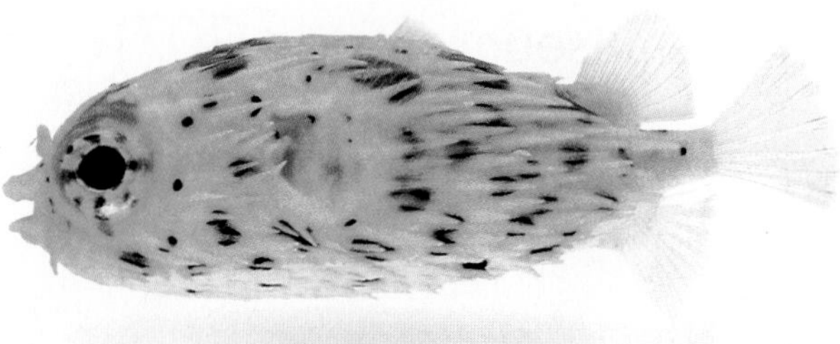

gravity (grav′ə tē) A force that pulls things toward the center of Earth. **Gravity** will pull the leaves back to Earth. (page 306)

H

hibernate (hī′bər nāt) To spend all winter sleeping or resting. Some animals **hibernate**. (page 186)

hurricane (hėr′ə kān) A storm that starts over warm ocean waters that has hard rain and very strong winds. A **hurricane** causes heavy rain and strong winds. (page 192)

I

insect (in′sekt) An animal without bones that has three body parts and six legs. It's fun to watch **insects.** (page 52)

invent (in vent′) To make something for the first time. Alexander Graham Bell **invented** the telephone. (page 399)

L

leaves (lēvz) Parts of a plant that use sunlight, air, nutrients, and water to make food for the plant. The **leaves** on the plant are long and thin. (page 8)

life cycle (līf sī′kəl) The way a living thing grows and changes. We studied the **life cycle** of a turtle. (page 106)

lightning (līt′ning) A flash of electricity in the sky. We watched **lightning** flash across the sky. (page 188)

liquid (lik′wid) Matter that does not have its own shape, but does have its own mass. **Liquids** take the shape of their containers. (page 244)

loudness (loud′nəs) How loud or soft a sound is. The **loudness** of some sounds can change. (page 336)

M

mammal (mam′əl) An animal with bones that usually has hair or fur on its body and feeds milk to its young. Chipmunks are **mammals.** (page 40)

manufacture (man′yə fak′chər) To make by hand or machine. Many countries in the world **manufacture** clothing. (page 408)

mass (mas) The amount of matter in an object. I use a balance to measure **mass.** (page 239)

meteorologist (mē′tē ə rol′ə jist) A person who studies weather. The **meteorologist** predicted sunny weather. (page 407)

migrate (mī′grāt) To move from one place to another in a regular pattern. Many types of birds **migrate** in the winter. (page 184)

mineral (min′ər əl) A nonliving solid that comes from Earth. Copper is a **mineral.** (page 147)

mixture (miks′chər) Something made up of two or more kinds of matter that do not change. Fruit salad is a **mixture** of different fruits. (page 250)

motion (mō′shen) Motion is the act of moving. A merry-go-round moves in a circular **motion.** (page 303)

N

natural resource (nach′ər əl rē′sôrs) A useful thing that comes from nature. Rocks are **natural resources.** (page 143)

nutrients (nü′trē ənt) Materials that living things need to live and grow. People get **nutrients** from the food they eat. (page 7)

nymph (nimf) A young insect that looks like its parent and grows wings as it changes. We found a dragonfly **nymph** in the pond by our school. (page 108)

O

orbit (ôr′bit) The path around something. It takes Earth about one year to orbit the Sun one time. (page 374)

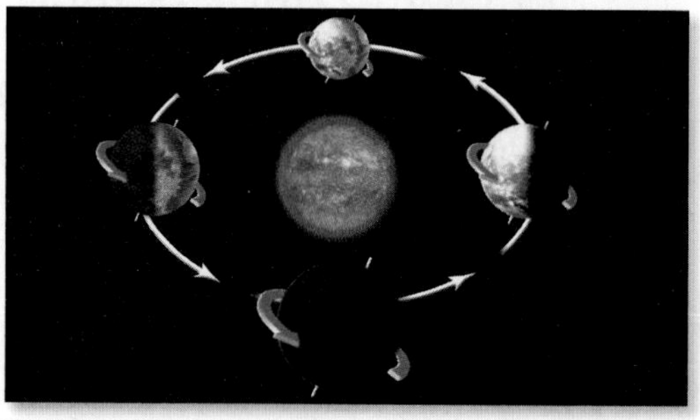

P

paleontologist (pā′lē on tol′ə jist) A scientist who studies fossils. **Paleontologists** study fossils to learn about life long ago. (page 207)

phase (fāz) The shape of the lighted part of the Moon. The Moon's **phases** can be seen best at night. (page 381)

pitch (pich) How high or low a sound is. The sound from the bullfrog had a low **pitch.** (page 338)

pollution (pə lü′ shən) Anything harmful added to land, air, or water. Many people work hard to reduce **pollution.** (page 154)

prairie (prâr′ē) Flat land covered with grasses and having few trees. A **prairie** has a lot of grass and few trees. (page 20)

predator (pred′ə tər) An animal that catches and eats another animal for food. A lion is a **predator.** (page 75)

prey (prā) An animal that is caught and eaten for food. Sea stars are the **prey** of sea otters. (page 75)

producer (prə dü′sər) A living thing that makes its own food. A kelp is a **producer.** (page 71)

property (prop′ər tē) Something about an object that you can observe with your senses. An object's color is one kind of **property.** (page 240)

R

recycle (rē sī′kəl) To change something so that it can be used again. My family **recycles** plastic bottles. (page 156)

reflect (ri flekt′) To bounce off of something. A mirror can **reflect** light. (page 282)

repel (ri pel′) To push away. The north ends of magnets will **repel** one another. (page 318)

reptile (rep′tīl) An animal with bones that has dry, scaly skin. Snakes are **reptiles.** (page 41)

roots (rüts) Parts of a plant that hold the plant in place and that take in water and nutrients from the soil. The **roots** of the old oak tree are deep inside the ground. (page 8)

rotation (rō tā′shən) Spinning on an axis. Earth makes one complete **rotation** each day. (page 370)

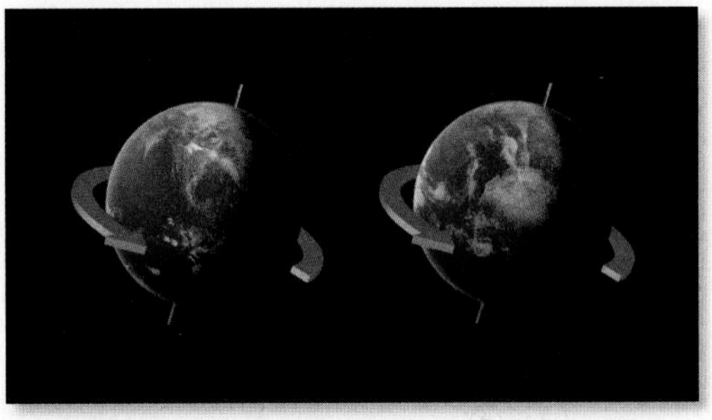

S

sand (sand) Tiny pieces of rock. People use **sand** to build roads. (page 146)

satellite (sat′l īt) An object that revolves around another object. Meteorologists study pictures taken by **satellites** to predict weather. (page 407)

seed coat (sēd kōt) The hard outer covering of a seed. The **seed coat** protects the seed. (page 114)

seedling (sēd′ling) A young plant. The tree **seedling** grows into a tree. (page 114)

shadow (shad′ō) A shadow is made when something blocks the light. The tree makes a **shadow.** (page 284)

simple machine (sim′pəl mə shēn) A tool with few or no moving parts that makes work easier. Workers often use **simple machines** to help them build things. (page 314)

solar energy (sō′lər en′ərjē) Solar energy is heat and light from the Sun. The house is heated by **solar energy.** (page 272)

solar system (sō′lər sis′təm) The Sun, the planets and their moons, and other objects that orbit the Sun. Earth is in our **solar system.** (page 382)

solid (sol′id) Matter that has its own shape and takes up space. The case that hold the supplies is a **solid.** (page 242)

source (sôrs) A place from which something comes. A lamp is one **source** of light. (page 278)

states of matter (stāts uv mat′ər) The three states of matter are solids, liquids, and gases. Water is a liquid **state of matter.** (page 242)

stem (stem) Part of a plant that holds it up and that carries water and nutrients to the leaves. The **stem** is long and green. (page 8)

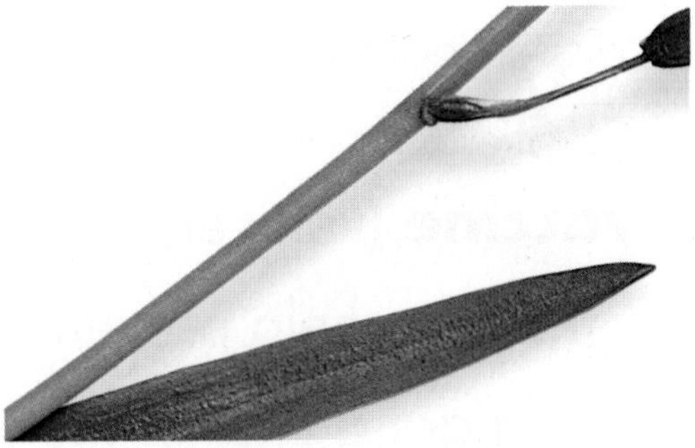

T

technology (tek nol′ə jē) Using science to help solve problems. People use **technology** every day. (page 399)

tornado (tôr nā′ dō) Very strong wind that comes down from clouds in the shape of a funnel. A **tornado** touched down near our town. (page 190)

transportation (tran′spər tā′ shən) Ways to move people or things from place to place. Today, **transportation** makes travel easier and faster than ever before. (page 400)

V

vaccine (vak sēn′) Medicine that can help prevent a disease. Mia got a shot of the flu **vaccine.** (page 402)

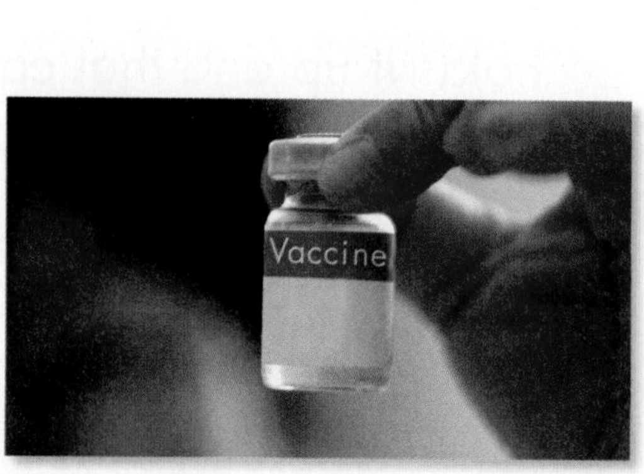

vibrate (vī′brāt) To move back and forth very fast. A flute makes the air **vibrate** to make sounds. (page 335)

W

water cycle (wȯ′tər sī′kəl) The way water moves from the clouds to Earth and back to the clouds. Water condenses and evaporates during the **water cycle.** (page 178)

weathering (weŦH′ər ing) The breaking apart and changing of rocks. **Weathering** causes sharp rocks to become smooth. (page 153)

work (wėrk) When force moves an object. It took a lot of **work** to push the sled up the hill. (page 308)

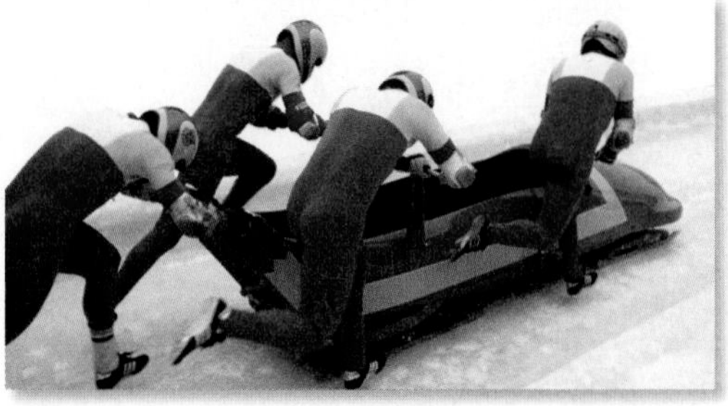

Index

This Index lists the pages on which topics appear in this book. Page numbers after a *p* refer to a photograph. Page numbers after a *c* refer to a chart or graph.

A

B

C

D

E

F

G

H

T

U

V

Credits

Text

"Little Seeds" from *The Winds that Come From Far Away and Other Poems* by Else Holmelund Minarik. Copyright ©1964 by Else Holmelund Minarik. Used by permission of HarperCollins Publishers.

"The Spring Wind" from *River Winding: Poems* by Charolotte Zolotow; Copyright ©1970 by Charlotte Zolotow. Reprinted by permission of S©ott Treimel, NY.

"This Happy Day" from *The Little Hill* by Harry Behn (Harcourt Brace, 1949).

"Apple Shadows" reprinted from *Black Earth, Gold Sun* by Patricia Hubbell with permission of Marshall Cavendish. Copyright ©2001 by Cavendish Children's Books.

Illustrations

29, 301, 327, 362, 367–368, 370–374, 376, 378, 380, 382, 388 Bob Kayganich; 69 Patrick Gnan; 201–203, 205-208 Big Sesh Studios; 344 Philip Williams; 365 Mary Teichman.

Photographs

Every effort has been made to secure permission and provide appropriate credit for photographic material. The publisher deeply regrets any omission and pledges to correct errors called to its attention in subsequent editions.

Unless otherwise acknowledged, all photographs are the property of Scott Foresman, a division of Pearson Education.

Photo locators denoted as follows: Top (T), Center (C), Bottom (B), Left (L), Right (R), Background (Bkgd).

Cover: (C) ©Chase Swift/Corbis, (B) ©Walter Hodges/Corbis, (Bkgd) ©Ralph A. Clevenger/Corbis, (Bkgd) ©George Grall/NGS Image Collection

Title Page: ©Tom Brakefield/Corbis

Front Matter: ii ©DK Images; iii (TR, BR) ©DK Images; v ©DK Images; vi (CL) ©David Middleton/NHPA Limited, (CL) ©Stephen Dalton/NHPA Limited; vii (CR) Tom Brakefield/Corbis, (B) Geoff Moon; Frank Lane Picture Agency/Corbis; viii (CL) Nigel J. Dennis/NHPA Limited, (B) William Bernard/Corbis; ix Andy Rouse/NHPA Limited; x (CL) ©Stone/Getty Images, (CL) ©Steve Terrill/Corbis, (B) ©DK Images; xi ©Jim Zuckerman/Corbis; xiii ©DK Images; xiv ©Charles Gupton/Corbis; xv ©Kelly-Mooney Photography/Corbis; xvi (CL) ©Lester Lefkowitz/Corbis, (CL) Getty Images; xvii (CR) ©John Gillmoure/Corbis, (Bkgd) ©Handout/Reuters/Corbis; xviii (CL, B) NASA Image Exchange, (CL) Getty Images, (BC) ©NASA/JPL/Handout/Reuters/Corbis; xix ©Reuters/Corbis; xxiv NASA; xxv Getty Images; xxix ©Royalty-Free/Corbis; xxxi ©Ed Bock/Corbis.

Unit A: Divider: (Bkgd) Digital Vision, (CC) Digital Vision; **Chapter 1:** 1 (C) ©David Middleton/NHPA Limited, (BR) ©Stephen Dalton/NHPA Limited, (TR) Brand X Pictures; 2 (BR) ©DK Images, (T) Corbis; 3 (BL) ©DK Images, (BR) Richard Hamilton Smith/Corbis; 5 (Bkgd) Corbis, (TR) ©Stephen Dalton/NHPA Limited, (CL) ©Eric Crichton/Corbis; 6 (C) Corbis, (TR) ©Stephen Dalton/NHPA Limited; 7 (BR) Brand X Pictures, (TR) Hemera Technologies; 8 (TL, BL, BC) ©DK Images; 10 Brand X Pictures; 11 (CL) ©Ted Mead/PhotoLibrary, (TR, BR) ©DK Images, (TL) ©Michael Boys/Corbis, (CR) ©ChromaZone Images/Index Stock Imagery, (BL) ©Scott Camazine/Photo Researchers, Inc.; 12 (TL) Peter Anderson/©DK Images, (CR) ©Cosmo Condina/Getty Images; 13 (CL) Steve Kaufman/Corbis, (CR) Ted Levin/Animals Animals/Earth Scenes; 14 Getty Images; 15 (TR, CR) ©DK Images, (TL) ©Bill Ross/Corbis, (CL) ©Ed Reschke/Peter Arnold, Inc., (BL) ©Ted Mead/PhotoLibrary, (BR) Getty Images; 16 (CR) ©M.P. Kahl/DRK Photo, (TL) ©DK Images; 17 (CL)©Royalty-Free/Corbis, (TR) ©DK Images; 18 (TL) ©Medford Taylor/NGS Image Collection, (BR) ©Eric Crichton/Corbis; 19 (TR, BR) ©DK Images, (C) ©Bob Wickham/PhotoLibrary; 20 (TL) ©Pat O'Hara/Corbis, (BR) Neil Fletcher and Matthew Ward/©DK Images; 21 (C) Getty Images, (TR) ©Pat O'Hara/Corbis, (BR) ©David Muench/Corbis; 22 (BR) ©Ronald Martin, (TL) Getty Images; 23 (C) Randall Hyman Photography, (BR) ©Patti Murray/Animals Animals/Earth Scenes, (TR) ©Steve Kaufman/Corbis; 24 (TL, BR) Brand X Pictures; 25 (TR) Image Quest 3-D/NHPA Limited, (BR) ©OSF/Animals Animals/Earth Scenes, ©David Muench/Corbis; 26 ©George D. Lepp/Corbis; 28 (CL, BL) Matthew Ward/©DK Images, (T) Hemera Technologies; 29 ©Klein/Hubert/Peter Arnold, Inc.; 30 (BR) ©Pat O'Hara/Corbis, (TR) ©Richard Hamilton Smith/Corbis, (TL, CL, CC, CR) ©DK Images; 31 (TR) ©DK Images, (CL) ©Roy Rainford/Robert Harding Picture Library, Ltd.; 32 (BL) Getty Images, (TL, CL) Hunt Institute for Botanical Documentation/Carnegie Mellon University, Pittsburgh, PA; **Chapter 2:** 33 (C) Tom Brakefield/Corbis, (CR) Brand X Pictures; 34 (BL) ©Don Enger/Animals Animals/Earth Scenes, (TC) ©Alan G. Nelson/Animals Animals/Earth Scenes, (BR) Getty Images; 35 (CR) ©Tom Brakefield/Corbis, (TR) ©Joe McDonald/Corbis, (BR) ©Buddy Mays/Corbis, (BL) ©Jean-Louis Le Moigne/NHPA Limited; 37 (Bkgd) ©Alan G. Nelson/Animals Animals/Earth Scenes, (TR) Brand X Pictures, (CL) ©Breck P. Kent/Animals Animals/Earth Scenes, (BCL) ©Joe McDonald/Animals Animals/Earth Scenes; 38 ©Alan G. Nelson/Animals Animals/Earth Scenes; 39 (BR) ©W. Perry Conway/Corbis, (TL) ©DK Images; 40 (BL) ©Joe McDonald/Corbis, (BC) ©George D.Lepp/Corbis, (BR) Getty Images, (TL) Hemera Technologies; 41 (BL) Getty Images, (BR) ©Tom Brakefield/Corbis; 42 (BL) ©Royalty-Free/Corbis, (TR) ©Joe McDonald/Corbis, (TL) Getty Images, ©D. Robert & Lorri Franz/Corbis; 43 ©Breck P. Kent/Animals Animals/Earth Scenes; 44 (TR) ©Jean-Louis Le Moigne/NHPA Limited, (B) ©Kent Wood/Photo Researchers, Inc., (TL) ©DK Images; 45 ©DK Images; 46 (CR, BL) ©DK Images, (TL) ©Comstock; 47 (TR, CR) ©DK Images; 48 (C) ©Stephen Dalton/NHPA Limited, (BL) ©Daniel Heuclin/NHPA Limited, (TL) Hemera Technologies; 49 ©Zig Leszczynski/Animals Animals/Earth Scenes; 50 (B) ©Carmela Leszczynski/Animals Animals/Earth Scenes, (TL) Hemera Technologies; 51 (CL) Getty Images, (C) ©Kim Taylor/Bruce Coleman Collection; 52 (TL, C) ©DK Images, (BL) ©Geoff Moon/Frank Lane Picture Agency/Corbis; 53 ©OSF/D. Clyne/Animals Animals/Earth Scenes; 54 (TL, C) ©DK Images; 55 (CR) ©Niall Benvie/Corbis, (TR, CR)©DK Images; 56 ©Dale Sanders/Masterfile Corporation; 58 (C, BC, BR) ©DK Images, (BL) ©Royalty-Free/Corbis, (CL) ©Carmela Leszczynski/Animals Animals/Earth Scenes; 59 (BL) ©DK Images, (BR) ©Daniel Heuclin/NHPA Limited; 60 (TR, CL, BR) Getty Images, (TL) ©Tom Brakefield/Corbis, (TCL) ©DK Images, (TCR) ©Joe McDonald/Corbis, (CR) ©Don Enger/Animals Animals/Earth Scenes; 61 (TR) ©DK Images, (CL, CR) Hemera Technologies; 62 (Bkgd) Map Resources, (C) ©Marian Bacon/Animals Animals/Earth Scenes, (B) Getty Images; 63 (TR) ©Andrew Syred/Photo Researchers, Inc., (T)©Royalty-Free/Corbis, (BR) MFSC/NASA, (C) ©Orbital Sciences Corporation/Photo Researchers, Inc.; 64 (BL) ©Niall Benvie/Corbis, (CL)©George Grall/National Geographic/Getty Images, (TR) ©Raymond Gehman/NGS Image Collection; **Chapter 3:** 65 (TC) ©Nigel J. Dennis/NHPA Limited, (TR) Getty Images; 66 (TC) ©Clem Haagner/Gallo Images/Corbis, (B) ©Kennan Ward/Corbis; 67 (BR) ©Randy Morse/Animals Animals/Earth Scenes, (CR) ©Stephen Frink/Corbis, (BR) ©James Watt/Animals Animals/Earth Scenes, (CR) ©Steve Bein/Corbis, (CR) ©Andrew J. Martinez/Photo Researchers, Inc., (TR) ©Sanford/Agliolo/Corbis, (TR) ©Amos Nachoum/Corbis; 69 (Bkgd) ©Clem Haagner/Gallo Images/Corbis, (TR) Getty Images; 70 Clem Haagner/Gallo Images/Corbis; 71 (R) ©Peter Johnson/Corbis, (TR) Hemera Technologies; 72 (TL) Getty Images, (B) ©Clem Haagner/Gallo Images/Corbis; 73 ©Ian Beames/Ecoscene/Corbis; 74 (BL) ©Royalty-Free/Corbis, (BR) ©Joe McDonald/Corbis, (TL) Frank Greenaway/©DK Images; 75 (BR) ©William Bernard/Corbis, ©Gaoil Shumway/Getty Images, (CR) ©Royalty-Free/Corbis; 76 (TR) ©DK Images, (TL, CR) ©Joe McDonald/Corbis, (BR) ©Stephen Krasemann/NHPA Limited, (CL)©Royalty-Free/Corbis; 77 (CL) ©Gaoil Shumway/Getty Images, (TC) ©Jim Zipp/Photo Researchers, Inc.; 78 (CL) ©Randy Morse/Animals Animals/Earth Scenes, (BC) ©Stephen Frink/Corbis, (CR) ©Andrew J. Martinez/Photo Researchers, Inc., (TL) Brand X Pictures; 79 ©Kennan Ward/Corbis; 80 (TC) ©James Watt/Animals Animals/Earth Scenes, (BR) ©Andrew J. Martinez/Photo Researchers, Inc., (CR) ©Stephen Frink/Corbis, (CL) ©Randy Morse/Animals Animals/Earth Scenes, (TL) ©Andrew J. Martinez/Photo Researchers, Inc.; 81 (T) ©Amos Nachoum/Corbis, (CR) ©Sanford/Agliolo/Corbis, (BC) ©Steve Bein/Corbis; 82 (T) ©Sanford/Agliolo/Corbis, (BL) ©Bettmann/Corbis; 83 ©Sanford/Agliolo/Corbis; 84 (B) ©Michael and Patricia Fogden/Corbis, (TL) ©DK Images; 85 ©Fred McConnaughey/Photo Researchers, Inc.; 86 (BL) ©Darrell Gulin/Corbis, (TL) Getty Images, (BR) ©Farrell Grehan/Corbis; 87 ©DK Images; 88 (CL) ©Pete Atkinson/NHPA Limited, (TL) NHPA Limited; 89 (CC) ©Eric and David Hosking/Corbis, (TC) ©Rob C. Nunnington/Gallo Images/Corbis, (TR) ©Richard Murphy; 90 ©Kennan Ward/Corbis; 92 (TR) ©Joe McDonald/Corbis, (BR) ©D. Robert and Lorri Franz/Corbis, (BL) Frank Greenaway/©DK Images, (Bkgd) ©William Manning/Corbis, (BL) Getty Images, (CL) Jane Burton/©DK Images; 94 (BR) ©Clem Haagner/Gallo Images/Corbis, (TC) ©Stephen Krasemann/NHPA Limited, (TR) ©Randy Morse/Animals Animals/Earth Scenes, (CL, CR) ©Royalty-Free/Corbis, (C) ©Joe McDonald/Corbis; 95 (CL) ©George H. H. Huey/Corbis, (CR) ©Norbert Rosing/NGS Image Collection, (TR) ©Andrew J. Martinez/Photo Researchers, Inc.; 96

(T, L) Getty Images, (B, BL) Brand X Pictures, (TL) ©The Image Bank/Getty Images; **Chapter 4:** 97 (C) ©Andy Rouse/NHPA Limited, (CR) ©Paul A. Sounders/Corbis; 98 (TL) ©Jonathan Blair/Corbis, (BL) ©Robert Thompson/NHPA Limited, (CL) ©Soames Summerhays/Photo Researchers, Inc., (C) ©Royalty-Free/Corbis, (BR) ©DK Images; 99 (BR) ©Carol Cohen/Corbis, (Bkgd) ©Tom Brakefield/Corbis, (TL, BR) ©DK Images; 101 (TR) ©Paul A. Sounders/Corbis, (CL) ©Royalty-Free/Corbis, (CR) ©David Young Wolff/PhotoEdit; 102 ©Tom Brakefield/Corbis; 103 Getty Images; 104 (TL) Getty Images, (CR) ©Peter Johnson/Corbis, (CL) ©Jonathan Blair/Corbis; 105 ©C. Allan Morgan/Peter Arnold, Inc.; 106 (CL) ©Jonathan Blair/Corbis, (BL) ©Soames Summerhays/Photo Researchers, Inc.; 106 Getty Images; 107 ©DK Images; 108 (BL) Neil Fletcher/©DK Images, (BL) ©DK Images, (TL) Courtesy of Digital Dragonflies, 109 ©DK Images; 110 (CL, CR) ©DK Images, (TL) Getty Images; 111 Bob Langrish/©DK Images; 112 (BL) ©Julie Habel/Corbis, (TR) ©Tim Davis/Corbis, (TL) ©DK Images; 113 ©Kevin Schafer/NHPA Limited; 114 (BL, BC, BR) ©DK Images, (TL) Brand X Pictures; 115 ©DK Images; 116 (TL) Brand X Pictures, (R) ©Robert Landau/Corbis, (BC) Getty Images; 117 ©DK Images; 118 (TL, BR) ©DK Images; 119 (CC, CR, BL, BC) ©DK Images; 120 (TL, C, BL, BC) ©DK Images; 121 ©DK Images; 122 (TR) ©Gladden William Willis/Animals Animals/Earth Scenes, (TC, TR) ©T. Kitchin & V. Hurst/NHPA Limited, (TR) ©Stephen Dalton/NHPA Limited; 124 (C) ©Albert Normandin/Masterfile Corporation, (B) ©DK Images, (CC) Getty Images, (C) ©Michael Newman/PhotoEdit, (CL) ©Robert Pickett/Corbis, (BL) ©Richard Shiell/Animals Animals/Earth Scenes, (BR) ©Kevin Schafer/Corbis; 125 (BL) ©DK Images, (CL) ©Stephen Dalton/NHPA Limited, (BL) ©George Bernard/NHPA Limited, (CC) Getty Images; 126 (TR, CL, CR, BL, BR) ©DK Images, (CR) ©Gary W. Carter/Corbis, (CR) ©Jonathan Blair/Corbis, (CR) ©Soames Summerhays/Photo Researchers, Inc., (TC) ©Robert Thompson/NHPA Limited, (CC) ©Carol Cohen/Corbis; 127 ©DK Images; 128 (B) ©Fred Bruemmer/DRK Photo, (TC) ©Carl & Ann Purcell/Corbis, (CL) NASA, (CL) ©Stone/Getty Images; 130 (BL) ©Tom Brakefield/Corbis, (TCL) ©Alan G. Nelson/Animals Animals/Earth Scenes, (TL) Corbis, (CL) ©Clem Haagner/Gallo Images/Corbis; 131 (TR) ©Andrew J. Martinez/Photo Researchers, Inc., (CR) ©Eric and David Hosking/Corbis, (CR) ©Don Enger/Animals Animals/Earth Scenes; 132 (TR) ©Theo Allofs/Corbis, (TR) ©Lynda Richardson/Corbis; 134 (Bkgd) ©Michael Boys/Corbis, (TL) ©Tim Wright/Corbis; 135 ©Bohemian Nomad Picturemakers/Corbis; 136 (BC) ©Image Quest 3-D/NHPA Limited, (CC) ©Michael & Patricia Fogden/Corbis, (Bkgd) ©Stone/Getty Images, (TC) Getty Images.

Unit B: Divider: ©Gavin Hellier/Getty Images; **Chapter 5:**137 (TC) ©Stone/Getty Images, (C) ©Steve Terrill/Corbis; 138 (BR) Grant Heilman Photography, (BL) ©DK Images; 139 (CR) ©Royalty-Free/Corbis, (BR) ©Pete Soloutos/Corbis; 141 (TR) ©Stone/Getty Images, (C) ©David M. Dennis/Animals Animals/Earth Scenes; 143 ©DK Images; 144 Getty Images; 145 (TL) ©Roy Morsch/Corbis, (BL) ©DK Images, (BR) ©Craig Tuttle/Corbis, (TR) Getty Images; 146 (B) ©Royalty-Free/Corbis, (TL) Hemera Technologies; 147 (TR, CL) ©DK Images, (BR) Brand X Pictures, (CL) ©Mark A. Schneider/Visuals Unlimited; 148 ©DK Images; 149 ©DK Images; 150 (CR) ©Donna Disario/Corbis, (CL, BR) Getty Images, (CR) ©Rob Blakers/Photo Library; 151 (CR, BR) ©Royalty-Free/Corbis, (TL, CL) Getty Images, (BL) Corbis; 152 (CR) ©Royalty-Free/Corbis, (B) Grant Heilman Photography, (TL) Hemera Technologies; 153 (CR) ©Joe McDonald/Animals Animals/Earth Scenes, (B) ©Lester Lefkowitz/Corbis; 154 (T) Digital Vision, (TL) ©ThinkStock/SuperStock, (T) ©Gary Meszaros/Visuals Unlimited, (BR) ©Charles E. Rotker/Corbis; 156 (TL) ©Corbis, (BC) ©Pete Soloutos/Corbis, (BL) ©Ryan McVay/Getty Images; 157 ©Eric Fowke/PhotoEdit; 158 (CL) ©Phil Schermeister/Corbis, (TL) Getty Images, (R) ©Steve Terrill/Corbis; 159 ©Momatiuk Eastcott/Animals Animals/Earth Scenes; 160 ©Robert Pickett/Corbis; 162 ©Susan Steinkamp/Corbis; 164 (TC) ©Mark A. Schneider/Visuals Unlimited, (B) ©Lester Lefkowitz/Corbis, (CR) ©Charles E. Rotker/Corbis, (CL) ©Owaki-Kulla/Corbis, (TL) ©Pete Soloutos/Corbis, (CC) Grant Heilman Photography; 165 (CL) ©Stone/Getty Images, (CR) Getty Images; 166 (BR) Corbis, (Bkgd) ©Royalty-Free/Corbis, (TR) Getty Images, (BL) ©Reuters/Corbis; 167 (TL, C) Getty Images; 168 (T) Getty Images, (TL) ©Lynda Richardson/Corbis, (CL) ©Jonathan Blair/Corbis, (BL) ©Macduff Everton/Corbis, (B) ©Royalty-Free/Corbis, (R) Tim Ridley/©DK Images; **Chapter 6:** 169 (C) ©Jim Zuckerman/Corbis, (TC) Getty Images; 170 (B) ©Sam Abell/NGS Image Collection, (T) ©Alan. R. Moller/Getty Images; 171 (BR) ©Joseph H. Bailey/NGS Image Collection, (BR) ©George McCarthy/Corbis, (TR) ©Annie Griffiths Belt/NGS Image Collection, (CR) ©A & J Verkaik/Corbis; 173 ©Alan. R. Moller/Getty Images; 174 (C) ©Otto Rogge/Corbis, (Bkgd) ©Bill Ross/Corbis; 175 (TR) ©Corbis, (B) ©DK Images; 176 (CL) ©Gene E. Moore, (TR) ©Phil Schermeister/NGS Image Collection, (TL) ©Stone/Getty Images; 177 (TR) Tom L. McKnight, (CR) ©Richard Hamilton Smith/Corbis; 178 (CC) ©Sam Abell/NGS Image Collection, (TL) Hemera Technologies; 180 (BR) Getty Images, (TL) Hemera Technologies, (BR) ©Tom Brakefield/Corbis; 181 (CL, BL) Getty Images, (TL) ©Dennis MacDonald/PhotoEdit; 182 (TL) Hemera Technologies, (B) ©John Conrad/Corbis; 183 (TL) ©James Schwabel/Panoramic Images, Chicago, (BL) ©D. Robert and Lorri Franz/Corbis, (CL) ©Michael Boys/Corbis; 184 (TL) Hemera Technologies, (BR) ©Gary W. Carter/Corbis; 185 (CL) ©Stone/Getty Images, (B) ©Lowell Georgia/Corbis; 186 (TL) Hemera Technologies, (BR) ©Marty Stoufer/Animals Animals/Earth Scenes; 187 (BL) ©Comstock Images/Getty Images, (TL, CL) Getty Images; 188 ©DK Images; 189 (CL) ©A & J Verkaik/Corbis, (TR) Getty Images; 190 (TL) ©Steve Bronstein/Getty Images, (TL) Hemera Technologies; 191 ©Alan. R. Moller/Getty Images; 192 Hemera Technologies; 193 (BL) ©Annie Griffiths Belt/NGS Image Collection, (CL) Getty Images; 194 Corbis; 196 (Bkgd) ©Gabe Palmer/Corbis, (BC) ©Stone/Getty Images; 197 (CL, CR) Hemera Technologies, (TL) Getty Images; 198 (TC) ©A & J Verkaik/Corbis, (TR) ©Marty Stoufer/Animals Animals/Earth Scenes, (CC) ©Annie Griffiths Belt/NGS Image Collection, (CR) ©Stone/Getty Images, (BC) ©Alan. R. Moller/Getty Images, (BR) ©D. Robert and Lorri Franz/Corbis; 199 (CL) ©Ariel Skelley/Corbis, (TR) ©Dennis MacDonald/PhotoEdit; 200 (BR) ©SYGMA/Corbis, (BL) ©Stocktrek/Corbis, (TR) ©MSFC/NASA; 202 ©DK Images; **Chapter 7:** 203 ©Richard T. Nowitz/Corbis; 205 Colin Keates/©DK Images; 207 (TR) Stephen Oliver/©DK Images, (BR) ©Richard T. Nowitz/Corbis; 208 (BL) ©DK Images, (BR) ©Scott W. Smith/Animals Animals/Earth Scenes, (TL) Tim Ridley/©DK Images; 209 (TC) ©DK Images, (CL) Colin Keates/Natural History Museum/©DK Images; 210 (TR) Natural History Museum /©DK Images, (BL) ©Dennis C. Murphy, (BR) Harry Taylor/Courtesy of the Royal Museum of Scotland, Edinburgh/©DK Images, (TL) Hemera Technologies; 211 Natural History Museum/©DK Images; 212 (TL, C, CR) ©DK Images; 213 (TR, CR) ©DK Images; 214 (BL, CR) ©DK Images, (TL) Natural History Museum/©DK Images; 215 (TL) ©DK Images, (C) Giuliano Fornari/©DK Images; 216 (TL, C) ©Francois Gohler/Photo Researchers, Inc.; 217 (Bkgd, TR) ©The Natural History Museum, London; 218 ©DK Images; 220 (Bkgd) ©Pat O'Hara/Corbis, (TL, BR) ©James L. Amos/Corbis, (CL) ©George H. H. Huey/Corbis, (BL) Colin Keates/Natural History Museum/©DK Images; 221 ©Lowell Georgia/Corbis; 222 (T, CR) ©DK Images, (CL) ©Richard T. Nowitz/Corbis, (BR) ©Layne Kennedy/Corbis; 223 (TR, CL) ©DK Images; 224 (BR) ©David Muench/Corbis, (BL) ©Peter Larson/Courtesy of the Black Hills Institute of Geological Research, Inc., Hill City, SD, (CR) ©Philip Gould/Corbis, (T) Senekenberg Nature Museum/©DK Images; 226 Getty Images; 228 Colin Keates/Natural History Museum/©DK Images; 230 Brand X Pictures; 231 Getty Images; 232 Digital Vision.

Unit C: Divider: ©Matthias Kulka/Corbis; **Chapter 8:** 233 (C) ©Charles Gupton/Corbis, (CR) Getty Images; 237 Getty Images; 239 (TR) Getty Images, (B) Brand X Pictures; 242 Hemera Technologies; 244 ©DK Images; 248 Steve Gorton and Gary Ombler/©DK Images; 250 Brand X Pictures; 252 ©Brand X Pictures/Getty Images; 253 ©Craig Tuttle/Corbis; 254 ©Nedra Westwater/Robert Harding Picture Library, Ltd.; 255 ©Royalty-Free/Corbis; 256 ©Royalty-Free/Corbis; 262 (B) ©ESA/PLI/Corbis, (TR, R) ©DK Images, (BL) ©John F. Kennedy Space Center/NASA, (BR) ©The Boeing Company; 263 (R) ©DK Images, (TR) Corbis, (C) NASA, (TL) NASA Image Exchange; 264 (Bkgd) Getty Images, (B) ©JPL/Cornell/NASA, (CL) NASA, (BR) ©NASA/Corbis, (TL) Corbis, (CR) ©ESA/PLI/Corbis; **Chapter 9:** 265 (C) ©Kelly-Mooney Photography/Corbis, (TC) ©Stone/Getty Images; 266 (T) ©Jim Cummins/Corbis, (BR) The Image Bank/Getty Images, (BL) Getty Images; 267 (CR) ©Richard Megna/Fundamental Photographs, (BR) ©Craig Tuttle/Corbis, (BL) Veer, Inc.; 269 ©Jim Cummins/Corbis; 270 ©Jim Cummins/Corbis; 271 (BR) Getty Images, (TR) Hemera Technologies; 272 (BL) ©Roger Ressmeyer/Skylab/NRL/NASA/Corbis, (TL) Hemera Technologies, ©Tom Stewart/Corbis; 273 Getty Images; 274 Hemera Technologies; 275 (TL) Corbis, (BL) ©John Conrad/Corbis, (TR) ©Laureen March/Corbis, (BR) ©Jon Feingersh/Corbis; 276 Hemera Technologies; 278 (TL) Dave King/Pitt Rivers Museum/University of Oxford, Oxford/©DK Images; 279 The Image Bank/Getty Images; 280 Hemera Technologies; 281 ©Paul Seheult/Eye Ubiquitous/Corbis; 282 (TL) Hemera Technologies, (B) ©Richard Megna/Fundamental Photographs; 283 ©Royalty-Free/Corbis; 284 (TL) Hemera Technologies, (BL) ©Craig Tuttle/Corbis, (BR) ©Lonny Kalfus/Getty Images; 285 ©DK Images; 286 Getty Images; 287 (TL) ©Randy Lincks/Corbis, (TR) ©Tony Freeman/PhotoEdit, Digital Vision; 288 (CL) Steven Gorton and Gary Ombler/©DK Images, (CL) Getty Images; 289 Getty Images; 292 ©Bryn Colton/Assignments Photographers/Corbis; 294 (CL) ©Richard Megna/Fundamental Photographs, (CC) Getty Images, (BR) Veer, Inc.; 295 (TR) Hemera Technologies, (TR) Getty Images; 296 (T, CR) Veer, Inc., (CR) ©Robert Landau/Corbis, (Bkgd) ©Ken Davies/Masterfile Corporation, (BL) ©Hans Neleman/Getty Images; **Chapter 10:** 297 (CC) ©Lester Lefkowitz/Corbis, (TR)

Getty Images; 298 (Bkgd) ©Paul Barton/Corbis, (T) Getty Images; 301 Getty Images; 302 (C) Getty Images, (Bkgd) ©Paul Barton/Corbis; 303 (TR) ©DK Images, (B) Getty Images; 304 (CL) ©Joyce Choo/Corbis, (R) ©First Light/Corbis, (TL) Getty Images; 306 (R) ©Chris Carroll/Corbis, (TL) Hemera Technologies, (BL) ©Stone/Getty Images; 307 (CR) ©DK Images, (CL, CR) Hemera Technologies; 308 (B) ©Wally McNamee/Corbis, (TL) Getty Images; 309 ©Stone/Getty Images; 310 Hemera Technologies; 311 ©Chapman/NewSport/Corbis; 312 Hemera Technologies; 313 (T) ©Mike Brinson/Getty Images, (B) ©ThinkStock/SuperStock; 314 Hemera Technologies; 316 (BR) ©DK Images, (CL) ©Laurie Campbell/NHPA Limited, (CR) Getty Images; 317 (CL) ©Juergen & Christine Sohns/Animals Animals/Earth Scenes, (CR) ©Jonathan Blair/Corbis; 318 Gary Ombler/©DK Images; 320 Hemera Technologies; 322 Digital Vision; 326 (C) Getty Images, (TC) ©Joyce Choo/Corbis, (BR) ©Michael S. Yamashita/Corbis; 328 (C) Corbis, (TL) ©Jeff Caplan/Langley Research Center/NASA; **Chapter 11:** 329 ©John Gillmoure/Corbis; 330 (B) ©Martin Harvey/NHPA Limited, (T) ©Thinkstock; 331 ©Mark Boulton/Photo Researchers, Inc.; 333 (Bkgd) ©Thinkstock, (C) ©Tom & Dee Ann McCarthy/Corbis; 334 ©Thinkstock; 335 (TR) Getty Images, (B) ©Thinkstock; 336 (CL) ©DK Images, (CR) ©Jeff Hunter/Getty Images, (BL) ©Walter Hodges/Corbis, (TL) Getty Images, (BR) ©George Hall/Corbis; 337 (CL, BL) Getty Images, (CR, BR) ©Royalty-Free/Corbis; 338 (TL) Hemera Technologies, (B) ©DK Images; 339 (TR) ©Mark Boulton/Photo Researchers, Inc., (TL) Getty Images; 340 (CL) ©Roger Wilmshurts/Frank Lane Picture Agency/Corbis, (BL) Digital Vision, (TL) Getty Images; 341 ©Jeffrey L. Rotman/Corbis; 342 (TR) ©Royalty-Free/Corbis, (BL) ©Stephen Dalton/NHPA Limited, (CC) ©Image Quest 3-D/NHPA Limited, (CL) ©DK Images, (TL) ©Ingram/Creatas, (CL) Getty Images, (CL) ©Stockbyte; 343 (CR) ©Brownie Harris/Corbis, (TR) Corbis; 344 ©DK Images; 346 ©DK Images; 348 ©Tom Tracy/Corbis; 350 (BR) Digital Vision, (CL) ©DK Images, (CR) Getty Images; 351 (TL) ©DK Images, (C) Getty Images, (TR) ©Image Quest 3-D/NHPA Limited; 352 (Bkgd) ©Royalty-Free/Corbis, (B) ©Photex/S. Maka/Zefa/Masterfile Corporation, (CR) ©Alejandro Purgue; 353 PhotoLibrary; 354 (BCL) ©Paul Barton/Corbis, (BL) ©Thinkstock, (CL) ©Jim Cummins/Corbis, (CL) Getty Images; 355 ©DK Images; 356 ©Darwin Wiggett/Corbis; 358 (C, BL) Getty Images; 360 (Bkgd) ©Steve Satushek/Getty Images.

Unit D: Divider: (Bkgd) ©Reuters/Corbis, (BR) Corbis; **Chapter 12:** 361 (C) NASA Image Exchange, (TR) Getty Images; 362 ©Roger Ressmeyer/Corbis; 363 (BL) NASA Image Exchange, (BR) ©John Sanford/Photo Researchers, Inc.; 365 (Bkgd) ©Roger Tidman/Corbis, (TR) Getty Images; 366 ©Roger Tidman/Corbis; 367 ©SOHO (ESA & NASA)/NASA; 368 ©SOHO (ESA & NASA)/NASA; 372 (CL) ©John M. Roberts/Corbis, (BL) ©Royalty-Free/Corbis, (CR) Getty Images; 373 ©James Randklev/Visions of America/Corbis; 376 ©Roger Ressmeyer/Corbis; 377 ©Jerry Schad/Photo Researchers, Inc.; 378 NASA Image Exchange; 379 ©Stone/Getty Images; 380 ©John Sanford/Photo Researchers, Inc.; 381 ©Goddard Space Flight Center/NASA; 384 ©Roger Ressmeyer/Corbis; 386 ©Scott Tysick/Masterfile Corporation; 388 (BR) ©Roger Tidman/Corbis, (TR) ©Jerry Schad/Photo Researchers, Inc., (CL) ©John Sanford/Photo Researchers, Inc., (CC) NASA Image Exchange; 389 (CC) Getty Images, (CL) ©SOHO (ESA & NASA)/NASA, (TR) ©Goddard Space Flight Center/NASA; 390 (C) ©Denis Scott/Corbis, (T) Getty Images; 391 (T) ©GSFC/NASA Image Exchange, (B) ©Jet Propulsion Laboratory/NASA Image Exchange; 392 (CL) NASA, (BL) ©Bill Ross/Corbis, (Bkgd) ©Greatest Images of NASA/NASA Image Exchange, (TR) Getty Images; **Chapter 13:** 393 (C) ©Reuters/Corbis, (TL) ©Stone/Getty Images; 394 (BR) ©David Ducros/Photo Researchers, Inc., (BL) ©Steve Raymer/Corbis, (T) ©Reuters/Corbis; 395 ©David Young-Wolff/PhotoEdit; 397 (TR) ©Stone/Getty Images, (CL) ©DK Images, (Bkgd) ©Reuters/Corbis; 398 ©Reuters/Corbis; 399 Hemera Technologies; 400 (TR) ©David Mace/Robert Harding Picture Library, Ltd., (BR) ©Giulio Andreini, (TL) Hemera Technologies; 401 (TL) Getty Images, (BL) ©Reuters/Corbis; 402 (CR) ©Steve Raymer/Corbis, (TL) Hemera Technologies, (B) ©Royalty-Free/Corbis, (B) Getty Images, ©Lester Lefkowitz/Corbis,©DK Images; 403 ©Bob Daemmrich/The Image Works, Inc.; 404 (BR) ©Science Museum/Science & Society Picture Library, (TL) Hemera Technologies, (BL) Getty Images; 405 (C) Getty Images, (TR) Unisys Corporation; 406 (B) ©DK Images, (TL) Getty Images; 407 (CR) ©David Ducros/Photo Researchers, Inc., (C) ©David Young-Wolff/PhotoEdit, (CL) ©Bob Daemmrich/Stock Boston; 408 (CL) ©DK Images, (TL) Getty Images; 409 ©DK Images; 410 ©Chuck Elliott/Getty Images; 412 ©Michael Newman/PhotoEdit; 413 (TC) ©Royalty-Free/Corbis, (CR) ©LWA-Dann Tardif/Corbis, (BL) ©Ariel Skelley/Corbis, (TL) ©Hutchings Stock Photography/Corbis; 414 (TC) ©Bob Daemmrich/Stock Boston, (TR) ©Reuters/Corbis, (C) ©Steve Raymer/Corbis, (CR) ©David Ducros/Photo Researchers, Inc., (B) Getty Images; 415 Brand X Pictures; 416 (B) ©Jet Propulsion Laboratry/NASA Image Exchange, (TL) NASA; 417 ©Arthur Tilley/Getty Images; 418 ©Roger Tidman/Corbis; 419 (TR) ©Stockbyte, (TR) Getty Images, (CR) ©Benelux Press/Index Stock Imagery; 420 ©Royalty-Free/Corbis; 422 ©Stone/Getty Images; 423 (C) ©Stone/Getty Images, (C) Getty Images; 424 (R) ©Stone/Getty Images, (C) ©John W. Bova/Photo Researchers, Inc., (B) Getty Images.

End Matter: EM2 ©Tom Brakefield/Corbis; EM3 (T) ©George D. Lepp/Corbis, (BR) Jean-Louis Le Moigne/NHPA Limited, (TR) ©Don Enger/Animals Animals/Earth Scenes; EM4 (CR) ©Clem Haagner/Gallo Images/Corbis, (BR) ©DK Images, (TR) Veer, Inc., (BCR) NASA Image Exchange, (TCR) ©Roger Ressmeyer/Corbis; EM5 (BR) ©Grant Heilman/Grant Heilman Photography, (TR) ©Jim Cummins/Corbis, (CR) ©Reuters/Corbis; EM6 (T) ©The Image Bank/Getty Images, (BR) ©DK Images; EM7 (TR) ©Royalty-Free/Corbis, (TR) ©Joe McDonald/Corbis, (TR) ©Gaoil Shumway/Getty Images, (CR, B) ©DK Images, (BCR) ©Joyce Choo/Corbis; EM8 (TR) ©Mike Brinson/Getty Images, (BR)©DK Images, (TR) The Image Bank/Getty Images; EM9 (B) ©DK Images, (TR) ©Stone/Getty Images, (TCR) ©Marty Stoufer/Animals Animals/Earth Scenes, (BCR) Getty Images; EM10 (TR) ©DK Images, (CR) ©Soames Summerhays/Photo Researchers, Inc., (CR) ©DK Images, (BR) ©A & J Verkaik/Corbis; EM11 (BR) Joe McDonald/Corbis, (TR) ©DK Images; EM12 ©Bob Daemmrich/Stock Boston; EM13 (TR) Getty Images, (TCR) ©Owaki-Kulla/Corbis, (BR) ©Robert Thompson/NHPA Limited; EM14 (TCR) ©Richard T. Nowitz/Corbis, (BCR) ©John Sanford/Photo Researchers, Inc., (CR, BR) ©Mark Boulton/Photo Researchers, Inc.; EM15 (CR) William Bernard/Corbis, (BCR) ©Stephen Frink/Corbis, (TR) ©Charles E. Rotker/Corbis, (BR) ©Randy Morse/Animals Animals/Earth Scenes; EM16 ©Pete Soloutos/Corbis, (CR) ©Richard Megna/Fundamental Photographs, (BR) Joe McDonald/Corbis; EM17 (TR) ©DK Images, (BCR) ©Owaki-Kulla/Corbis, (BR) ©David Ducros/Photo Researchers, Inc.; EM18 (TCR) ©DK Images, (CR) ©Craig Tuttle/Corbis, (BR) Getty Images; EM19 ©DK Images; EM20 (TR) ©Alan. R. Moller/Getty Images, (CR) ©Giulio Andreini, (BR) ©Steve Raymer/Corbis; EM21 (TR) ©Thinkstock, (TCR) ©Sam Abell/NGS Image Collection, (BCR) ©Owaki-Kulla/Corbis, (BR) ©Wally McNamee/Corbis

End Sheets: ES2 ©Tim Flach/Getty Images

EC CRU 10 9 8 7 6 5 4 3 2 1